Praise from Filmmake
Making Documentary Films

SECOND EDITION

"Guided by Barry Hampe's first edition, I embarked into the world of documentary film-making with zero background but lots of practical advice. The result was an award-winning film, *The Kidnapping of Ingrid Betancourt* (with co-producer Karin Hayes). Now into my third documentary, I find *Making Documentary Films and Videos,* Second Edition, has become an even more valuable handbook."

—Victoria Bruce, documentary filmmaker

"Barry Hampe's *Making Documentary Films and Videos,* second edition, is a joy to read. With his welcome emphasis on the primacy of the idea, Mr. Hampe guides the nascent filmmaker amusingly, clearly, and concisely through all the pitfalls of documentary construction. I recommend it heartily."

— Professor Alan Rosenthal, filmmaker and author, *Writing, Producing and Directing Documentary Films and Videos*

"The second edition is more than an improvement on the previous version. We enlarged the bullet points at the start of the chapter on research and stuck them up on the wall. That's our Bible from now on when we start a new documentary."

—Henk Lamers, documentary filmmaker, Loftmatic, Eindhoven, The Netherlands

"When I started to make my first documentary film, I ordered six books from Amazon. The best, by far, was Hampe's *Making Documentary Films and Videos.* This new edition is fabulous. The thing that sets this book apart is that Hampe is a real writer, a beautiful writer. Even someone not interested in documentary film would enjoy reading this book."

—Caren Cross, documentary filmmaker, *Lost and Found in Mexico,* San Miguel de Allende, Mexico

"In this second edition, Barry expands and deepens his original premise that visual evidence, truth, and ethics are the documentarian's only silver bullet. Audiences and critics will choose to act, react, or pass based on the veracity of the presented evidence. Play by the rules or break them, but know the potential consequences by reading this book."

—Richard Dixon, producer/director, *Rare America*

"Enjoyable and practical, with a valuable emphais on documentary truth and the nature of visual evidence."

—Sheila Curran Bernard, filmmaker and author, *Documentary Storytelling*

"When I first outlined a course on creating media for education, I anticipated needing several texts, one each for the design process, production techniques, and professional standards and ethics. Then I discovered that Hampe's first edition covered it all, with an accessible, engaging, and admirably concise approach. Now I look forward to teaching with *Making Documentary Films and Videos,* Second Edition, which continues these strengths while updating to include more contemporary trends and examples."

—Joseph Blatt, Harvard Graduate School of Education

Also by Barry Hampe

Making Videos for Money

Video Scriptwriting

MAKING DOCUMENTARY
FILMS AND VIDEOS

SECOND EDITION

BARRY HAMPE

MAKING DOCUMENTARY FILMS AND VIDEOS

SECOND EDITION

A Practical
Guide to
Planning,
Filming,
and Editing
Documentaries

A HOLT PAPERBACK

HENRY HOLT AND COMPANY

NEW YORK

Holt Paperbacks
Henry Holt and Company, LLC
Publishers since 1866
175 Fifth Avenue
New York, New York 10010
www.henryholt.com

A Holt Paperback® and ⓕⓟ® are registered trademarks
of Henry Holt and Company, LLC.

Distributed in Canada by H. B. Fenn and Company Ltd.

Library of Congress Cataloging-in-Publication Data

Hampe, Barry.
   Making documentary films and videos : a practical guide to planning,
filming, and editing documentaries / Barry Hampe.—2nd ed.
        p. cm.
   "A Holt Paperback."
   Rev. ed. of: Making documentary films and reality videos. 1997.
   Filmography: p.
   ISBN-13: 978-0-8050-8181-7
   ISBN-10: 0-8050-8181-X
   1. Documentary films—Production and direction.   2. Video recordings—
Production and direction.   I. Hampe, Barry. Making documentary films
and reality videos.   II. Title.
   PN1995.9.D6H26 2007
   070.1'8—dc22   2006053175

Henry Holt books are available for special promotions
and premiums. For details contact: Director, Special Markets.

Originally published in 1997 by Owl Books as *Making Documentary
Films and Reality Videos: A Practical Guide to Planning, Filming,
and Editing Documentaries of Real Events*

Second Edition 2007

Designed by Victoria Hartman

Printed in the United States of America

10 9 8 7 6 5 4 3 2 1

This book is lovingly dedicated to my grandchildren, some of whom do not yet read, in the hope that they may someday be pleased to see their names printed in a book, and may even say, "Papa wrote this? Cool."

In order of appearance:

Austin Michael Hampe
Sterling Thomas Hampe
Ryan Haulani Kaleookapule Hampe
Elizabeth Lourdes Florence Kahali'aaloha Unemori Hampe
Barrett Kekamakuikapono Hampe
Catherine Sylvie Maria Unemori Hampe
And any others who may later join the clan

I love you all, and I am grateful for your presence in my life.

CONTENTS

PREFACE TO THE SECOND EDITION

"Barry, I read your book. Then I made a documentary. And I just sold it to HBO."

Let me tell you, that's about as good as it gets for an author. The occasion was a reception for filmmakers at Silverdocs, the documentary festival created by the American Film Institute and Discovery Channel. The person talking to me was Victoria Bruce, a journalist and author who had never made a film until she and Karin Hayes made the award-winning documentary *The Kidnapping of Ingrid Betancourt*.

Today, a lot of people who don't know anything about video or film technology, and whose only knowledge of how to create a documentary has come from watching television, have begun making documentary films and videos.

You may be one of them.

As I write this, I'm working with a producer/director who went halfway around the world to shoot a film of a unique event that he hoped would be the pilot for a TV documentary series. It was only after he returned home and sat down with the footage he had shot that he realized he didn't quite know how to turn what he had into a finished program.

I regularly get e-mails from readers who say they are about to start their first documentary. Some are already working in video or are experienced photographers. The others just have a piece of truth they want to explore and are determined to proceed with their project, learning as they go.

Two changes in the world of documentary have made this possible:

1. Relatively inexpensive digital video cameras and truly inexpensive desktop editing systems have removed all economic barriers to making a documentary. Not long ago making a documentary required access to about $100,000 worth of film or video equipment. Today it can be done—with the same, or better, technical quality—using a $4,000 camera and a $200 desktop editing system.
2. The market for documentaries has expanded on television and through DVD distribution. Cable channels have an insatiable appetite for documentary films, and DVD distributors welcome independent documentaries.

But even those who have knowledge and experience with video and film technology—for example, from producing sales or training videos or TV commercials—can find themselves lost when they turn to documentary. Unfortunately, many people think that because they are making a film about actual events, the *truth* will jump inside their cameras and will automatically reveal itself on the screen to their audience.

This never happens.

Making a documentary film is not as difficult as making a night landing on an aircraft carrier—I've done both—but it does require thought, knowledge, and planning, as well as talent and luck. This book can help you with the first three. And if you get those under control, you'll have a good chance of finding success with the other two.

The major change in this edition is a new emphasis on truth and credibility in making a documentary. The factual style of the documentary form has often been used by government agencies to make propaganda films. And now some independent filmmakers have appropriated the form to make single-issue, one-sided partisan attack films that not only don't tell the whole truth, but sometimes don't tell the truth at all.

As I was finishing the manuscript for this book, a journalist doing a story on documentary ethics asked me if I thought there should be a code of ethics for documentaries. I told him I thought kindergarten rules would do just fine:

Don't lie.

Don't hurt people.

PREFACE TO THE FIRST EDITION

I got into making documentaries by accident because I was looking for a better job. I had been working as a copywriter at the old *Philadelphia Bulletin* and doing lunchtime job interviews with ad agencies around town, all of which seemed to end with the statement, "You're a good writer, but you don't know anything about film, so we can't use you. If you get some film experience, give us a call."

Through a lot of financial juggling and a certain amount of sacrifice by my wife, my sons, and my father, that fall I entered the master's program at The Annenberg School of Communications* at the University of Pennsylvania to learn enough about filmmaking to get a better job. Annenberg is not now and never has been a film school. But it offered a course called the documentary film laboratory, taught by Sol Worth, a photographer, filmmaker, and painter, who was nursing a secret desire to be a scholar.

That year we both achieved our goals. Sol wrote the proposal for the study with anthropologist John Adair that would result in their book, *Through Navajo Eyes*. And I got a better job.

Unfortunately, it was not one that paid better; it was a labor of love. I became Sol's assistant in the documentary film lab on a graduate fellow's pittance. It was a good time. From Sol I learned a way to think about film and filmmaking. I learned how to see what was really there in the footage. And I learned some important things about doing creative work—that you must combine the playfulness and desire to experiment of a young child with an absolutely adult willingness to persist at the

---

*Now for some reason called the Annenberg School for Communication.

task until you get it right. During this time I made my first documentary, *The Trouble with Adults Is . . .*

You'll find references to Sol throughout the book. He was a great teacher, who offered thought-provoking questions in place of authoritative answers. He was a mentor, who always had time to listen and advise. He was a friend, who died way too young. This book is a means of giving back some of what I have learned.

A Note on Usage

Throughout this book I have made distinctions wherever necessary between the process of producing a documentary on film and the quite different process of doing it on video. But the distinction between the two media becomes less clear every day. Today, most programs, even if originally recorded on motion picture film, are shown on a video screen. Language usage has extended the verb *to film* to refer to the process of recording any sort of sound-image material. People talk of *filming* a video, and I have used the term this way.

I have also used the term *film* interchangeably with documentary, even though a documentary film may be an all-video production.

Video once meant videotape, and still usually means that as I'm writing this. But digital video can be recorded to many different media, including DVDs, hard drives, flash drives, and certainly two or three other neat things that are being developed which I don't yet know about as I write this, but you may know about as you read it. I have used the word *video* rather than *videotape* throughout the book to refer to whatever video recording medium may be in use by the time you are making your documentary.

Sex and Gender

I have tried to keep my manuscript as gender-free as I could without getting into the syntactic distortions that have become the style of memos written by faculty committees on diversity. I usually refer to people in the book as *he or she* or *him or her*. If I haven't done it everywhere, it is because I think of myself as a writer first, and I sometimes just can't face stuffing in a *himself or herself* to demolish the rhythm of an otherwise well-crafted sentence or piling up multiple uses of *he or she* without end, like a legal brief.

I have also occasionally taken advantage of the convention in spoken English of using the third person plural—*they, them, their*—to refer to one person whose sexual identity is unknown or indefinite. That's probably the only way we'll get out of this cumbersome *he or she, him or her* usage.

Therefore, if you find a *he* without an *or she* or a *him* without an *or her,* please accept that this is grammatical gender only and still the convention in English, but can be read, if you so desire, as *she or he* and *her or him.*

FEEDBACK

In appendix 1 you'll find an e-mail address to which you can send me questions or comments about this book, along with the address of a website devoted exclusively to the book. I invite you to check it out.

ACKNOWLEDGMENTS

Everything I know about making documentaries begins with my great teacher and good friend the late Sol Worth. Sol taught me to love filmmaking and how to look at films. And he paid me the supreme compliment a teacher can give to a student, when he went on sabbatical and asked me to teach the class in documentary filmmaking that he had created.

As a teacher, I have had the opportunity to learn from the work and questions of many very bright and truly creative students. As a documentarian, I have been privileged to work with some fine film- and video-makers over the course of my career, and I must acknowledge the contribution that Jack Behr, Andy Dintenfass, and Tim Bradley have made to my understanding of making documentaries. I am also indebted to the late Calvin Pryluck for forcing me to think about documentary ethics when I would much rather just get a signed release and move on.

I want to thank Cynthia Vartan, my original editor at Henry Holt and Company, for her friendship and encouragement, and Flora Esterly and Lindsay Ross, my editors for this edition, both for their enthusiasm about this edition of the book and their flexibility about deadlines when the real world intervened in the writing process.

Thanks to Peter Vogt for reviewing the section on postproduction and for bringing interesting projects my way over the years; to Marty Sonnenberg who has involved me in projects about interesting people from stonemasons to fire fighters; and to John Bell, Michael Buday, Steve Harnsberger, and Mark Sugg for permission to quote from proposals, treatments, and scripts they gave me the chance to write.

Special thanks to a group of thoughtful people who were kind enough to take the time to review and comment on the manuscript prior to publication. They are: Sheila Curran Bernard, author of *Documentary Storytelling;* Joseph Blatt at the Harvard Graduate School of Education; Clark Bunting, president, Discovery Networks U.S. Production; Alan Rosenthal, author of *Writing, Producing and Directing Documentary Films and Videos;* and documentary filmmakers Victoria Bruce, Caren Cross in Mexico, Richard Dixon, Robin Johnson, Henk Lamers in The Netherlands, Richard Randall, and Susan Shankin.

Finally, I must express my heartfelt gratitude to Sylvie Leith Hampe—my partner in life and work and the go/no-go editor on everything I have ever written—for her unswerving belief in and support of my writing, which has never gotten in the way of her ability to say, "You need to change this." (And I always do.) Sylvie is my most valuable critic, loving supporter, and best friend.

PART I

WHAT IS A DOCUMENTARY?

I used to think that the documentary films
I was making were real. But as I looked
at what I was doing, I saw I was
making analogs—I was making models
of the situation I was filming.

• • •

—*Bob Young, documentary filmmaker,*
118th Technical Conference of the Society of
Motion Picture and Television Engineers

IT LOOKS SO EASY

From the outside, making a documentary seems like the easiest thing in the world. You just go where something interesting is happening, turn on the camera, and record it.

Looked at that way, the most successful American documentarian would be Abraham Zapruder, the Dallas garment manufacturer whose home-movie camera was pointed at President John Kennedy as he was being shot. His three-hundred-plus frames of Super-8 film have probably been the most talked about and widely shown bit of footage in the history of nonfiction film.

Certainly, if you can get camcorder shots of a tornado flattening a town, or a wildfire wiping out million-dollar homes, you can be on TV.

And yes, if you can put together a series of interviews with the right kinds of people sounding concerned about the right kinds of social problems—from AIDS to zoolatry—you can become the darling of the special interest video festivals.

But unfortunately, reality footage of a tornado isn't a documentary. It's a news clip. And long interviews with earnest proponents of any sort of social change usually don't make a documentary, either. What they make is a dull video sermon, acceptable only to those who already side with the speakers. That's called preaching to the choir.

It Takes More

Making a successful documentary film or video requires much more.

It starts at the camera. You have to have good footage—visual evidence that sets forth the statement of the film in visual terms. And you need more than a simple event. Tornado footage is good, but it is not sufficient. Just saying, "Look at this destruction that happened!" is journalism, not documentary. You need a concept that organizes the material and expresses the point of view of the film. In their *VolcanoScapes* documentaries about the destruction of the lovely Hawaii coastal town of Kalapana by Kilauea volcano, Artemis and Mick Kalber had incredible footage of homes destroyed by a slow-moving river of lava. And they used it. But they focused their story on the people who had chosen to live and build their homes downhill from an active volcano.

Interviews are not enough. Interviews may help define the point of view, but they are usually a terribly cumbersome way to get the documentary idea across, because they don't *show* the topic; they show people *talking about* the topic. A documentary film needs pictures. For instance, immediately after the opening title, Ken Burns's *The Civil War* shows a series of dramatic photographs of war after a battle. The camera moves slowly across each photo, letting you know that in this film much of what you will see will come from still pictures, and you will be given time to see what is there. On the sound track we hear a violin—no speech—as the documentarian shows us that the pictures can speak for themselves.

The Camera Won't Do It for You

I once worked as house audiovisual guy for a teacher-training project. When the project put on a conference, I'd take snapshots of each day's activities and display them on the bulletin board the next morning. The teachers told me how much they liked the pictures. And, invariably, the next thing they'd say was, "What kind of camera did you use?"

As if that mattered.

It was a simple, inexpensive, wide-angle-lens, no-frills camera that recorded what it was pointed at. But it wasn't the camera that made the pictures interesting. It was what the people were doing.

A persistent problem for the modern documentary has been the almost mystical belief of many would-be documentarians that the *camera* somehow does it all. I vividly recall one academic authority on documentary who questioned whether I was "in sympathy with the cinéma vérité filmmaker's desire to shoot a wealth of footage as a passive observer, in order to report as self-effacingly as possible as a journalist."

Well, no. Because that formulation reduces the documentarian to something of a media janitor in charge of an image vacuum machine. Just turn on the machine and it will suck the essence of the event through the lens and store it on film or video. Then all you have to do is reverse the flow and blow your film back in the audience's faces.

If only it were that easy!

Yes, I'm in favor of shooting a lot of footage, but always as an active, decision-making participant in a process of communication that begins with an idea and ends with an audience. Inexpensive video equipment has placed the possibility of making a documentary within the reach of anyone. But the equipment won't make your footage interesting. And digital effects and editing systems can't turn random shots or hours of talking heads into a dramatic documentary statement.

Good Images Don't Just Happen

I began planning the original version of this book in the mid-'90s while working on the script for *Defenders of Midway*, a documentary focused on a group of veterans of the famous World War II naval battle. At the start of that project, UPS delivered to my apartment two boxes of VHS windowprint dubs covering 120 half-hour field tapes shot at Midway Atoll. The problems I found with this footage are typical of the problems to be avoided in making a documentary:

- Lack of planning
- Inadequate visual evidence
- Poor interview technique
- Obtrusive crew interference with the people in the video

Much of the footage was shot by an award-winning commercial director who wouldn't dream of shooting a 30-second spot without extensive preproduction planning. But who, at least from the evidence in his footage, went off to shoot an hour documentary with little or no preparation.

It is precisely when you don't *know* what is going to happen that preproduction planning is most important.

A group of veterans had returned to Midway fifty years after the historic battle. They had been young Marines, sailors, and airmen in 1942.

Fifty years later they were men in their late sixties and seventies who had come to dedicate a memorial and reminisce with one another. I'm sure the producers believed that if the video crew just followed these veterans around and recorded whatever they did and said, they'd have a great film. And the notes I received from one of the producers suggest that he believed they had accomplished exactly that. Unfortunately, his optimism wasn't borne out in the footage.

Lack of preproduction planning left the project without a unifying concept. And without that, there was no apparent strategy for gathering visual evidence related to the theme.

Half of the tapes were interviews with the veterans. Now, a major problem with interviews is that they're about people talking when your goal should be to show things happening. Still, this was a historical documentary, and each of these men had a story to tell. Unfortunately they were asked to tell their stories in a static interview conducted by a historian who specialized in oral histories.

Two problems there: First, a static interview is visually boring. Nothing happens. It's a talking head. Plus the interviews were all filmed in the exact same location—like school yearbook pictures. There was no attempt at making them visually informative. Second, an oral history gathers the facts of a story to be listened to on tape or to be published. That makes it the exact opposite of a documentary interview. In an oral history the interviewer usually has a checklist of items to cover and often will use leading questions, since a yes or no answer still provides the facts. But showing someone listening to an interviewer read a question and then answering yes or no—or possibly just shaking his head—does not make dramatic footage.

In other footage, the veterans go on a boat trip to visit Eastern Island, where several of them had been stationed. And the camera crew goes along—with the camera operator asking questions, giving directions, and generally talking all over the sound track. This would have been an excellent opportunity to do some good on-site interviews as the veterans reminisced about their service on the island, but that opportunity was never taken.

In spite of the problems in the footage, *Defenders of Midway* ended up a good film, and I'm proud of my part in making it. But if the producers, and the crew that shot the footage, had known more at the beginning about making a documentary, it could have been far better.

And that's how this book got started.

About This Book

This book is written for the person who wants to make a documentary, for whatever reason, and especially for those interested in recording behavior out there in the real world, either for production of a documentary or for research of some sort.

It brings into focus what I have learned from making and watching documentaries and from trying to help others organize the documentaries they've shot. It's based on a lifetime of love for the nonfiction film in all its permutations.

I have loved making documentaries from the first time I sat down at an editing table and spliced selected pieces of film into a visual statement. I have shot, directed, edited, and written scores of documentary films and videos. And in the quiet hours of the night while I cut film or edited video, I've thought a lot about what goes into a successful film. And by "successful" I mean a documentary that communicates to an audience exactly what you intended.

What You Won't Find Here

This is not a book about using equipment. For one thing, technology changes too quickly. A camera or editing system will be the flavor of the month only until a new one comes along. (On a previous page I mentioned a $4,000 camera, but by the time you read this there may be an equally good one available for less.) But more important, I don't think of making a documentary as a technical—by which I mean equipment— problem. It is always, from initial concept to final release, a communication problem.

Most of us learn how to operate our technology long before we really have any clear idea of what we want to do with it. Put another way, we can get so caught up in the problems of shooting that we forget about showing. And it is the film the audience sees, not the one the documentarian shoots (or wishes he or she had shot) that counts.

This is also not a book about how to make moneymaking documentaries. I hope that the book will help you to make a good documentary, and that you will be rewarded for your effort. But I have to confess that the financial side of making documentary films is not where my interest lies. Making a documentary takes far too much time and effort to be wasted on anything other than a project you are passionately interested in. "Important" documentaries often become important only after the fact. Initially, they were just something someone fervently wanted to do.

And What You Will Find

This is a book about thinking your way through the documentary process. It starts from the position that *truth* is the essential element in documentary. And that means documentable, verifiable truth.

Recording a lot of people—even famous people—saying that they do like something or someone, or that they don't like something or someone, proves *nothing* about the something or someone except that there are people with strong opinions on the topic.

A documentary must always be an analog of the larger truth. When a film shows something that actually happened, but that is not truly representative, it may be the truth, but it's not the whole truth. In these days of highly partisan, gotcha politics, that's an important distinction to remember.

Making a documentary requires:

- Planning the visual evidence that needs to be recorded
- Recognizing it when it occurs
- Selecting and organizing what has been recorded to present a visual argument to your audience

So a substantial portion of this book is devoted to (1) planning what you're going to do before shooting, and (2) after shooting, selecting and organizing what has been shot into the visual evidence of your film.

Much of what I have learned about documentary filmmaking has been learned under pressure—on location with a small budget and a tight schedule, where every mistake cut deeply. So for every chapter in the book, somewhere I've got a scar.

Shooting a documentary is a lot of fun. I'm always up when I set off for a new location to start a film. There's a kind of automatic status that goes along with being a documentarian. When you walk in with the lights, the sound equipment, and the camera, people assume you know what you're doing. Even if it's your first documentary, you are automatically accorded the status of professional. That's pretty heady stuff.

But a documentarian must never forget that the end of this exciting process is a program that an audience is going to look at—without any explanation from you. The audience will never know how much fun—or how much trouble—you had in getting the pictures. Nor should they.

The audience can be concerned only with the documentary you show them.

2

WHAT *IS* A DOCUMENTARY?

I've spent my professional life working from a kind of operational definition of documentary films that I got by osmosis from my friend and teacher Sol Worth. Sol loved films, and he worked with a big-tent definition. He was willing to accept as a documentary almost anything that wasn't clearly a work of fiction. I don't go quite that far.

It Is an Act of Communication

Like Sol, I start from the position that a documentary film must be an act of communication between the filmmaker and the audience. A documentary can also fall into other categories—work of art, investigative report, personal memoir—but it should first be judged on how effectively it has accomplished the task of communicating with the audience.

If a documentary fails to communicate, it's not doing its job.

It Tells the Truth

Equally important, a documentary must be grounded in truth, so that one of these conditions will obtain:

- What it presents is true, in the sense that its truth is documented and can be verified.
- The documentary itself is a quest for the truth, and it honestly presents its findings as evidence for the viewer to evaluate.
- It purports to show events or behavior as they happen, and therefore shows an accurate and honest analog of the events or behavior that occurred.

In the first edition of this book, I dealt with the issue of truth in documentary mainly in terms of the tension between truth and reality, something I go into in more detail in chapter 13 of this edition. When I wrote the first edition, the line between documentary and propaganda seemed reasonably clear. I expected that the makers of historical and biographical documentaries would base their works on documentable facts or reasonable historical speculation that was clearly labeled as such. I was mainly concerned that filmmakers documenting the present would fall into the trap of thinking that what was real was true, or that sound bites could be used as evidence of the truth of whatever the speaker was saying.

Today, truth in documentary is something that every viewer should worry about and every documentarian should practice conscientiously. I am convinced that truth is the ethical and moral imperative that sets documentary filmmaking apart from other kinds of film and video projects. When truth is sacrificed—for whatever reason—the result may be video pamphleteering or public relations or just plain propaganda. But it is not a documentary.

Problems with truth can also be a combination of ignorance and laziness. Every week I get e-mails—you probably do, too—with the latest e-rumor or urban legend. They may tell about something bad about to happen (Congress is about to tax e-mails on the Internet in order to recoup lost postage costs) or they show someone from "the other side" in a bad light or make someone from "our side" look good. There are several websites such as TruthorFiction.com where one can check out these e-rumors quickly and easily, but the senders never do. They just click on FORWARD and send them on. And if they are willing to accept this sort of silliness uncritically in an e-mail from an anonymous source, how much more likely are they (and we) to accept as truthful the assertions presented in a documentary film?

WHAT EVERYONE KNOWS

You and I are far too sophisticated to be taken in by silly e-mails. But what about the things we *know* are true—because everyone we know *agrees* they are true?

Such as? Well, most people on the religious right *know* that the Supreme Court outlawed prayer in public schools. (It didn't.) And most people on the liberal left *know* that President Reagan's tax cuts didn't increase revenue to the government. (They did.) That's old stuff, of course, but the point is that we all carry around some unexamined notions that we accept as true. And if you start from one of these and look only for evidence to support it, while ignoring—or failing to seek out— any evidence to the contrary, you aren't trying to learn the truth.

For example, a documentarian asked my partner and me to view and comment on a twelve-minute promotional cut of a film he was working on about the cost and availability of health care in America. We did, and sent him a four-page analysis, which said, in part:

> The biggest problem is that you present no evidence. . . . Interviews are not proof. They are only visual evidence of the fact that the person shown said the words that are spoken, but tell us nothing about the truth value of the words. . . . In the highly partisan political climate today, statements of politicians and activists are always highly suspect, because we *know* they will spin the facts to fit their political positions.

Among the sound bites were two dealing with the profits of health care providers. The first was by the health columnist of a major newspaper, who said, "If you have a system where you have to produce a 20 percent rate of return on your investment from Wall Street, then something is going to have to go. And what that is is patient care, because the patient is the most vulnerable person, and the least able to fight for themselves."

The second came from an academic activist speaking at a rally. She said, "Doctors and nurses know just as clearly that the unbridled greed of a corporate-driven health care system is killing our patients and squeezing every ounce of humanity out of the U.S. health care system, and we aren't going to take it anymore, either."

Relating to these in our comments, we wrote:

> We'd like to know at what point in time health insurers were racking up 20 percent profits. If it's now, we'd like some company names so we could buy their stock. The evidence for or against this assertion of 20 percent profits is readily available. Public companies have to file quarterly financial statements and annual reports. Any reasonably competent stock analysts should be able to go through that data and analyze what's really happening.

I don't know if health care companies actually were earning a 20 percent return on investment at some time in the last twenty years. But I do know a documentarian has a responsibility beyond the sound bite. In this case to determine: (1) if the assertion is true; and (2) if it turns out to be true, whether this is necessarily a bad thing. Since the economics of health care are an important part of the documentary, a responsible documentarian probably should include evidence from economists about the effect of profits on prices. This is Economics 101: As profits in a specific field go up, other providers will enter that field, creating increased competition that brings prices down.

Making a documentary about health care—or any topic—requires knowing a lot more about the topic than just the names of some authorities to interview. That's one of the reasons excellent documentaries are sometimes made by people with no film experience, but who are experts on the subject of the film.

The rest of us have to make a commitment to learning what the truth actually is. And that is surely going to involve many interviews, if only for research purposes. If the subject is at all controversial, the film must include interviews with the best available representatives from all sides of the issue.

It Makes a Visual Argument

Ideally, a documentary will make its case with a structured argument composed of visual evidence. Film and video are visual media, and their purpose in a documentary is to show the viewer things he or she either hasn't seen or hasn't previously paid attention to.

The organization of the documentary argument will include an early indication of where the film is going, a presentation of evidence—the truth, the whole truth, and nothing but the truth—and a summing up and resolution of the issues raised in the film.

Regrettably, too many documentarians, rather than going out and finding compelling images that show an audience what the subject is all about, are content to show interview after interview in which people tell what they think, believe, know, or in the best TV tradition, what they *feel* about the topic.

Talkumentaries.

DOCUMENTARY GENRES

Throughout its history, the documentary has followed two different approaches. One is behavioral and anthropological—showing people, institutions, and cultures as they are, or at least as they seem when a camera is pointed at them. The other is historical and biographical—trying to bring to life on film or video significant people and events from the past.

Robert Flaherty took his camera into the frozen arctic in the early 1920s to observe behavior for *Nanook of the North*. At about the same time, in the Soviet Union, Sergei Eisenstein was "documenting" the history of the Bolshevik Revolution with reenactment films such as *Battleship Potemkin* and *October: Ten Days That Shook the World*.

John Huston's combat cameramen shot *San Pietro* as the battle happened in World War II Italy. Marcel Ophuls went back to re-create the sense of that tragic time in occupied France in *The Sorrow and the Pity* through interviews conducted two decades after the war.

Hoop Dreams followed the lives and athletic careers of two young basketball players as they unfolded before the camera over a period of several years. *Baseball: A Film by Ken Burns* used interviews with players, fans, and friends of the filmmaker, along with photographs and stock footage, to portray the director's lengthy view of the history of the sport.

The Hobart Shakespeareans showed a single fifth-grade class, led by a brilliant teacher, as they worked their way through an academic year. *The French Revolution* used reenactment, realistic locations, and, of course, many interviews with experts to distill the essence of an earthshaking event into less than two hours.

Nanook, San Pietro, Hoop Dreams, and *The Hobart Shakespeareans* are behavioral. *Potemkin, The Sorrow and the Pity, Baseball,* and *The French Revolution* are historical.

These two basic approaches to the nonfiction film—recording the present and recalling the past—have existed within a wide range of variations from the earliest days of documentary.

Recording the Present

Documentaries recording the present are filmed as the activities they record unfold in real time. This is the genre known variously as cinéma vérité, direct cinema, or spontaneous cinema (I prefer the final term), recording an event in progress with the outcome unknown or recording human or animal—or even machine—behavior.

It may also be a more formal process of creating a record of things as they happen.

Recalling the Past

History and biography fall easily into the genre of documentaries recalling the past, which also includes investigation of past events. Today, television and the education market make these prime areas for documentarians.

Past and Present Combined

Obviously, some documentaries will combine past and present, visiting past occurrences as a way of understanding—or influencing—events in the present. This is what James Burke did brilliantly in the documentary series *Connections*—taking seemingly unrelated events out of the past and showing how they are tied together in present-day phenomena.

In the unfinished film I mentioned about health care in America, the filmmakers trace the evolution of health care in the twentieth century from the kindly old doctor who made house calls—whom most of us know only through movies of the 1930s and '40s—to the much more impersonal managed health care system of today. The filmmakers show that an important development occurred during World War II. Because of wartime wage and price controls, employers were unable to raise wages to attract workers, but they gained government permission to offer health care as a fringe benefit for their employees. That historic change from individual responsibility to the expectation that a third party—employer or government—would provide health care led to the current situation explored by this documentary.

Investigative Documentaries

Every documentary is—or should be—a rigorous search for the truth. Digging for all the facts. Evaluating the evidence. And presenting a set of well-thought-out conclusions. The excellent documentary *The Sinking City of Venice* on *NOVA* starts its investigation with the observable fact that the city is flooded by the sea more often at the present time than it had been in the past. The filmmakers then endeavor to find out why and to explore what can be done to save the city.

The simple answer would be to say it's a city built at sea level, and the level of the ocean is rising, so blame global warming. Instead, the film explores the situation from many perspectives. Among other things, we learn from archaeologists that the water level has risen about five inches a century since the area was first settled two thousand years ago. From geologists we find out that the city is built on a giant geological sponge, and as the weight of Venice and its surrounding area pushes moisture out of the ground beneath it, the city is actually sinking. And yes, global warming also plays a part, because any solution to Venice's problem must take into account that in addition to Venice sinking, the level of the ocean is rising.

The Sinking City of Venice is also a beautifully visual documentary. Even though a substantial amount of information comes from interviews, it's not just talk; the visual evidence is there on the screen.

THE WHOLE TRUTH

Making an investigative documentary also means disclosing to the viewers whenever the evidence isn't conclusive—even though it may be sensational. For example:

Was Thomas Jefferson the father of one or more of the children of his slave Sally Hemings?
Possibly.
Is there historical evidence suggesting he was?
Yes.
Is it conclusive?
Probably not.
Don't the DNA tests show that Thomas Jefferson was the father?
No, they showed that some Jefferson was, but were not conclusive as to which one.
Are some historians and scholars convinced that Thomas Jefferson fathered Sally Hemings's children?
Yes.
Does that make it so?
No.

Even if we can record them on camera giving this as their expert opinion?

Still no; their testimony would be *evidence*, but it would not be conclusive.

WHAT ABOUT SPONSORED ADVOCACY DOCUMENTARIES?

Until very recently, making a film was an expensive activity. Even today it can still cost a lot of money to get a serious documentary completed. So the question of sponsorship is almost always with us. Someone or some entity has to put up the money to get the thing made, and it usually isn't the filmmaker. But the problem with sponsorship is never about cost; it's about control.

Control is always a problem for documentarians whenever someone else contributes money to a film project. Usually, the filmmaker finds a sponsor who shares his or her enthusiasm for a particular idea and is willing to contribute funds to help the process along. Part of the negotiation will be about how much and what kind of control the sponsor's contribution has purchased. Ideally, from the filmmaker's point of view, the sponsor should put up the money and then go away until the premiere of the film. That's rarely possible, so there is always a certain amount of tension between filmmaker and funder.

In some cases, it is the sponsor who has decided a film should be made, and who contracts with a filmmaker to make it. For the sponsoring entity, commissioning a documentary is a way of bringing the attention of the public to issues and events that people either don't know about or have ignored. It is also a way to get out "the other side of the story," especially when it appears that the truth—or part of the truth—has been ignored, distorted, or suppressed.

Here is the problem: The sponsoring entity wants to get its version of the truth out to the public. So, while it may be interested in the truth, it may not always want—or be able to deliver—the whole truth. For example, several years ago I wrote the script for an advocacy documentary about the invasion and occupation of Cyprus. The film was sponsored by the government of the Republic of Cyprus. One difficulty was that since the Republic of Cyprus did not recognize the government installed by Turkey in the occupied area of Northern Cyprus, it was not possible for us as documentarians to deal with the Turkish side of events, except at very long distance. I am confident that what we put into the film was true. But I am less confident that we were able to tell the whole story.

The biggest problem in making a sponsored advocacy documentary is that the sponsor always has the last word. Since the documentary is essentially work made for hire, perhaps it would be better to call these information videos rather than documentaries.

3

WHAT IS *NOT* A DOCUMENTARY?

First let me make a distinction between bad documentaries and films that are not documentaries. A bad documentary sets out to explore the truth about something but fails to do it well. Perhaps it lacks depth. Perhaps it lacks structure. Perhaps it is simply the product of filmmakers with no talent.

It's still a documentary. Just not a good one.

But there are other kinds of films and television programs that have encroached on documentary territory but are really not documentaries.

Docudramas

The term docudrama is a television invention, coined in 1961 to refer to a TV program using actors and scripted dialogue in a dramatic portrayal of an actual historic event. Over the years the term has evolved to mean almost all dramatic films about actual people or events. Among these are films from *The Aviator* to *Zulu,* including such docudramas as *Cromwell, Hotel Rwanda, In the Name of the Father, JFK, Kinsey, A League of Their Own, The Longest Day, Patton, Quiz Show, Schindler's List, Thirteen Days, World Trade Center,* and many others, along with a plague of made-for-TV movies, which reached epidemic proportions with three separate films about Amy Fisher, the "Long Island Lolita." That's right, *three:* one each for ABC, CBS, and NBC.

There is nothing new about this. Historical dramas have always been a staple of the theater, and they quickly moved into film. Less than four years after the Lumières projected a motion picture before an audience for the first time, French filmmaker Georges Méliès presented his feature-length biographical film *Jeanne d'Arc*. In 1912 Sarah Bernhardt played the title role in *Queen Elizabeth*. In 1915 D. W. Griffith made *The Birth of a Nation*. While this film has earned its place in film history as a pioneering effort in the evolution of film techniques, it was also a terribly flawed, racist history of the Civil War and Reconstruction, foreshadowing the problems with many docudramas to come.

These films, and others from *Revolution in Russia* (1905) to *Munich* (2005), are not documentaries. They are works of fiction derived from the lives of real people and the history of real events. The test of a docudrama is that in it the truth of the real event will always be subordinated to the dramatic needs of the film. One small example: In both *Gunfight at the OK Corral* and *My Darling Clementine*, Wyatt Earp's brother James is shown as the youngest of the Earps, killed by the Clantons prior to the famous shootout. In both films, a major reason the Earps meet the Clantons at the OK Corral is that they are seeking justice for the murder of young Jimmy. Actually, James Earp was Wyatt's oldest brother. He was forty, not eighteen, at the time of the gunfight in 1881, and he lived another forty-five years before dying of natural causes in 1926. But the myth makes a better drama than the truth.

A docudrama, therefore, is no more a documentary than a can of "real draft" beer is a draft beer.

Reality Television

The earlier edition of this book was called *Making Documentary Films and Reality Videos*, but for this edition I've dropped the word *reality* from the title. The reason is to avoid confusion with "reality TV," which has nothing to do with documentary filmmaking.

Reality television is where dodgeball went to live when they kicked it out of the public schools. Each week someone gets knocked out of the game. Reality television is *The Price Is Right* writ large. The participants in a series such as *Survivor* understand that they are making a TV show, not living their lives. They are contestants, competing for a big prize. They go someplace other than where they live, become involved with a group of strangers, and act out a sequence of events according to the rules of a game.

Here's the question that distinguishes all of this sort of programming from documentary: Would any of this have happened if there wasn't a camera present? The presumption is that the events recorded in a documentary (except, perhaps, for the interviews) have a life of their own that would have occurred naturally regardless of the presence or absence of a film crew.

Yes, what you see on a reality TV show is more or less real, in the same sense that what you see on the Game Show Network is real. It actually happened. But it happened in the totally artificial environment of a TV production. Without the TV money and impetus, these events would not have occurred.

We also know that events on reality TV are heavily manipulated. This is what writer David Rupel, who describes himself as "a showrunner for reality TV," had to say in an article posted on the website of the Writers Guild of America, West:

> The first thing to realize is that the term "unscripted" is a fallacy. No, we don't write pages of dialogue, but we do *create formats, cast people based on character traits, and edit scenes to tell a powerful, intriguing tale.** In short, we are storytellers just like you. We just get there a little differently.
>
> So with the caveat that no two reality shows operate identically— *CSI* isn't produced exactly like *Everybody Loves Raymond*—here are some general rules:
>
> Most reality shows fit into one of two categories:
>
> A. It is a show with very little structure, where everyday events become the stories, such as *The Real World, The Osbournes,* and A&E's *Airplane.* On these shows, story editors sift through days (and sometime weeks) of footage to find compelling stories after the shooting has occurred. These shows tend to have longer shooting schedules, because you can't predict when something interesting is going to happen. (In) my early days on *The Real World,* we usually shot about six days to generate one 30-minute episode.
>
> B. It is a show that is heavily formatted, where events are planned before shooting begins. Examples of this are *Survivor, The Amazing Race,* and *The Bachelor.* Writers—usually getting some kind of producer title—create beats for the show that generate

---

*My italics.

the dramatic structure. These shows tend to have much shorter shooting schedules. Two to three days is typical to create a one-hour episode.

Even in Rupel's Category A programs, what you see may be some sort of real, but it's not always true. He writes:

> When I worked on *Bug Juice* (a show for Disney Channel about kids at summer camp), we faced a major problem with our big boy-girl love story. After weaving this storyline through nine episodes, we were caught flat-footed when our boy Connor had the nerve to dump his girl, Stephanie, off-camera! We had enough interview bites to explain what happened, but we needed a good visual to make it work. If you catch a rerun of the show, you will see a happy Stephanie obliviously bounce up to Connor, who solemnly takes her hand and leads her off, as his interview bite explains he needs to end things. With the help of a tender music cue, it turned out to be a touching and bittersweet end to our summer romance. The reality: Steph walked up to Connor, gushed about his Adidas T-shirt and they headed off to have lunch. We used the interview bites and music cue to shape the otherwise innocuous scene to approximate the reality that we failed to shoot.

> Question: Would you do something like that in a documentary?
> No?
> Neither would I.

Docuganda

Using the conventions of the documentary film for propaganda certainly goes back at least as far as Leni Riefenstahl's *Triumph des Willens* (*Triumph of the Will*), made in 1935 at the request of Adolf Hitler. The archives of ad agencies and public relations firms are full of films and videos that have used the documentary form to present a favorable image of their clients—corporations, political candidates, products, and even countries.

What seems to have gotten out of hand today is the attack piece, posing as an impartial documentary report. That's *docuganda*.

I suspect that a legacy of the social documentary of the midtwentieth century is some notion that it is the documentarian's responsibility to point the finger and assign blame. The problem is that our society has moved into a period of extreme partisanship, with shrill voices crying "Gotcha!" from both ends of the continuum. Today, partisan filmmakers are using the form of the documentary to do a hatchet job on people and things they don't like, winning applause from all those who agree with them.

There is really no other reason why Michael Moore should have won an Academy Award for *Bowling for Columbine*. He took a sensitive social issue and trivialized it, but in a way that obviously appealed to his like-minded peers in Hollywood. In the film, he raised some interesting questions about gun deaths in the United States, and then proceeded to stage ambush interviews with Dick Clark, Charlton Heston, and a PR person from Kmart, as if these would in some way lead to answers. Far more can be learned about the probable roots of the Columbine tragedy by reading *Another Planet,* Elinor Burkett's excellent study of life in a suburban high school in Minnesota, than one will ever find in *Bowling for Columbine.*

It's not that Moore doesn't have ideas. He does—too many of them. It's that he doesn't follow through. Moore is a *provocateur*—a performance artist—not a documentarian. At their best, his works are personal essays. In the first edition of this book I described his film *Roger & Me* as "a brilliant satire on corporate public relations and municipal mismanagement." At their worst, however, his films are inaccurate polemics that have so freely distorted the facts that they have produced an avalanche of websites devoted solely to debunking them.*

If you were to search the word *docuganda* online as I did in early 2006, you would have found that most references dealt with Moore's *Fahrenheit 9/11,* followed next by Robert Greenwald's *Outfoxed: Rupert Murdoch's War on Journalism*. Greenwald specializes in unrelenting attack films that show clearly that he thinks Fox News or Wal-Mart (*Wal-Mart: The High Cost of Low Price*) are all bad, but fail to go beyond finger-shaking and name-calling.

Watching a nonfiction film by Robert Greenwald is like eating a pot

---

*I Googled "Michael Moore" and "truth" and got over seven million hits. While I certainly didn't have time to read them all, the first few pages of listings were mainly concerned with questions of inaccuracies in Moore's films and books.

pie with no filling—all crust and no meat. In *Outfoxed* he takes Fox News to task for practices that CNN pioneered years ago. But he hardly acknowledges that CNN exists, let alone that it was once so liberally biased that it was known as the Clinton News Network, which may be one of the reasons Fox News stole its audience. He uses negative sound bites from former employees of Fox and Wal-Mart, but never indicates whether they quit voluntarily or may actually be disgruntled former employees who were fired. And he doesn't seem to have looked very hard for employees with good things to say about either company.

In *Wal-Mart: The High Cost of Low Price,* he faults Wal-Mart for receiving subsidies from local and state governments that other businesses don't receive, but never really explores why these subsidies have been given or what, if anything, the communities actually received—or expected to receive—in return. When you compare Greenwald's *Wal-Mart* with the PBS *Frontline* program, *Is Wal-Mart Good for America?,* it's clear that the former is docuganda and the latter, while critical of Wal-Mart, has the analytical completeness of a documentary.

What makes docuganda not documentary is its blatant one-sidedness. It's as if a jury had to decide guilt or innocence based solely on the case presented by the prosecutor without the defense even being present in court. Advocacy films, even those made with the best intentions in the world, may fall into the docuganda trap if they rely too much on evidence from the side of the angels and don't go out and get the devil's side of the story. It's for this reason I would include a film such as Carlton Sherwood's *Stolen Honor* in this category. Its purpose was to "get" John Kerry and prevent his election as president by linking his antiwar activities in the 1970s to the prolonged hardships endured during the Vietnam War by former prisoners of war. The former POWs clearly believe that Kerry's statements as a member of Vietnam Veterans Against the War put their lives in peril, added to the torture and abuse they received from their captors, and indirectly caused the deaths of some of their fellow prisoners. It's a strong indictment. But it's only an indictment, since Kerry is given no chance to defend himself.

I want to add that there are times when a documentarian has a responsibility to point out clear cases of abuse and injustice even if the report is one-sided. There is nothing the government of Nazi Germany could possibly say in defense of death camps such as Auschwitz, and

Alain Resnais's horrifying documentary *Nuit et Brouillard* (*Night and Fog*), which revisits Auschwitz ten years after the war, presents what happened without asking the Nazis for justification.

But when these techniques are used against a politician one disagrees with or a company one dislikes, it is like calling Democrats "communists" or Republicans "fascists." It's docuganda, not documentary.

DOCUMENTARY FILMMAKING VS. TELEVISION JOURNALISM

Documentary filmmaking was a mature medium long before television journalism existed. Today, when so many documentaries appear on TV, it's easy to connect documentaries with TV news. But the truth is that putting the news on the air and making a documentary are two quite different things.

Documentarians are, or should be, analysts who take time to think about whatever it is they are doing, so that they can present a coherent picture to an audience. Television journalists often are more interested in the buzz than the truth. They are used to working against deadlines reckoned in minutes or hours rather than weeks or months. And often they lack the background and knowledge to evaluate the information they receive.

One example: Throughout the summer of 2005 TV journalists were all atwitter about the high price of gasoline. But not one of them went beyond the price at the pump to compare the current prices with the rate of inflation so they might know whether we were actually paying a higher or lower percentage of our income for gasoline than we were ten or twenty or thirty years ago. That is the sort of investigation I would expect to be pure reflex action for a documentarian.

By mid-2006, gasoline prices had reached an all-time high, and most journalists followed the lead of Congress in deploring windfall profits, rather than analyzing why prices were up and might not go back down. I would expect a documentarian to explore the economics of the issue— to look at the actual return on investment, to examine how high gasoline prices would probably lead to exploration of new sources of petroleum previously considered too expensive to develop, and to further development of alternative energy sources.

By October 2006, when gasoline prices had dropped by almost a dollar, TV journalists had lost interest. That's chasing the buzz, not investigating the problem.

Yes, there are good journalists just as there are bad documentarians. But the goal of electronic journalists, as it has been for their print brethren, is to be the first on the air with the story, rather than to investigate it thoroughly. Another problem with TV news is that it is formatted as a stand-up statement by the reporter, a sound bite from an interview, and a stand-up summary by the reporter, along with footage to illustrate what is said, called "B-roll." It lasts just forty-five to ninety seconds. Not much depth. The difference between television journalism and serious documentary filmmaking is the difference between a newspaper article and a book.

An important aspect of documentary is that it is always past tense, never present tense; always after the fact, never now. Journalism tries to work as close to the present as it can, with live reports from the scene of the event. It sometimes even presumes to step into the future, which is why election campaign coverage is all about who will probably win the horse race and only rarely about who the candidates really are, what they actually stand for, and how they might be expected to govern.

Since documentary is unabashedly after the fact, that means there is time for the sort of research, analysis, and structuring of the documentary model that is not possible in a journalistic report. Time to make sense of the events that were filmed.

Later in the book I tell the story of filming a very young child named Zeke, sitting on a rug and playing with his bottle. Eventually I used this scene to introduce a film about the way children learn, showing how (as I saw it) Zeke found a wet spot on the rug and looked for what caused it. He formulated a hypothesis about wet spots and bottles and tested it to his satisfaction. All at the age of thirteen months.

The most important thing about this story is that as the documentarian and the director of the film, I had no idea all of that was happening as we were filming. I was just waiting for the child to try to walk or try to talk, which were the reasons we'd come to his home to film him in the first place. I looked at that scene in the editing room many times, over several weeks, before I got a hint of what might be going on behaviorally. And that's what, in my opinion, a documentarian does. Given the time constraints of journalism, a journalist would have had to be extremely lucky or incredibly brilliant to pick up that piece of behavior in footage that had already been shot for a totally different purpose. I'm not saying it couldn't happen. But I am saying that all too often journalists shoot illustrative B-roll while a documentarian looks for visual evidence.

4

A LITTLE HISTORY
(OR HOW THINGS GOT THIS WAY)

In order to go forward, it's good to know where we've been, and how we got to where we are now. These days, when a digital camcorder fits in the palm of the hand and can render crisp pictures of a ghost in a cave, it is hard to imagine the problems of early filmmakers, especially documentarians, who wanted to record real people and real events in the real world. Many of the interesting aspects of making documentaries are related to the evolution of film, sound, and video technology, and the ways in which the available technology caused documentarians to think about what they were doing.

Great visual films were made in the silent era because all the filmmaker had to work with was the image. Almost all of the techniques for telling a story visually had been worked out in the first two decades of the motion picture medium's existence. By the 1920s, film was a sophisticated art form and communication medium. Robert Flaherty's *Nanook of the North* remains a classic. Joris Ivens's *The Bridge* is a clinic on observing actuality with a movie camera. And Walter Ruttman's *Berlin, Symphony of a Great City* became the model for all subsequent city films.

In some ways, making a documentary in the silent era was similar to making one today; filmmakers went out with their hand-cranked cameras and recorded whatever interested them.

But then things changed.

The Hollywood Model

Starting with the sound era in the 1930s, the model for all filmmaking became the way films were made in the big movie factories in Hollywood. They were—and still are—technological marvels. Battalions of expert technicians could create a frontier town or burn Rome overnight. If the light outdoors wasn't exactly right, they moved the production onto a huge sound stage, where it could be high noon twenty-four hours a day.

Slow film, bulky cameras, and masses of sound equipment kept the scene being shot pinned down to a tightly defined location. Actors had to "hit the mark" where the light was right and a microphone was positioned to record what they said. Film was shot in short takes, starting with the master scene—a wide shot showing all of the actors and all of the action. Then the set was relit and everything was moved around for the next take, and so on.

In making historical documentaries, documentarians emulated the cumbersome studio system. For documentaries made away from a studio, they would shoot silent footage with a relatively lightweight camera, record some wild sound with a nonsynchronous recorder for use in the background, and limit sound-on-film shooting—if used at all—to a few carefully staged, convenient sequences that would give an air of naturalism to the film.

There were good technical reasons for this. Equipment to synchronize camera and sound was heavy and unwieldy. It was also expensive. Shooting sound on film raised the cost of a film by an order of magnitude. It meant that a lot more film had to be shot, because people speaking the lines of a script would make mistakes. Or, if there was no script, the crew had to keep shooting until the person being interviewed said something worthwhile. The problems of editing sound on film also raised the film editing time by several fold.

As a result, narration and music dominated the sound tracks of nonfiction films from the 1930s well into the 1960s. There were many good films made this way. These include classics such as John Grierson's *Night Mail,* Pare Lorentz's *The Plow That Broke the Plains* and *The River,* and Willard Van Dyke's *The City* in the '30s; the many great war documentaries of the '40s; and the early television documentaries of the

'50s, such as the *Victory at Sea* series at NBC and the long-running series *The Twentieth Century* at CBS.

But there were a lot more bad ones. The pictures were technically perfect. The sound was crisp and clear. The narrator was lucid and informative. But all too often the film itself was a dull illustrated lecture.

According to the Hollywood model, a picture had to be perfect, or it couldn't be used. Everything was scripted. Suppose the documentary was about a world-famous author, a Nobel Prize winner who would never let anyone else write, or change, a line in his books. Nevertheless, a scriptwriter would write the words for the famous person to say, and the world-famous author would memorize them—and say them as written.

Believe it or not, actors were often used instead of the actual personalities, because the actors were considered "more believable on film."

Hollywood Rules

Filmmaking—and later television—was boxed in by *rules* that everyone knew and everyone followed. A stray sunbeam in the lens, a long pause while someone thought of the answer to a question, the wrong kind of light, ambient noise on the sound track—anything that would take away from the high gloss of the finished product—was justification for a retake, or to stop filming.

The statement of the film often had to be subservient to the technology with which it was being made.

FILMING BY THE RULES

My friend and documentary film teacher Sol Worth knew all the rules by heart and firmly believed they had *nothing* to do with making a documentary. Here's a story he liked to tell from the rules period.

He swore that it was true.

Once upon a time there was a film company in New York that had a contract with a major airline to produce travel films. It had an immense library of stock footage from all over the world. It had thousands of feet of color film of the airline's planes taking off, landing, and flying over scenic countryside. And each year it would send a film crew to several foreign cities to update the stock footage.

One year it scheduled a film crew to shoot in Rome and Tokyo. Almost a year before the trip to Rome, the company had sought, and been granted, permission to place a camera in the best possible position for filming the Vatican. This was a balcony that commanded a view of everything.

Just before the crew arrived in Rome, the pope died. And the day the perfect balcony was reserved was the day of the election of a new pope. Suddenly the location from which they planned to shoot some scenes for a travelogue had become the premium piece of real estate in Rome for news coverage of the election.

"Great!" said the director. "We'll shoot all the film we've got, and sell it to the news media. It's a once-in-a-lifetime chance."

He had a Mitchell 35mm camera, a first-class union camera operator, and a lot of very slow color stock. In these days of fine-grain, high-speed, color film—and video cameras that can record an acceptable image by candlelight—it's hard to imagine there was once a time when color stock had an exposure index of ten, which meant getting a decent picture took bright daylight or massive studio lighting. But there was, and this story takes place back then.

"Hold on," said the camera operator. "I'm a first-class union cameraman. I have to guarantee the footage that I shoot. If there's enough light, I shoot. If not, I won't."

"I'll take the responsibility," said the director. (He had already tried to buy some high-speed black and white film, but there was none available. It was sold out to the newspeople.) "Look, if there isn't enough light, we'll shoot at sixteen frames per second, or eight frames per second. Just so we get pictures of the smoke coming up, signifying the election of a new pope."

"Hold on," replied the camera operator. "If you think I'm going to change the speed of this camera when I've got to take it all over the world, you're crazy. This isn't a toy. Once the speed is changed, we might never get it right again. I'll shoot at twenty-four frames per second if there is enough light to expose the film properly. Otherwise, I don't shoot."

The day the new pope was elected was dark, dull, and overcast. The director stood on the perfect balcony, next to his adamant camera operator, watching a once-in-a-lifetime opportunity and praying the sun would come out. He pleaded, begged, commanded, and tried to bribe the camera operator to shoot. But the sun never came, and the camera operator stood there all day long and never exposed a frame of film.

Technology had triumphed over common sense, and the opportunity was lost forever.

That story seemed ridiculous when I first heard it, and I'm sure it seems downright impossible to believe today. But it is part of our filmmaking heritage and illumines the mind-set that led up to the spontaneous cinema revolution.

The epilogue to the Rome story occurred a month later in Tokyo. The director and camera operator had filmed everything in the script except for a shot of the Imperial Palace with Mount Fuji in the background. It was their last day in Japan—a perfect day—clear sky, a light haze in the valley, a few white clouds over the mountain—a day like a Japanese silk print.

The director thought the shot of the palace would be more interesting if the clouds over Fuji seemed to be moving. But their movement was so slow they appeared stationary in any take of a reasonable length.

If we shoot at a slower speed, he reasoned, the clouds will seem to be moving.

Once again he asked the camera operator to change the speed of the camera. "I'll take the responsibility," he said. "It's the last shot before we go home. If the camera jams, we haven't lost anything. We already have the scene at normal speed. Slow the camera down to eight frames per second, and we'll have an even better shot."

"Hold on," said the camera operator. "I'm supposed to shoot at twenty-four frames per second, and I won't take a chance on jamming the camera. Besides, if I slow the camera speed now, and nothing goes wrong, you'll say I should have done it in Rome."

And that was that.

The spark of life was missing from films made this way, crushed out under the pressure of technology. I don't think we realized this completely, back then. Perhaps we sensed that something was missing. But the audience—no less than the filmmakers—knew that this was how nonfiction films had to be.

The Traditional Documentary

Whether filmed in process or re-created, the documentary film until the 1960s was a show-and-tell affair. It was John Grierson who in the 1930s first used the term *documentary,* derived from the French word *documentaire*, which then was used to mean travelogue. Even the highly acclaimed CBS *See It Now* documentaries of Edward R. Murrow and Fred Friendly were closer in structure to the dull travelogues that used to be shown in church basements and junior high social studies classes than to modern documentary videos and films.

These films did let you see things you might otherwise never know about, but always as an after-the-fact report, with little or no sense of immediacy. The nonfiction film was like the nonfiction magazine article or book, a report from those who knew what had happened to those who didn't.

BREAKING THE RULES

But a counterculture was developing that was breaking the Hollywood rules—taking cameras into hot situations and filming whatever happened. By hot situations I mean those in which the filmmaker is present with a camera running, but has no control over what happens.

Army Signal Corps cameramen went into battle in World War II armed with spring-wound, one-hundred-foot capacity, 16mm Bell and Howell or 35mm Eyemo cameras. They shot what was happening and brought it back. They risked their lives to get the picture as it happened. And not all of them returned.

Anthropologists were experimenting with film. Even silent footage, they believed, was a better document of behavior than their laborious note-taking systems.

And then, in the late '40s, television arrived.

THE INFLUENCE OF TELEVISION

Until the advent of television, people lived in a world of communication that depended primarily on words. News came from newspapers with brief bulletins reported on radio. In contrast to this, the strength of the documentary was that it let viewers *see* powerful images of people, things, and events that they had never seen before, or that they had ignored until projected on a screen before their eyes.

In the 1950s television changed the way we encountered the world. Information came to us not just in words but in moving pictures that poured into our homes from around the world. For the first time, we had the ability to sit at home and witness events happening a continent away—as they occurred. The nature of television—live television—is the instantaneous transmission of whatever happens in front of the camera. Some selection is possible, of course, but no editing, no polishing and refining, and no delay in presentation to the audience.

Live television could seem exciting even when it wasn't, because *we didn't know what might happen next.*

TV's Effect on the Classic Documentary

The environment of spontaneous presentation created by television changed forever the way we looked at the traditional documentary. The technical polish, the carefully worded script spoken by a mellifluous voice-of-god narrator, and the obvious pretense that the camera wasn't there, all contributed to a structural message that seemed to say, "We know something you don't know." When what was shown had some importance, this came across as arrogance. When it wasn't very important, it seemed almost silly that so much effort could be expended with so little result.

TV Sports

It is the sense of process, of watching while it happens with the outcome in doubt, that has raised television coverage of sporting events to an art form. A live broadcast on TV is not just the next best thing to being there in person. It's an entirely different experience. When it is well done, you can see, hear, and know far more about what is happening at the event than would ever be possible from a seat in the stands. When it is not done well, of course, it can be just as bad as anything else on TV, with only the outcome of the event itself to redeem it. I do not understand, for instance, why it is deemed necessary to have three commentators for figure-skating competitions, who then chatter all through the skater's performance. That's something you would not have to endure if you were at the event itself. But on the other hand, you wouldn't have slow-motion replay.

Cinéma Vérité Changed
the Documentary World

By 1960, filmmakers had available relatively lightweight 16mm cameras synchronized to high-fidelity tape recorders. This new technology opened a new world for documentarians. They could go into the field and capture on film people as they were and events as they happened. The only limitations were the sensitivity of the film—you had to have *some* light—the cost of film stock and processing, and the cooperation of those involved.

At *Life* magazine, Robert Drew put together the first direct cinema production company and with other pioneers such as Ricky Leacock, D. A. Pennebaker, and the Maysles brothers began to shoot a new kind of documentary that broke all the rules. I can still remember the physical shock of seeing the French cinéma vérité film *Chronique d'un été* (*Chronicle of a Summer*) as a student at The Annenberg School, the exultation I felt at viewing Wolf Koenig's *Lonely Boy*, my incredulousness at the intimacy of the Drew Associates' classic direct cinema documentary *Primary*, and the potential I saw in Arthur Barron's *The Berkeley Rebels*. These films might seem fairly tame today—after all, documentarians have been copying their techniques for more than forty years—but they were earthshaking at the time because they showed a completely new way of making a documentary. In essence, these documentarians put their research on film and showed the audience whatever they found.

As the technology improved, it became easier and easier to go almost anywhere and record actual events as they happened. To make visible that which had been unseen or ignored. The social documentary moved out of church basements and art theaters to a new home on television, first on the major networks, and later, when commercial broadcasting tired of airing bad news about social problems, on the newly created Public Broadcasting System.

Then along came cable television, which was hungry for original programming that matched its tight budgets. Documentary filmmakers found a new home for their work on A&E, Bravo, Discovery, the History Channel, Home Box Office, the Learning Channel, the Travel Channel, Turner Broadcasting, and other cable channels as they emerged.

Proud Heritage, Challenging Future

Documentaries in the twentieth century have shown us the ugly face of discrimination based on race, sex, age, nationality, or sexual orientation. Documentarians were among the first to show the tragedy of AIDS. They brought mental illness out of attics and closed wards and made it something that at last could be discussed. They showed us child abuse and spouse abuse.

It's important to realize, however, that whatever the future of documentary may be, it is not simply to reprise the documentary topics of the past century. It is always easier to copy that which has already been done than to come up with new ideas. But I am certain that the important documentary work of this new century—or even of the next twenty-five years—will be in areas most of us probably haven't been thinking about.

Making documentaries in the twenty-first century means actively seeking out and revealing the truth. It means the documentarian must be more than a propagandist for one political philosophy or for one side in any of our great social controversies. And this can be really tough, because America has grown more partisan, with less room in the middle.

Making documentaries in the twenty-first century means you have to do your own independent research. You can't just interview the experts, because these days the experts often have an ax to grind. I have become convinced that people on opposing sides of almost any political, social, or even scientific controversy are often more interested in winning than in telling the truth.

Which opens up a lot of room for documentarians, if we care to accept the burden.

PART II

PLANNING YOUR DOCUMENTARY

It is not the will to win that's important. It's the
will to prepare to win that really separates those who
wish and dream from those who make it happen.

. . .

—*Coach Dick Tomey*

5

STEPS IN PRODUCING
A DOCUMENTARY

How do you get from that wonderful moment when you say, "I want to make a film about . . ." to the point where you sit in a darkened room and show an audience the film *you* made?

With current technology, the entire process can take just a few days. Or with a documentary such as *Hoop Dreams,* it can take several years. Director Luc Jacquet spent a year on the ice in Antarctica shooting 120 hours of film for *March of the Penguins* (none of which he saw until he returned from Antarctica).

It can cost a few hundred dollars or hundreds of thousands. It can be a wonderful experience or a terrible one—and you never know in advance which it will be.

Each documentary project is unique. If it isn't, you need to change jobs, because you probably aren't learning anything new. As a friend of mine used to say, "Do you have twenty years of experience—or one year of experience twenty times?"

That's why this book devotes a number of these early chapters to how to think your way to the film you want to make before it deals with how to shoot it. The truth is, the mechanics of photography are not that difficult. I taught a friend how to use a 16mm camera one afternoon, and he went off on an adventure and brought back perfectly acceptable footage. And yes, the difference between perfectly acceptable footage and great cinematography can be huge, requiring a lifetime of study and practice. But the point is, even the greatest camera operator in the world can't help you if you don't know what you're looking for.

So let's see what has to be done to make a documentary happen.

Preproduction

The preproduction period is crucial to the success of a documentary. Failure here sends you out on the wide ocean in a leaky boat with no charts and few provisions.

Different types of documentaries will emphasize different things in preproduction. A documentary of a unique event requires planning to maximize the probability that you'll have the camera in the right place at the right time to record critical events as they happen. A historical re-creation may require extensive background research to select settings, costumes, and props that are authentic. A behavioral documentary means thinking about the sorts of behavior you hope to find and film, and the sorts of people who might both exhibit that behavior and give you permission to film them.

Concept

Your starting point is the *concept,* or documentary idea. It tells why you want to make the film, what it will be about, and what effect you hope it will have on an audience. In general, you should be able to state the concept in not more than a hundred words. Be specific, but don't get bogged down in details. These belong in the treatment or script.

More on the documentary idea in chapter 6.

Treatment and Script Preparation and Approval

The *treatment* for a film is often called an outline, but it really should be thought of as an explanation of the documentary you intend to make. For many documentaries, the treatment is the basic shooting document. It tells what is to be shot and why, and how the film will be organized to make a statement to an audience.

Because it sets the visual approach to the documentary, the treatment should be written by a film- or videomaker or by a writer with a good film sense. The problems with the Midway documentary began with the lack of a proper treatment. All that existed were several pages of the hopes and dreams of the producers—who were not filmmakers.

For some, a *script* will also be written. The script is a blueprint, as detailed as possible, for shooting and editing. For each scene it tells what is shot, how it is shot, who is in the scene, and what is said. You need a script for a historical documentary or a re-creation, while you would expect to go with a treatment for a documentary of a unique event or a behavioral documentary.

More on writing the documentary in Part Four.

Budget

The budget details the cost of the documentary and is usually developed along with the treatment. Sometimes the budget will have a strong influence on the treatment, for instance, when there is a specific amount of money available to produce the film. Then, unfortunately, you have to tailor the treatment to the budget.

There is no truth whatever to the notion that a film or video should cost so many dollars per minute. The cost of a documentary depends entirely on what is to be shot, how many days it will take to shoot it, how large a crew is required, the equipment that will be used, and all the other things that may go into a production, such as the cost of actors, props, makeup, special effects, and special items such as original music.

More on budgeting a documentary in appendix 5.

Scouting and Preproduction Planning

With the script and budget approved, the real work begins—getting ready to shoot.

Scouting. Scouting is usually necessary if the film is to be shot on location. The director and camera operator need to know about the places they'll be shooting in: what they look like, what the light and sound levels will be, and whether there are going to be any constraints on shooting. More on scouting in chapter 21.

Casting. If actors will be used, the director needs to audition them. Similarly, the director may need to meet and talk with any people who are not actors who will be appearing in the documentary to select those who will look and sound good on camera, and who won't freeze up when the lights come on. More on working with people who are not actors in chapter 25 and on casting in chapter 26.

Scheduling. A production schedule has to be worked out, which will make the most efficient and effective use of time, money, people, and equipment. Scheduling is covered in chapter 21.

Crew. A production crew has to be selected. While it is possible to shoot a documentary with just a camera operator and sound recordist, the normal minimum crew for a nonfiction film may also include a director and a production assistant or camera assistant. More complex films will require additional people. More on crew selection in appendix 3.

Film or Video? Will you be recording on film or video? Until recently, film offered better quality, but video provided greater economy. High-definition video (HDTV), however, gives you the image quality of film with the convenience and cost effectiveness of digital video. Film once had a slight edge over video if the documentary might be released to television in other formats, such as PAL, in addition to standard NTSC used in the United States, but the shift to digital video has changed that. You can shoot on digital video and release in any video format, including HDTV, but be aware that digital video not shot in high-definition may seem coarse in comparison to actual HDTV footage.

If you have any idea of releasing the documentary to theaters, you should give thought to film, although the shift to digital projection in theaters has started as I write this and will doubtless continue. Therefore documentaries shot in high-definition video, which is digital, will be able to go to the big screen fairly easily.

Equipment and Supplies. The appropriate equipment has to be chosen and reserved or rented. The appropriate film stock or video recording medium has to be ordered. If the documentary is to be shot on film, arrangements need to be made with a processing lab.

More on equipment and supplies in appendix 4.

Production

Production, sometimes called principal photography, is the period during which you are focused on recording the visual evidence and sound that will make up your film.

Filming and Recording

Shooting film or recording video for your documentary can occur in quite limited time and space or may take place over months or years, at many different locations.

Shooting Ratio. Normally, far more footage is shot than can be used in the final version. This allows for retakes, changes in camera angle or position, and some risk taking—filming of scenes or events that could be great if they work out, or could be nothing. The relationship of the amount of footage shot to that used in the final print is the shooting ratio. With film, I anticipate a shooting ratio of at least 10:1.

Recording video permits a much higher shooting ratio than film does. Since the video recording medium is much cheaper to buy than film and requires no processing, it could be 20:1, or even 50:1 or 100:1. But overshooting in video is not without cost of another sort, which is the time it takes to work with more footage. For example, it takes twice as long to view and log fifty hours of video as it does to view and log twenty-five. And twice as long to search for that one shot you remember but can't seem to find in the log.

On the other hand, with video you can keep the camera running without worrying about cost, even when nothing seems to be happening, in the hope that the behavior or events you are looking for will eventually occur. That's a big advantage.

Film Processing and Sound Transfer

If your documentary is being shot on film, the camera original is sent off to a processing laboratory to be developed. At the same time, the sound that has been recorded on audiotape is transferred at a sound laboratory to magnetic film. This is a film stock base that has been coated with a magnetic emulsion for recording. The *mag film* is used in editing and postproduction.

The camera original is carefully stored until it is needed to make the final print of the film—either in a vault at the lab or in a safe place where you are—and a copy is made for you to work with. Until recently, this copy would have been a film work print, which is a low-cost print from the original for use in editing. Today, however, the film will most likely be transferred to video for viewing and editing.

Viewing Video Footage

If you have been shooting on video, you don't have to deal with laboratory processing and sound transfer since video is ready for playback immediately after recording. But even though video usually can tolerate much more handling than film original, most documentarians make copies of all the original video to work with. With digital video, the copies are essentially clones of the camera original with no loss of quality. The originals go in the vault for protection until they are needed.

POSTPRODUCTION

Preproduction is full of hopes and dreams. Production is all potential. But it is in postproduction that you have to deal with reality. This is where you discover what you really have in the footage as opposed to what you thought you shot.

Look and Log

The first thing to do is to find out what you've got. Everything that was shot must be viewed with a critical eye and logged for later reference. A written log is essential, because as the footage piles up—and in a documentary this can mean hours and hours of film or video—it's impossible to remember what film reel, tape cartridge, or other medium each shot is on. Both film and video come with reference numbers that can be used in preparing the log.

More on this in chapter 30.

Editing

Editing is the heart of the documentary process. This is where you shape the material you've recorded into a coherent visual statement for presentation to an audience.

Rough Cut. The good takes are organized into a rough cut—or video string out—which is the first edited version of the documentary. The rough cut is edited to see how things go together. Since the editing may not be much more than joining the takes together, the rough cut will usually be longer than the intended final length of the print. Such refinements as music, narration, titles, and optical effects may only be suggested.

Fine Cut. The rough cut teaches you what your footage is like, while editing to fine cut may be a slow process of seeing what scenes go together in what order to make the documentary statement. Getting to a fine cut usually involves a series of successive approximations, each of which gets closer to the documentary lurking in your imagination. This may be a long, slow process.

Titles, Music, and Narration. These visual and sound elements are added during postproduction. Music, if it is to be used, is composed or selected and scored to the fine cut. If there is to be a narration, it should be written (or rewritten), recorded, and transferred at this point.

More on editing in chapter 31.

Review and Approval of Offline or Interlock

When the fine cut is completed, there is usually a step in which the documentary is reviewed in its current state and approved for completion.

If it has been edited on film, this step requires an *interlock,* which is the showing of the fine cut with all the picture and sound in its proper place. This is a critical formal step in film production, because following approval at interlock the filmmaker will cut the camera original, mix the sound, and have a print made—all of which are expensive. Interlock is, therefore, the last point at which changes can be made to a film inexpensively.

If the fine cut has been done on video, this stage simply involves viewing the edited video. Approval moves the production to the final stage of editing, which also can be expensive.

Finishing on Film

The process of completing the documentary is different with film than it is with video. My assumption is that if you are going to shoot on film you either know film technology or have someone working with you who does.

Finishing on Video

Video is edited by rerecording rather than splicing. Therefore each approximation—or edited version—is, in a sense, a finished product. The first step in editing is the offline edit, usually done either with a desktop editing system or in a small—and relatively inexpensive—offline editing suite. Either one can handle the normal editing functions but may lack all of the effects, graphics, and other expensive support found in an online editing studio.

Sound Sweetening. Original recording normally offers only a limited number of sound tracks. Digital editing systems, however, may provide multiple sound tracks so that each audio source can be separated, controlled, and mixed individually. To have the kind of sound complexity in video production that film editors have long taken for granted, video editors have developed the process of *sound sweetening*. Once the video is frozen, either as an offline template for online editing or as a completed online, it is taken into a sound studio, where the multiple tracks are synchronized with the picture, and layers of sound can be added as needed.

Video Sweetening. It is also possible through digital processing to improve and enhance the video image, much as sound sweetening improves the audio tracks.

Online Editing. The final editing stage is the online edit, in which the edited video master for the finished documentary is created with all of its components—picture, graphics, narration, titles, and sweetened sound and video—in place.

Duplicate Master. A duplicate video master may be made from the edited master if copies in quantity are desired. Its purpose is the same as that of the printing negative with film: to protect the original from being worn out by repeatedly passing through the equipment as copies are made. A DVD master may also be created.

Video-to-Film Transfer. It is possible to do a transfer from video to film, resulting in a printing negative and sound track from which prints on motion picture film can be made. This is an expensive process and the quality of the film print made from video other than HDTV may not be as good as a print made from original film stock.

More on finishing the documentary in chapter 32.

Distribution

This is the last step—getting a usable print of the film or copy of the video in the hands of the intended audience.

And that's the process—all the steps that have to be gone through to take a film or video from idea to audience. Some of the steps are more fun, more interesting, or just plain more like filmmaking than others. Some involve a great deal of skill and creativity. Some are more or less mechanical. And some are mainly administrative. But each step is important to the full realization of the finished documentary.

6

THE DOCUMENTARY IDEA

Planning begins with the documentary idea. And this may begin with nothing more than a vague urge in some direction. For instance, I noticed that some of the pedestrian WALK lights in a town I used to live in were on for no longer than four seconds. One time, as I tried to walk across a seven-lane boulevard on a four second light, three cars—one right after the other—made a right turn on red without stopping, keeping me from even trying to cross while I had that oh-so-brief WALK light. And the thought flashed across my mind, "I wish I had that on videotape. I'd like to show it to the county council."

Maybe that urge will grow until it becomes forceful enough to result in a documentary on pedestrian safety, or dumb traffic engineering, or bad driving. And maybe it won't. Making a documentary requires time, energy, and money. So the documentary idea has to be important enough to you for you to put in the time and energy to gather the money and do the work.

What Is the Concept?

A documentary idea is some sort of notion of what the film will be about. As the idea evolves, it will come to determine, more and more, what will be shown on the screen in the final print of the film.

My idea about videotaping what happens at a traffic light might result in several different documentaries. Because I'm interested in behavior, I'd probably state the idea initially in terms of filming the behavior of pedestrians and motorists at traffic lights. Then there's the business of that four-second WALK light. I'd want to find out why that was permitted—it's too short to do any good—and what the rationale was.

It might turn out that the people responsible don't even realize that the WALK light is on for so short a time. They may be working from some formula that says the steady red DON'T WALK light must be on for so many seconds for each lane of traffic, and before that the *flashing* red DON'T WALK light must be on for a specified period of time, so all that is left is four seconds of WALK time. If that were the case, then the documentary idea and the resulting film might lurch in the direction of exploring bureaucratic rules and unanticipated consequences.

It might be that in the course of researching and filming the traffic light idea, a community group—senior citizens, perhaps—would try to call this to the attention of responsible lawmakers in order to have the situation corrected. In my experience, calling government's attention to something silly it is doing rarely results in immediate rectification of the error. So the documentary might look at the process of trying to get a stupid situation corrected when government agencies are involved.

At this point, what started as a random thought about documenting a stupid and dangerous situation has begun to evolve into the kind of film I like—a documentary of human behavior with the outcome in doubt.

Why Do You Want to Make This Documentary?

At a workshop sponsored by the International Documentary Association, Mitchell Block, a University of Southern California professor and head of Direct Cinema, Ltd., said, "I submit that all works, whether they are fiction or nonfiction, are made for one of two reasons—either to do good or to make money."

What is your reason?

The best documentaries are undoubtedly made because the documentarian had a driving desire to deal with the topic. Still, there's nothing wrong with making money. It's just that if you approach making your documentary primarily from the point of view of making money, you're faced with one set of questions:

- What is the market for this kind of documentary?
- What is this market buying?
- How can I make my project attractive to this market?

Whereas if you approach your documentary with a burning desire to get it made, the important questions are somewhat different:

- What do I want to show?
- What do I need to show?
- What will it cost to do this?
- How can I raise enough money to get this documentary made?

The Things We Do for Love

My own bias is always to go for the film you burn to make. There are plenty of good reasons, and the first is that those projects I have taken on just for the money have never been satisfactory, either artistically or financially. But those I have done because I really wanted to do them have paid off in many unexpected ways.

It takes an enormous amount of time and a substantial amount of money to make any film or video—even a very bad one. So why invest your creative force in something you're not in love with? The annals of filmmaking are stuffed with examples of highly successful projects no one wanted except the filmmaker—until after they were done. But nobody makes lists of the dull, mediocre, and sometimes unfinished projects that were taken on to make a buck.

I'm distinguishing here between serious documentaries and commercial videos. I have been known to write, and sometimes produce and direct, sales and corporate videos for clients. And I invest very little of myself in these other than my demonstrated professional *skill* at getting such projects made. If the client wants changes, I rarely argue; I just make them. Unless, of course, they are absolutely stupid. In which case I point out that these changes will be bad for the final product. Even so, if the client insists, I make the stupid changes, because this is not *my* project, it's the client's.

But when I'm making a documentary, I'm in charge, and it has to be done my way. And no one brings that kind of passion to a project undertaken just to make money. The story is that *Woodstock*, the movie—which was a tour de force documentary project about Woodstock, the event—almost didn't get made. With time running out before the concert, negotiations almost broke down between the promoters and

Michael Wadleigh, who directed the film. At the last moment, the film-makers managed to explain that Wadleigh wasn't asking for a bigger piece or more money, "he just wants creative control." With that agreed to, the film was made, and it became a part of documentary history.

On average, it's probably going to take three years to get funding. Who wants to spend that kind of time and money for anything less than a project you believe in?

BUILDING A BODY OF WORK

Your body of work and your documentary reputation begins with your first project, so make it something you can build upon. If you want to make nature documentaries in remote locations, start with a nature documentary, even if it's in your backyard or the park across the street. Like it or not, to the outside world—especially sponsors, underwriters, and funding agencies—you are what you do.

Each documentary is a learning experience. So it's important to be learning the things that let you demonstrate that you are able to do the kind of work you *want* to do.

Why Should an Audience Want to View Your Documentary?

Unless you have a reasonable answer to this question, your documentary idea still may not be worth pursuing. It's hard to inform or persuade an audience that's not interested in your idea.

Considering the audience leads to two essentials in developing the documentary idea.

STORYTELLING

The first of these is telling a story. A documentary must be more than a collection of facts—more than bullet points and sound bites. To be effective, it needs to pique the audience's curiosity, capture their interest, and engage them in a process they will want to see through to its conclusion and resolution.

You have a better chance of doing this with a question than with an assertion. A question leads to a search for answers with the outcome not necessarily known. Questioning is a process that can carry the audience with you to a conclusion. An assertion, on the other hand, starts from the conclusion and then piles up facts as proof. When the audience knows the outcome at the start, they may decide they don't need to watch how you arrived at your preordained conclusion. If they disagree with your conclusion, they may not care how you got there. If they agree, they may say to themselves, "I already know this stuff."

Working Backwards

If you can imagine what the finished documentary will be like—not in all its glorious detail, but in the ways in which it would have an appeal for an audience—then you should be able to work backwards to the concept for, and the means of arriving at, that finished documentary.

What do you imagine happening when the film ends and the lights come on? What do you expect viewers to think—or to say to one another?

Both storytelling and working backwards put the emphasis in developing a documentary concept where it belongs: on the finished product. I have seen countless proposals, both from students and from people who actually plan to spend money on making a documentary, that go into raptures about what they will shoot and how they will shoot it, but offer little or no clue as to what will eventually appear on a screen for an audience to see.

Does this mean you have to compromise the integrity of your message to pander to an audience? No. It means that if you don't find a way to attract an audience and hold them to the end of the film, they'll never receive your message.

Can You State the Concept in a Few Words?

Sol Worth would ask his film students to begin the process of planning their documentaries by writing a short statement that began, "I want to make a film about . . ." Sol always asked for it in a hundred words or less. That was good discipline, especially for graduate students who were more accustomed to writing several pages than one paragraph. But it's also realistic. You should be able to describe the bones of a workable documentary idea in two or three sentences—something a little longer than the blurb in *TV Guide* but somewhat shorter than a letter to a friend.

Try it. If you have an idea for a documentary, see if you can state it in a hundred words or less.

Here's mine. I want to do a documentary about . . .

> . . . why my town has too brief WALK lights where it takes twenty sec-
> onds to cross the street. Public figures are alarmed by a rise in pedes-
> trian fatalities. These wouldn't happen, they say, if people would use
> the WALK lights. We'll show that WALK lights on many wide avenues
> are on for just four seconds. We'll show that drivers making turns of-
> ten don't check for pedestrians, so intersections may be the most
> dangerous places to cross. Then we'll explore who knew about the
> short WALK lights, why the situation has persisted, and whether gov-
> ernment helps or resists common sense change.

That's ninety-nine words. The statement tells what I am thinking
about and what the thrust of the documentary will be. Each sentence
evokes additional ideas for amplification and suggests images that could
be recorded to make up the visual evidence of the documentary. But it's
only a first draft. As the concept evolves through research, thought, discussion, and the process of getting it down on paper, it is bound to
change.

Here's another. My documentary *A Young Child Is* . . . was to be a
film about learning in children too young to go to school. I had absolutely no idea how the final film would begin or end, or what it would
look like. But I had a statement of what the film was about, and what it
was supposed to do:

> The film will show the tremendous amount of learning that children
> do on their own, long before they ever get near a school. It will
> demonstrate to teachers and school administrators (the intended au-
> dience) that children are not born on the steps of the kindergarten at
> the age of five.

Note that this "I want to make a film about . . ." statement is for the
documentarian's use. It is the concept from which everything else that
goes into the documentary will eventually flow. It is not what you would
write for a fund-raising proposal. That might begin with the details of
one of the pedestrian fatalities or with an example of out-of-school
learning in small children. Nor is this a treatment—although it might be
the start of a treatment.

Does the Concept Lead to Concrete Images That Can Be Recorded on Video or Film?

The documentary idea should help you to develop a shot list for your film. It should suggest where you have to go, and what you need to shoot to record the visual evidence you need. This should lead you to imagine the kinds of concrete images that would serve as evidence of what you want to show.

In Sol Worth's documentary class, this was the point at which the students would normally ask, "How can I do that? It will all depend on what happens when I get there."

Sol would say, "Make it up. Make up a list of ideal scenes that would show exactly what you want." Doing this is a process of fine-tuning yourself as an observing and decision-making instrument. It is not that you will try to shoot the scenes that you have made up. But the exercise of listing possible scenes will help you be ready to recognize the kinds of images you should record when they happen.

If you can't make up a complete hypothetical shot list based on your documentary idea, the idea isn't good enough.

CONVENTIONAL CONCEPTS

I think there's a Hollywood way of looking at documentary, which often is to see it as a stepping-stone to doing feature films. Which means making a film with big-screen production values.

In the first edition I was certain there is a PBS way. But I'm less certain in the twenty-first century. The network that has brought to the air such outstanding work as the *NOVA* series, James Burke's *Connections,* and Ken Burns's *The Civil War,* has also aired some less distinguished work, but I think PBS has benefited from the competition cable channels have given it over the past decade.

I'm sure there's a cable TV way, as seen on the Discovery Channel, A&E, the History Channel, The Learning Channel, and so on. Their documentaries have tended to deal with biographical figures, historical events, and gadgets—including the weapons of war and Hollywood special effects—possibly just because there's interesting footage available of gadgets at work. The History Channel is now doing some interesting documentaries involving reenactment, and Discovery Networks have branched out in all directions.

Then there are "actuality videos"—made by putting a camera crew in the back of a cop car or in an emergency room or anywhere else that interesting and exploitable footage may be recorded.

Finally, theatrical documentaries have recently found new favor. They can be on almost any topic that will find an audience. Many theatrical documentaries make the rounds of film festivals, spend a week or more in a theater in New York or Los Angeles to qualify for Academy Award consideration, and then go to DVD.

Documentary Categories

In the worlds of network and cable TV, where the way you describe an "original" idea is to name the other films it is *like*, and where you can't get a script read unless you are willing to sign a release which acknowledges that there are no new ideas, you are going to be asked to fit your documentary into a precast set of categories—historical, biographical, social commentary, unusual events, travel, nature, or behind-the-scenes, for example. At that International Documentary Association workshop, Mitchell Block suggested that all documentaries fit into one of the four Ps: *portrait, performance, place,* and *poetry.* To which I would add *process* to include the documentary of a unique event with the end in doubt, although I think Block might include that under his category of performance.

But I'm also convinced that in documentary—just as in feature films, book writing, painting, music, and drama—there are the exciting and unexpected results that come from dedicated artists immersed in impossible projects that seem totally reasonable to them. And these aren't easy to categorize.

One of the reasons that a series like *FDR* on PBS's *American Experience* was able to raise over two million dollars in funding is that it was easy to categorize. That made it easy for underwriters to know what they were putting money into, and what they could expect to see when it was done.

It certainly took a lot more courage for the Michigan Council for the Arts to put money into *Roger & Me,* back before Michael Moore had gained an Oscar for *Bowling for Columbine* and notoriety for *Fahrenheit 9/11,* than for any funder to give money to *FDR.*

Terry Zwigoff had great difficulty in raising money from conventional sources over the seven years he was working on his offbeat documentary *Crumb*. He said that every now and then he'd put together a short sample tape and travel from San Francisco to L.A. looking for money. And it was available—if he were willing to change the concept to a more conventional portrait of an unconventional artist. Which he wouldn't do.

Victoria Bruce and Karin Hayes used their credit cards to finance their first documentary, *The Kidnapping of Ingrid Betancourt,* rather than go through the red tape and delays involved in getting grants.

Overdone Ideas

In spite of the voracious appetite of cable TV and DVD, it is very hard to get funding for, or to license the distribution of, a documentary on a subject that has already been covered. At least not until a lot of years have passed since the first film was made.

AIDS awareness, problems of the homeless, environmental pollution, and many other subjects are certainly worthwhile, and a righteous way for a documentarian to spend his or her time, except . . .

. . . they've already been done.

If your documentary idea is about a hot topic that is getting a lot of coverage in the newspapers and popular magazines, you're too late. You can be sure documentaries—or proposals for documentaries—on that topic are already in the works. And if the topic is so hot that you saw something about it on TV, forget it; it's already old and done.

On the other hand, if you have a truly original slant on an old topic, then it becomes new again, and you may be able to get both funding and distribution. I recently heard from a Belgian journalist in London who is working on a documentary about "love amongst the homeless." That's a new slant on an old topic. More about this in chapter 19.

The point is that for conventional support, your idea has to be conventional enough to be understood, but different enough that it hasn't been done before.

Unconventional Concepts

Crumb got made and has enjoyed decent success in theatrical release and on DVD. It's a dark, moody, revealing story of three brothers from a very strange family. Zwigoff's concept for the film is so much stronger than any conventional biography would be that he was right to wait it out, even though it took seven years to complete the film.

Woodstock became a legend in its own time.

The Kidnapping of Ingrid Betancourt started out to be *The War Room* to a Latin beat, a political film set during a presidential election in Colombia. It became, instead, a documentary about evil, corruption, and family loss.

The March of the Penguins was an impossible task that nonetheless got made. And once made, won an Academy Award.

If you want it badly enough, you'll find a way to get it made. And if your documentary idea is good, your filming is honest and effective, and your editing skillfully organizes the footage to present the idea clearly to an audience, you'll have a film you can be proud of.

And if you've gone that far, then this documentary—or the next one—will make you some money.

7

DOCUMENTING BEHAVIOR

When my oldest son, Jeffrey, was about six years old, I took him to the TV studio at The Annenberg School, where graduate students were prepping a project in which several artists would demonstrate their work.

We arrived before taping began. In the center of the studio a sculptor had set up an armature loaded with wet clay that he was smoothing with a curved tool. Jeff was enthusiastic about anything to do with art, and he was fascinated by the sculptor. He stopped to watch, while I wandered off to talk with some friends.

The next time I noticed my son, he was standing on an apple box with a wire tool in his hand, reaching up over his head to smooth the clay just as the sculptor had been doing. He appeared to be totally absorbed in the work and made such an interesting picture that the students moved in video cameras to photograph him for practice before the class started.

I went to master control to watch on the monitors there. You could see Jeff's intense concentration as he carefully worked the clay, and the students working as control room crew were ecstatic. "Look how natural he is!" they said. "How unself-conscious! He's not even paying any attention to the cameras."

In a little while I went back down to the studio. Jeff had been working with the clay for at least fifteen minutes.

"How's it going?" I asked him.

"My arms are killing me," he said without looking up, barely moving his lips.

"Then quit," I said, "and we'll go up to my office and get a Coke."

"I can't," he said.

"Why not?"

"The cameras are still on."

It makes you wonder what the truth is about recording behavior. Does it require a hidden camera to get real behavior? Or can we go into a situation with camera running and expect to record behavior that not only looks genuine but has the ring of truth to it?

Recording Human Behavior

From the early Edison short *Mother Washing a Baby* to Flaherty's *Nanook*, to *In the Street* by Levitt, Loeb, and Agee, to Rouch and Morin's *Chronique d'un été* (*Chronicle of a Summer*), to the body of work by Frederick Wiseman, the Maysles brothers, and others, to contemporary documentaries such as *Hoop Dreams* and *Lalee's Kin: The Legacy of Cotton*, the goal of many documentarians has been, and is, to discover people as they are. To record, reveal, and learn from human behavior.

In the early days of spontaneous cinema a lot of films were made about ordinary people living out their ordinary lives. Films such as the Maysles' *Salesman*, Alan King's *A Married Couple*, Frederick Wiseman's *Titicut Follies*, *High School*, and *Hospital*, and the PBS series *An American Family* became a kind of anthropology of ourselves.

A tremendous body of work was created by film and video documentarians as they tested, revised, and refined the behavioral documentary through practical experience in the field. And while it was possible to see the results of the work of these early practitioners, it was not at all easy to determine how the results were achieved. In the beginning it seemed like magic, and we often asked, "Did the people know the camera was there?" We had never seen everyday people bare their souls so completely on film.

Today, the shock value of personal revelation has been blunted by tabloid TV and talk shows whose hosts and guests hold *nothing* sacred. But the desire—and the need—to document behavior as it happens, remain.

One of my first films, and the one I remain the proudest of, *A Young Child Is . . .* , made in 1972, set out to observe how very young children grow and learn. Until then, those who wanted to look at the behavior of children were stuck with works such as the McGraw-Hill *Ages and*

Stages series, which took prevailing child development theory and *illustrated* it by having children act out whatever the experts said children did at that age. One unforgivable offshoot of this series was hanging the name "the terrible twos" on two-year-olds, when they are actually terrific, not terrible. Anyone observing without preconceived expert theory would recognize that this is the age when babies become people in their own right. And people don't always do what someone else wants them to.

The behavioral documentary is very much with us today, and so much easier to do because we now have inexpensive and technically marvelous tools with which to record behavior. After I made *A Young Child Is . . . ,* I thought it would be fascinating to follow a two-year-old—or several of them—around for a year, to document on film why these are the terrific twos, not the terrible twos. But the budget to do so, including a basic crew, equipment, film stock and processing for a minimum of 100 hours of film, and all the costs of postproduction would have been close to $250,000. Adjusted for inflation, that would be more than a million dollars today. And while million dollar budgets are not unknown in documentary now, that kind of money was very hard to come by in the '70s. Today a year's worth of behavioral footage could be recorded by a dedicated documentarian for lunch money.

There is a way to film people so that their speech and behavior are consistent with their personality and beliefs, even when they know that a camera and recorder are running. It's not such a difficult task that it requires spy technology and hidden cameras. Nor is it so easy that anyone can do it just by turning on a video camera and letting it run. Recording human behavior takes work, intelligence, an understanding of human nature, a cooperative crew—and practice.

And there are dozens—maybe hundreds—of ways to do it wrong.

What It Takes

Recording behavior requires sufficient mastery of the recording technology—whether video or film—to allow you to concentrate on the people being filmed.

It requires a contract—not only unwritten, but perhaps never spoken—with these people that you will be a professional and will not abuse their amateur standing. You will let them do whatever they are doing without bothering them with your production problems.

It requires a separate contract with the audience that you will show them the truth as you know it to be, and will not knowingly fool them.

It requires the ability to plan for the unexpected and the ability to discard preconceptions when they don't fit what people are doing in front of the camera.

It requires a high tolerance for uncertainty—a willingness to turn the camera on and keep recording with the clock running and production costs mounting in the optimistic belief that something interesting will happen.

It requires an understanding of what is happening in the filming situation, and how that relates to the edited film that will be shown to an audience.

Building an Invisible Wall

In his excellent book on the documentary movement of the 1960s, *The New Documentary in Action,* Alan Rosenthal profiles the intimate portrait of a marriage in Alan King's documentary *A Married Couple.* The film was shot over ten weeks, mainly in the couple's home, and was a pioneering event in spontaneous cinema. Richard Leiterman, photographer and associate director, tells how they handled filming in such an intimate situation for such a long time:

> We went in with a kind of ground rule that we would have no communication with them nor would they communicate anything to us. We put up an *invisible barrier* [my emphasis] between us. . . . If we came at any time, they were not to act surprised or to change what they were doing to something else, and they would not make any exception to what they were doing just because of our presence. (p. 46)

While not every documentary requires such an invisible wall, it is essential whenever you are serious about recording behavior. And it is a good practice at all times when you are working with regular people in their regular habitat. The more you are able to keep the process of filming behind an invisible wall so it does not intrude on the people you are filming, the better—and more natural—the footage that will result. More on the invisible wall and recording people who are not actors in chapter 25.

How Not to Record Behavior

I was shooting a simple interview with a police captain in Wilkes-Barre, Pennsylvania. I had hired a highly professional film crew that had shot many industrial films. But we had never worked together. The camera operator turned out to be the best I've ever worked with at getting clean, well-exposed, nicely composed footage. The camera assistant was an obsessive about keeping the slates and camera log in order, and a tyrant about cleanliness. The sound recordist could get a usable sound bite inside a cement mixer.

The film was focused on community reaction to a plan to provide care and treatment for mental patients in their home communities rather than in large, state-operated institutions. We had picked Wilkes-Barre because this subject had already evoked strong feelings there. I was after community reaction, and I wanted people to be as spontaneous as possible on camera. In briefing the crew, I had told them I wanted an invisible wall between us and anyone we were filming, so that the subjects would not try to act for the camera.

On that first day, we went to the center square of Wilkes-Barre to interview the police captain. He was a man in his late forties, responsible for police-community relations and also a member of the board of directors of the local mental health organization. I was after his comments on reports that former mental patients had been gathering in the square and annoying other residents.

A Crack in the Invisible Wall

Because I hoped to use his answers to my questions as a kind of running narrative, I was not in the picture. The captain wore a wireless microphone, but I didn't. As we got ready to shoot, the sound recordist said, "Captain, would you repeat the question before you start to answer, so I'll get it on tape?"

That's not my style, because it's a crack in the invisible wall, but it didn't seem too much to ask, so I let it pass. I certainly wasn't going to *prompt* the captain to repeat the questions, but if he could remember to do it, editing the film might be a little easier.

We slated the first take and began walking and talking. After I had gotten his name and occupation, I asked, "Captain, what about the reports of former mental patients hanging out in the square? Has this been much of a problem?"

"Well, it really hasn't been a problem," he started.

"Repeat the question!" yelled the sound recordist.

"Oh, right," said the captain. "Well, let's see. Has there been much of a problem—"

"Could you walk a little faster?" asked the camera operator.

At that point, with the invisible wall already crumbling, I yelled, "Cut!"

"It looks terrible," the camera operator said. "You're hardly walking."

"And try to remember to repeat the question," the sound recordist added.

We started again, got through the next couple of questions, and were in the middle of the third when the camera operator took the camera down from his shoulder.

"The film ran out," he said.

Although the film camera was an Eclair NPR, which boasted a five-second magazine change, we stood around for about two minutes while the camera assistant pulled the lens, checked the gate for cleanliness, changed magazines, and set a new slate.

"The walking just doesn't look good," the camera operator told me.

"OK," I said, "let's pick a spot and stand there and talk."

Death of an Interview

We found a good spot in front of some old people sunning themselves on a bench and started again.

"What was I saying?" the captain asked.

"You were answering the question about police training," the sound recordist told him.

"Better start again," the camera operator said. "It's a new location."

CAPTAIN: Well, the officers—
SOUND: Repeat the question!
CAMERA: Could you cheat this way a little more?
CAPTAIN: How's this?
CAMERA: That's good.
SOUND: Remember to repeat the question.

CAPTAIN: What was I saying?

SOUND: Police training.

CAPTAIN: The Wilkes-Barre Police Department has implemented a comprehensive, communitywide, innovative program of . . .

We got through it with several more interruptions. The tape ran out and we had to wait while the sound recordist put in a new reel. A noisy truck went by and we had to repeat a question and answer. But by then it didn't matter. I was no longer interviewing a police captain who knew a great deal about the problem we had come to film. I was playing a bad scene with an amateur actor who was trying to please my crew. In the rushes, the picture was sharp and well composed and the sound was clear. But the captain had been reduced to a boring bureaucrat, spouting officialese and qualifying every statement. His film debut had to be postponed indefinitely.

And yes, the crew and I did have a conversation about who would talk and who wouldn't when filming an interview.

A Set of Ideas About Documenting Behavior

In directing and editing my own documentaries, in viewing hundreds of videos and films made by others, and in teaching documentary production, I've come up with a set of ideas about documenting behavior. Let's look at these one at a time.

When We Photograph People, It Is Behavior That We Record on Film or Video, and Nothing Else

We don't record personality, or the way people are, or what they believe, or what they think. Those things must be *inferred* from the behavior we observe. We *see* physical behavior, including the way in which a person dresses and grooms himself. We *hear* verbal behavior; not just the words themselves, but the way in which the words are spoken. And that is all. In documentary, as in life, this is the evidence from which we infer the essence of a person's character.

People Behave Differently in Different Situations

How people act, their body posture, facial expression, tone of voice—even the way they dress and the language they use—are situation-specific in accordance with social rules. We *expect* people to act differently in different situations—so much so that when people do not alter their behavior to fit the situation, we say, "They don't know how to behave." So it is not surprising if people alter their behavior in front of a film crew and camera. As we'll see, this is not really a problem.

People's Behavior Will Remain Consistent with Their Beliefs About Themselves and Their Place in the World

While we can expect situation-specific variations in behavior, it is the overall pattern that counts. If we have had a chance to observe someone's behavior in one situation fairly carefully, we should be able to make pretty good inferences about that person's beliefs about himself and his world. Therefore, we should be able to make fairly strong predictions about how he will behave in other situations. Naturally, the more we can see someone in different situations, the more powerful are the inferences about him that we can make.

Most People Are Unable to Maintain a Pose or Act Out a Role for Any Length of Time

Most people just aren't very good actors. In fact, many people may not have much of an idea of what their normal behavior is. They never see themselves as others see them, so they have no authentic baseline from which to alter their behavior.

Try to role-play a personality different from your own for an hour or so. To do so with any credibility—and without a script—without going out of character even once, requires intense concentration. Much more than people are willing to give just to fool a camera. And that is the point to this section: People's behavior in front of a camera will be consistent with their behavior elsewhere. Even if they start out playing a role, they'll soon fall back on their normal pattern of behavior.

It Is Hard for People to Be Themselves When They Have Nothing to Do

You can't just plop people down in front of a camera, tell them to be themselves, and start recording. What you'll get is people trying to re-member how they act when they are being themselves.

The Presence of a Video or Film Crew Becomes a Factor
in the Documentary Situation

The pretense that the camera is not there, which was so much a part of the traditional documentary, simply distorts the evidence that is recorded in a behavioral documentary. That's why I often include in a film at least one shot of the crew at work. It reminds the audience that what they are seeing took place in front of a camera and microphone, possibly under production lights, and with one or more strangers tiptoeing around behind the scene.

If the people in the scene are busy doing familiar things, they'll get interested in what they are doing and let the camera take care of itself. Even in an interview, where people are essentially talking for the camera, most are able to overcome their camera-consciousness and talk directly to the interviewer. Certainly they are aware of the camera, but this awareness becomes a part of their behavior.

When I was shooting an interview with a self-described "mentally ill" patient, the first thing he asked after the camera rolled was, "Are we being on TV now?" In editing the film, I left in that statement. It showed he was aware not only of the fact that he was being filmed, but also of the intended use of the footage. It made his statements about himself, which followed, even more powerful and credible.

But sometimes the camera gets in the way. For *Schools for Children* I wanted the principal of one of the schools in which we were filming to tell about how his school had been designed to support young learners. I hoped to use it as a narrative to tie the scenes in the school together. What he had told me in the preinterview was so in keeping with the philosophy underlying the film, and so well said, that I just knew he'd be great. Unfortunately, he wasn't. When the lights came on, he began talking for the record. His informal statements of the day before were transposed into the safe, polysyllabic jargon of an educrat, and nothing I did as the interviewer could make him change.

The Behavior of the Production Crew Can and Will Affect the
Behavior of the People in the Shooting Situation

This is most dramatically shown with the police captain in Wilkes-Barre.

Hubert Smith, who shot 160,000 feet of film documenting the behavior of Mayans in the Yucatán Peninsula, said that one of the hardest things he had to do was to convince his subjects that he and his crew were not guests in their homes, but were working. It took incredible patience, he said, just to sit in a room and keep insisting, "Whatever you do is interesting," without yielding to the temptation to suggest some activity. But that's what they did. They also refused all offers of refreshment during the shooting period, promising to come back later—after all the shooting was finished—to eat with the family. Eventually this would pay off, and the family would be able to go about its business in the presence of the film crew without attempting to include the documentarians in its activities.

In Order to Avoid Controlling the Behavior of the People in the Documentary, You Must Control Yourself and Your Production Crew

A good model for shooting a behavioral documentary is the live television coverage of a football game. The program documents an event in progress with the outcome in doubt. Shooting concentrates on the behavior of the subjects in the scene with a heavy emphasis—instant playback, isolated cameras, slow motion—on presenting evidence of that behavior.

There is a well-defined line of demarcation between the production crew and the subjects in the shooting situation. For instance, the camera operator cannot go out on the playing field to get a better shot. Nor can the director ask the quarterback to run the play that resulted in a touchdown again—but this time at the other end of the field where the light is better, and with a three-beat pause before the pass is thrown.

All the football director can do is prepare carefully, select the crew and equipment that will do the best job, give each crew member a specific assignment, try to be ready for anything, strive for excellence, and above all, forget a poor shot or missed opportunity as soon as the moment has passed.

Making a documentary of behavior is very much like that. You have to do your homework. You have to know why you are going to this location to shoot. And you should have a good idea of the kind of visual evidence you are looking for. You have to make sure your equipment is in good working order and is appropriate to the job at hand. You have to brief the crew on what you expect from them—not just on what you want them to do. You also have to make clear precisely what you *don't* want them to do. You have to make certain that cameras and recorders are loaded appropriately. There's nothing worse than running out of tape or film right at the height of the action.

You Can't Worry About Behavior That Happens Off-Camera

You have to be willing to shrug off a missed shot or the fact that an interesting piece of business happened off-camera, out of the lights, or while you were reloading. The best you can do is note it, remember it, and try to be ready if it happens again. Every documentarian knows that interesting behavior always seems to happen immediately after the camera has been turned off. I *expect* that I'll see something that I'm going to *wish* I had shot. That way I don't get depressed when it happens and begin to wonder if, just this once, I should intervene and try to get the people to re-create the scene. As the producer, I say to myself as the director, "If you don't have the footage, then as far as this film is concerned, it never happened. Don't worry about it. Work with the visual evidence you do have."

What Is Actually Recorded Comes as the Result of a Combination of Preparation and Luck

You have to know what you eventually want to show to an audience. This defines the purpose of the documentary. It may be quite vague, such as, "I want to show evidence of early learning in young children." Or it could be quite specific, for example, "I want to show the different ways in which husbands and wives talk to each other when they are angry."

Careful preparation should lead you and your crew to a location where you have a high probability of observing the behavior you want to record. And a sensitivity to the material you're looking for will increase the probability that you'll have the camera turned on when it does happen. But since you don't have control over what happens in front of the camera, there always remains an element of luck.

Maybe nothing interesting happens the day you're there. That's bad luck. Preparation, planning, and control of yourself and your crew can hold this to a minimum, but there will be times when you burn film or video with no apparent results. That's why the shooting ratio for a behavioral documentary is high. You just keep shooting and smiling, never letting the subjects know that you're not getting what you want.

There's also good luck. Sometimes you'll get a piece of behavior that is so much better than anything you could have dreamed up that you can hardly believe it happened. Earlier, I promised to tell you about filming Zeke, a thirteen-month-old boy who was just starting to walk and just beginning to experiment with making sounds in the pattern of English sentences. Since these were both things that I wanted for the film *A Young Child Is . . .* , we went to his house and filmed him playing on the floor.

At one point he was playing alone with some toys—occasionally taking a drink from his bottle. It seemed like a good establishing shot, even though I couldn't see that anything we were looking for was happening. But behavior is behavior, and besides, I thought that at any moment he might start to do something important, like talk. So we kept the camera on him and running. In a couple of minutes he crawled over to his mother, then stood up and tried to walk. Great! Just what we'd come for!

Much later, I began trying to edit this sequence. On about the fifth or sixth time through the footage, I began to realize that something truly important was going on in that "establishing shot." The child was engaged in behavior that I was convinced—from watching my own kids—was the key to learning in young children, but had never before been able to prove.

Here's what he was doing:

While he was playing alone, he kept rubbing a wet spot on the rug. Then he picked up his bottle, lying near the spot, and sucked on it. He put the bottle down and touched the wet spot. Then he picked up the bottle and shook it until some drops fell out onto the rug. Finally, he rubbed the spot he had just made.

As far as I was concerned, that thirteen-month-old baby had formed a hypothesis about how the wet spot got on the rug, had tested it empirically with his bottle, and had satisfied himself as to the results of his experiment. And when he was done, he crawled off to play with his mom.

This became the opening of the film. I had the original footage duplicated so I could run it twice. The first time, I said to the audience in narration, "Here's a baby playing on the floor. What do you see?" The second time, I explained my interpretation, step by step, as we watched the child's behavior.

In effect, this scene became the topic sentence for the rest of the film. An audience could disagree with my interpretation. What they couldn't do was ignore the behavior that they had seen.

Shooting a Behavioral Documentary Is an
Active Process of Selection and Decision Making

Cameras don't make movies—people do. There is absolutely nothing of the "passive observer" in the efforts of a behavioral documentarian. There is no way to avoid the responsibility for what is shot. Everything that is recorded is the result of a deliberate series of decisions:

To go here, and not there.
To take a camera along.
To load it.
To point it at something—this, and not that.
To shoot at eye level, floor level, or standing on a ladder.
To bring in lights, which may be distracting, or to shoot with available light.
To frame a medium shot rather than a close-up or long shot.
To turn the camera on.
To turn the camera off.

Even when the camera is locked off and you stand frozen, holding your breath to keep from intruding even minutely into the scene, there is an active, totally engaged, decision-making process going on below the surface. It began with the decision to make this documentary, and not some other. Then there were the decisions to be in this location at this time, to shoot this scene, and to do it with a locked-off camera rather than handheld and moving about, to turn the camera on at a certain time, and either to turn it off at some point or to let it go until you run out of whatever you are recording on.

As the complexity of the shooting situation increases, the number of decisions to be made increases. Some of the things the documentarian must continually keep in mind are:

- the purpose of the film
- the kind of behavior he or she is trying to capture
- what is happening in the scene being shot
- the fact that the footage will be edited for presentation to an audience
- how what is being shot in this scene might go with what has been shot before and what is to follow
- how to get the best possible images and sound as visual evidence of the event being shot
- how far the crew can go with all this and still remain on their own side of the invisible wall

The process of editing the footage you've shot is, if anything, even more deliberate than shooting the film.

You start with nothing but an estimated running time and gradually build the documentary out of images and sounds selected from the raw footage, choosing and organizing what the audience will see from what has been recorded.

In the end, there is nothing in the final version of your documentary that was not put there deliberately.

What About a Hidden Camera?

The question of using a hidden camera often comes up in the initial stages of planning a behavioral documentary. And the more interested you are in the behavior of people, the more likely it is to arise, and the tougher it will be to dispose of. Someone will always want to know if you don't think it's a good idea to shoot with a hidden camera.

Filmmakers doing animal documentaries may sometimes use a hidden camera, although hiding the camera and camera operator is often unnecessary. And hidden cameras with humans can be a lot of fun, as the programs *Candid Camera, Totally Hidden Videos,* and others have proven since the early days of television. But the use of a hidden camera in shooting a behavioral documentary is rarely practical, often impossible, usually unnecessary, and probably unethical.

Problems with Hiding the Camera

The obvious problem with the use of a hidden camera is that you have to hide it. However you do that—by placing it behind a one-way mirror, by camouflaging it to look like something that would naturally be in the setting, by shooting through a peephole in an adjacent wall, or by concealing the camera in a vehicle—you have given up the one great advantage of modern equipment: its portability. Essentially you have gone back to the shooting situation used in Hollywood during the early days of sound films—locking the camera away in a separate room, so that the action in the scene has to come to the camera, instead of the camera following the action.

A normal lens covers an arc of about 24 degrees. That means a locked-off, hidden camera with a normal lens can record only one-fifteenth of the activity available to a portable camera placed in the center of the action and able to point anywhere. Going to a wide-angle lens might double the viewing arc, but the increased viewing angle is gained at the loss of detail. So much for facial expression and subtle nuances of behavior.

Even if the camera is placed behind a one-way mirror or the equivalent, so that a camera operator can point it more or less anywhere within a 180-degree radius, you're still shooting from a fixed position. You can change focal length, you can follow focus, you can pan and zoom, but you can't change camera angle. If someone is standing with his back to the camera, you're going to spend your shooting time getting pictures of the back of his head and the texture of his shirt. If someone moves in close to the camera position, so that his body covers your field of view, you're out of business until he moves away.

LIGHTING PROBLEMS

The second problem with a hidden camera concerns lighting. If you're shooting outside in daylight, you're probably OK. But few films of human behavior can limit themselves to exterior shooting. Which means you're going to have to shoot under artificial lighting at some point. Fast video cameras can shoot in low light, but I notice that whenever we have control of the environment, the camera operator still prefers to set production lights to get a better picture.

The ambient lighting in most public buildings and offices with even illumination from overhead fluorescent lights generally falls within a range of about 16 to 40 footcandles. In homes and other informal settings it may be much less. In low light you may have to use a fairly wide-open aperture, resulting in a narrow range in which the picture is in focus. This is because the depth of field of any lens decreases as the size of the aperture increases. Depth of field also decreases as the focal length of the lens increases. So as you move from a wide angle to a longer focal length for a two-shot or a close-up, you again have a very narrow range in which the image will be in focus.

Therefore, if you want your pictures in focus—and that's the point to the exercise, isn't it?—you have to have enough light to shoot by. If you bring in production lights to raise the ambient light in the room, there's hardly any point in hiding the camera.

The question, of course, is not whether it can be done—*Candid Camera* proved it can years ago, when a lot more light was needed than today—but whether it is worth the extra effort and the sacrifice of mobility and image quality just to fool the subjects of your film into believing there is no camera present.

ETHICAL PROBLEMS

Another problem with the use of a hidden camera falls within the still not very well defined area of image ethics. Clearly, our society still frowns on invasion of privacy. Deliberate eavesdropping is a social no-no. And filming someone without that person's knowledge or consent—or even simply observing someone, whether you are recording or not—is deliberate eavesdropping. At some point you have to come out of your hiding place and admit you've been filming.

And at some point you have to ask the person to sign a release so that you can show the footage you shot while you were invading their privacy. When do you do that? At the end of the day's shooting? But suppose you want to come back to shoot in that location again. Suppose the footage you got is so good you want more. Suppose you want to shoot some of the people again but not all of them. Do you ask the ones you won't need anymore to keep the secret from the others? Suppose they refuse. What do you do then?

If anyone in the scene you've shot from hiding refuses to sign a release, you can't use the footage. That's it. Do you keep shooting, piling up expensive production days and a lot of video or film, in the hope that everyone will agree, later on, that the project is worthwhile? Could you find a sponsor to fund a documentary project under such conditions?

And do we have the right to observe and record what someone does when he thinks he is alone? That's a tough question to try to answer. The one thing I'm certain of is that the ethical resolution turns on what the person believes the situation to be, not on what he was doing while we were observing.

Candid Camera and its successors have gotten away with filming from hiding because they are, primarily, just big practical jokes, and a joke is one of the few acceptable ways to violate social rules. Even so, I'm sure that some people they filmed failed to see the humor, and at the very least refused to sign a release. But such programs plan on shooting many, many setups to get a few that can be used on television. I'm also willing to bet the producers' liability insurance has a large amount built in to cover lawsuits from unhappy hidden camera subjects.

No Real Need

Actually I've never felt the need to use a hidden camera. The powerful images of *Chronique d'un été* (*Chronicle of a Summer*) or *My Brother's Keeper* or *The War Room*, all shot with cameras in the open, have convinced me that there is no advantage to hiding away. I've viewed videos of psychotherapy and family therapy sessions shot both with a concealed camera and with a small camera mounted in sight but out of the way, and I saw no difference in the behavior of the subjects.

And I've seen films such as Ed Mason's *Referred for Underachievement,* in which the camera operator sat in a chair right in front of the members of a family during an initial intake interview for family therapy. Again, there was no difference in the kinds of behavior recorded between the hidden and the obvious camera. But there was a big difference in the kind of documentary that resulted. The footage shot by an active, participating, decision-making documentarian working in the open was better because of the freedom to capture the best images possible.

One Final Reason

The final reason I'm against using a hidden camera is that I've always been more than a little suspicious of the motives of the people who have suggested it. A very thin line separates the behavioral scientist from the Peeping Tom. I grew up in the tradition of the social documentary, in which there are often good guys and bad guys. I've always wanted to be on the side of the good guys.

And good guys don't shoot from hiding.

DOCUMENTING AN EVENT
WITH THE OUTCOME UNKNOWN

Whereas many documentaries, notably historical documentaries, tend to focus on the events leading to an already known outcome, a spontaneous cinema documentary records process and intention before knowing how the story will turn out.

Not knowing the outcome provides much of the fascination in watching sports, and I'd suggest that one model for documenting an event with the outcome in doubt is sports on TV, because there is conflict followed by a clear outcome and resolution. This may be why so many documentaries in this category are built on the events of some kind of competition—although not necessarily sports. *Primary, The War Room,* and *Staffers '04* cover the stressful grind of election campaigns. *Spellbound* was nominated for an Academy Award for its study of eight teenage contestants in the 1999 National Spelling Bee (the Oscar went to *Bowling for Columbine,* however—go figure). *The Cliburn: Playing on the Edge* takes us through the final days of a prestigious piano competition. *Mad Hot Ballroom,* winner of an International Documentary Association award, shows urban schoolchildren in New York City becoming "ladies and gentlemen" as they prepare for and take part in a citywide ballroom dance competition. John Huston's World War II classic, *San Pietro,* filmed during the fierce battle for the Italian town, shows a life-or-death struggle in which 1,100 Americans lost their lives. And *Six Days to Sunday,* produced by NFL Films, documents a week in the lives of the Minnesota Vikings and the Dallas Cowboys as they train for and then play a football game.

Still, there are important differences between a documentary film and a televised sporting event. These are the differences between watching the Olympics on NBC and watching a Bud Greenspan documentary about the Olympics. Sports are shown live, and when the winner is known, it's all over. A documentary, on the other hand, is never live, *always* after the fact. Even though the outcome is unknown during most of the filming, it certainly will be known—at least to the documentarian and often to the viewers as well—long before the documentary is shown to an audience. And this knowledge will influence what will be selected for inclusion during postproduction. A documentary should aspire to a deeper understanding of the process than simply who won or lost, so that competition provides the element of dramatic conflict around which the documentarian builds a more complex story.

While conflict of some sort is almost always an element of good filmmaking, not all spontaneous cinema documentaries involve some kind of competition. The incredible documentary *9/11* by Jules and Gideon Naudet and James Hanlon began as a film about the learning process, growth, and behavior of a rookie fire fighter. It became a documentary about heroism under pressure in one of the worst disasters in American history—made as it happened.

Victoria Bruce and Karin Hayes planned to make a film modeled after *The War Room* about Ingrid Betancourt's campaign for president of Colombia, run against an entrenched, corrupt establishment. Just before leaving for Colombia, the filmmakers saw on CNN that Mrs. Betancourt had been kidnapped by the Revolutionary Armed Forces of Colombia (FARC), a guerrilla group that has operated more or less freely in the country for many years. In that moment, competition as a theme evaporated, but dramatic conflict increased. The result was the award-winning documentary *The Kidnapping of Ingrid Betancourt*.

A truly delightful film, *The Hobart Shakespeareans* directed by Mel Stuart, tells the story of a fifth-grade teacher, Rafe Esquith, who uses preparing his students for a year-end performance of a Shakespeare play as a catalyst for excellence. The film records a year in the life of the class, ending with their performance of *Hamlet*. Along the way, we learn a lot about the children—and their teacher. And no one knows, until the school year ends, how it will all turn out.

Other films might document an event involving research or exploration of some kind. The outcome is always in doubt, and the film itself is the visual evidence of what happened.

PICTURES, PREPARATION, AND PERSISTENCE

Today, the economic barriers to making documentaries of events as they occur are gone. But the critical elements remain. They are pictures, preparation, and persistence.

You Need Solid Visual Evidence

What makes this sort of documentary effective is that it is a process of discovery, which shows the event as it is happening. This requires solid visual evidence, not just sound bites and B-roll. You wouldn't, for example, do a documentary about the Super Bowl using just interviews with players, coaches, sportswriters, and fans, illustrated with B-roll from various football games.

A documentary of an event with the outcome unknown requires being there with camera running, recording events as they occur. It usually means gathering a lot of footage, because you don't know in advance which is the good stuff. In *The Hobart Shakespeareans* there is a moment in which Rafe Esquith is reading to his class from *The Adventures of Huckleberry Finn*. It's the point at which Huck is trying to decide what to do about his friend, Jim, a runaway slave. At first he determines to do the "right thing" and participate in the return of the slave. He says, "I felt good and all washed clean of sin for the first time I had ever felt so in my life." And then he thinks about his friendship with Jim and changes his mind.

As Rafe is reading, the camera tilts down from him to a boy in the class, following along in his book. As Rafe reads, "I studied a minute, sort of holding my breath, and then says to myself: 'All right, then, I'll GO to hell . . . '" tears well up in the boy's eyes. A moment later Rafe asks a girl named Danielle to continue reading. She starts reading and then is overcome with the emotion of the moment and can't go on.

It's in the film because it's a great scene. It's available to be in the film because the camera was on—recording what could easily have been a nothing event, Rafe reading to the class.

Planning Is Critical

Capturing unscripted, unexpected moments such as that takes planning. Preparation for a documentary of an event with the outcome unknown requires both analysis and imagination.

When you are documenting an event of some sort, whether it's a year in the life of a fifth-grade class or a weekly poker game in your neighbor's basement, you're not working completely blind. You know a lot about the event before you start filming. You know things that are going to occur and where and when they'll be happening. Which means not only that you can be there with a camera when they happen, but also that you can develop a fairly comprehensive plan for filming them. That's analysis.

Then you try to imagine the sorts of things that might happen that you'd like to have in the film. You probably won't come up with *Rafe reads, and the class cries,* but your list might include looking for ways a good teacher touches the hearts as well as the minds of his students. And you might even have a list of possibilities. None of the possibilities on your list may happen. But making the list will help you be ready to recognize valuable things not on the list that do happen.

A PLANLESS DOCUMENTARY

I got a call from a good friend, a producer-director in Honolulu, who said his company had shot a lot of video documenting a unique event. A chain of restaurants had opened several new locations and had added some new items to their menu. They decided to make a special day out of officially opening, or reopening, five of their restaurants. They had the restaurants blessed by a minister—which is a tradition in Hawaii—and they offered live music, balloons, prizes, and freebies at each of the five locations. Customers were encouraged to visit all five restaurants that day and get a special "passport" stamped at each one to win a prize.

Members of the company's executive staff traveled from location to location accompanied by a Dixieland band and my client's video crew. My friend (and client) told me that originally the public relations firm that handled the restaurants was going to write the script, but now they wanted him to bring in a writer.

I found out why as soon as I got a look at the footage. In spite of the fact that there were two camera crews in operation all the time, and that the same procedure was gone through at each of the five restaurants, the footage was woefully incomplete. For instance, it didn't contain a complete sequence of a blessing, a complete statement of the purpose of the event by someone from management, or even a complete song from the Dixieland band. It just showed the same set of mistakes being made five times.

Along with the footage, I got some written information about what this special day was supposed to be, including the PR firm's own game plan for the event. So I had a pretty good idea of what was missing. These are excerpts from a letter I sent to my client about the footage:

> There are no shots whatsoever of the special passports (500 to be given out at each restaurant). No shots of anyone receiving a passport. No shots of anyone explaining the passport. No shots of a passport getting stamped at a store.
>
> Although six different radio stations participated, there is only limited footage of two radio DJs, and no radio broadcast audio.
>
> There is only one shot of a drawing for a door prize (which is also one of the two shots of the DJs).
>
> Too much camera time is spent on people from the PR firm riding the bus.
>
> No close-up of an employee wearing the Celebration Day button.
>
> I don't see in the footage any evidence that "each restaurant will be decorated professionally" as indicated in the game plan.
>
> There is . . . no systematic coverage of the new menu items. There is one shot of the menu, close-up of the word NEW, and no return to what is NEW.
>
> There is no complete coverage—establishing shot, medium shots and close-ups, while the sound continues—of the country and western band at Westridge Shopping Center or the Hawaiian music group at Windward City Shopping Center.
>
> No footage of the 20 × 30 posters announcing Celebration Day.
>
> We have no interviews or statements from (company executives) such as:
>
> "This is an important marketing test for use on the mainland."
>
> "We're introducing a new image—brighter, more complete restaurants, rather than takeout places—and a new menu."
>
> "This is going to be great for business."

I want to stress that this footage was not shot by a bunch of amateur wannabes who went out with their camcorders and got into trouble. The work was done by a highly regarded film and video production company in Honolulu. The production involved a director and a camera operator who had created many award-winning commercials, but who had no experience with unscripted productions, especially a documentary of a unique event. They had never developed a clear documentary idea, and therefore had not made a plan, a shot list, or even a guess list of what to shoot.

What About a Script?

Scripting will likely be no more than a well-planned treatment prior to principal photography. The treatment will describe what you are looking for and list the things you know you are going to shoot. It should give you the latitude to follow interesting developments as they occur during filming. Depending on your working style, you may want an editing script prior to postproduction, or you may "find" the film as you are editing, making do with a narration script, if required, written either during the editing process or after you have a first cut or offline version of the documentary.

Persistence Pays Off

If you've analyzed carefully, imagined creatively, and planned thoroughly (with room for serendipity) then once you've started filming, stick with it. Even though the outcome is unknown when you start, there definitely will be one. And, unless you've completely misjudged the situation, interesting things will happen along the way.

9

REMEMBERING PEOPLE AND EVENTS

In 1993, when I wrote the script for *Defenders of Midway,* I was looking back to an event that had occurred in 1942. I had available to me whatever we might have learned about the battle in the intervening fifty-one years. And that included footage shot during the famous battle by director John Ford for his film *The Battle of Midway.*

My Midway film was a historical documentary, while Ford's was a documentary of a unique event with the outcome unknown. What's the difference? Documentaries remembering people and events are after-the-fact reports, created by looking in a rearview mirror. I was probing the past, while John Ford was so much involved in filming present events as they unfolded that he was wounded during the battle.

He shot the footage he needed. I had to search for it.

What to Show and How to Show It

The first problem facing a documentarian making a film about the people or events of a prior time is finding a way to keep the film visually interesting. If the documentary is set in the twentieth century, there may be stock footage. Still photographs extend our visual resources back to the mid-nineteenth century. Earlier than that there may be a few paintings or drawings, but hardly the wealth of visual material needed to fill a serious documentary.

Words

Mostly what will exist will be precisely what you'll find in books of history and biography—words. So there's always a strong temptation to compensate for the lack of visual evidence by showing clips from interviews with experts or by using an on-camera spokesperson. Experts may contribute important information to the content of a documentary, but the sudden appearance—amid scenes of Romans in togas or Ming Dynasty Chinese—of a twenty-first-century professor in contemporary dress is not only anachronistic, it breaks the flow of the story. As to the use of a spokesperson, very few have the knowledge and charisma to match the intensity and excitement that, for example, James Burke brought to his role as a guide to time travelers in the series *Connections*. Most are just volunteer docents leading a guided tour through the museum of the past.

Words are obviously an important part of documentary storytelling. But words by themselves, no matter how well written, no matter how eloquently spoken, simply do not make a film. Having someone talk about a person or event on camera may be the easiest way to provide a picture to go with the story, but it's seldom the best.

Only on very rare occasions will what someone has to say about a person or an event be the best possible way to present that person or event. The accounts and recollections of eyewitnesses or participants usually work best, because they have the ring of authenticity. *Watermarks,* directed by Yaron Zilberman, is a sad, beautiful story of the champion women swimmers of Hakoah, a Jewish sports club in Vienna in the 1930s, told mainly by the women themselves.

On-camera eyewitness testimony obviously limits the historical reach of a film to the lifetime of any living eyewitness. Ken Burns extended eyewitness testimony in his landmark documentary *The Civil War* by quoting extensively from the letters, diaries, and memoirs of civil war participants. But he did this in voice-over, meaning he had to find something to show at the same time, while limiting on-camera talk to the ubiquitous experts.

In *Benjamin Franklin* (2002), scriptwriter Ronald Blumer put Franklin's own words in the mouth of actor Richard Easton, playing Franklin, while co-directors Ellen Hovde and Muffie Meyer found images to illustrate the account of Franklin's life. As a result, *Benjamin Franklin* is a story well told in words and illustrations, like a good children's book.

Even with an eyewitness, the documentarian still needs to search diligently for ways to bring the story to life visually. And the further we move away from eyewitness testimony, the more likely it is that the person speaking becomes just another talking head.

Keep It Visually Interesting

The documentarian always has the responsibility to find a way to portray a person or event in a manner that is visually interesting. And this should mean more than just finding some *visuals* to illustrate the words. Visually interesting footage is revealing. It shows us something we otherwise wouldn't know. And it goes beyond illustrating the text.

It ain't easy. But, as the saying goes, if it were easy, everyone would do it.

STOCK FOOTAGE

If it happened in the last hundred years, there's a chance it may have been captured on film. The National Archives is an incredible resource for film and still pictures of historical significance, available usually with no royalties or use fees, so that your only cost is the cost of making a broadcast-quality duplicate.

In addition, all television news organizations have stock footage libraries and will license the use of their footage to documentarians for a fee.

And don't overlook home movies and videos. Asking for such materials should be part of your interview checklist.

In some cases, where the archived footage contains copyrighted material from other sources, such as music, you may have to get clearance from the copyright holder. Clearance issues apparently caused the temporary disappearance of the highly acclaimed documentary miniseries *Eyes on the Prize*. Licenses for the use of news footage, various photographs, songs, and lyrics (including "Happy Birthday") used in the film expired in 1995, and the film company Blackside could not afford to renew these licenses at fees that I'm told ran into the high six figures. As I write this, the problem has been solved, and the series returned to PBS in the fall of 2006. A boxed set of DVDs is available from PBS.

STILLS

The National Archives is also a treasure trove of still pictures, going back to the Civil War and beyond. Other sources are countless private galleries and collections of photographs, plus the archives of all news organizations.

As you are researching the facts and events that will make up your historical or biographical documentary, always ask the people you are talking with for personal photos and snapshots.

ILLUSTRATION

Most of human history occurred before the invention of photography. But the documentarian may be able to find drawings or paintings dealing with the film's historical topic. Unfortunately, this all too often has meant an unending series of camera moves over the same handful of illustrations—often portraits—which provide cover for the narration and expert interviews but add little to the audience's understanding of the topic.

The documentarian can also commission drawings to represent the people and events being chronicled. And can create maps and graphics to show, for example, the disposition of forces and how a battle played out, whether it be Thermopylae or the Zulu Wars.

In a new approach to illustration, documentarians today have begun to use the sort of animated graphics found in video games to illustrate stories for which there are no images.

FICTION FOOTAGE

Filmmakers making historical or biographical documentaries will sometimes take footage from fiction films about their subject and use it to illustrate their topic. Motion picture studios used to give away this footage at a small cost, considering its use a form of promotion for their movies. Then, as documentarians found that they could make very professional-looking documentaries—mainly about film and TV stars—using this material, and as the economics of the film industry changed from ticket sales to ancillary profit centers, the cost of fiction footage went up—way up.

Obviously, if you are going to use fiction footage, you need to be sure it accurately portrays the situation presented in your film. And you should identify its source on screen.

Use a Specialist

The stock footage and still photo resource is so rich and varied that it often pays to add an archival researcher to your production team. This is a person whose profession is knowing where to look for visual materials of all sorts in government archives, in stock libraries, and in public and private collections. The fees for archival researchers are not only reasonable but can be a downright bargain both in the time researchers can save you and the possibility that they will know where to find far better footage than you are likely to turn up on your own.

Reenactment

Another way to show the story is through reenactment, re-creating the historical period or the people and events of the biography using actors, costumes, and sets. Many filmmakers who hope eventually to do feature films itch to do reenactments as a way of showcasing their writing and directing skills.

Reenactments can range from a fully dramatized presentation of the documentary topic to the use of re-creation with historical characters and dialogue in some scenes, to silent footage that illustrates whatever is being said on the sound track, such as marching soldiers in the uniforms of the period. (And why are they so often shown marching in slow motion? It makes no sense to me. Real soldiers don't do that.)

In attempting a reenactment, a documentarian assumes the responsibility for what is shown. Reenactment in documentary should follow the same rules as re-creation in a historical or biographical text. What is shown should be accurate, verifiable, and the truth as the documentarian understands it.

Research: Getting It Right

Research is the bedrock upon which you build a historical or biographical documentary. This means getting the dates, facts, and names right, of course. It also means researching the way things were—and the way they were not. It means forgetting what you think you know—or at least putting it on hold—while you search for the truth.

Be a skeptic. Almost any historical event you can think of didn't happen in the way it is portrayed in the popular wisdom. In fact, it probably didn't happen in the way it was taught in school. To inoculate yourself against accepting myth and fantasy as historical fact, take a look at James Loewen's fine book, *Lies My Teacher Told Me: Everything Your American History Textbook Got Wrong*.

Getting it right means going to several sources, and when sources conflict, looking even further. It means if you don't know the period yourself, you need to get someone on your team who does.

Don't Trust What Others Say, Do the Math

History is full of numbers—years, ages, dates, population, sizes of armies, and distances, to name just a few. A documentarian who doesn't pause to do a little adding and subtracting from time to time is likely to make some foolish mistakes. And you can't take for granted that others have done the math for you.

Here's what I mean: A few years ago I did some research for a possible documentary about Montgomery C. Meigs, an outstanding engineer and brilliant individual, who became quartermaster general of the Union Army during the Civil War. A graduate of West Point, Meigs was assigned in 1852 to design and build what became the Washington Aqueduct, ensuring an adequate supply of fresh water for Washington, D.C. Before the year was out he was also given the task of supervising the expansion of the U.S. Capitol, and adding wings to the post office building.

Meigs was an Army lieutenant at the time. Almost invariably, those writing about these events refer to Meigs as a "young lieutenant." It's just such a good story, this bright, fuzzy-cheeked boy lieutenant taking on the responsibility for these huge projects. Until you do the math. Montgomery Meigs was born in 1816. He graduated from West Point with the class of 1836, at the age of twenty. But when he took on these projects in 1852, he was thirty-six years old and had sixteen years of experience as an officer and an engineer. The Army was quite small—only 16,000 men at the start of the Civil War—and for the few hundred officers on active duty, promotions were abysmally slow. Far from being a young lieutenant, the man supervising these projects was a very *old* lieutenant.

The Way Things Were

Getting it right also means understanding the way things were at the time your film is documenting. How things worked. The social contracts that existed. The pecking order. Who did what sort of work, how, and with what. Especially if you are going to re-create the period, you—or someone—must account for hundreds of details that were a part of daily life at the time, from clothes to food to manner of speech and forms of address.

You also must put aside your twenty-first-century sensibilities and work within the values of the time you are showing. For example, there is no question that slavery is always wrong. But for most of recorded history, it was an accepted fact of life throughout the world, not just in the American South before the Civil War, but also in Africa before the arrival of the Europeans, throughout Asia for most of its history, and in ancient Egypt, Greece, Rome, and England. Portray it as it was, not as you might wish it to have been. Let your experts or your narrator comment on its immorality, if you feel a comment is necessary. Your audience, after all, already knows just as well as you that slavery is wrong.

SCRIPTING

For most historical documentaries, a full script will need to be written prior to principal photography. The script provides the structure within which the story will be told, identifies the visual evidence that needs to be shown, and specifies what will be said. (See chapter 20.)

For a narrated documentary with interviews, the script will provide the structure, visual evidence, and narration, but may simply indicate the information expected to be gained from interviews. After the interviews have been shot, the sound bites to be used will be selected and written into the script.

The script for a reenactment will be similar to a screenplay or teleplay, showing the complete action and dialogue organized in scenes to tell the story.

Double-Check Your Facts

Remember that there usually will be people in your audience who know more about some parts of the story than you do. Treat the information that goes into your script just like the notes for a master's thesis or a doctoral dissertation. Keep track of who said and did what, when, and under what circumstances. And have others check your script.

In an early draft of my script for *Defenders of Midway,* I relied on memory and wrote that dive-bombers from the USS *Hornet* and USS *Enterprise* attacked the Japanese fleet. Fortunately, as others checked the script, I got e-mails saying the bombers from *Hornet* never found the enemy fleet. It was planes from *Yorktown* (sunk at the end of the battle by a Japanese submarine) and *Enterprise* that sank the enemy carriers. Red-faced, I made the corrections, and no harm was done.

These days I sometimes embed backup data in hidden text within the script. And I recently read about a filmmaker dealing with a controversial historical topic who said he had one version of the script with every fact footnoted, so that he'd be prepared to answer any questions about anything that appeared in the film.

There is a widely expanding market for historical documentaries, and a great career awaits filmmakers who can tell good stories about people and events from the past—and get it right.

PART III

WHAT WILL
YOU SHOW?

Film is a visual medium that dramatizes a
basic story line; it deals in pictures, images,
bits and pieces of film. We *see* a clock
ticking, a window opening, a person in the
distance leaning over the balcony, smoking;
in the background we hear a phone ringing, a
baby crying, a dog barking as we see two
people laughing as their car pulls away
from the curb.

. . .

—*Syd Field*, Screenplay (2005)

10

VISUAL EVIDENCE

Communicating with an audience through an existential, visual medium is far different from communicating in a face-to-face or voice-to-voice situation. Audiences have the perverse habit of assuming that the way they think you are communicating is the way that you intended to communicate. As far as they are concerned, the message they get is the only message there is. And you have no opportunity to defend yourself—to revise, clarify, or explain what you actually meant.

Therefore, it is important to think of the images you shoot as visual evidence. It is not enough that you can argue the case for what your images mean. You'll never get the chance. The only real test is whether the images can stand on their own and argue the case themselves.

For instance, in a documentary about a protest march, there was a shot of a cold-looking police officer standing by a police barrier. Behind him was a completely empty street. The narrator said, "Twenty thousand people took to the street in protest . . ." But the visual evidence said *nobody was there.* Imagine if the voice had come from an interview rather than from the narrator. The use of this shot would have suggested to the audience that the person in the interview was not telling the truth.

This, for me, is the essential difference between visual evidence and B-roll. B-roll merely illustrates what is being said, while visual evidence works to tell your story in visual images. Silent films were great on visual evidence, because that's all they had. Go back and get a look at some of the classics, run at the proper speed. Films of the silent era were shot and projected at sixteen frames per second. Following the silent era, they were often played back on sound film projectors at twenty-four frames per second, which caused everyone to walk funny and bounce around sort of herky-jerky. Fortunately, silent films released on DVD play at the right speed, giving you the opportunity to see how visual evidence communicates.

A perfect example of visual evidence is a beautiful short film, *89mm from Europe,* which won an International Documentary Association award some time ago. The film shows how trains arriving at the border between Poland and the former Soviet Union must have all their wheels changed to proceed because of an 89mm difference in the width of the rails. Shot like a silent film—although there is voice, natural sound, and music—it is *all* visual evidence.

There Is No Substitute for Good Footage

You have to shoot the best analog of the actual situation that you can manage and then edit the footage into a single, coherent print that will clearly communicate your intentions to the people who will see it.

Advances in film and video technology have given us the ability to record images from reality that would have been impossible just a few years ago.

Cameras attached to telescopes and cameras mounted on satellites look outward into space.

Cameras using fiber optics, cameras mounted on microscopes, and cameras and video repeaters hooked up to electron microscopes, fluoroscopes, and God knows what else, are examining inner space.

Cameras take pictures in the dark using infrared film or light-gathering lenses.

Cameras operating at high speed slow down events that occur too quickly for the eye to follow.

Time-lapse photography speeds up action that occurs over too long a time for the process of change to be noticeable.

In the area of re-creation, models and miniatures are used to abstract significant details from events that are too complex to be observed in full.

Digital computer animation systems create three-dimensional pictures as if a camera were moving around—inside or outside—

structures that do not exist, presenting images of events that never happened.

Therefore, if you can think of an image, you, or someone, can make a picture of it.

Concrete Nouns and Action Verbs

The more concretely you can describe your documentary idea in terms of visual images, the better your chance of communicating it through film or video. Similarly, the more abstract or interpretive your idea is, the more important it becomes to build up evidence for the idea through specific, concrete images.

To be filmed, an image has to be solid, tangible, existential. For instance, there's no problem in filming the image-idea:

The boy runs toward the camera.

Just turn the camera on, yell, "Action!" and shoot what happens.

But it gets trickier with the addition of adjectives. How would you film this image-idea in one shot?

The frightened *boy runs toward the camera.*

Probably you'd try to have the boy act frightened—his face contorted, breathing heavily, looking over his shoulder, bumping into things, and so on. You might also try to film in a situation that helps the audience infer fright from the boy's actions: At night on a dimly lit street. In a dark forest. On a battlefield.

Let's try one more. In one shot, how can you film this image-idea?

The intelligent *boy runs toward the camera.*

You can't.

You need two scenes in sequence. First a scene that establishes the boy's intelligence, and then the shot of the boy running.

You can't film abstractions, such as:

Economics is the dismal science.

Nor can you film the absence of something:

On Tuesday, the mail didn't come.

Yes, of course, you can film two actors talking. One says, "Happy Tuesday, did the mail come?" The other says, "No." You could also put the statement in narration. You just can't shoot a picture of it.

The best you can do, in either case, is to shoot and organize a sequence of concrete events from which you hope the audience will infer your meaning.

But getting it shot is not all there is to making a documentary—not even when you are shooting events as they actually happen in the real world. Because it is not what *you* see happening that counts. It's not even what you aim the camera at that matters. It is the actual scene as it's recorded on film or video that provides the visual evidence for the audience.

Miss Darling and the Scene That Wasn't There

We were working on a documentary about open education in a classroom of third and fourth graders. The teacher was a beautiful young woman, very likable, very photogenic, who got along well with the kids. My crew immediately nicknamed her "Miss Darling."

One of Miss Darling's strong points as a teacher was that she related well to the boys in her class. Fourth-grade boys can be difficult, and some teachers have trouble with this. So I wanted to show what happened in Miss Darling's classroom.

We filmed a group of boys playing with dinosaurs in a diorama they had made until we used up the film in the camera. While Jack Behr, my camera operator on that film, reloaded the camera with a fresh 400-foot magazine, I looked around for another bit of behavior to shoot. In a quiet place, away from the other children, a husky ten-year-old boy in a football jersey was sitting with Miss Darling, learning to knit.

I liked the look of the scene and motioned to Jack and the soundman to move in and shoot. At first, I didn't have much more in mind for the scene than a few shots of a young, would-be football player and an attractive teacher, sitting together and knitting. But as we started to shoot, I began to realize that they were carrying on a conversation in low voices. From where I was standing I couldn't hear what they were say-ing, but the scene was so poignant—the boy looking up with wide, trust-ing eyes, the teacher bent toward him with a tender look on her face, the quiet conversation—that I whispered to Jack, "I don't know what's going on, but I like it. Shoot the whole magazine."

I was convinced that we were capturing an intimate and personal moment in the relationship between a teacher and her student. It would serve as a shining example for teachers everywhere that (1) the class-room won't go to hell if you spend some quiet time with one student; and (2) boys, even rough-and-tumble boys in jock sweatshirts, can be interested in more than sports and all-male activities. Beyond that, it was such a charming scene that I was convinced it would enhance the film and please the audience. In my mind, I made space for as much as five minutes of this scene in the twenty-five-minute running length of the finished film.

Unfortunately, I neglected to tell any of this to Jack while he was shooting. He had started out concentrating on close-ups of the teacher and the boy and of their hands as they were knitting. From his point of view, through the viewfinder of the camera, he was too close to them to see what I felt was going on. As a result, the footage consisted of a set of related close-ups and two-shots that covered the process of learning to knit far more extensively than was needed, but barely hinted at the deeper, more personal sharing that I thought had been there. I spent three weeks trying to edit that footage to show what I wanted, and then gave up in defeat. No matter what had actually happened in that class-room during the eleven minutes we were filming, what we had on film was a rather prosaic sequence of a boy and his teacher knitting.

And that's all.

I remain convinced that the tender, almost loving, moment between Miss Darling and the boy actually occurred in the way I witnessed it, but there was no way I could use the footage we had shot to communi-cate to an audience what I had seen and felt. Even describing it in nar-ration wouldn't do. The evidence simply was not in the footage.

A Great Opening Scene

Later, Jack found and photographed a scene so powerful that we used it as the opening shot to represent the theme of the documentary.

We were in the playground of a nursery school. The children had been tie-dyeing T-shirts, and one five-year-old boy was trying to hang his on a low clothesline to dry. He had the T-shirt in one hand and a clothespin in the other, with the clothesline bouncing up and down in front of him. The boy knew what he wanted to do. But he lacked the experience to hold the clothesline steady, drape the T-shirt over it, and secure it with the clothespin. He experimented with several different approaches, but always seemed to need one more hand than he had to complete the job. The more he tried, the more frustrated he became. This was such a clear example of the difference between knowing about something and having the skill and experience to do it, that we used the entire two minutes, uncut, as the opening scene of the film.

No audience has ever misunderstood that scene. At first they laugh at the child's difficulty, but after about thirty seconds, a large part of the audience is leaning forward as if to help him. The scene is so visually compelling that it serves as a defining moment that sets the audience on the right track to understand the rest of the movie.

That's visual evidence.

Seeing What Is There

Being able to see what you have actually recorded can be tough, even for an experienced professional. I wanted the footage of Miss Darling and the boy to be usable so badly that I worked at trying to edit it long past the point where I should have admitted to myself that the evidence simply wasn't there.

And for the person who is new to documentary, learning to see what is there can be especially hard. Most of our experience in looking at films and videos, from grade school on, has been in interpreting them. And I take the word *interpreting* quite literally to mean translating from visual imagery to some form of verbal response.

For example, I was working with a graduate class in the use of visual communication in education. I showed them *The Birth of Aphrodite,* a short, somewhat abstract and artistic film about the myth of Aphrodite rising from the sea. Then I asked, "What did you see?"

At first their responses were either generalities about beauty, art, mythology, and the human condition, or had to do with creative writing, the classics, and how to use film in the classroom.

"Yes," I said, "but what did you *see*? What is in the film? What happened within the frame? What was the first shot? What was the next shot?"

With a great deal of difficulty, and with everyone contributing, the students slowly were able to start re-creating and describing from memory the sequence of shots that made up the film.

As they worked on it, they got better. When they came to the last few shots, where we see the naked Aphrodite dancing in the moonlight at the edge of the sea, several people remembered that the "just-born" goddess had the white outline of a swimsuit on her otherwise beautifully tanned body.

We can only speculate as to whether the filmmakers noticed that flaw when they were putting the film together. Perhaps they did, and thought they could get away with it. They almost did. Or perhaps they didn't see it at all. It takes time, training, and experience to look at your own work and see it for what it is.

Behavior Is Visual Evidence

Films of behavior have to be made up of visual evidence, because no one today is willing to settle for an illustrated lecture. For instance, *The War Room* shows the behavior of people working on the 1992 Clinton campaign. There are no interviews. There is no narration. *It's all visual evidence.* I love this kind of documentary. I wish there were more of them.

Reading People

Making documentaries—and to me that usually means filming the behavior of people—gets you involved in trying to capture pieces of a process on film or video. People are seen in the middle of the process, between their history and their hopes. The documentarian can choose to trap them in roles—the manager at his desk, the housewife at the supermarket—or to explore them more fully as individuals.

It's not simply a matter of getting a lot of background footage of these people in other situations. That's the solution most often proposed by film students when they sense a caricature in the footage rather than a portrait. "If I could only see her at breakfast, or playing with her children," they say, "then I'd understand her better."

Could be. And I'm not opposed to fleshing out a portrait with anything you can get that works—if you've got the time and space in your film. But a cardboard background of a cardboard person will simply lend cardboard detail to the caricature.

When the visual evidence is well realized, however, you can get a sense of the situation in a flash. The fact is that we are all skilled at reading people. We attend not only to what is said but to the way it is said and the nonverbal behavior occurring in the situation.

Even though a documentary is not the same as face-to-face interaction, it is similar when we show a person talking with an interviewer or speaking directly to the audience. The difference is that there is no feedback channel for the audience to test their impressions of the person. They can't say, "You frowned when you said that. Are you angry about it?" What they see is all they've got. And that makes it all the more important for us, as documentarians, to record and show as accurately as we can the visual evidence in the scene.

Remember to shoot people doing what they do, even if you're mainly interested in what they have to say. Plan the location so that it becomes a part of the evidence of the scene. If you're filming an expert on juvenile delinquency who is proposing alternatives to putting adolescents in adult prisons, film her at the prison rather than in her office. You'll have the visual evidence that says this woman is talking about concrete reality, not just some theory she's concocted.

Words and Actions

Remembering that what is said and what is done should both be considered behavior, what happens when people's actions seem to contradict the words they are saying?

Here's a situation from a video of a counselor working with a husband and wife whose marriage was in trouble: If you simply had a transcript or an audio recording of the words being spoken, you could easily come away with the feeling that while all was not right with the marriage, at least the couple was trying. But if you looked carefully at the body posture and behavior of the husband and wife—with or without sound—you couldn't escape a quite different conclusion. The wife was eager to please the marriage counselor, trying to put a good face on things, quick to cooperate. The husband said little and did nothing.

At one point the counselor asked them to turn their chairs to face each other and talk to one another about their problems instead of talking to him. The wife immediately moved her chair. The husband didn't budge. He sat slumped down, hands in pockets, present—but not there. It was clear from the visual evidence of their behavior that she was living on hope, desperately clinging to the marriage, while he was already gone.

FILMING VISUAL EVIDENCE
TAKES PREPARATION

Making a documentary with visual evidence requires the filmmaker to go out and find something happening in front of the camera that tells the story to the audience far better than any interview with an expert. And that depends on the filmmaker being prepared to find the visual evidence, or to recognize it when it happens. You have to plan for filming in situations and at locations likely to provide useful visual evidence, and you must also be prepared to recognize visual evidence when it occurs, even when it doesn't show up in the way you might have expected.

A critical part of the preparation for any documentary project should be to ask yourself what you can show your audience that will help them to understand the subject. What can you show that will catch their attention? What can you show that will make them want to know more?

I regularly receive e-mails from people who want to make a documentary on some subject, but are having a hard time figuring out what to film as visual evidence and wonder if I can help. The e-mail is almost always accompanied with some statement about the people the filmmaker has lined up to give interviews. Which to me means the person is thinking about the project, which is good, but hasn't distinguished between basic research and principal photography.

One of the things you should do is to ask your interview subjects, "What can I film that will show an audience what we are talking about?" They know. They'll tell you.

Another would be to imagine you have to shoot with a silent camera. What could you film that would show the story of the documentary to your audience? What would make them say, "Wow!"?

I'll give you a hint: It isn't an interview with an academic expert.

In Sol Worth's documentary film class, when we would talk about our film ideas—and these were often pretty strange, esoteric, not very visual ideas; we were graduate students, after all—Sol would ask, "OK, how are you going to show that?" And we would kind of flail around until we finally thought up some sequence of images that we thought might convey the idea we were talking about.

Sol would listen, and if we had come up with anything that someone might conceivably record on film and edit into a communicative sequence, he'd say, "Good. That's good."

And just as we were going, "Phew, got away with that OK," Sol would ask, "How else could you show it?"

It was a way of tuning us to look for images to tell the story. And it was also a way of reminding us that even if we didn't get the perfect picture—the one in our imagination—we should be on the lookout to find something else that might work.

Quite often, the images we found were far better than the ones we had thought up.

Visual Evidence Is Not the Same as B-roll

Some filmmakers might argue that what I call "visual evidence" is the same as what they call "B-roll," but most of the time it's not. For instance, suppose they were filming my documentary idea about short WALK lights and cars that turn on red without stopping so pedestrians can't cross even when the WALK light is on. If they've shot some good visual evidence, they won't say, "I've got great *B-roll* of cars turning right on red without stopping." They'll say, "I've got some great *shots* of cars that don't stop before turning right on red. One almost hit a pregnant woman." Because they really think of B-roll as cover footage, just as I do, and they know their "great shot" is visual evidence.

Much more about B-roll in the next chapter.

Gathering Evidence

It's not enough to know what you want to shoot. It's not even enough to know what really is happening in the situation you shot. You have to have the evidence on film or video.

This has two important implications for the documentarian: First, during shooting, it's important to keep firmly in mind that the documentary is going to be edited in order to organize it to communicate with an audience. And second, during editing, it's necessary to forget, for a while, what you intended to shoot and look at what you've actually recorded.

Editing Visual Evidence

Obviously, you can't show everything you've shot. In editing, you abstract visual evidence that will serve as an accurate analog of the events that were filmed. And you organize it into a statement that will communicate to your audience—honestly, directly, and forcefully—what you know about the event.

Clearly, you have to be careful, in editing, not to distort the evidence. And that can be hard. You were there when the footage was shot. You know everything that happened. It takes only a little bit of the footage to spark your memory of the entire event. But your audience wasn't there. So the footage you choose for the scene has to stand as an accurate analog for everything you remember.

Cutting the Part Where Nothing Happens

Suppose the marriage-counseling sequence had been edited into a scene in a documentary, ending with the marriage counselor giving a summary of the case. And suppose, as so often happens, it had been edited to keep what was being said flowing smoothly. The long pauses where the husband said nothing might be cut out because the editor found them uninteresting. And the scene in which the husband didn't move his chair might be eliminated because nothing's happening. The visual evidence would have been altered so that it seemed to support the verbal statements that everything was going to be OK.

Then it would unquestionably come as a shock to the audience for the marriage counselor to state—as he actually did to me—that there was very little chance of this marriage lasting, and that a divorce might be the best solution for both parties.

Good Mother—Bad Mother

Here's a problem that came up in one of my documentaries. I had separate sequences of two mothers and their two-year-old children working and playing together. Let's call one the Bad Mother. Her own behavior was pretty neurotic, and she tended to see only her little boy's faults, never his good points. She often couldn't understand what he was doing or make sense out of what he said.

The other was clearly a Good Mother. She talked freely with her daughter, paid attention to her, and encouraged her to do things on her own. She was also a person who liked everything clean and neat. I filmed her daughter helping her mix the batter for a cake.

In editing the film, I put the two mother and child sequences back to back, the Bad Mother first. Each sequence ran about four and a half minutes, cut down from nearly two hours of original footage.

In the sequence with the Bad Mother, I had focused on the little boy. It was his behavior I was interested in. I had sidestepped and cut around the mother's neurotic outbursts as much as possible, because I wanted the audience to watch the behavior of the boy and not waste time psychoanalyzing his mother.

In the Good Mother sequence I was especially interested in one point, where the daughter is handing eggs to her mother to crack and put into the mixing bowl. Then the daughter tries to crack an egg herself. The mother exclaims, "No! Please, dear! Let me do that." But the little girl persists, and finally does crack one egg. I had been concentrating on the talk between the two, leaving in as much as possible.

When I ran the two sequences, I realized I had made a big mistake. I had included almost all of the footage in which the Good Mother clucked about the mess, worried about neatness, and said "Don't . . ." to her daughter—a total of about a minute out of the forty-five minutes of original footage.

As a result, while I had neutralized the Bad Mother, I had inadvertently ended up making the Good Mother look pretty bad. Enough that, by the time the daughter tries to break an egg on her own, an audience was quite likely to miss the point that the mother could have stopped her, but didn't. I was afraid they might see it instead as just one more case of a fussy mother worrying about the mess. So I reedited.

In the final version, the concern of the Good Mother for neatness is shown, but it doesn't overpower the important behavior of the child. And it doesn't turn a really good mother into a villain. The visual evidence of the sequence is in balance with what actually happened.

When Pictures Contradict What Is Said

When I talk about visual evidence, I'm concerned primarily with the images that are an integral part of your documentary. Every documentarian knows he's got something going if he has evidence on film or video that contradicts what the speaker says. Suppose you're doing a documentary on industrial waste. The president of a chemical company says in an interview on camera that his company is not polluting the river. But you've got footage that shows raw chemicals being discharged from his plant directly into the river. You're going to use that footage, along with the company president's statement, to show that either he is lying or he doesn't know what he is talking about. That's an obvious situation and needs no comment.

CONTRADICTION IN NARRATION

But what happens when the images and the narration are in conflict, as in the protest march film showing an empty street while the narration talked about a huge crowd? These elements are under the control of the documentarian, and the effect is to put image and sound in contradiction. Visual evidence shows what the film is about. When the images show an empty street, then that's what the film is about no matter what the narration says.

LYING BY EXCEPTION

Or let's take this situation from a public relations film made to recruit students for a famous university. Many of the strong points of the school are brought out in the film. But two scenes stick in my memory. The university is located in a cold northern city with a long, bitter winter. But there are no shots of cold, snow, and wind in the film. None. There is, however, a rather idyllic sequence of students sunbathing and swimming at a lake which almost certainly was shot during summer school, not during the regular academic year. The narration explains that the students enjoy their outings at the lake, and adds, almost as an afterthought, "Of course, it's not always like this. It can get pretty cold in winter."

In a sequence on the life of a student, the filmmakers chose to shoot an attractive female graduate student living with two other young women in an expensive townhouse close to the campus. Again the disclaimer in narration, "Of course, not all students live like this," followed by a reference to the availability of student dormitories for most undergraduates—although these are never shown.

Such disclaimers in narration mean next to nothing. The visual evidence is that if you go to that university, you'll live in an expensive townhouse and enjoy sunny afternoons at the lake.

Because that is what is shown.

Misrepresentation

A documentarian was doing a social documentary on teenagers. He had done a highly successful film about the college protest movement and wanted to look at younger people of high school age to see if he could find the roots of protest in a suburb that sent most of its children to college.

The opening scene of the film shows a lot of sixteen-year-olds, dressed up, looking very somber. The boys look sad; the girls seem on the verge of tears. I think this was used without comment as the title background. Although nothing is said, certainly the visual evidence of the footage is that being a teenager at this place at this time is a pretty serious thing.

After the film was shown on TV, the charge was made by residents of the town that this scene had been filmed at the funeral of a classmate. I don't know whether that's true or not. My point is, if a documentarian takes a scene like this out of context and uses it as evidence to give a false impression, that's lying on film.

Sure it's real; it really happened. But it's not the truth in the visual argument of the documentary.

Similarly, taking statements made by one person, but at two different times and two different locations for two different purposes, and putting them together as if they were one statement made at one time for one purpose is at least misrepresentation and probably lying. More on this in chapter 14.

UNREAL IMAGES

The modern documentarian has available a number of tools that simply did not exist a few years ago. Or even if they did exist, they were too expensive to use in a documentary. But today, when it's an easy thing to rearrange the location of the pyramids by computer, digital effects and computer animation make it possible to create images of *anything*.

I think this is wonderful, and the documentarian has every right to make use of these images, as long as they are used honestly. That means labeling made-up images as simulations. It means not using digitally enhanced images as if they had been recorded in an actual situation.

Fiction Footage

I've already mentioned documentarians using footage from fiction films to illustrate historical documentaries. I have no problem with this *as long as the audience knows what they're looking at*. But if scenes are taken from fiction and used as if they were actuality footage, so that the audience is led to believe that what they are witnessing really happened, then the documentarian has left the truth behind in order to serve some other purpose, such as keeping the story interesting. Unfortunately, that's what docudrama does, and why it is fiction based on fact and not documentary.

Reenactment

Reenactment has been a technique of documentary from its earliest days. It can be an extremely effective way of showing an event for which no footage exists. In reenactment as with any other footage not documenting real events, the documentarian must be honest and accurate. It might make a great dramatic scene to show Thomas Jefferson having a lover's quarrel with Sally Hemings, but it wouldn't be honest.*

If you are going to dress people up in costumes and give them the tools and weapons from an earlier time, be sure what you show is correct for the period.

---

*As I write this the Jefferson-Hemings issue still has not been completely resolved by historians and may never be.

11

B-ROLL AS ILLUSTRATION, METAPHOR, AND VISUAL WALLPAPER

The concept of B-roll comes from the film days in TV news. Two rolls of film would be loaded on film projectors feeding into TV cameras. One was called the A-roll, which showed the reporter on camera talking or interviewing someone who was talking. The other was the B-roll, which carried the "visuals" that illustrated the story the reporter was talking about.

B-roll is cover footage, pictures that run while someone is talking. It's like the children dressed up as shepherds or wise men in a Christmas pageant—there to provide something for the audience to look at while they listen to the words. It's not evidence, just illustration.

For example, in the first hour of the miniseries *FDR* on *American Experience,* the story is told entirely through narration and sound bites from interviews. At the very opening of the film, we see newsreel footage of the train carrying President Roosevelt's body to Washington and the people lining the tracks to pay their respects. After that, what we see consists of camera moves on still pictures, a few atmosphere shots from the Roosevelt estate at Hyde Park, a few newsreel shots of political events in the last ten minutes or so, and, of course, the talking heads of interviewees. Watched with the sound turned off, the images tell no story, although one can occasionally infer key points in the life of young Franklin Roosevelt.

The B-roll Mentality

What troubles me about the whole concept of B-roll is what I might call the B-roll mentality:

- Planning a documentary around a series of interviews. (More on that in chapter 12.)
- Thinking that the verbal statement (the A-roll) is the more important thing.
- Thinking of all noninterview footage as "B-roll" and all non-interview filming as "getting some B-roll."
- Which leads to believing that as far as the images are concerned, close enough is good enough.
- And, perhaps the biggest problem of all, accepting what people tell you, rather than going out with a camera and seeing for yourself.
- Because, if you consider the message of the documentary to be in the interviews and narration, why take the time and trouble to locate and record strong visual evidence, when all that's needed is to cover twenty seconds of talk so the screen won't be blank?

Any time you see action in a documentary in slow motion for no reason, it's B-roll. But if the shot is in slow motion so you can better see what actually happened, it's visual evidence.

Any time a shot in a documentary could be taken out of the film and replaced with something completely different, it's B-roll. If it has to be there, it's visual evidence.

When you see the same shot used over and over again, it's B-roll.

The B-roll mentality is what allowed the filmmakers making a documentary about a historical figure in the American Revolution to shoot a steel-hulled sailing ship for a scene set in the early eighteenth century, and put that shot in the film. I mean a close-up of the hull—bow wave curling back as the ship goes through the water— so that you can see it's made of steel. Wrong century.

Before making my documentaries on kids and schools, I screened all the films I could find on early learning in children. Many of these films had obviously had the narration written before the film was shot, so that the script followed the child development theories of whatever expert was the consultant to the film. Then shots of children illustrated the narration. But quite often the behavior shown was not the behavior described. The narration might say that at a certain age young boys join together in inseparable gangs. Which was accepted child development dogma at the time. What we actually saw on the screen, however, was several boys on a playground, but each boy was playing by himself. The film offered absolutely no visual evidence to support the gang thesis. It was all B-roll, as if the filmmaker, or the expert, or both, had decided that everyone knows that at a certain age young boys gang together, so it would be enough to show a bunch of boys—no matter what they were doing—for everyone to get the point.

B-roll and TV

Try watching TV news with the sound (and closed captioning) turned off. Usually you can make only a wild guess at what's happening. B-roll illustrates talk. If you can't hear the talk, it makes little or no sense.

In some circles—and even some university documentary courses—it is conventional to plan principal photography for a documentary in terms of how many interviews need to be shot, and how much B-roll will be needed. That's exactly how you make a TV show and stay within budget and on deadline, but it is not, in my opinion, how to make a documentary.

I'm a big fan of the competitions on the Food Network, where several master chefs compete in producing phenomenal cakes, pastries, and sugar structures. These are not documentaries, of course. They are reality TV game shows. But when these programs started a few years ago, we viewers got a good chance to see all of the hard work that went into the chefs' creations.

Then as the shows got popular and began to be produced on an assembly line, the B-roll mentality took over. Today the shows are all about the talk, with lots of fast cuts, swish zooms, and constant camera motion, so that we don't really see what is happening, as much as we get a sense of activity, while the host tells us in voice-over how the competition is progressing. The only time we get any solid visual evidence is at the end of the competition, when the chefs must move a fragile five-foot-tall sugar sculpture from their kitchen area to a display table for final judging. This is the riskiest time of all, because these creations can—and often do—shatter and crash during the move.

That, the cameras cover from every angle.

B-roll as Illustration

Well, you might ask, if B-roll is so bad, why use it at all? The short answer is that you use B-roll to illustrate what is being said in interviews or narration when you don't have other footage. Documentaries remembering the past face this problem constantly. There may be stock footage or photographs of the period, person, or event. But these were almost always shot for some purpose other than the one the documentarian now has in mind. So they must be used, not as evidence, but as illustrations of the time and the people being talked about.

The challenge for the filmmaker is to make illustrative B-roll more than kids in towels playing shepherds. You have to dig for images that help to advance the story, that give the viewer information as well as something to look at while someone talks.

Bringing a War Story to Life

Here is an example: I was approached about writing/revising the script for a documentary called *The Borinqueneers* about an infantry unit during the Korean War. These men had attacked and taken Hill 391 several times, while sustaining heavy casualties. Each time they had been driven off the hill by devastating enemy artillery fire. Finally, some of the men refused to go up the hill again, and they were later court-martialed.

The filmmakers, Noemi Figueroa Soulet and Raquel Ortiz, had hours of interview footage with former members of the unit and with a military historian. They knew a lot about the people in the unit and the injustice that had been done to them, but probably less about what it was like to be in the Army in the 1950s or to serve as an infantryman in combat. In the rough cut they sent me, the illustrative B-roll was mostly rear-echelon footage: soldiers living in tents, going through a chow line, riding in trucks, that sort of thing. There was little combat footage.

While I did not become involved with the production, I thought it was an extremely worthwhile project and a story that should be told. And I thought it needed better footage to bring to life the events the interviews described. I wrote:

> The documentary needs more of a sense of what war is about—
> especially the war of the infantryman. It is hell. It's hell when you're
> winning and hell when you lose. It is just terrible. I think we need to
> see this. We need to see and hear artillery and mortar shells landing.
> The Chinese were very accurate with mortars. And when the viewers
> get to Hill 391 they need to know that there was a lack of artillery

ammunition, and because of this the unit did not receive artillery support in the form of counter-battery fire, which would have suppressed some of the Chinese fire. Without it, the Chinese were free to fire on the unit at will. Viewers need a stronger sense that the unit went up Hill 391 and held it for five days against terrifying fire, and went back again and again and again, before some men decided that this was suicidal. That the refusal to go was less cowardice than a grim appraisal of reality. They need to get a stronger visual sense of war on that hill.

On the other hand, *Devil's Playground*, a documentary about the time in their late teens when Amish youngsters are free to experience the world outside the Amish community, uses lots of shots of Amish life to cover voice-over from interviews. While this functions as illustrative B-roll, it is also visual evidence of the nature of Amish life, which is a big part of the story.

B-roll as Metaphor

A visual metaphor is an image that stands for something else. In a film about New York fire fighters following 9/11, the filmmaker used a shot of three firemen's turnout coats hanging alone on a long row of coat pegs as a metaphor for dead firemen lost in the 9/11 tragedy.

Metaphor is a kind of symbolic B-roll. As the sound track talks about the strength of the nation, for instance, the filmmaker might show visuals of rugged mountains or towering redwood trees.

Metaphor is always explanation, never evidence. It is not even circumstantial evidence. If we say, "John is a tiger," we may mean many things: John is strong or brave or aggressive or ruthless or a killer. What we do *not* mean is that John is literally a tiger.

In a script I reviewed for an information video about pharmaceutical software, the writer used the visual metaphor of a jigsaw puzzle, and showed a picture of each component as a piece in the puzzle. This illustrated the idea that all of the components fit nicely together. However, a metaphor either gets the concept across quickly or not at all, and in this case, the point was made the first couple of times pieces of the puzzle graphic clicked snugly together. But the image continued over and over for the rest of the film until the puzzle was complete. While the puzzle metaphor was apt, it was hardly compelling. It was just another way of telling the audience the same information that was being said on the sound track, rather than showing the audience evidence of the ways the components of the program actually worked together.

B-roll as metaphor can seem like truth in a different package, because the metaphoric explanation may feel like evidence, even though it isn't. When a metaphor works, it helps us to understand something, to clarify and expand our way of thinking, but it is never proof.

Of course, when a metaphor doesn't work, it often seems like nonsense.

The new-age documentary *What the #$*! Do We (K)now!?* is full of metaphor as a way to explain concepts for which the filmmakers simply offer no evidence. So we see a lot of high-end graphic animation along with a little allegory featuring Marlee Matlin as a woman named Amanda, who has a lot of questions about her life.

Graphics are illustration, never evidence. And a made-up story about a fictional character, when coupled with statements from interviews or a narrator, is not proof of anything.

I am not opposed to visual metaphor as a form of explanation. I just don't want it confused with visual evidence.

B-roll as Visual Wallpaper

Talk-talk documentaries often use neutral images to provide filler to cover the continuation of an interview as voice-over, or as cutaways to cover an edit in an interview. Outside, shots of trees and sky are favored. Or any nature scene—a stream, flowers, whatever. Inside you have the long tilt down a wall to arrive at nothing in particular, or furniture, books, whatever. These scenes may be very pretty, even occasionally dramatic, but they are shot as filler—visual wallpaper—not as evidence to make a visual argument.

For example, in *FDR* we see an exterior of the house at Hyde Park, at dusk, with light showing through a single window in the upstairs. The camera pushes in to a close-up of that one illuminated window as the narrator says, "While Franklin was at Harvard, his father, seventy-two years old and grown frail and weak from heart disease, died. Sara wrote in her diary, 'All is over. He merely slept away.'"

I have no idea what that shot is supposed to mean. I can conjecture that it is supposed to symbolize the room in which Franklin's father died. But if he died in his sleep, why was the light on? Or why didn't it go off at the end of the scene? As it is, it's visual wallpaper, no better, or more informative, than a hundred other images that might have been used to cover that bit of narration.

When we've seen the same portrait of George Washington or Napoleon or Catherine the Great several times, but the documentarian keeps coming back to it whenever the person's name is mentioned, that's visual wallpaper.

If people in a documentary are traveling by ship or boat, then the first time we see a shot of the wake or the curl of the bow wave, it's illustration, possibly even a metaphor for moving on. The second time we see the same shot, it's visual wallpaper. The same with shots of the rails on which a train is traveling. Or a plane flying through the clouds.

Show the Visual Evidence

As a documentarian, your job is to find, record, and organize visual evidence to make a powerful, dramatic statement on the screen. Evidence shows the audience something both real and true which they can understand to be a portion of the documentary argument. A strong visual demonstration will almost always be the best evidence you can use.

The minute you find yourself thinking about visuals or B-roll footage, an alarm should go off in your head to tell you that you lack the visual evidence you need and are relying on words to tell your story.

Show us what happened, instead.

12

A SHORT SERMON
ABOUT INTERVIEWS

This is a marvelous time to make documentaries. We have lightweight, inexpensive video cameras that can run for up to several hours without changing recording media and can record a broadcast-quality image in almost any light. It is equipment that allows a documentarian to go into virtually any situation and record visual evidence—activities, behavior, and events as they happen. And yet, many would-be documentarians think first of using this marvelous technology to record interviews.

Why?

Could it be because it is so much easier to ask an expert than to go out and learn about the subject on your own—with a camera?

Promiscuous Interviewing

When all documentaries were shot on film, and it cost about $150 (equivalent to $500 today) to shoot and process a 400-foot magazine of color film to get an eleven-minute interview, we could not afford to shoot interviews promiscuously. We needed that expensive footage for visual evidence. But the switch from film to video, and the bargain-basement cost of cameras and recording media, have made it possible to record hour upon hour of interviews for almost no direct, out-of-pocket cost. This has turned the ratio of visual evidence to interview footage upside down.

I cringe when I hear a producer or director talking about shooting lots of interviews and then having them transcribed so he or she can work from the transcript in editing the documentary. Because usually what will result from this sort of promiscuous interviewing is something that may be more than a Q&A magazine article, perhaps even more than the sort of thing you might hear on talk radio, but it will definitely be something less than a film. It will just be people talking.

A Modest Crusade

My modest crusade is to return the documentary to filmmakers who deal in visual evidence. I don't think much of talkumentaries. Yes, the testimony of eyewitnesses is important and may be the only evidence available in some cases. But too much of the talk in modern documentaries is there, I fear, because it's so much easier to do an interview than to go out and find a compelling image.

Don't get me wrong, I believe in interviews. I've done thousands of them as a documentary filmmaker, as a scriptwriter, and as a book and magazine writer. I think they are an extremely helpful research tool. In researching a documentary, I expect to gather a lot of information about the topic prior to shooting, much of it from interviews. But I am constantly looking for the visual evidence that will permit me to tell the story with pictures.

Interviews Usually Aren't Evidence

Interviews present special problems that many documentarians seem not to be aware of. For instance, when interviews in a documentary use what is said as evidence, then the rules regarding testimony come into play, starting with the caveat that just because a person—even an important person—said something, that doesn't make it true.

TALK WITHOUT VISUAL EVIDENCE

Here's a scene from *What the #$*! Do We (K)now!?*: A man (identified in the closing credits, but not before, as Dr. Joe Dispenza, D.C.) sits in what looks like a rustic lodge, with a huge fireplace behind him, and talks about perception, memory, and reality. He says:

> Scientific experiments have shown that if we take a person and, uh, hook their brains up to certain PET scans or computer technology, and ask them to look at a certain object, and they watch certain areas of the brain light up. And then they've asked them to close their eyes

and now imagine that same object. And when they imagine that same object, it produced the same areas of the brain to light up as if they were actually visually looking at it. So it caused scientists to back up and ask this question: So who sees then? Does the brain see? Or do the eyes see? And what is reality? Is reality what we're seeing with our brain?

This dissolves to a large public area where we see "Amanda" (played by Marlee Matlin) looking at images on a computer. The man continues, voice-over:

Or is reality what we're seeing with our eyes? And the truth is, is that the brain does not know the difference between what it sees in its environment and what it remembers, because the same specific neural nets are then firing.

Dissolve to a young boy blowing a string of soap bubbles, as the man concludes, voice-over:

So then it asks the question: What is reality?

The opportunity for visual evidence—showing the "scientific experiments" the man describes—is ignored. Instead we have only his statement, which is evidence that he said the words, but not that the words are true, along with some B-roll metaphor that might loosely allude to the great mystery of the nature of reality.

LESS THAN THE WHOLE TRUTH

One of the techniques of docuganda is to build a case for or against something by selecting only the sound bites that the filmmaker agrees with and ignoring any statements to the contrary. This is like the witness in a TV courtroom scene who is asked a loaded question and instructed to answer yes or no. When she tries to explain that a simple yes or no is insufficient, she's told to "just answer the question." Everyone knows her answer may be *true*, but it's not the whole truth.

In a documentary interview, you have to probe for the full story, not just the favorable parts. And if you leave out the stuff that hurts your case, you're really not making a documentary.

The Rules of Evidence

So, suppose you are shooting a documentary about a subject that has become controversial. One side makes charges. The other side denies them and makes countercharges. Being a modern documentarian you shoot interviews with people from both sides. What sort of evidence do you have?

The fact is that while an interview is prima facie evidence that the person shown said the words that were spoken, it carries no evidence whatsoever about the truthfulness of the statements the person makes. Even in court, where the interview form—questions by an attorney, answers by a witness—is the way virtually all information is elicited, there are complex rules governing what information can and cannot be used. This is because the courts know that what people say is terribly unreliable.

- They may not remember things correctly.
- They may leave out something that should be included.
- They may include or imply something that is not accurate.
- They may not tell the truth—or the whole truth.
- They may not really understand what they are talking about—even if they are credentialed experts on something or other.

HEARSAY

Under some circumstances, courts will exclude testimony about what someone else said. This is called the hearsay rule. If Alice, as a witness, says, "Tiffany told me she got home at one a.m.," the statement is inadmissible as evidence about what time Tiffany actually got home. Why? Because Alice doesn't know what time Tiffany got home. She only knows what Tiffany told her. But the statement might be acceptable as evidence that Tiffany actually said these words. For example, if Tiffany said, "I told Alice I didn't get home until four," Alice's testimony about what time she was told would be relevant.

But note that we still don't know which of them is lying. Possibly both of them are.

CROSS-EXAMINATION

Rules of evidence also require that the speaker be subject to cross-examination. He or she is not allowed to drop a verbal bombshell and simply walk away, as happens in so many one-sided documentaries. In court, the other side gets to ask questions.

Some filmmakers use interviews with people identified as former employees of the company or agency that is the target of their investigation. Doing so suggests they have inside information about the day-to-day operations of the target. And well they may. But as opposing counsel, I would want to know why this person is a *former* employee, and whether he or she has an ax to grind.

In chapter 2 I wrote about a film on health care my partner and I reviewed. The questions we raised about the assertions that health care companies are making a 20 percent return on investment and are motivated only by greed are the kind of cross-examination completely missing in this film. A speaker may sincerely believe every word he or she is saying. It may be unquestioned common knowledge among the people the speaker hangs out with. But on cross-examination, you would want to test the validity of that knowledge. You'd want company names. You'd want to hear actual numbers. You'd want to be sure the 20 percent actually referred to return on investment, rather than, say, a 20 percent increase in profit. A company whose profits went from 5 to 6 percent has made a 20 percent increase in profit, but just a 6 percent return on investment. I don't know what the truth is about profits in commercial health care. But these statements raise questions in my mind that are not answered in the film.

A little cross-examination would help most interviews. Playing devil's advocate—asking hard questions, indeed, questions that may be counter to your purpose in making the documentary—can either help you prevent inaccuracies from being included in the film or bolster the truth value of what a speaker is saying.

Behavioral Evidence

An audience, like a jury, is not above using behavioral cues to decide whether or not to believe an interviewee. The speaker's dress and manner, as well as the logic of the statements made, can have a powerful effect on an audience.

I once did an interview with two employees of a mental institution. Both of them were leaders of the committee to keep the institution from being closed down. One was a lay therapist who dressed in hippie chic, tilted his head at a crazy angle when he talked, and spoke in a mixture of street slang and social science jargon. He made several good points in favor of keeping the institution open. But in the course of an eleven-minute interview, he also made two or three totally outlandish statements.

The other man was the union shop steward and a member of the janitorial crew. He had a full beard, neatly trimmed, and was wearing his working clothes. What he said wasn't elegant, but he spoke in an even voice and stated the facts as he knew them. Most important, his attitude and behavior indicated that he believed what he was saying.

This was a sponsored documentary, and the sponsor was trying to remain neutral but actually leaned toward closing the institution. So it would have been an easy thing to use the interview with the weird lay therapist. Most audiences would find him unlikable and difficult to believe, not so much because of what he said but because of the way he said it. Fortunately, the sponsor agreed with me that doing that would be stacking the deck. We chose to keep the visual evidence neutral and use the statement by the shop steward instead.

SUBTITLES OR SIMULTANEOUS TRANSLATION?

Behavioral evidence is the reason I favor use of subtitles rather than simultaneous translation when the person being interviewed speaks in a foreign language. I also advocate subtitles when the interviewee speaks English with a heavy accent. The subtitles let us know the words that have been said, while also hearing the original statement lets us know *how* they were said.

In simultaneous translation, the voice of the speaker fades under, and we hear only the translator. For example, a program called *Natasha and the Wolf*, shown on PBS's *Frontline* some years ago, is a film constructed from interviews. Much of what is shown, visually, is reenactment, and often seems to bear little relationship to what is being talked about. Therefore there is no convincing visual evidence, just B-roll. The interviews are conducted in Russian with simultaneous translation into English. Without the ability to hear the way the speaker talks, since the voices are covered over by simultaneous translation, there is no way to use behavioral clues to evaluate the information.

Best Evidence

Occasionally, interviews provide the best evidence about events that happened for which no footage exists. My friend Sy Rotter created a compelling series of documentaries about the rescuers who saved Jews from the Nazi extermination machine during the Holocaust, mainly by interviewing actual rescuers and Holocaust survivors. Their memories of those events, often filmed at the actual locations, were a powerful way to tell the story. And as Sy points out, the interviews provided not just the facts, but the emotion of the event.

Evidence That the Words Were Said

In our highly partisan political arena, there seems to be a news story every week (even more often close to an election) about a politician or candidate who said something he shouldn't have. The speaker often claims later to have been misquoted or to have had the statements taken out of context.

If an interviewee in a political film likens the president to Adolf Hitler and his administration to the Third Reich, that doesn't make the statements true, but the footage is evidence that this person actually made those outrageous accusations. The interview is visual evidence of what words were said, who said them, under what conditions, and in what way—as long as it is run uncut or we have access to the original footage to determine that the sense of the statement in the interview has not been changed by editing.

Pitfalls of Planning a Film Based on Interviews

The first and most obvious problem with basing a documentary primarily on interviews is that you have given up the major advantage of filming, which is the ability to *show* your audience something. There's a reason interviewees are called talking heads. That's what there is to see: a head, talking.

Dull, Duller, Dullest

Don't think that my prejudice against making documentaries out of interviews stems solely from my early days of shooting with a silent film camera and later adding nonsynchronous sound. As a documentary scriptwriter for hire, I've spent hours and hours looking at interview footage and reading transcripts, because that's what the director had. And here's the truth: Most people are not very good in interviews. They don't speak in short, clear, convincing sound bites. They talk too much and say too little. They can't get to the point. They make grammatical errors. They use the wrong words. They repeat themselves. They say things in a way that doesn't make sense. Their statements often lack any real depth. They can be boring. They can be *very* boring.

Here's an excerpt, right off the transcript from an interview with a contract worker who was spending a year at Midway Atoll, helping to clean up the environment so the Navy could turn it over to the Park Service:

WORKER

The Navy's conducting environmental programs on Midway that are, ah, predominant. That's gonna be primarily linked to installation restoration or environmental cleanup. Um, since the Navy came to Midway a number of, ah, which we are learning now, bad decisions, were, bad decisions were made. The same as back in the States. Ah, we used to think asbestos was not harmful. We, also, used to think that lead paint was not harmful. Ah, so, we, like so many other places back in the States, we now have to clean up.

There's a bit of good information in that clip, but it's buried in a meandering response that runs for forty seconds. Sure, you could edit it to make it usable, especially if you were to use it in voice-over. Or you could place the good information economically in narration, while you show the cleanup work that is actually being done.

INDIRECT COSTS

While interviews may be cheap to shoot, many documentarians don't count the indirect costs of extensive interviewing.

The first of these is time spent managing footage after it has been shot. It takes longer to view and log interviews than visual evidence. A short description will often suffice for visual evidence, but some sort of transcript—or at least a summary of what is said—is required for interview footage.

Adding to the actual cash cost of shooting interviews, many documentarians now send out the interview footage for transcription by a stenographer. A whole new industry has sprung up to provide documentarians with transcriptions keyed to the time code of the video.

Second, since interviews are so inexpensive to shoot, documentarians tend to let each interview go on longer than they probably should, and to shoot more of them, because, hey, it's just video. Which results in a bigger pile of interview footage to manage *after* shooting.

Third, interview statements can be time-consuming on the screen. They may slow down the flow of the film. And obviously a talking head is usurping screen time that might better be used for visual evidence.

Fourth, and the most damaging from my point of view, time spent shooting interviews is time *not spent* finding and shooting visual evidence.

LEARNING THE WRONG THING

You learn from what you do. But you learn nothing from what you don't do.

If you plan and shoot your documentary around doing interviews, that will be what you learn how to do, and that will become your comfort zone.

But it won't help you learn how to find, shoot, and tell your story using visual evidence.

End of the Sermon—Somebody Say Amen

The best use of interviews is as a way to amplify upon, and help the audience understand, what is being shown. When used in moderation, interviews can provide the audience with background information, technical details, history, and, sometimes, eyewitness accounts. Statements from recognized experts can be used as a supplement to narration and will often add credibility to the documentary argument when they are combined with compelling visual evidence.

So yes, you are probably going to use interviews. We all do. What I am pushing for is that you don't settle for showing clips from an interview before you have explored other visual options. What would you do, for example, if the interview existed only on audiotape, and the interviewee was no longer available to be filmed?

Try starting with the question, "What will I show?" rather than "Who will I interview?"

No, it's not easy.

Yes, it will make you a better documentary filmmaker.

Talk is cheap.

Good footage is hard.

But it's worth it.

13

WELL, WHAT ABOUT REALITY?

As technology changed the way documentaries were shot, filmmakers could—and did—record events as they happened. And because they filmed real people (not actors) doing real things in a real situation, it was almost inevitable that they began to think of nonfiction filmmaking as documenting reality.

Recording "Reality"

The undeniable fact that spontaneous cinema and behavioral documentaries were shot in a real situation became the justification, if not the outright excuse, for any number of conceptual errors.

CONFUSING ACTUALITY WITH TRUTH

One was the error of trying to stuff reality into a box, which came from confusing the truth of the documentary with the *actuality* of the situation in which it was shot. If it happened, it's real, the argument went. And if it's real, it's true.

Not really.

It may be worth noting that the French chose the term *vérité*, not *réalité*, to describe *cinéma* as found in the behavioral documentary. What is shot bears only an ideal relationship to what is shown. The documentary shown to an audience is a carefully constructed analog that has been abstracted from the footage that was shot. It has been tempered by the overall truth of the situation as the documentarian understands it and, indeed, by the *honesty* of the documentarian in constructing the program.

The distinction between truth and reality was an obvious and necessary one in the early days of documentary film. The technology simply didn't permit much direct filming of actual events. So a documentary was expected to be *true* in the sense that it was based on fact and its accuracy could be verified. But it wasn't expected to be *real*. Most documentaries were re-creations of events, using actors and written scripts, and were often shot in a studio just like fiction films.

The documentary film—from *Battleship Potemkin* to *The River* to *Harvest of Shame*—was clearly an analog to the event being shown. It was "documentary" because it was based on documented facts that were a matter of record and not just the product of a scriptwriter's imagination. In those days a documentary was expected to be true, but not necessarily to be real, because reality was usually too fleeting and elusive to be captured by slow film stocks, heavy cameras, and cumbersome, inadequate sound systems.

Cinéma Vérité and the Question of Reality

Cinéma vérité showed a new way to film behavior. A subtle shift developed, away from the technological stance in which the film that was to be made controlled the action in front of the cameras, toward a new notion of letting the action control the film. Naturally, what you might anticipate happening, did happen. Everyone wanted to try it, and as the 1960s passed into the '70s, there was a rush to take cameras somewhere—anywhere!—turn them on, and let events record themselves.

In various communities, kids were given 8mm cameras and a few minutes' instruction and were told to go out and make a movie. Hospitals and mental health institutions bought video equipment and began to record hours and hours of human behavior. Public schools jumped into film and video with a vengeance.

The "subtle shift" had become a vicious backswing away from technological control and all that went with it. And that, unfortunately, included technical competence and planning. In a sense, filmmaking was trapped in a new kind of technological tyranny, which posed as complete freedom. These beginning filmmakers quite literally were saying, "We don't need all that. We'll just point the camera at something interesting, and it will make the film for us."

In the early '70s, Public Broadcasting commissioned a landmark spontaneous cinema documentary series about the members of a single family. And when the furor over *An American Family* died down, the notions of cinematic truth and cinematic reality had taken some heavy blows to the body, and all that remained was the conviction that what was shown in the series had, in fact, happened—somewhere, sometime—while a camera was running.

But the belief in the "realness" of a documentary came—as it always has—from the way in which the director, camera operator, and editor selected what was to be shot and shown, and organized it for presentation to an audience as an accurate analog of the situation that was filmed.

GLORIFYING GRAB FOOTAGE

The new film technology provided the illusion of recording reality by letting filmmakers shoot candid, unstaged, undirected, sound footage of people, events, and places that previously had been impossible to get. And this led to the error of justifying poor footage on the basis that it was shot in a real situation—on the fly, as it were. I'm guilty along with the rest. I shot with high-speed, color reversal film under fluorescent lights and sometimes got images that looked like fifty-year-old wallpaper.

In fact, in a triumph of form over content, I stuck a swish pan and focusing zoom that went nowhere into the final version of my first spontaneous cinema documentary just because I thought it gave the feel of actuality filming to an otherwise fairly humdrum scene.

Would I do that today?

No.

WINGING IT

There is the recurring error of believing that recording an event as it happens does away with any need to plan the shoot in advance. Quite the opposite is true.

Serendipity plays a part in documentary just because you are working with actuality. And every now and then, someone chances to turn on a camera just as something interesting happens in front of the lens. But the good stuff—including the "unplanned" good stuff—is most often the result of a shooting plan that puts camera and crew in situations where something interesting is likely to happen. Indeed, the less you know about what will happen, the more essential it is to plan for what *might* happen.

Reality Is Not Enough

If you're serious about doing documentary, you're going to have to come to grips with the reality problem. You can start by getting rid of a couple of notions that have had great influence on making documentaries but simply don't hold up on close examination.

THE CAMERA DOESN'T LIE

The first of these is the naive belief that the camera doesn't lie. Which is nonsense. To paraphrase Edsger Dijkstra: *The question of whether a camera can tell the truth is no more interesting than the question of whether a submarine can swim.* That's not what a camera does. What a camera does is to record a very coarse analog of the light patterns in front of the lens.

What is a picture? On film it's the result of the clustering of silver halide or dye molecules into black dots or points of color. Look closely enough, and the image disappears. On videotape it is a magnetized signal that will cause a video tube to create a pattern of light, dark, and color on a television screen. In digital video it is a stored pattern of ones and zeroes yielding the same effect: a display of light and color on the screen.

It is only the mind of the viewer, making inferences from these shadows and color patterns, that gives them meaning.

ACTUALITY EQUALS TRUTH

The second notion, in all its eloquent and complex permutations, has accounted for thousands of silly, unintelligible, and stupid films and videos. It is this: *What was filmed really happened, therefore it is true, and will be accepted by an audience as true.*

Which is simply not true.

Even if we define reality as whatever happens when the camera is on that is spontaneous, unplanned, unrehearsed, and undirected—which neatly sidesteps several thousand years of philosophical speculation about the nature of reality—there is no reason to assume that what was captured by the camera is *true*.

At the most obvious level, if we film someone telling a lie, then what is the truth of the scene? We've documented that the person said whatever was said. But we may have no way of knowing whether what was said is true. Even if we know the person is lying, we may not know why. Perhaps it's just a joke. Perhaps the person is psychotic and doesn't know he is lying. Or perhaps the interviewee is simply repeating what he has been told and believes to be true. While we have recorded a piece of what happened, its mere existence tells us little or nothing about its truth value.

How about this: In a dusty village, a person with his hands bound behind his back kneels in a dirt road. A man in uniform takes a pistol from his holster and shoots the kneeling man through the head. Cold-blooded murder? Perhaps. Or maybe a legal execution according to the laws of that country or the mores of that culture. Again, we have recorded a piece of what happened, but may need a great deal more information to communicate meaning, and to define the truth of what we've filmed.

Even if what we've recorded *is* documentably true, it is dangerous to assume that an audience will judge the truth of a sequence in a documentary on the basis of its objective *realness*. The person telling the truth may behave on film like a liar. The scene of an execution in the middle of the street may look staged to an audience.

THE FORM OF REALITY

A nonfiction video or film, every bit as much as a Hollywood movie or a Broadway play, must work within the framework of audience beliefs, conventions, and expectations. The images on the screen may be both *real* and *true,* but if they lack the appearance of truth, you are setting up a credibility gap with your audience that you may never overcome.

For example, in the early days of the cinéma vérité movement, documentaries were shot on film. The only way to record any kind of an image in the low light of most practical locations—even with some minimal production lighting—was to shoot what was then called high-speed black-and-white film. The resulting images were coarse-grained, often very contrasty, and with little or no production value to the lighting. And for a time this became the *look* of the reality documentary: black and white, grainy—often scratchy—images with bad lighting.

And now we have *shaky-cam,* which yields a jumpy image that never settles down to let the action unfold in front of it, because it is too busy emulating a camcorder in the hands of a hyperactive child. This is the urban myth of reality video: That actuality comes handheld, badly lit, and with muffled sound, even though today's technology allows us to record rock-steady, well-lit scenes with decent audio—even in hot situations.

Does this mean you have to use the shaky-cam convention to make a believable documentary? No. Which is why I wouldn't use that swish-pan, focusing-zoom shot today. But you should be aware that there are formal elements in shaping the documentary communication you will eventually show your audience. It means you may even have to be cognizant of conventions from fiction such as *verisimilitude*—the appearance of truth—in order to make a documentary statement that is not only true, but believable. More on verisimilitude in chapter 28.

If you think of your documentary as a model of the actual situation in which you filmed, then you have a responsibility to your audience to make it the best, most accurate model you possibly can. And that's not done in the camera, it's done on the screen.

High Degree of Abstraction of Film and Video

Earlier in this chapter I suggested that a picture is a pattern of molecules, iron filings, or digital formulae, arranged to create light and shadow, which can be recognized as an analog to something the viewer might recognize.

A viewer looks at a snapshot and says, "Yes, that's Aunt Mary."

Well, no, it isn't. It's a piece of paper with a dot pattern on it. It is a highly abstract analog of a small piece of something that may have existed in the real world. Indeed, this picture doesn't even show all of Aunt Mary. It shows only her head. And not all of her head—just one side of it.

The core of the matter is not the picture, but the human being who looks at this tiny bit of data and says, "Yes, that's Aunt Mary."

Another example. In your office is a blank, white wall. You want to show the reality of this wall to someone. You take a motion picture camera and carefully record your wall. Have you captured its reality on film?

Let's take a look at the film, before it is projected. Is there a white wall recorded there for all to see?

No, there isn't.

What *is* recorded on the film?

Nothing.

Nothing?

That's right. In order to represent the white wall you photographed, the motion picture film has nothing on it. The light of the projector shines through the empty plastic of the film to represent your white wall as simply light falling on a white screen.

There is no reality recorded on the film. There is only a high level of symbolic abstraction, which by implication may be made to represent an analog of something that was recorded in the real world.

I'm carrying this to an extreme because if you want to make good, believable, useful documentaries of things as they happen, you have to get over the idea that you can suck reality into a camera and blow it back at your audience.

Digitally Enhanced Images

Not long ago, the existence of an image was at least evidence that what was shown had happened. No longer. Digitized images and powerful computers can create scenes of things that never were, in such a way that no one may be able to judge whether what is shown is a record of something that exists or an artist's fantasy.

Kirk Douglas, who produced and starred in the epic film *Spartacus* (1960), said years later that it would now be impossible to make a film like that because of the cost. The final battle scene used 10,000 extras, including 8,000 from the Spanish army. Flash forward to *Troy* (2004). Was Helen's the face that launched a thousand ships? No. Just two. The other 998 ships in the Spartan fleet were digital images, as were almost all of the 50,000-man army. Could you tell? Yes, at least part of the time. But that will change.

In the first edition of this book, I quoted from a scene in the book *Rising Sun,* by novelist and filmmaker Michael Crichton, and a decade later it is still a cogent description of the problem surrounding the accuracy of images. In this scene, Detective Peter James Smith, who tells the story, talks with Dr. Phillip Sanders at the University of Southern California, about some videotape:

I said, "These copies are exact?"

"Oh, yes."

"So they're legal?"

Sanders frowned. "Legal in what sense?"

"Well, as evidence, in a court of law—"

"Oh, no," Sanders said. "These tapes would never be admissible in a court of law."

"But if they're exact copies?"

"It's nothing to do with that. All forms of photographic evidence, including video, are no longer admissible in court."

"I haven't heard that," I said.

"It hasn't happened yet," Sanders said. "The case law isn't entirely clear. But it's coming. All photographs are suspect these days. Because now, with digital systems, they can be changed perfectly. *Perfectly*. And that's something new. . . .

"Photographs always had integrity precisely because they were impossible to change. So we considered photographs to represent reality. But for several years now, computers have allowed us to make seamless alterations of photographic images. A few years back the *National Geographic* moved the Great Pyramid of Egypt on a cover photo. The editors didn't like where the pyramid was, and they thought it would compose better if it was moved. So they just altered the photograph and moved it. Nobody could tell. But if you go back to Egypt with a camera and try to duplicate that picture, you'll find you can't. Because there is no place in the real world where the pyramids line up that way. The photograph no longer represents reality. But you can't tell. Minor example."

"And someone could do the same thing to this tape?"

"In theory, any video can be changed."

Every Frame Requires a Decision

For the present, at least, reality is out of the box, and documentarians can return to their proper job of recording good images and organizing them in a forceful way to make a statement to an audience. Reality is not enough. We are obliged to document as well as to record.

So let's agree that whatever the terms mean, *reality* in the external world and *truth* in documentary are not the same thing.

The verifiable truth of a video or film depends on the honesty of the documentarian in presenting an accurate analog of the situation as he or she understands it. But that is still no guarantee that the audience will accept the documentary as *true*. It takes a lot of hard, professional work to turn your record of what happened when the camera was on into a documentary that will be believed by an audience.

14

THE GROWING PROBLEM
OF CREDIBILITY

In the twenty-first century we can no longer trust that "seeing is believing" or "the camera never lies"; we know otherwise. And the willingness of highly partisan filmmakers to subordinate honesty to ideology has shown that even when the form of a documentary is factual, the content may not be. When truth matters, credibility counts, and the next big event in the evolution of documentary filmmaking may well be about dealing with an erosion of confidence in the truth of documentaries.

Threats Against Credibility

What happens to the credibility of documentary films when what is shown isn't what it seems to be? What happens when the evidence presented may be based on fact, but has been put together in a way that implies something other than the truth of the situation? What happens when a documentary film presents only one view of a controversy, as if no other interpretation were possible—or even existed? What happens when the documentarian cheats, even though it is in what he or she perceives to be a good cause? What happens when people calling themselves documentarians lie, and persist in presenting the lie even after its falsity has been demonstrated?

Fudging Reality

How big a step is it from manipulating the people and events in a reality TV series—to make the show more interesting—to manipulating the people and events in a documentary for the same reason? Unfortunately, history teaches that the path to corruption often starts as an apparent shortcut, a little bit easier way to reach your goal. But it's a slippery slope, perhaps shallow at first but gradually growing steeper. Once on, it's hard to get off. And once caught, it's hard ever to be trusted again.

In any documentary of events as they occur, the temptation is always there to nudge things in a preferred direction. But the moment that happens, you are no longer documenting a unique event with the outcome unknown. You're influencing the outcome. And what might be learned from the film has been tainted. It can no longer be considered valid.

As the television audience learns more about the nature of producing reality TV programs, they can't help but realize that even though what is shown is real in the sense that it happened, it's still a TV show. They know that people and events have been fiddled with to make a better story. Or most of them do. There still are some people who believe televised professional wrestling is a competition in which the best man or woman wins, and that a Nigerian official wants to park several million dollars in their bank account in order to do business in the United States.

But most people by now have some doubts about reality TV, and these may begin to carry over to documentary films that purport to have been made in reality situations. Which means documentarians must be even more careful during filming and editing to present not only what is real, *but also what is true*.

Digital Images Morph Easily

It has always been possible to alter pictures through special visual effects, but until quite recently the results were both expensive to achieve and often not completely convincing. The marriage of filmmaking to digital technology has made it possible to alter images of things that are, and create images of things that never were, sometimes with just the press of a button.

The technology exists to create any setting in any way one likes, or to show any person—living, dead, or imaginary—doing and saying whatever one wants. In the feature film *Sky Captain and the World of Tomorrow*, Gwyneth Paltrow and Jude Law perform in a digital world created by computer. It's all in good fun, but it demonstrates a highly developed technology for fakery. In television commercials, Budweiser horses play football, and dead movie stars shill for products that didn't exist when they were alive. Audiences know anything is possible, and we can't tell the truth of what we're seeing by looking at it. The picture no longer automatically speaks the name of its referent.

In the History Channel documentary *The French Revolution,* thirty-eight actors become a cinematic mob of hundreds of peasants storming the Bastille. In a *The Making of* . . . featurette for a recent feature film, the director happily explained how a hundred extras became the audience for a public event in the story, digitally duplicated until they filled the entire public space. So technology now provides techniques that could turn a handful of actual supporters or protestors into an apparent multitude for or against some issue in a political or social documentary.

Biased Sources

I browse through four newspapers every morning: one liberal, one conservative, one center left, and one center right. And of this I am certain, partisanship has increased in almost every area of public discourse, and the proponents of one side in a controversy—even if they are credentialed experts—are often willing to say or do almost anything to further their cause. Interview documentaries are especially susceptible to people who are willing to lie—or at least fudge the truth. This means a documentarian in search of the truth cannot simply interview the experts on a topic, because the "experts" often have an ax to grind.

Global warming offers an excellent case in point, and I use it as an example several times in this book. First, because it is a complex topic that brings together scientists from many disciplines and involves research conducted over a century and a half. Therefore, making a thorough documentary investigation of the subject would almost certainly exceed the filmmaker's own knowledge, requiring additional research, most likely through interviews with a number of scientists believed to be authorities on the topic.

Second, because global warming clearly is a controversial issue, what you are likely to learn about it depends on whom you ask. On one side is a group of scientists, politians, and journalists who are committed to the position that global warming is a looming crisis caused by human activity, and that extreme measures are required immediately to prevent a global catastrophe. Their motto seems to be "Scientists Agree!" On the other side is a different group of scientists, politicians, and a few journalists who agree that there has been recent warming of the planet, but who are not convinced that it constitutes a crisis, that human activity is the only cause, or that the remedies that have been proposed will be much help. Their motto might be "Not So Fast."

As an example of the severity of this split, let's consider two recent books:

In *The Discovery of Global Warming* (2003), Spencer R. Weart, director of the Center for History of Physics of the American Institute of Physics, traces the study of climate change from research done as early as 1859 to the present. Weart clearly leans in the "Scientists Agree" direction, and his book is an excellent study of how that agreement came about. In his conclusion, he writes:

> Of course climate science is full of uncertainties, and nobody claims to know exactly what the climate will do. That very uncertainty is part of what, I am confident, is known beyond doubt: our planet's climate can change, tremendously and unpredictably. Beyond that we can conclude (with the IPCC) that it is *very likely* that significant global warming is coming in our lifetimes. This surely brings a likelihood of *harm, widespread and grave* (my italics). Those who contest these facts are either ignorant or so committed to their viewpoint that they will seize on any excuse to deny the danger. (p. 199)

But in a fascinating and well-documented book, *Meltdown: The Predictable Distortion of Global Warming by Scientists, Politicians, and the Media* (2004), Patrick J. Michaels, research professor of environmental sciences at the University of Virginia, piles up chapter after chapter of examples of exaggerations and distortions made by scientists regarding global warming. He writes: "When it comes to climate change, there's a culture of distortion out there. But it shouldn't surprise you. Its development was logical, predictable, and inevitable." He points out that there is little grant money or possibility of tenure for scientists who go against the prevailing paradigm of disaster. ("Scientists Agree.")

Note: IPCC=Intergovernmental Panel on Climate Change, established by the United Nations.

Michaels agrees that the earth is warming, and that much of the warming is caused by increases in carbon dioxide in the atmosphere, but he is not convinced that the consequences are all bad. ("Not so Fast!") For example, a modest increase in temperature could be economically beneficial, rather than resulting in disaster. And, contrary to some reports, melting of the ice at the North Pole will not raise the level of the oceans because "the North Polar icecap is a floating mass, and melting that will have absolutely no effect on sea level; a glass of ice water does not rise when the cubes have melted." (p. 203)

My point to all this is that if you based your global warming documentary solely on the expert testimony of either one of these scientists—and his like-minded colleagues—you would have less than the full story.

That's the flaw in *An Inconvenient Truth,* directed by Davis Guggenheim, which shows former Vice President Al Gore trying to raise the consciousness of the world about global warming, one audience at a time. Taken as a performance documentary, the film accurately portrays what are clearly Gore's beliefs, as presented in what can only be called a sermon—he did attend Vanderbilt University Divinity School for a year—about an impending planetary crisis. This may be the best look we've ever had at the man and his convictions. He seems sincere. He seems well informed. And he often makes an emotional appeal straight from the heart. The deaths of his son and his sister are shown as events that motivated him to try to do more to help the world.

But taken as a documentary about global warming, it is not only totally one-sided, it also lacks the sort of scientific documentation you'd hope to see in a film about a serious geophysical problem. Voices from the other side are dismissed as misinformed skeptics or as the stooges of corporations with an economic interest in discrediting global warming. Not once does Gore address any of the questions or comments from serious scientists who may not be in complete agreement with his position.

And, as he has so often done before, he damages his own credibility through exaggeration. Just one example: Painting a picture of environmental damnation, he tells us if either the Greenland glacier or the ice shelf in West Antarctica were to melt completely—or if half of each should melt—then the level of the oceans would rise by twenty feet. He then shows us what the resulting flooding would do to the coast of Florida and the island of Manhattan. But, having previously scared us with stories of past abrupt geophysical changes that, he says, occurred in anywhere from a few days to as little as ten years, he somehow fails to mention exactly how long it might take for the ocean level to rise by twenty feet. We're left believing if we don't turn out the lights and buy a hybrid car right now Florida's a goner.

Actually, it turns out that Gore's statement about sea level rise is probably true. That is, *if* glacier melting of the magnitude he describes were to happen, the rise in ocean level would be on the order of twenty feet. But it's not the whole truth, because the time line is way out of whack. Climatologists say it won't happen the day after tomorrow (as in the film by the same name), but in anywhere from one thousand to five thousand years—if it happens at all. And even the IPCC, the leading advocate of the potential disasters of global warming, only predicts a rise in the level of the oceans *over the next hundred years* in a range from just four to less than thirty *inches*. This is never mentioned in the film.

Work Both Sides of the Street

Therefore, it is crucial that a documentarian not limit his or her interviews to those who line up on only one side of an issue. Not only does this expose our biases, it walls us off from learning anything from those who don't necessarily share our views.

What are our biases? Many of us, unless we are overtly political, believe we don't have any. We like to think we're in the center, or at least where the center ought to be. We think of those we agree with as centrists like us, and those with whom we disagree as -wingers of the left or right.

Here's the fastest way to find out where in the political spectrum you *actually* stand. Take the World's Smallest Political Quiz at:

http://www.theadvocates.org/

In an article about this quiz, *The Washington Post,* June 17, 2001, wrote, "The quiz has gained respect as a valid measure of a person's political leanings; [during the 2000 election year] Rasmussen Research used the quiz in a poll about how likely voters viewed themselves."* (In

---

*If, by the time you read this, the quiz no longer shows up at www.theadvocates.org, do an Internet search for "World's Smallest Political Quiz." You're sure to find it somewhere.

the interest of full disclosure, every time I have taken the test I have scored Libertarian, which means I favor both economic freedom and freedom of behavior. Or to put it another way, I think the government should stay out of our lives as much as possible.)

Once you know what your leanings are, you can take care to include those who lean the other way in your research and your filming.

Avoid Polarizers

Be careful about your sources. Try to avoid those that polarize your viewers. When I was working on the sponsored documentary *Beyond Division: Reuniting the Republic of Cyprus,* our contact in the Embassy of the Republic of Cyprus gave us a list of political figures we might interview. Most were Democrats, since this was the final year of the Clinton administration. Included were Senator Edward Kennedy and Senator Barbara Boxer, both of whom, I'm sure, had positive things to say about the Republic of Cyprus.

We were making a film in an election year that would not be released until after a new administration took office. Since there was a statistically even chance that the new administration would be Republican, it did not make sense to me to use two highly partisan figures who would automatically alienate Republican viewers. No matter what Senators Kennedy or Boxer might say, their mere presence would polarize a film meant to inform the American people and U.S. government officials of the plight of Cyprus.

(If you don't understand why this is so, you *really* need to take the World's Smallest Political Quiz.)

Ignorance

Documentarians who are not knowledgeable about the subject matter of their documentaries are at the mercy of those who might want to manipulate them. This is a growing problem as more and more documentaries are being made, and the documentarians making them come from the fields of communication (filmmaking or journalism, for example) but lack a background in history, economics, political science, anthropology, sociology, physics, biology, or whatever might pertain to the content of the films they are doing.

If you won't know whether a person you're interviewing is telling you the truth, or if the evidence you're being urged to film is relevant, you're not ready to make the documentary. You need to read, study, ask questions, and reflect on what you're learning in order to become knowledgeable about the topic. If it's so esoteric that it requires a specialist's knowledge, then you need to attach a specialist you can trust to your documentary unit. Someone, if possible, who can explain the positions of various factions involved in whatever you are documenting in such a way that he or she does not seem to be favoring any specific position. Someone, if possible, who is as open-minded as you should be about the outcome.

Overcoming ignorance is one good reason for staking out an area of interest that you would like to make films about and becoming an expert on it.

Docuganda

As we have seen, there are filmmakers willing to use the form of the documentary without regard for the truth in order to present their own one-sided, biased, or partisan views. When people calling themselves documentarians believe their mission is more important than the truth, we all suffer.

Documentary as Personal Essay

In those four newspapers I work my way through each morning, it is understood that there is a distinct separation between what should be considered factual reporting and what should be considered personal opinion. Reporting runs in the main news pages and is expected to be both truthful and, as far as possible, unbiased. Opinion pieces are found close to the newspaper's editorials and, while they certainly should contain factual information, they are there to bolster the views and opinions of their authors.

Problems occur when readers—or television viewers or radio listeners—perceive that a bias that rightly belongs in an opinion piece has crept into a news story. It happens more often than most journalists like to admit, which may be one reason the approval rating for journalists in public opinion polls is about the same as for politicians. It is also happening in documentary.

MICHAEL MOORE PRO AND CON

I thought that Michael Moore's *Roger & Me* (1989) was a brilliant example of documentary as personal essay. Yes, it was sometimes over the top, and no, getting an interview with General Motors CEO Roger Smith was not going to make much of a difference to the fate of Flint, Michigan. But this was clearly personal commentary starting with the word *Me* in the title.

But it's also worth noting that Moore's trip down the slippery slope began here. As Hal Hinson wrote in *The Washington Post,* January 12, 1990:

> When I first saw the film, it struck me as the most impressively articulated response to the Reagan era I'd seen. Since then it has come out that Moore has—either intentionally or through lack of skill—fuzzied the chronology of events, creating the impression that the plant closings and layoffs took place all at once, around 1986 and '87, instead of over a period of more than a decade. In other instances too, Moore may have fallen short of factual accuracy.
>
> Though this doesn't invalidate his political points, it does cast them in a more dubious light—and Moore along with them.

When Moore has been attacked for similar inaccuracies, and a lack of integrity, in *Bowling for Columbine* (even the title is based on a false assumption) and *Fahrenheit 9/11,* there have been those who defended these films as personal essays, and who argued that essays and opinion have a proper place within the documentary genre.

While I agree that there is room within the documentary big tent for personal films of essay and opinion, I don't agree that calling a documentary a personal essay is a license to lie or cheat, either overtly or by implication. Information presented as factual should be accurate and complete. Editing of sound bites should *never* change their meaning.

As I write this, Michael Moore is still a large presence in the world of independent filmmaking, whether one regards his work as documentary, personal essay, or docuganda. By the time you read this, it is entirely possible that he will have fallen out of the public consciousness.

But the damage to films called documentary has already been done. In a recent newspaper article, the writer, after citing certain facts pertaining to his story, said he couldn't be sure how accurate they were, as they had come from a documentary.

Three rebuttal films to *Fahrenheit 9/11* have been produced:

- *Michael Moore Hates America,* directed by Michael Wilson
- *Fahrenhype 9/11,* directed by Alan Peterson
- *Celsius 41.11: The Temperature at Which the Brain . . . Begins to Die,* directed by Kevin Knoblock

Yes, these are also partisan attack films, but they have the virtue that their purpose is to point out the errors, inaccuracies, false implications, and outright falsehoods in Moore's film. And they do so with a much more rigorous documentation than Moore has ever applied to his own work. Just one example is the story of Sgt. Peter Damon, which you'll read about in the next chapter.

Online, numerous websites assay the truthfulness and importance of Moore's work. Many of these, as you can imagine, are obviously conservative and clearly opposed to Michael Moore. These tend to document alleged distortions, false implications, and untruths in his work. You can survey the pros and cons fairly quickly by looking up the entry for Michael Moore in Wikipedia, the free encyclopedia (http://en.wikipedia.org/wiki/Michael_Moore).

But it is not only the political right that takes exception to Moore's work. On the website of the Democratic Leadership Council, which thinks of itself as center left, I found this statement about Michael Moore by Peter Ross Range, the editor of *Blueprint* magazine, which is published by the DLC. In an article entitled "Michael Moore's Truth Problem," a review of Moore's book, *Dude, Where's My Country?,* Range wrote:

Is Michael Moore a courageous political documentarist who unmasks the chicanery all around us—or just a charlatan in a clown suit? Is he an entertainment genius or a dangerous ideologue? The answer, of course, is all of the above. The problem is that you never know which of the four is doing the talking in Moore's movies and books. The end result is that the writer-filmmaker spreads a fog of misbegotten notions about America, politics, business, and international affairs among his youthful, left-leaning following at home and, indeed, around the world. Uninformed readers and viewers tend to believe everything he says.

And when the truth comes out, as it always does, will the disenchanted blame the messenger? Or the medium?

Credibility Matters

These are questions twenty-first-century documentarians should be grappling with, because the strength of the documentary genre has always been its grounding in truth. Take that away and you have *The Daily Show* or *Saturday Night Live*—commentary without corroboration.

A documentary can't just be about what *everyone knows*. If *everyone knows* global warming is a problem, there's no need to make a film saying so. But if everyone doesn't know this—or doesn't believe it, or believes the planet is getting warmer, but isn't sure what's causing it—then a documentary on the subject needs to be accurate, truthful, and complete. First, because it's the right thing to do. And second, because today you can't get away with anything.

Whatever your topic, if you manipulate the facts, use biased sources, draw false conclusions, or lie, *you'll be found out*. The bigger the splash you make, the better the chance that someone will be looking into the facts you have presented and checking the credentials of your sources. The more important the topic, the more likely it is that the other side will come back in rebuttal.

And here's the scary thing: Even when you do everything right and tell the truth as you know it, if your topic is at all controversial, the other side will attack your credibility.

Restoring Credibility

Now that pictures can be altered so easily that an audience can't immediately tell that it has been done, and advocates and propagandists have been shown to be willing to present unreliable or altered information as if it were the truth, it will become both harder and more important to be able to prove the validity of what is being shown. The solution, I think, will be part technology and part personal integrity. One without the other won't work.

Documentarians must seek the truth, be able to recognize it when they find it, and have the skill and integrity to present it to an audience. New technology makes it possible to embed context interactively in a documentary. DVDs of a documentary have the capacity to carry complete interviews, not just the sound bites used in the film. Or they could store all the footage that was shot of an activity or behavior, so that a viewer wanting to know more could click on an icon and see everything the documentarian had to work with.

When you can do that, you completely change the producing and viewing equation. If propagandists use the documentary form without embracing the truth ethic, then it may become necessary for the truth tellers to make *everything* available to their audiences, as a way to show they aren't cheating. For example, all of the raw footage could be posted on the documentarian's website.

If that were to happen, propagandists who take sound bites out of context and edit them into sequences where they don't belong would have a harder time making their case with the audience. And those who refuse to make everything available would automatically become suspect.

15

DOCUMENTARY ETHICS

The field of documentary ethics is an emerging one, and, as we've seen in the previous chapter, one that is probably long overdue. The original set of concerns had to do with image ethics: Were people who agreed to appear in documentaries sufficiently protected against various harms they probably weren't even aware of, which might come their way as a result of appearing in a documentary?

To this I would add the area of information ethics: What are the documentarian's responsibilities toward the information he or she presents and toward the audience that receives it?

Image Ethics

Who owns my image?

That, in brief, is a question you should give some thought to as you set about the business of producing a documentary.

If (you might ask) this film were being produced by strangers—people about whom I knew little or nothing at all—and if I were a subject in it, just how much freedom would I give them to use the images of me that they record?

Never mind about what *you* plan to do with, for, and to the subjects of *your* documentary. Naturally, you are honest, honorable, benevolent, a seeker after truth, and one who intends harm to no one. But how much slack would you cut for the other guys to use your image in any way they please if *they* were documenting *you*?

Today, anyone with access to a little bit of video equipment can make a "documentary" of virtually anything he or she decides to point a camera at. The behavioral documentary poses some ethical problems simply because it is *the people themselves* who are the subjects of the film. Unlike other artists and communicators, behavioral documentarians *require* the spontaneous and personal behavior of their subjects in order to do their work.

Therefore, what is—or should be—the relationship of the documentarian to the people whose behavior is being recorded? What is—or should be—the responsibility of the documentarian to these people?

Frankly, until I met Professor Calvin Pryluck at a conference of the Society for the Anthropology of Visual Communication, I felt it was enough to get a release in advance and to tell the truth as I understood it. The late Cal Pryluck was one of a handful of documentarians and communications scholars who had concerned themselves with the ethical use of people's images by documentarians.

The Question of Releases

The question of the rights of the people who appear in a documentary usually has been resolved through the expedient of getting a signed release from each person that grants all rights—or limited rights—to all recordings of the image and voice of the subject either to the documentarian or to the sponsor of the documentary.

As far as I know, the legality of such a release has never been fully tested. Television news crews, and even some television documentary crews, often don't bother to obtain releases on the grounds that they are reporting newsworthy events and are therefore protected under the First Amendment right to a free press. In ambush situations, like some of those on *60 Minutes,* the probability of getting signed releases is remote.

Producers who hope to earn money from a documentary in theatrical release usually get signed release forms from everyone who is recognizable in the footage. But this is typically a matter of economics, not ethics. The people in a theatrical documentary are the talent in the film, and as such are entitled to compensation. In the absence of a signed release form, a court would probably award compensation not lower than minimum scale for the Screen Actors Guild or the Screen Extras Guild. Not only will few documentary budgets tolerate that rate of pay, but the time and expense involved in a court case would usually be prohibitive.

As for the remainder of documentarians—those making films or videos with neither television backing nor the hope of theatrical profits—the signed release is their insurance policy. It protects them from nuisance suits by people appearing in the film who either hope for additional compensation or who decide, after the fact, that their privacy has been invaded.

IF YOU DON'T WANT TO BE FILMED, LEAVE

In lieu of releases, some documentarians record the subject's verbal consent at the start of shooting. With the camera running, they briefly explain the purpose of the production and ask the subject if he or she is willing to be recorded. Or, at the start of a meeting or other group event, the documentarian will record himself announcing to the audience that the meeting is being recorded for use in a documentary. He briefly explains the purpose of the film, and then states, "Your continued presence here indicates your consent and willingness to be recorded as part of the documentary."

In essence, under this system the only way an individual can guarantee the protection of his or her rights is to refuse to appear in the film. If people don't want to give someone else control over the use of their images, they can refuse to have them recorded. They can refuse to sign a release. They can refuse, on camera, to give their consent. They can get up and leave a meeting or other event—even though they may sincerely want to attend—if to remain is to give implied consent to be a part of the documentary being made. They need not complain that their privacy has been invaded if they have refused to participate. And that, in general, is the answer to the legal question of the rights of subjects.

But it doesn't come close to resolving any of the ethical questions. Nor does it absolve us as documentarians of our responsibility toward the subjects who appear in our productions.

The Need for a Documentary Ethic

Although people who are potential documentary subjects may protect themselves from unwarranted invasion of privacy by refusing to appear on camera, few of them actually do. The only refusals I have ever had came from people who had a vested interest in one side of a conflict and who, I think, felt there was a chance that their position might not be presented fairly. In other words, they were people with a fairly sophisticated awareness of the risks of giving up control of their images to an outsider.

Most people, however, are not nearly so sophisticated. Or perhaps they just don't care. The question most often heard by a documentary producer is not "How will you use the footage?" but rather "When will this be on TV?" Many people seem to be more than willing to trade their dignity for their fifteen minutes of celebrity—at least before the fact. Again, most documentarians report that the people in the film love it when they see it—until the reviews come in.

My own experience is that most people will do almost anything to *appear* on camera. Some examples:

A production company was shooting a commercial for a bank, which centered on a young couple having their first baby. And they needed a baby. They were shooting in a hospital, and it took less than ten minutes to convince the parents of a newborn infant, just six hours old, to permit their baby to be taken from the newborn nursery to a nearby room to appear on camera. Yes, the filmmakers kept the baby in a newborn isolette except for the few seconds it was on camera in each take. And yes, they had a nurse in full-time attendance. And yes, they explained all this to the parents. But the parents gave their consent without any hesitation and with only minimal consideration for any potential risks involved.

A friend of mine had no problem finding couples willing to appear in a medical school–sponsored behavioral documentary entitled *Sexual Intercourse*. The behavior to be filmed, of course, was sexual intercourse.

When such is the situation, one is tempted to question whether documentarians have any ethical responsibility at all toward the subjects who appear in their films. But the fact is that most people who agree to appear in a documentary are not involved in anything nearly so dramatic as the examples above. And few people who give their consent to appear on camera have any notion of the potential that exists for a damaging portrayal.

THE DOCUMENTARIAN'S INTENTIONS

Earlier, I gave some examples of potential image victims: the policeman in Wilkes-Barre whose interview went badly, the school principal who babbled bureaucratese about his program, and the Good Mother and Bad Mother in *A Young Child Is*. . . . They willingly consented to my use of images of themselves that could have proven highly unfavorable and not at all what they had expected. And those were all situations in which I was operating with the best of intentions.

In an article entitled "Ultimately We Are All Outsiders: The Ethics of Documentary Filming," which first appeared in the *Journal of the University Film Association* (Winter 1976), Calvin Pryluck cites several examples from the literature of documentary in which the intentions of the documentarian may have been less than 100 percent aboveboard. He quotes Marcel Ophuls (*The Sorrow and the Pity*): "If you have moderate gifts as a fast talker or a diplomat or if you appear moderately sincere, you should be able to get cooperation. . . . It's a con game to a certain extent."

Pryluck continues:

> Regardless of whether consent is flawed on such grounds as intimidation or deceit, a fundamental ethical difficulty in direct cinema is that when we use people in a sequence we put them at risk without sufficiently informing them of potential hazards. We may not even know the hazards ourselves. Filmmakers cannot know which of their actions are apt to hurt other people: it is presumptuous of them to act as if they do. (p. 23)

What Is a Documentarian to Do?

What, then, is the documentarian to do? Part of the documentarian's responsibility, as I see it, is to *do no one harm unintentionally*. I state the case that way because, clearly, there are times when the very purpose of the documentary under production is to get the goods on some person, organization, or institution with malice aforethought.

But most of the time, especially in the behavioral documentary, the purpose is to show real people as they are, not as someone or other might think they should be.

In the same article, Pryluck writes:

> In one important respect the ethical problems of actuality filmmakers are identical to those faced by research physicians, sociologists, psychologists, and so on: scientific experiments and direct cinema

depend for their success on subjects who have little or nothing to gain from participation. The use of people for our advantage is an ethically questionable undertaking; in its extreme it is exploitation in the literal sense. (p. 24)

In effect, the documentary of behavior has moved away from journalistic protection under the First Amendment and placed itself within the canons of social science and medical research. These documentaries carry with them a potential for the abuse and exploitation of the people who appear in them for which few ethical models exist. Even in the social documentaries of the recent past, the people shown were there less as individuals than as representations of the effects of social problems on specific human beings.

There is a distinct difference between the migrant workers who permitted themselves to be interviewed about working conditions for the Murrow-Friendly documentary *Harvest of Shame* and the members of the Loud family as they consented to be filmed for *An American Family*. The migrants knew the risks they were running. They knew that in telling about their plight as migrant workers they risked the possibility of brutal retaliation, and that the loss of their jobs might be the least of their worries. But they went ahead in full knowledge of the potential consequences.

The Loud family, on the other hand, had no idea what they were getting into, clearly did not understand the process as they were being filmed, and were unprepared for the impact the documentary had on their lives when it was released.

It would probably be fair to say that the producers of *Harvest of Shame* were well aware of the risks they were asking the subjects of their documentary to assume. The same cannot necessarily be said of the producer of a behavioral documentary. Quite often he or she has no way of foreseeing the way the film will come out, let alone what the risks to the participants might be. How, then, does the documentarian go about seeking consent from people he or she would like to have appear in the film?

Informed Consent

Informed consent in scientific and medical research depends on at least three elements:

- the absence of coercion and deception
- thorough explanation of the procedure and its anticipated effects
- competence of the subject to give consent

In the quest for consent, should the producer detail all of the horrible possibilities, from obscene phone calls to public ridicule, that might conceivably occur, and take a chance that the potential participant will say no?

Or is that more than is required? In order to get a signed release, should the documentarian downplay the possible risks to the participant in order to go ahead and make the movie? And if he does, is that really informed consent? In research, consent is flawed when it is obtained through the omission of any fact that might influence the giving or withholding of permission.

That sounds clear-cut, but it isn't. What is a fact that might influence the giving or withholding of permission? Do you have to tell every potential participant that "some people have found that their neighbors laughed at them after they appeared in a documentary"?

At the other extreme, isn't requiring someone either to give implied consent or to leave a public meeting a form of coercion?

The Eye of the Beholder

One year my friend Chris Speeth and I both made sponsored documentaries about two different educational programs in two different cities for two different clients. Each film featured an administrator who was responsible for the educational programs shown in the film.

What I remember about Chris's film is that his man was always on the go. Chris showed him riding in every available type of transportation. When he was afoot, he walked briskly. And as he traveled around, he talked about his hopes and plans for the educational programs of his city. He often used the language of overstatement common to people who operate in a political arena. At one point he expressed the belief that his city's tax-supported college could become "the Sorbonne of the Midwest."

The educator in my film operated in a smaller arena, administering several grant-supported programs within a single high school. In style he was solemn and super-sincere. His commentary on the program was an uncomfortable mixture of student slang and pedagoguese, with an overlay of the mechanistic psychobabble of special education.

Sol Worth asked us to show the films to his documentary film students and talk about the making of them. The students found it hard to believe that Chris and I had been able to "get away with showing" the administrators as we did. To them, the educators came across as pompous bureaucrats talking nonsense, and the film students interpreted each film as a put-down of the man in charge. They couldn't believe that we had gotten approval from our clients for films such as those.

But—and this is the important part—in each case, the administrator was quite pleased with the way he was shown in the film. The man in Chris's film saw himself as a forceful, active person getting the job done. The one in mine thought he came across as a well-informed expert who cared about young people. Remember, these were sponsored films, which had been reviewed by the clients, including these administrators, before they were completed.

I don't know how Chris felt about the administrator in his film. I didn't much care for the man in mine. But I would argue that the behavior shown in each film was an accurate and honest analog of the everyday behavior of those two men in similar situations.

Proof Within the Frame

That a segment of the audience finds the way an individual is presented within a documentary unflattering may indicate that the documentarian is not a Pollyanna, finding the best in every situation. But it is certainly not proof of unethical conduct. And there is usually no evidence within a documentary to prove whatever a critic may think reflects an ethical problem.

Suppose I had left the Good Mother and Bad Mother sequences as they were originally edited, with the Bad Mother neutralized but the Good Mother looking pretty bad. In my opinion it would have made the film dishonest, a less-than-accurate analog. *But no audience would have known that.*

On the other hand, suppose that I had concentrated on the neurotic behavior and negative attitude of the Bad Mother toward her son. The film was a documentary about the way children learn. And, certainly, the relationship between mother and child is a factor in early learning in young children. In my opinion, to have done so would not have made the film dishonest—it would have been showing the mother as she was—but it *would* have been unethical. It would have been changing the intent of the film as I had originally conceived it—and, more important, as I had explained it to the parents in seeking their permission to film them and their children—in order to take a cheap shot at a target of opportunity. The film was not a psychological study of the interactions between mothers and their children. Since it wasn't, the behavior of the mother had, in a limited sense, come under my protection. But, again, no audience would know any of this from watching the film.

If the day should come when documentarians post all of their footage for the interested to see, as I suggested in chapter 14, then the audience might begin to understand more about the subjects and the way the filmmaker has used them. And while this device may serve as a way to deal with the growing issues of credibility, it will open a new Pandora's box of ethical issues.

Areas of Confusion

I suspect that much of the criticism on ethical grounds of the behavioral documentary comes from a confusion over such concepts as *objectivity, reality,* and *truth*. To be fair, this confusion isn't at all limited to critics. There are a lot of documentarians who are equally confused about how these concepts relate to the films and videos they shoot and eventually show.

CONFUSION ABOUT OBJECTIVITY

The very notion of objectivity in documentary is a fairly recent development in the history of the genre. It is an outgrowth of the peculiar rules governing American network television and a basic misunderstanding of both the requirements of journalistic objectivity and of the nature of scientific objectivity.

Certainly the pioneers of documentary made no pretense of using a journalistic approach in their films and would have found any discussion of journalistic "objectivity" totally irrelevant. They unashamedly used the documentary to make as powerful a statement as they could manage about something they considered important. And this continues among contemporary documentarians who take up a specific social or political point of view. They are not objective; they are advocates. But so long as their work is truthful (the whole truth) and honestly documents their position, they remain documentarians.

Scientific Objectivity. Objectivity in science means that a scientific investigation can be verified independently. If it is an experiment, the results can be replicated by another scientist using the same procedures and materials.

Journalistic Objectivity. Objectivity in journalism came about as a reaction to the highly opinionated, politically positional press of the eighteenth and nineteenth centuries. It seeks to separate fact from opinion, assumption, and evaluation, and to make clear which is which. News reports are expected to be founded in fact and capable of independent verification. Opinion, conclusion, evaluation, interpretation, speculation, and so on are dealt with in editorials, signed opinion columns, and bylined feature stories. In areas of controversy, TV journalists try to present "both sides of the story" and attempt to give equal weight to each. The television documentary evolved within this tradition.

Cinéma vérité and spontaneous cinema are, if anything, a reaction to the journalistically objective television documentary.

Does this reaction to objectivity mean anything goes? No. Factual information must still be both accurate and complete. And context counts. If you show a protester at a rally saying, "The president is a traitor to the American people," that's opinion. If you show a professor of political science, so identified on screen, in an office interview setup saying, "The president is a traitor to the American people," the context suggests the presentation of fact through expert testimony, rather than opinion, and opening this door requires further evidence, without which the professor's statement remains just his opinion.

CONFUSION OF ACTUALITY WITH REALITY

A behavioral documentary is shot in an actual situation, not on a staged set, with actual people, not actors, doing whatever it is that they actually do, not acting out a script. The resulting film can have such immediacy that both documentarians and the audiences who view their work have often made the erroneous assumption that the documentary showed reality.

This assumption is simply not valid. The best you get is bits and pieces of whatever happened, filtered through the eyes, ears, and minds of a film crew and the recording capabilities of their equipment. When we are present, and everything is right, we can record the image and sound of the behavior that takes place in front of the camera. We do not penetrate to the thoughts, instincts, history, social conditioning, and all the other complex elements that underlie behavior. We do not even record the taste, feel, or smell of the situation. At best, we try to imply these. Often we ignore them.

Imagine, for example, a documentary interview in which:

- the person being interviewed is from a culture that prefers a fairly close social distance for conversation and
- has incredibly bad breath, while
- the interviewer prefers a wider social distance and
- has an extremely sensitive nose.

Such a situation might well produce visual images of a dance of approach-avoidance on the part of the interviewee and interviewer quite unrelated to the subject matter of the interview. How do you handle that? That's actuality, but are the images that result *reality*?

CONFUSION ABOUT TRUTH AND HONESTY

Such a scene would certainly be an interesting—and true—piece of behavior. But the next bothersome question is: Does it belong in the film? If an obvious inference from the scene is that the interviewer does not care for the person being interviewed when in fact the interviewer simply doesn't want to stand as close as the interviewee prefers, what is the honest thing for the documentarian to do? Probably the director has to find some solution that won't give the wrong impression—either a fix in editing, such as use of the interview as voice-over, leaving out pictures of the interview altogether, or, if it is crucial to the documentary, shooting it again in a way that avoids the problem.

Information Ethics

What about the documentarian's responsibility to the audience? Documentary ethics need to address the use of deceptive practices in a film purporting to be a documentary.

Partisan Attack or Impartial Investigation?

A documentarian has an ethical responsibility to his or her audience to make clear to them the type of documentary they are watching. If the film is a partisan attack on someone or something, then the documentarian should not pretend that it is objective, or nonpartisan, or a personal essay, or simply a presentation of the facts. Robert Greenwald makes this sort of partisan film, but he at least makes his intentions clear right from the title in works such as:

Wal-Mart: The High Cost of Low Price
Outfoxed: Rupert Murdoch's War on Journalism
Uncovered: The Whole Truth About the Iraq War

The same is true of Michael Wilson's Michael Moore Hates America.

You can't pick up one of these films expecting an impartial appraisal of Wal-Mart, Fox News, the Iraq war, or Michael Moore. And you won't be disappointed; they go on the attack from frame one. These films are the cinematic equivalent of books such as Lies and the Lying Liars Who Tell Them: A Fair and Balanced Look at the Right by Al Franken or Treason: Liberal Treachery from the Cold War to the War on Terrorism by Ann Coulter.

The ethical question for partisan films is this: If a documentarian is going to tell only one side of the story, is it ethical—or even fair—to pretend this is a factual/investigative documentary? Should there be something (the title obviously is a good start) that lets the viewer know immediately that this film represents a fixed position? If the film has been sponsored by a partisan organization, should this be in the opening titles, not buried in the closing crawl? When people in interviews have not only an official position (doctor, professor, governor, senator) but also a partisan leaning that bears on the information presented, should this information be shown?

The burden on the documentarian may be to recognize that the documentary he or she is making is actually a partisan attack film.

- If everyone you know agrees that A is bad and Z is good, and you're making a film in support of Z and attacking A, be careful. It's probably not an impartial investigation.
- If at any time in working on your film, you say—or even think— "Gotcha!" you're probably making a partisan documentary.

Is It Enough That What Is Shown Actually Happened?

This is the reality-in-a-box argument: It happened so it's true and therefore can go in the film. But, as shown by the Good Mother/Bad Mother examples, the ethical question is never: Did it happen? The ethical question should be: Is what is shown an accurate analog of the situation being presented? If I show this to the audience, will I be telling them the truth about this person, this behavior, this situation, or will I be giving them a false impression?

THE CONTEXT QUESTION

Give me enough footage and a good editor and I can show you a sequence of a saint consorting with the devil. That doesn't make it true. It just means that if you remove something perfectly innocent from its context of innocence and place it in a context of guilt, it's going to look a lot less innocent than it did before. That's the foundation for jokes based on a double entendre. One definition of a word is innocent, another risqué. Use the word's innocent definition in a risqué context and the meaning changes.

Must the documentarian provide context? Certainly enough context is needed to make clear the situation being shown. If you show a sound bite without the surrounding context, you can make a person appear to be saying the exact opposite of what he meant. So context counts.

WHEN THE INTERVIEWEE ISN'T TELLING THE TRUTH

What is the documentarian's ethical responsibility when he or she knows or suspects that an interviewee is not telling the truth? Or is not telling the complete truth? Or knows—or should know—better, but is actually lying?

You cannot ethically include statements you actually know to be untrue as part of the package of factual information you present to the audience. It doesn't matter whether the statement is made by a crack dealer or a United States senator. Using it as if it were true is dishonest.

During the interview, you might want to give an interviewee a chance to correct an untrue statement. You might even want to point out why the statement is not accurate and see what the interviewee's response is. Just as an example, suppose an interviewee were to tell you, "I know for a fact that the mortgage on former President Clinton's New York home is being paid by the federal government. The way it works, the government rents space from the Clintons to house their Secret Service detail, and the Clintons have set the rent for that space at the same amount as their mortgage payment. So we taxpayers are paying for the Clintons' luxury home."

This is all pure baloney, of course. It's an anti-Clinton e-rumor that's circulated from time to time on the Internet. According to the fact checkers at TruthOrFiction.com:

> Presidents are reimbursed for any area of the home that is used by Secret Service agents. The amount is based on a formula, however, not defined by the homeowner. Based on that formula, Mr. Clinton would be eligible for more than $1,000, but he has declined the money for his New York home.

If you actually knew this, you might point it out to the interviewee, and see what happens. The response might range from, "Oh, I didn't know that," to "Well, even if it isn't true, I still don't like Clinton," to "No, that can't be. I know this for a fact." In the first two instances you might still get something useful. In the third you have a quote you can't use.

If you didn't know the truth about this quote during the interview, it's certainly something you'd want to check out before including it in your documentary.

The one situation in which you might ethically run a sound bite that you know to be untrue would be when your purpose is to show that the speaker actually *is* lying.

Ethics of Using Footage Shot for a Different Purpose

In *Fahrenheit 9/11* there's a brief scene with Sergeant Peter Damon at Walter Reed Army Medical Center. Sgt. Damon lost both hands in Iraq when a Black Hawk helicopter exploded in front of him. The scene comes in the center of a montage of injured veterans, designed to show the pain and suffering resulting from the Iraq war, and to suggest that the government is neglecting them. The scene is set up by Representative James McDermott (Democrat, Washington), a doctor:

> They say they're not leaving any veterans behind, but they're leaving all kinds of veterans behind.

The antecedent of "they" in the congressman's statement is not clear, but apparently means either the Army or the Bush administration.

Two other amputees speak, apparently about the lack of news coverage of wounded soldiers, and then Sgt. Damon is shown in a bed, his arms bandaged, receiving medication. He is not identified by name. He says:

> I still feel like I have hands. And the pain is like my hands are being crushed in a vise. But they do a lot to help it. And they take a lot of the edge off it. And it makes it a lot more tolerable.

The antecedent of "they" in this statement is not clear, either. By implication, it's a continuation of the Army or the system, as in the preceding sound bites.

This is followed by a close-up of a soldier, also not identified by name, at Blanchfield Army Community Hospital, Fort Campbell, Kentucky, who tells about being injured and the pain he's in. Then in a wide shot, the soldier continues:

> I was a Republican for quite a few years. And if, for some reason they uh . . . They conduct business in a very dishonest way. I'm going to be incredibly active in the Democratic Party down where I live, once I get out. I'm gonna definitely do my best to ensure the Democrats win control.

Sgt. Damon says he had no idea he was in a movie. And not just any movie, but a very political movie about the Bush administration and the

Iraq war. And he was not just in the movie, he was sandwiched between a politician scoring points and a veteran making an overt political statement.

You see, the clip that appears in *Fahrenheit 9/11* is from an interview Sgt. Damon gave to Brian Williams for NBC News. In it, according to the *New York Post* (May 31, 2006), "he discussed only a new painkiller the military was using on wounded vets." The "they" in his sound bite referred to the painkillers.

According to the *Post*, Damon and his wife filed a lawsuit against Michael Moore. "Damon is asking for up to $75 million because of 'loss of reputation, emotional distress, embarrassment, and personal humiliation.' In addition, his wife is suing for another $10 million because of the 'mental distress and anguish suffered by her spouse.'"

Sgt. Damon is not antiwar at all. According to the lawsuit, Williams ends the NBC clip by adding, "These men, with catastrophic wounds are . . . completely behind the war effort."

It may be legal to buy interview footage from news organizations such as NBC News (although Sgt. Damon's lawsuit may change that). But it is certainly not ethical to take a sound bite from an interview shot for one purpose and use it for an entirely different—and in this case, contradictory—purpose.

It's wrong. Simple as that.

Misleading Footage, Half-Truths, Innuendo

These are all techniques of docuganda:

Showing a scene that suggests things are a certain way, when in fact they are not that way misleads the audience and is unethical.

Telling only the part of the story, even if true, that helps your side of the argument, while leaving out the parts that may help the other side, is dishonest, knowingly misleads the audience, and is unethical.

Editing or sequencing sound bites in a way that gives a false impression to the audience is unethical.

MAKING OUR OWN ETHICAL JUDGMENTS

In the final analysis, resolution of the ethical questions, like that of all the other questions pertaining to the production of a documentary, lies with the documentarian.

There can be no help for it. The documentarian must take the responsibility for that which is shown. The ethical milieu surrounding the production of a documentary of human behavior is the product of the integrity of the person or persons responsible for the production.

There will be abuses, as there have been in the past. And there will be brilliant documentaries made by thoroughly honorable people. Sometimes subjects will become collaborators in the organization and editing of the material, and sometimes they'll be locked out of the editing room.

What I hope is that, as you go about the planning, production, editing, and presentation of any documentary, you will do so with a heightened awareness that your actions have moral consequences.

In the last analysis, you will have to make your own ethical judgments.

There is no other way to practice our craft.

PART IV

WRITING A DOCUMENTARY

So why a script? Because using a script
is usually the most logical and helpful way to
make a film. . . . To put it very simply,
a decent script makes the task of filmmaking
a hundred times easier.

• • •

—*Alan Rosenthal*, Writing, Directing,
and Producing Documentary Films and Videos

16

DOCUMENTARY WRITING

A modern documentary may run from beginning to end without a word of narration or dialogue and without anyone acting out a written scenario. Which is good. A large part of the fascination of doing documentary is this: What happens in the real world is often far more interesting—and usually more exciting and astonishing—than anything that could be made up by a scriptwriter.

So what's to write?

Quite a bit. Writing a documentary film may extend from preproduction all the way to the final stages of postproduction. The writing may be done by the producer, the director—sometimes even the editor—or by a designated scriptwriter.

Even when the documentary is filmed and edited in an "unscripted," spontaneous style, some kind of written plan usually gets made. It may be called a proposal, a concept paper, a treatment, or something else entirely. Whatever it's called, it expands the original documentary idea into a plan for shooting and, at the very least, a theory for editing.

Of course, "unscripted" in relation to this kind of film means it wasn't shot to a script written in advance of principal photography. It doesn't mean "unplanned." Also, most documentaries are not spontaneous cinema productions.

WHAT DOES THE WRITER DO?

So what does the scriptwriter do in making a documentary?

The answer depends on the kind of documentary. If it's a historical documentary, a biography, or a re-creation or reenactment of some event, the scriptwriter's work will be very similar to writing a feature film. The writer must gather and organize the information and then write a screenplay containing a well-structured series of scenes that can be created on film or video. If archival footage exists, reviewing it becomes part of the research process.

On the other hand, if the production is a spontaneous cinema documentary, showing some kind of behavior or a unique event, there may never be a script in the sense of a screenplay, because no one knows ahead of time exactly what is going to happen. In writing this sort of documentary, the emphasis is on visualization and organization, not on writing narration or dialogue. This is what I call the art of writing without words.

It is also true with a spontaneous cinema documentary that, as has happened to me on several occasions, the writer may not be brought into the production until some time after shooting and before editing to try to bring order out of a mass of footage that was shot on the fly. In most cases the script, and the film, would be better had the writer joined the team earlier.

The least productive use of a scriptwriter is for the director to wait until the footage has been shot and edited and then show the writer the cut and indicate the narration that needs to be written. That makes the writer nothing more than a translator, turning the director's notes into a narration script. Limiting the writer's involvement to doing a polished draft of the words to be said uses less than a fourth of the talent an experienced scriptwriter potentially brings to a production.

The Writer's Gifts to the Production

These are the things that documentary scriptwriters do:

- Research and planning
- Visualization
- Organizing a structure for the film
- Writing the words that are needed

RESEARCH AND PLANNING

Good images don't just happen. You have to plan for them. And you have to be ready to recognize them and, even more important, be ready to record them on film or video when they do occur. Then you have to select and organize them to present a visual argument to an audience.

Making a documentary is an exercise in model building, creating an analog of some event. And a scriptwriter is a film architect. Which is why, if a writer is to be used at all, it's important that he or she is brought into the process as early as possible.

Someone has to do the same kind of research for a documentary that a print writer would do for an article or book: Visit the location, talk to the people, and get the facts—the who, what, when, where, why, and how of the event to be documented. Out of this should come, at a minimum, an outline of the information, a list of copy or story points, and a shot list of people, places, and events that could or should be filmed.

If no one does this, the result is a body of video with no head, like the film about the restaurant openings in Honolulu (chapter 8).

In that situation, I came in after the fact, with the mistakes already recorded on video and the production budget spent. I wrote an editing script that organized the chaos of the footage into a reasonable presentation of information, wrote some new scenes   which could be shot inexpensively in the production company's small studio—to cover the missing pieces. And I got us all out alive.

The thing is, prior to shooting, *any* competent scriptwriter—or any experienced documentarian—could have spent less than an hour with nothing more than the written background information I received with the footage and written a treatment that would have eliminated *all* of the problems I listed in my letter to the producer.

A good scriptwriter could have spent a little longer and very likely come up with some suggestions of concept and coverage that would have made this into an exceptional piece.

Visualization

The writer's research should be focused not just on the facts of the documentary topic but also on ways to show it clearly to an audience. What will make up the visual evidence for the argument presented?

If you can show a picture of the topic, you can cut down substantially on the words that must be spoken. If you're doing an environmental documentary, you could go and interview an environmentalist who says a chemical plant is polluting the river. Then you could interview an official from the chemical plant who says they're not. That's a standoff. It's what you get on local TV news. Talking about a problem is not documenting the problem, it's documenting what people have to say about the problem.

But if you've got footage of ugly stuff pouring out of a pipe into the river, you're beginning to *show* the problem, not just talk about it. And if you can get some neutral party to test the ugly stuff on camera and demonstrate through the tests that it either is or isn't pollution, you're building a chain of visual evidence.

I've said it elsewhere, and I'll say it here again: *There is no substitute for good footage.*

Organizing a Structure for the Documentary

Making a documentary is an exercise in storytelling, and as Sheila Curran Bernard writes in the first edition of *Documentary Storytelling,* "Structure is the foundation on which story is built, whether the story is being told in person, in a book, or on screen. It's the narrative spine that determines where you start the story, where you end it, and how you parcel out the information along the way." (p. 42)

A good story builds from an attention-getting opening through a series of important—and interesting—incidents to a satisfactory conclusion. Creating this sort of structure is what scriptwriters do. Much more on structure in chapter 18.

Writing the Words That Are Needed

Almost every documentary requires some sort of a proposal. Usually there will be a treatment, which may function as the shooting script for a spontaneous cinema documentary. There may be a full script or screenplay written before principal photography as the blueprint for filming. Or there may be a script written prior to postproduction to organize what has been shot into a storytelling structure.

We'll look at all of these in more detail in the next few chapters.

17

RESEARCH

Making a documentary is, or should be, a process of discovery that begins with questions rather than answers.

First you question yourself to help define the quest you are embarking on:

- Exactly what is it that you are wondering about?
- Why are you interested in this?
- Where could you begin to look for answers to your questions?
- What possible explanations can you think of for whatever it is you are wondering about?
- How can you test the truth, accuracy, and validity of the things you find out?
- Where can you find the facts?
- What could you film that will show the truth?

Then you go out into the real world and keep asking questions. You have to be open to things that you may not want to hear. You have to ask people how they know the truth of what they are telling you. You have to look for evidence; for proof.

And you have to accept that the search for truth may put you at odds with your friends and colleagues who are convinced things are one way and don't want to hear any evidence to the contrary. You hope it won't. But it could.

The best documentaries are made by people who set out to learn the truth about something. If you don't learn anything in the process of researching, writing, recording, and finishing your film, then making the documentary will probably have been a waste of time.

Read

I can't imagine starting a documentary project without reading one or more books related to the subject of the film, along with as many articles as I can get my hands on, plus searching the Internet for information related to the topic.

I often start with a topic search at Amazon.com. It's a quick way to get the names of authors who have written something about the topic, along with a useful description of the contents of their books. And on Amazon there's often the opportunity to browse inside a book.

I'll also click over and do an online search at my local library. In addition to Internet access to the library system's catalog, many libraries today offer their online members access to *Books in Print*.

Then there's LexisNexis, a powerful online search system for legal, business, scholarly, and journalistic sources. LexisNexis Ala Carte! allows a researcher to search for free and pay only for the documents that are used.

And, of course, I Google every search descriptor I can think of. As I find articles and items of interest, I download them to the project file so they'll be available for reference. Out of this may come a list of people I want to talk with and possibly other lists of places I might want to visit and things I'd like to see.

I'm looking for several things:

- A broader and deeper understanding of the topic of the documentary, whatever it may be
- Names of people (and organizations) involved with the topic
- Controversy. Are people taking opposing positions on the topic? If so, why? How do they differ?
- Visual evidence

Talk with People

Then I start to do interviews. These may be by phone, by e-mail, or in person. In some cases they may be done on camera.

Part of research interviewing is purely administrative. This includes getting the correct spelling and pronunciation of the person's name, a title if he or she has one, and an affiliation, such as a university, company, or advocacy group. In short, you begin to gather the information for an identifying graphic should this person appear on camera.

Then you may have a list of questions you'd like to ask. Your list should start with the five or six most important questions, because you may never get past these. One or two should be general questions about the topic. The rest should try to focus on this person's area of expertise.

GOALS IN A RESEARCH INTERVIEW

A research interview is a mining operation, not a conversation. It has several specific goals.

To Increase Your Knowledge About the Topic

This is your primary goal. Assume there is far more that you don't know about the topic than you do know. If you are not open to the possibility that all or part of what you think you know is wrong, you're not seeking the truth.

To Find Additional Sources of Information

Each person you talk with knows others who may be able to add to your knowledge. And they may suggest books or articles you should read or films that you should view. If they don't volunteer the information, ask.

To Evaluate This Person as a Possible On-Camera Interviewee

You're saying to yourself, "Hampe, I thought you didn't like on-camera interviews."

No, what I don't like is building a documentary out of interviews. But you probably are going to shoot some, so each person you talk with is a potential on-camera interviewee. How do they speak? Can they get to the point? Do they tell interesting (and brief) stories? Do they make a good appearance? Do they truly seem to know the subject? Do they have an ax to grind? Are they so firmly on one side of a controversy that they may lack credibility?

To Learn About Opposing Positions

There probably are more sides to the story than the one(s) you started with. You need to find out about them. What are they? Who speaks for them? How credible are they? You really have to talk with people representing all sides, not just those on whichever side you might favor initially. You might find that each has a valid argument, but about a different part of the issue, and that the truth lies somewhere in between.

To Identify Visual Evidence

Every interview will probably give you a lead to visual evidence that you can film. But you have to be listening for it. Just suppose you were interviewing Dr. Joe Dispenza from the film *What the #$*! Do We (K)now!?*, mentioned in chapters 11 and 12. When he started talking about experiments where scientists hooked people's brains up to PET scans to see what part of the brain lights up when they looked at—or merely imagined—an object, the visual evidence portion of your brain should have lit up also. As a follow-up question, you would want to ask him where you might be able to film those experiments or how you might get copies of existing film or video showing this interesting phenomenon. Also, in such a situation, if the interviewee can't provide this kind of background information, you may want to probe deeper to try to discover whether this person is talking from facts or passing on an urban myth.

To Gather Documentation

The more research material you can get in writing—either on paper or recorded electronically—the better off you will be when you start to organize your research results into a proposal, a treatment, or a script for a documentary. If the interviewee mentions a report on the topic you're investigating, ask for a copy to take with you or to be e-mailed to you. Gather paper like a pack rat. At a minimum it will help you out with names and titles along with useful addresses and telephone numbers. And more often than you might think, you'll find interesting items in the text that never came up in the interview. I scan much of this information into my computer to make it easier to search for specific items later on.

Questions Lead to Questions and Answers
Lead to More Questions

If you don't get answers to the questions you are asking, it may be because they're the wrong questions. Or because you are asking the wrong person. Or because you're relying on people to tell you the things you need to know, when perhaps you need to do more reading and searching first. So keep probing to find out what you should be asking about or whom you should be talking with.

The answers you receive will often lead to a new set of questions as you define the project better and refine your research approach. I always think of the research phase as a trial-and-error process. The more I learn about the kinds of things I need to know to handle the project, the better I become at getting the information I need. And the better I become at getting the information I need, the higher the quality of the information I have available to work with in developing and producing the documentary.

Never Show Off Your Knowledge

A research interview is not an opportunity for you to impress the expert with the depth of your knowledge. You may need to demonstrate a sufficient grasp of the basics of the topic to convince the interviewee that talking with you will not be a waste of time. But in general you should be an empty vessel waiting to be filled.

Always Ask for More

Never forget that the interviewee probably knows far more about some aspect of your documentary topic than you do. But you may not get the good stuff unless you ask for it. I always end an interview with these two questions:

1. *Is there anything I should have asked you but just didn't know enough to?* This admits my relative ignorance and asks the expert to enlighten me.
2. *Is there anything else that you would like to tell me that I haven't given you a chance to?* The interviewee may have some things he or she would like to talk about, but you may never know about them unless you ask.

The Central Question

All through the research process you are seeking the answer to the central question for a scriptwriter, which is:

What is there about any of this that will interest an audience?

Is there a story here? Is there a question begging to be answered? Are there interesting things for the viewer to see? Are there the elements of dramatic conflict? Are there interesting people? Is there a human story?

And probably most important: Is there a truth that needs to be told?

18

STRUCTURE

Structure is one of the most important—and least understood—aspects of documentary production. Bad structure is worse than bad writing, bad cinematography, and bad acting. It can lose you your audience almost before you start. And you will *never* know why.

Documentary structure is an ordered progression of images and sounds that catches the interest of the audience and presents the point of view of the film as a visual argument. Its purpose is to keep the audience interested from the beginning through the long development of the middle to the resolution and closure at the end.

B-M-E

Everyone knows about beginning-middle-end, but how exactly does that translate into scenes in a documentary? In a creative writing class at the University of Pennsylvania, Dr. Bruce Olsen explained beginning, middle, and end this way:

> The beginning is the point in your work *before which* nothing needs to be said. The end is the point *beyond which* nothing needs to be said. And the middle runs in between.

The only modification I would make would be to substitute *shown* for *said*.

Beginning: The Point Before Which Nothing Needs to Be Shown

Defining the beginning this way eliminates the problem of having two or three opening scenes, one right after another, which plagues so many documentaries and information videos. Does the audience have to know this right now? No? Then leave it for later. Do they really ever need to know it? If not, maybe you can leave it out.

The beginning is critical. It is that brief moment in which you must both capture the attention of your viewers and teach them how to view your film. The beginning states the theme, asks a question, or shows something new or unexpected. It gets the film started and raises the expectations of the audience.

OPENING SCENE

In her excellent guidebook for screenwriters, *Making a Good Script Great,* Linda Seger says that most good films begin with an image: "We see a visualization that gives us a strong sense of the place, mood, texture, and sometimes the theme. . . . Films that begin with dialogue, rather than a particular visual image, tend to be more difficult to understand. This is because the eye is quicker at grasping details than the ear." (p. 21)

In structuring a documentary your job is to make your audience want to see what will happen next. The structure might be chronological, starting with a precipitating event. Or it may start in the midst of events—with a question or conflict or problem of some sort—and work out from there in as many directions as it takes. If you can unsettle the world of your audience, just a little, in the first couple of minutes, you're going to find them still with you a half hour or two hours later, when the film is ending.

A LITTLE EXPOSITION—VERY LITTLE

Within or following the beginning, you weave in a brief presentation of the theme of the documentary, the problem(s) it deals with, the main people involved—whatever the viewer needs to know for the film to go forward. Keep this short! Trust your audience and limit this section to the absolutely essential information without which the audience won't understand the documentary.

Inexperienced documentarians have a tendency to stop the film *dead* right after the opening titles and try to explain everything. But if you don't get caught up in the idea that you have to impose an order on your documentary based on some sort of exterior logic—first you have to know this, then you have to know that—you'll find that this sort of exposition will take care of itself.

Instead, get on with exploring the problem and let essential information come in when it is needed and relevant. You may play hell with chronology, but your documentary will flow smoothly from point to point. And that, I'm convinced, is the key to good understanding and retention on the part of the audience. Audiences, I believe, can handle a lot more ambiguity and uncertainty than most producers can.

Middle: The Presentation of Evidence

You've gotten the audience interested. You've given them a notion of what the documentary is about. Now you need to present some hard information to keep up their interest. This is the middle. It is a logical and emotional argument constructed out of the visual evidence that you've shot or will shoot. It builds the story you have to tell, while exploring conflicting elements of the situation.

The middle is hard. It comprises most of the film, and you have to live with constant decisions about what to include and what to leave out. This always means leaving out something you'd like to include. And it may sometimes mean including something you'd rather leave out.

The middle shows all the good stuff dealing with the documentary topic that you have room to include. Ideally it will consist of a well-blended combination of factual information, dramatic events, and human emotions.

CONFLICT

The middle often will explore conflicting elements of the situation by showing visual evidence in support of and in opposition to the theme. Or it may show progress toward a goal, along with barriers to that progress and how they were overcome.

The purpose of this is to introduce something like dramatic conflict into the structure of the documentary. Dramatic conflict doesn't mean some kind of encounter situation with adversaries yelling at one another. It is a structural tension that keeps the outcome of the film somewhat in doubt—and keeps the audience interested.

For instance, in *The War Room*, we see Gennifer Flowers holding a press conference saying she was Bill Clinton's lover, and then Governor Clinton saying the charges are false. He tells reporters, "It's sad that this sort of thing can be published in a newspaper like the *Star*, which says Martians walk on the earth. You've never asked me if Martians walk on the earth."

Overcoming Barriers

"Who wants to do what and why can't they?" is a description of conflict I read a long time ago. While directly applicable to screenwriting for feature films, it's a reminder to documentarians that human goals and the barriers to those goals are also a part of nonfiction storytelling.

- In *Watermarks* young Jewish athletes in Austria in the 1930s want to compete, but are barred from membership in Aryan athletic clubs.
- In *Spellbound* youngsters want to win the National Spelling Bee, but face stiff competition.
- In *The Hobart Shakespeareans*, teacher Rafe Esquith wants to help his fifth graders achieve excellence in what they do, in spite of the school's low expectations for its students.

Controversy

A documentary is expected to explore conflicting elements of a situation. This doesn't mean that it has to be passively neutral. But even when it takes a strong position in its theme, it should be able to acknowledge that this position isn't universally accepted. If it were, there would be little reason to make the documentary. One of the differences between information and propaganda is the willingness of the former to acknowledge that other points of view may legitimately exist, even if they are considered wrong.

Conflict is an element of any film about a controversial topic when the film shows more than one side of the controversy.

- *Is Wal-Mart Good for America?* first asks a question and then explores the positions of both pro-Wal-Mart and anti-Wal-Mart partisans.
- *Wal-Mart: The High Cost of Low Price* less convincingly contrasts allegations made in interviews by partisans opposed to Wal-Mart with positions taken publicly, although not necessarily in interviews for the documentary, by Wal-Mart officials.

Contrast

You can also provide dramatic conflict without playing opposing scenes against each other if the evidence you are presenting runs counter to the expectations or experience of the audience. In a documentary of behavior, it's the behavior that is important. But even here, you may be playing actual behavior against audience expectations. In *A Young Child Is . . .* , I showed Stevie, a little boy a year-and-a-half old, amusing himself for a long time by climbing over a low brick wall, getting a handful of sand, climbing back over the wall, throwing the sand in the lake, and then repeating the process again and again and again. The narrator says:

> You've probably heard it said that young children have a short attention span. We've come to doubt whether the concept of attention span has much meaning when the child initiates his own activities. We think attention span only refers to how long a child will tolerate doing something someone else wants him to do. If you don't believe us, believe Stevie. This went on all afternoon.

In *It Was a Wonderful Life* the present state of the homeless women is contrasted with their relatively comfortable middle-class lives before events made them homeless.

Actions vs. Intentions

Conflict in a documentary may also come from contrasting actions with intentions or actions with expectations.

- *The French Revolution* contrasts the revolutionaries' zeal for liberty with their horrifying abuse of the power they have gained.

- *Devil's Playground* compares the life Amish children find outside the Amish community with the life they've known within it, at a time when they must decide whether to stay or go.
- *March of the Penguins* sets the determined trek of the emperor penguins to their traditional breeding grounds against the incredibly harsh Antarctic conditions they must endure.

Process

In a documentary of a unique event, it is the process that counts. *The War Room*, for instance, is about an election campaign, a unique event with the end in doubt. Dramatic conflict comes, first, because the participants don't know how the event will come out; second, through problems that occur and the way they are overcome; and third, by finding other points of tension within the event.

GO WITH THE FLOW

Organizing the documentary so that it seems to flow effortlessly from one interesting topic to the next is what structure is all about. Otherwise you find yourself in the position of the person who says, "I'm no good at telling jokes" (but goes ahead and tells one anyway), and when he gets to the punch line and no one laughs, says, "Oh, I forgot to tell you . . ."

But by then it's too late.

Recurring Themes

In *The Cliburn: Playing on the Edge* we meet each of the contestants and learn something about their personal and professional lives and their hopes and dreams, all within the context of preparing for the final competition. Much the same is true of *Spellbound*.

In *Roger & Me* Michael Moore will show someone from business or government making an optimistic prediction about the future of Flint, and then cut to a sheriff's deputy evicting people from their homes. And between these milestones, he'll go off to explore some new facet of his story.

In *Basic Training: The Making of a Warrior* we see the recruits learning various aspects of infantry training and then applying them in practical situations.

End: The Point Beyond Which Nothing Needs to Be Shown

In one of Hollywood's many fairy tales about itself, there's a producer who says, "All I want is a picture that ends with a kiss—and black ink on the books." Take it as a metaphor. You want to end your documentary in a way that satisfies the expectations of your audience. It doesn't have to be a happy ending. But it does have to bring a sense of completion to the viewer.

Structurally, the end of a documentary has two elements, the resolution and the closing. These may occur together or in sequence.

THE RESOLUTION

Resolution is really the point to the documentary, toward which all of the evidence has been leading. In a documentary of a unique event with the outcome in doubt, it is the point at which the audience learns the outcome. In *Unzipped*, a documentary about designer Isaac Mizrahi, it's the successful presentation of the Mizrahi collection. In *The Hobart Shakespeareans* resolution comes with the end of the school year and the performance of *Hamlet*, which symbolizes the growth we have seen in the students throughout the year.

In a historical documentary it is the climax of the historical event. In *Defenders of Midway* it's the outcome of the battle, the point where the film totals the devastating enemy losses and compares them to the light American casualties. In *The French Revolution* it is Robespierre beheaded at the guillotine, to which he had unsympathetically sent so many others.

THE CLOSING

This is a final sequence within or after the resolution that ties up the loose ends, drives home the theme, and completes the documentary for the audience. In *Defenders of Midway* it's the point where the veterans reflect on the meaning of the battle and are seen dedicating Midway as a national historic landmark.

In *Hoop Dreams* it's the end of the process, as the two boys go off to college and talk about their dreams of playing in the NBA. William says, "If I had to stop playing basketball, right now, I think I'd still be happy. I think I would. That's why when somebody say, you know, 'When you get to the NBA don't forget about me,' and all that stuff, I should say to them, 'If I don't make it don't you forget about me.'" The resolution ends with a denouement in which roll-up titles inform the audience what has happened to the two boys at college.

In *March of the Penguins* it's the return of the new chicks to the ocean to begin the life cycle once again.

Sex in a Cold Climate, the documentary that directly led to the award-winning feature film, *The Magdalene Sisters,* closes with each of the three women whose stories were told commenting bitterly on the way her forced internment as a penitent in the Magdalene laundry impacted her life. One of the women says there was nothing "godly" about the nuns. "All I saw was a bunch of bullies . . . dressed up in nun's habits."

Getting Organized

In many ways a film is like a mosaic, made up of many little bits and pieces, which when put together properly let you see the big picture. Any documentary of a decent length will involve a lot of these little bits and pieces, for which you must find an organizing structure.

The Existential Outline

The first time I had to write a script for an hour-long program, I borrowed a technique screenwriters often use and wrote each event—scene, specific shot, sound bite, graphic, and so on—on a 3×5 index card. Then I stuck each card up on the wall with a piece of Scotch tape. The first organization of all these cards was just to put things that seemed to go together into little clusters without worrying too much about which came first or which was more important. The second organization was then to arrange the cards in a sequence from the beginning through the middle to the end.

What I like about this system, as opposed to a written outline or even an outlining software program—and I've tried both—is that it gets *everything* that may be going into the script right out in front of me. I call it an existential outline. I don't have to try to remember something that may be item IV-B-1-c on page 7 of a written outline. It's right up there on the wall to remind me of its existence.

The first time I used this system, it worked fine, except for one thing. Several weeks later, when I had finished the script and went to take the index cards off the wall, I found that they brought little bits of wallpaper with them, stuck to the tape. This left me with a pockmarked wall. Today I use Post-its—or Post-it size printout strips and removable tape—instead of index cards and stick them to a 30×40 foam-core planning board instead of the wallpaper.

FAMILIARITY BREEDS SUCCESS

Why go through all this? Well, you certainly don't have to. All I can say is that this is a system that has worked for me for more than twenty years. And I continue to use it because it accomplishes several important things on the way to writing a proposal, treatment, and script:

*It Helps Me to Become Thoroughly Familiar
with the Research Material I'll Be Using*

As part of this process, I type up my notes from research interviews and from my reading, and in many cases I scan printed background materials and convert them to text. In the next step I print everything out in two-inch-wide strips. These I cut into film events, like the screenwriter's index cards. I stick them in clusters of similar things on the planning board using removable tape, which lifts off and resticks easily just like Post-its.

Figure 18.1 shows an excerpt from the notes I made from Pietra Rivoli's book, *The Travels of a T-Shirt in the Global Economy,* in getting organized to write a proposal and treatment for a documentary based on it. The items in the column can be cut apart and moved about as needed.

In the process of reviewing, typing, and handling these bits of information I have a chance to become thoroughly familiar with the various elements that may eventually go into the film.

It Lets Me See How Things Go Together

I start with the things I'm fairly certain about. This may be the opening scene. It might be the closing. Or it may be a critical section somewhere in the middle. I stick those Post-its and printout bits in the appropriate spot on a clean planning board—opening of the film on the far left, closing on the far right, middles in the middle. From there, I

Figure 18.1. Printout of Notes for Planning Board

Chapter 8 Perverse effects and unintended consequences of T-shirt trade policy [p.139]

No more doffers [p.139]

. . . the influence of politics in redirecting trade has had a number of other consequences—mostly perverse and unintended—but both positive and negative, for rich and poor countries alike. [p.139]

Textile and apparel jobs in the United States have been vanishing and will continue to vanish, with or without protection from imports. [p.140]

Figure 8.1 Employment and productivity in the U.S. textile industry, 1990 to 2003. [p.140]

Figure 8.2 Employment and productivity in the U.S. apparel industry, 1990 to 2003. [p.141]

While the rationale for the series of "temporary" trade arrangements has always been to save jobs by giving U.S. industry breathing room in which to become competitive, the only hope for becoming competitive is to get rid of jobs. [p.142]

The charge that America's textile jobs are going to China also must square with a remarkable and inconvenient fact: China is losing textile jobs too, and losing more of them more rapidly than has ever been the case in North or South Carolina. [p.142]

In short, textile jobs are not going to China, textile jobs are just going, period. [p.142]

Figure 18-1: An excerpt from the notes I made while reading *Travels of a T-Shirt in the Global Economy*, prior to writing the treatment. The notes have been formatted into a two-inch column for the existential outline. Included are subheadings within the chapter, figures that were used, and excerpts from the author's words.

proceed to put together other segments leading into or out of the items already on the board, following my own structural rule of dealing with a topic once and moving on. As I work with each segment, I consider all the bits dealing with that topic, select the ones I want to use, and return the discards to the cluster they came from, where they are available in case I change my mind.

And that's how I build up the outline for the script. Do I get it right the first time? No, of course not. As I'm putting the bits for, say, sequence number five on the board, I may realize that some of the information won't make sense unless the audience is aware of something contained in a cluster I had planned to use later on. So I have to reshuffle, moving that information into an earlier sequence so that the film will flow smoothly and the audience will understand what is going on.

Keeping Track of What's In and What's Out

With this system, I can keep track of everything that needs to go into the proposal, treatment, or script because I can see it in front of me. Information still in notebooks or file folders or somewhere on the hard drive is not really accessible. And as every writer should know, ideas in your head are nothing but vaporware—they have no validity until they've passed the test of being able to be written.

This way, nothing important gets left out, because I regularly check the "outs" clusters to be sure I'm not overlooking anything critical. And if I get a new idea about how to handle something in the film, I just jot it on a clean Post-it and stick it up on the board. The bits on the planning board become a paper edit of a film that has not yet been shot. And when I like the way it plays out on the wall, I go to writing.

Preparation Is a Huge Part of Creativity

About the time I created my first existential outline, I appeared on a panel at an all-day workshop about writing documentaries and information videos. In one session we were asked to tell how we worked. I said that by the time I had researched and organized the material and written the treatment, I had done probably 80 percent of the creative work, because by then I knew what the video would look and sound like. Then I naively suggested that the other writers on the panel would probably agree with me.

They didn't.

One said he didn't really get into the creative work until he began writing the script. He was a writer-director who liked to do dramatizations, and it wasn't until he got to the script stage that he began to deal with what his characters had to say. Another disagreed, saying that creativity was in the clever way the narration was written.

Nevertheless, I stand with Richard Walter, screenwriter and UCLA professor, who says in *Screenwriting: The Art, Craft, and Business of Film and Television Writing*:

> While all the elements of a screenplay are important, and none exists independently, the most important component of all, and certainly the most difficult to craft is story.
>
> The three most important facets of story craft are: (1) structure; (2) structure; (3) structure. (p. 37)

For me, at least, finding the structure depends on becoming thoroughly familiar with the material and how different pieces may go together. Once you've found the structure and organized the material within it to tell the story, the rest is relatively easy. But if you put too much reliance on being *creative* with the words said by your characters, spokesperson, or narrator, you probably haven't organized the script to make a visual argument.

A footnote to this story is that some time after that writing panel, I was hired to analyze and eventually rewrite a script that the director declared was unshootable. The problem was lack of structure. The script had been written by my friend from the panel who didn't get creative until he got to the script. Most of his experience had been in writing very short videos, mostly commercials. When he had to craft a piece running almost an hour, his lack of structural concern caught up with him. He had written lots of clever dialogue for the film, and I kept much of it in the rewrite. But his script lacked an organized framework on which to hang his cleverness.

RUNNING TIME

One final element of organizing material into the structure for a documentary is timing. A documentary for television is going to have to be a certain length, whether it's a commercial hour (which is forty-some minutes), a noncommercial hour (which is fifty-some minutes), an hour and a half, two hours, or a series of fixed-length episodes. A theatrical documentary will normally be longer than an hour and less than two hours.

Running times for commercial television vary, depending on how many commercials a specific network currently runs in its documentary programs. The only way to know is to call and ask, or to time some current programs of the sort you hope to do.

Once you know the running time, you can begin to structure the content of the documentary in terms of time as well as flow. When I'm setting up the planning boards for my existential outline, I divide them into columns, with each column representing a certain number of minutes of running time. That way I know I can put only so much content into each column. This is a big help in deciding what can be included and what doesn't make the cut.

Acts for Commercial TV

Documentaries for commercial television, including cable, must be structured in acts, which run between the commercial breaks. Again, watch similar programs to see how many acts they have in a specific time period and what their average length is. Then establish the structure of your documentary around those acts.

The program may start with a short tease or grabber, a sort of pre-opening designed to catch the attention of the viewers. This leads up to the opening titles and possibly a commercial break. The first act functions as a beginning, getting the story under way. Each act after that usually deals with just one or two topics, and all but the last act will tend to end with something that keeps the viewers interested so they'll stay through the commercial break. The last act functions as the end of the documentary and contains the resolution and closing.

A documentary for noncommercial television or theatrical release must pay attention to overall running time, but can tell its story in any logical and effective way without the arbitrary structure of acts built around commercial breaks.

Sure It Seems Like a Lot of Work, But . . .

The function of a script is to organize the information that must be covered and present it to an audience in an interesting way. You must have a way:

- to know what information you have available
- to choose from this the information to be used—and that to be ignored
- to place the information in a sequence that will convey the message to the audience

You can take the time to do this before you start writing. Or you can write a draft and then take the time to revise it afterward, when the draft doesn't work. I've done it both ways and, frankly, I much prefer to know where I'm going before I start writing.

I use an existential outline for everything. Every script is planned this way. Each chapter of this book goes up on a board and is shuffled around until it offers an organization that covers the information economically and organizes it logically.

Do I write the manuscript exactly as it is outlined on the planning board? Hardly ever. Every writer knows that the work takes on a life of its own. What seemed like a good idea days or weeks ago when I was constructing the outline sometimes doesn't seem so great when I've written my way up to it. No problem. I just shuffle the Post-its until I find something that works. That's what I love about this system. It's out in front of you where you can see it. And it always maintains its flexibility. A Post-it on a piece of foam-core board is not very intimidating. It can be moved easily. So you are not being controlled by some arbitrary outline. You are in control of what you write.

Two Final Points

First, this is simply one way of planning your work before writing. It's certainly not the only way to do it, and if you have another, use yours. If not, try mine.

Second, when I was teaching a college writing course, I showed this system to my students, most of whom had never made a plan before writing. Some used it; some didn't. Those who did usually were writing better by the end of the semester. Those who didn't, often weren't.

19

PROPOSAL AND TREATMENT

Before there is a script for a documentary, usually there is a script treatment. And for many documentaries a comprehensive treatment serves as the blueprint for filming, with the actual script written after principal photography—if at all.

Before there is a treatment, there may have to be a proposal to describe the hoped-for documentary. And sometimes even to raise the money for research and treatment writing.

Proposal

There's an enormous difference between a neat idea in your head and a workable plan for a production. Somehow, what seems so pure and simple in your imagination gets a lot tougher to describe when you begin writing about the way the film will actually be made. So it's a good practice to do a proposal even if you're doing the documentary all by yourself with your own money. Getting it down on paper can be a worthwhile reality check and a big help in moving forward.

And, of course, if you're trying to raise money, a proposal is essential. It's a selling document. Documentaries can be expensive to produce. The organizations putting up the money have to be convinced that the benefits of financing a documentary justify the cost, either in profitable distribution or by doing good in some way. So you have to take the idea that is so beautiful in your mind and bring it out where others can see and react to it.

Some funding organizations may have a standard format for a proposal.

But regardless of whether it is written to format, done as a letter, or written as a report, the proposal, in a few pages, has to engage the fantasy life of the sponsor, stress the benefits of making the documentary, and shake loose the money.

How long is a proposal? The best rule is to be as brief as you can, but be complete. Keep the proposal short, and save the details for the treatment.

Getting Started

How hard it can be to take that first step! Especially if you have lived with the idea for some time. I received an e-mail from Ann-Eve Fillenbaum, a Belgian journalist in London, embarking on her first documentary that, she said, "aims to be a love story amongst the homeless of London."

She had an interesting idea for a documentary. Her problem was getting something written. She wrote:

> The project is moving forward, but people and my producer keep literally harassing me for a script, and I just feel incapable of providing this to them! I want to follow three couples for up to a year and observe how their condition affects something that is hard to maintain for all of us, even under a roof—a relationship! Through this, I would also like to suss out the multiple other issues that underlie homelessness such as mental health, drug use, family, and employment. Although I personally know the couples I am wanting to work with (I have volunteered in a shelter for over two years), I do not yet know anything about the way their relationship works (or doesn't) and therefore do not know how to provide the dreaded script!

What she really needed at this point was a proposal, something in writing that would begin to solidify a neat idea into a workable documentary project. And that's what I told her:

> The reason you can't write the dreaded script is quite simple: You are doing a behavioral documentary, and, quite properly, you don't know what the behavior will be. What your producer and others probably want, in asking for a "script," is some description of the documentary in your head that they can use to raise money, plan a budget, etc.
>
> So try this. Start with the Sol Worth exercise: "I want to make a film about . . ." and write out what you want to make your film about.

Don't worry about length in the beginning; get it all down. Since this is a behavioral documentary, describe the behavior you hope to film. Give examples of the sort of behavior you hope to find and to film, and make it clear that these are made-up examples. Think about how you are going to do your investigation with a camera, because that's what this is. You are going out with a camera and a microphone to investigate the behavior of six people. You are especially interested in the behavior of "a love story," and you are going to have to think deeply about what that means. Do you hope to film two people falling in love? Or do you want to explore an existing love relationship, which just happens to be among homeless people? Are you going to explore why these people are homeless? And how this affects whatever relationships they may have? And how things might be different if they were no longer homeless?

When you've gotten all this figured out, then you are going to have to boil it down to a one-page statement. This usually takes me anywhere from a day to a week to write. I do a lot of drafts. The one-pager should start with a short, *TV Guide* description of the film. Shoot for 14 words, and don't go over two typed lines. The rest of the page describes the exciting documentary you plan to make in a way that makes everyone who reads it want you to hurry up and get it done so they can see it.

Keep It Brief

One of the reasons people have trouble with a proposal is that they want to tell everything. But the purpose of a proposal is not to tell everything, but to tell just enough to get the recipient of the proposal to express interest and ask for more information.

For example, marketing experts talk about "the elevator pitch," which is a way to tell about your product or service in the time it takes an elevator to get to the tenth floor. It starts with the words, "Do you know how . . ." and a description of a problem. This is followed by, "What I do . . ."

You don't have to do this on an elevator, of course. Actually, you're more likely to do it in other settings where it would be natural for someone to ask, "What do you do for a living?" According to the experts, you don't say, "Oh, I'm a mortgage broker." You say:

Do you know how some people look all their life for the perfect home? And then they finally find it. But they just can't make the monthly payments work. They can't get a loan. They can't get the right interest rate. They can't get approved?

Well, **what I do,** I work with hundreds of lenders around the country. We even do those new "no doc" loans, where there's no documentation, no income verification. Low interest rates, hundreds of lenders, we get people in that home of their dreams at a price they can afford.

That's your goal: to have a brief, complete description of your film that you could tell someone in an elevator. Most of us, when we're asked, "What's your documentary about?" want to take the person through our whole thought process, from when this idea hit us while walking across the street to the names of the film festivals we'd like to enter it in. And long before we get to the good stuff, the other person has gotten off the elevator.

Try describing your documentary in terms of a problem and a solution. Or a problem and an investigation:

Do you know how when crossing the street, you wait for the walk light, and then as soon as you start to go it changes to don't walk? And how cars turn in front of you so you can't walk anyway? My documentary investigates why that happens. Is it bad engineering, bureaucratic indifference, stupidity, or something else?

Once you are able to describe the documentary you want to make with an elevator pitch, you will have a pretty good idea of the essence of your project. And that's what goes into the proposal.

Example of a Proposal: Lost Legend

I got an e-mail from Steve Harnsberger, who wanted to make a documentary about a disastrous flood in China in 1931, and the part that members of his family, missionaries in China, played in the recovery. He was on his way to China to help open an exhibit commemorating the event. We agreed on a consulting fee and he started sending me material. Included was a "Documentary Outline" which ran some thirty pages, along with many pages of background information and photos. Eventually, I wrote a proposal that fit, single-spaced, on one page. This is shown in figure 19.1.

Figure 19.1. *Lost Legend* Proposal
The Lost Legend of the World's Worst Flood

The devastating flood that killed 3.7 million Chinese in 1931 was largely un-remembered, even in China, until a missionary's son and grandson brought the story home.

A Proposal for a Documentary Film

"Imagine Lake Erie set down on top of Massachusetts, a mammoth lake stretching as far as the eye could see, smiling peacefully over drowned homes." Those are the words of Anne Morrow Lindbergh, describing just one portion of a giant flood that she and her husband witnessed. A flood that killed nearly 4 million people—*and then almost completely vanished from memory!*

The worst weather disaster of the 20th century occurred when typhoons stalled over Central China in August 1931, following eight weeks of heavy rain. The Yangtze and Huai rivers ran wild, breaking through the dikes and flooding an area of 70,000 square miles. Lake Gaoyou, elevated above the sur-rounding countryside, tore a 700-meter gap in the levee containing it, killing thousands instantly. Throughout the flood area, an estimated 140,000 people died in the first few days. Some areas remained flooded for up to six months, resulting in extensive disease and starvation. Called "the greatest flood on his-torical record" in the report of the Chinese National Flood Relief Commis-sion, the tragic event caused an estimated 3,700,000 deaths over the course of a year.

Yet it was a disaster that, incredibly, much of the world, and even many people in China, had all but forgotten as worldwide depression, civil war, the Japanese invasion of China, World War II, and the resumption of civil war piled one catastrophe upon another. The memory of the flood was preserved, however, in the family lore of the descendants of Thomas "Lyt" Harnsberger. A Presbyterian missionary to China, he played a key role in rebuilding the al-most half-mile-long breach in the levee at Gaoyou.

The proposed documentary is the story of the great flood, of the heroic effort to rebuild after the disaster, and of the lifelong dream of Hutch Harns-berger, son of the missionary, to see the story of the flood—and his father's contribution—restored to China. As Hutch fell ill, the dream passed to his son Steve, and was finally realized when the lost legend of the world's worst flood was reborn in a new museum along the Grand Canal in 2005, just eight months after Hutch Harnsberger died.

Among the museum's exhibits are never-before-seen photographs of the flood taken by Charles and Anne Lindbergh, who had flown a single-engine

Figure 19.1 (*continued*)

float plane from the United States to China via Alaska and Russia, as recounted in Anne's book, *North to the Orient*. The Lindberghs arrived in China shortly after the flood and volunteered to conduct an aerial survey of the devastated area, photographing it from their plane, *Sirius*. The photos were found in the home of a 93-year-old American woman who had kept them since 1931.

Three dedicated men led in rebuilding after the flood. Lyt Harnsberger realized that the waters would not recede in the flood area until the massive break in the levee was repaired. He put his missionary duties on hold for a year while he managed the levee repair. Missionaries are often portrayed as spiritual creatures with no grounding in the real world. Those who made their way to China in the early 20th century and survived were adept at handling adversity. Harnsberger moved his family to the flood area in a Chinese houseboat, where he managed, paid, and fed 15,000 laborers who rebuilt the levee by hand. Hermit Lin, a Chinese Buddhist who had renounced the world, sold everything he owned and donated $200,000—equivalent to two million dollars today—to fund the Gaoyou dike project. In his donation letter, he wrote, "To save others is truly to save myself." Wang Shuxiang, a retired Chinese general and engineer, who had a lifetime of experience with dike building and management, provided the technical expertise to plan and execute the project.

The dike rebuilding project was completed in about a year, with the project cost kept under the budgeted amount. Steve Harnsberger proudly notes, "My grandfather returned about 10 percent of the original funds to the Relief Committee in Shanghai. They said it was the first time in a hundred years that had happened. Then he returned to his Christian ministry work."

Visual Evidence: A 30-minute program appeared on China Central Television, produced at the suggestion of Steve Harnsberger and using his materials. A 20-minute program appeared on Gaoyou television. In addition there are more than 200 photographs from the Harnsberger family, the Lindberghs, and the Nanjing Archives, showing the flood and the reconstruction. Steve Harnsberger has video and audio interviews with his father Hutch and his uncle Jim Harnsberger.

Production Team: Executive producer for the proposed documentary is Steve Harnsberger. Production partner is Dreamtime Entertainment, which has produced many documentaries for PBS, the History Channel, the Travel Channel, and others. Scriptwriter is Barry Hampe, documentary filmmaker and author of *Making Documentary Films and Videos*.

Revise, Improve, Rewrite

Another reason people have trouble writing a proposal is that they somehow think they can get it done in one draft. And when the first draft isn't perfect they say, "I just can't write a proposal."

My time log shows that getting that one page written for *Lost Legend* took about a day and a half of my time, spread across four calendar days. Each new day I started with a fresh look, and every sentence was revised, shortened, or completely rewritten several times.

As I write this, the project is still developing. The one-page pitch may become a more formal proposal tailored to the preferred style of the funding or distribution source. Eventually a treatment will be written, and then a script.

TREATMENT

If the written script is the blueprint for a film, the treatment is the blueprint for a script. The treatment sets forth the idea of the documentary comprehensively enough to be understood, but with enough flexibility to allow for chance, change, and the occasional flash of creativity. Approval of the treatment by the producer, sponsor, or network is approval of the concept and approach set forth in the treatment.

Length

How long is a treatment? As long as it takes to do the job. And this will vary according to what stage of the planning and filming process you may be in. Early in the process the treatment may simply elaborate on the proposal to show that you understand what you are trying to do. As you get closer to either writing a full script or beginning principal photography without a script, the treatment will become more detailed.

The treatment should be specific enough that it can be used as the basis for developing a preliminary budget for the documentary. Most of the information on the Post-its and printout strips on my planning board will eventually make it into the treatment—sometimes summarized for brevity, sometimes in detail for clarity.

Elements of a Treatment

A treatment is often referred to as an outline for a script. But it's more than that. It's really an explanation of the documentary. It describes the content of the film—what it is about, what will be included—and what it will look like, including the style in which it will be shot and the way it will be edited. It includes all the content items—the people, places, things, and events—that must be a part of the film. And it tells how the documentary will be organized to communicate with an audience.

Example of a Proposal and Treatment: Travels of a T-Shirt

Producer Mark Sugg optioned the rights to make a documentary based on the book *The Travels of a T-Shirt in the Global Economy* by Pietra Rivoli, a professor of economics at Georgetown University. Sugg had written a first draft treatment, which he wanted to use as a pitch to PBS, but he wasn't completely happy with it and asked me if I'd be interested in taking a crack at it.

First I started reading the book and couldn't put it down. It's a real-life economics thriller with a surprise in every chapter. Then I went back through the book and pulled out chapter titles, subheadings, and various bits of text that seemed significant to me. These notes, keyed to the appropriate pages in the book, along with Mark's original treatment and some thoughts I had while reading, became the printout bits to go up on the planning board. (An example was shown in the previous chapter as figure 18.1.) The notes printed out on seven marginless pages, each with four two-inch-wide columns of single-spaced, nine-point type. A lot of stuff.

This was organized into a set of proposal information posted on one planning board while the bits and pieces to make up a two-hour documentary were posted on another.

The proposal tells why a film based on this book would make one heckuva documentary. The first paragraph says:

> *The Travels of a T-shirt in the Global Economy* by Pietra Rivoli is a journey in search of the truth, the very essence of documentary film-making. It's also a fun read—a rare thing in an economics book—and

destined to be a classic. The author's sense of humor shines through as she reveals that many things the popular wisdom assumes to be the case, are wrong. That the story of our global economy is often a zany one, full of contradictions and unexpected, sometimes foolish, out-comes.

The treatment that follows tells what will be shot and what will be shown, breaking the story into an opening at Georgetown University

where Professor Pietra Rivoli heard a student at a protest against the International Monetary fund and the World Trade Organization ask the crowd, "Who made your T-shirt? Was it a child in Vietnam, chained to a sewing machine without food or water? Or a young girl in India earning eighteen cents per hour and allowed to visit the bathroom only twice per day?" As the speaker continued to paint a grim picture of the lives of workers in T-shirt factories around the world, Prof. Rivoli reflected, "I did not know all this. And I wondered about the young woman at the microphone. How did she know?" Thus began a search for answers that resulted in the book *The Travels of a T-Shirt in the Global Economy: An Economist Examines the Markets, Power, and Politics of World Trade.*

Then four sections:

Cotton Come from Teksa—which tells the remarkable story of cotton farming in Texas, where we meet an eighty-year-old man who farms 1,000 acres of cotton, more or less by himself.

Enter the Dragon—which takes us to China where cotton lint is turned into T-shirts, and we ask the question, "How can the American textile industry be losing jobs to China, if the Chinese textile industry is also losing jobs?"

The Protection Racket—which traces the history of protectionism in the textile industry, and what has been called "the long race to the bottom," as manufacturing moves from country to country to find cheap labor. And we discover some reasons why this may not be such a bad thing.

Afterlife—**A Free Market**—which follows the T-shirt, now worn and discarded but with plenty of wear left in it, to an outdoor market in Dar Es Salaam, Tanzania.

The treatment concludes with this thought:

> "As I followed my T-shirt around the globe," Professor Rivoli writes, "each person introduced me to the next and then the next until I had a chain of friends that stretched all the way around the world: Nelson and Ruth Reinsch, Gary Sandler, Patrick and Jennifer Xu, Mohammed and Gulam Dewji, Geofrey Milonge, Augie Tantillo, Ed Stubin, Su Qin, and Tao Yong Fang. . . . The Texans, Chinese, Jews, Sicilians, Tanzanians, Muslims, Christians, whites, blacks, and browns who passed my T-shirt around the global economy get along just fine. Actually, much, much better than fine, thank you very much. All of these people, and millions more like them, are bound together by trade in cotton, yarn, fabric, and T-shirts. I believe that each of them, as they touch the next one, is doing their part to keep the peace."

The second draft of the treatment also included the option of a five-part miniseries. Single-spaced, the proposal fit on one page and the two-hour treatment on four additional pages. Adding the suggestion for a miniseries kicked the treatment up to five pages. I spent thirty-nine hours reading, researching, writing, and rewriting.

The complete proposal and treatment can be found in appendix 6.

A Treatment Instead of a Script

In writing a behavioral documentary the emphasis is on organization and visualization, not on writing narration or dialogue. For a behavioral documentary or a documentary of a unique event, a comprehensive treatment usually will take the place of a script. The treatment will show that you know what to look for and how to use it in the film you are planning, and that the documentary crew is well organized to cover whatever happens.

Example of a Shooting Treatment: A Young Child Is . . .

A Young Child Is . . . was planned as a documentary of behavior, in which the images that would make up the film would be found in the behavior of the people we filmed. The treatment had to deal with the fact that while we didn't know specifically what would be filmed, we had a strong concept of both what the documentary would be about and how it would look.

The treatment sets out a series of purposes for the film, such as "to show the tremendous amount of learning accomplished by these very young children before they ever come in contact with schools and teachers." The approach to filming is summarized as "what we get is what you see." And finally it sets out a list of content points to be covered during filming.

I don't know how long I spent writing this treatment. Certainly several days of thought, writing, and revising went into it. And it is the document from which the film was shot. The only script was a narration script that I wrote on a typewriter I kept on a little desk behind my Moviola film editing table. When I came to a place that needed narration, I wrote whatever was needed, went next door to the sound room and recorded it as a scratch track for temporary use in editing, brought it back, and edited it into the film.

An excerpt from the treatment for *A Young Child Is . . .* is presented in appendix 7.

The Script Treatment

A lot of scriptwriting goes into creating a complete treatment for a script. It will describe in detail the content that will go into the finished script, including scenes to be shot. Where footage has already been shot, it describes the types of shots that will be used, and may refer to specific shots or sound bites. For interviews still to be shot it indicates what the interviewee can be expected to talk about or what information the interviewer should try to elicit.

Well, if it's that complete, you might ask, why bother doing a treatment? Why not go directly to script? The truth is, occasionally you might. But starting with a treatment has some advantages.

First, because you summarize—rather than detail—the scenes, narration, and interview sound bites that will go into the documentary, a treatment will be shorter than a script and consequently easier to write and faster to read. For example, the treatment I wrote for an hour documentary about the lost warship, USS *Perry,* ran eighteen pages. The final script is fifty pages in length.

Second, the treatment is the first comprehensive look at how the documentary will be organized and what will be included. Once it is done, there almost always will be changes. And it is much easier to make changes in a treatment than in a script.

Example of a Full Script Treatment:
Lost Warships—U.S.S. Perry

Producer/director John Bell had completed the videotaping of deep-water dives on the U.S.S. *Perry* when he contacted me about working on the script. So I had footage that had been shot and transcripts of interviews with survivors from the *Perry* to work from. The planned documentary would combine history from World War II with the story of deep, technical diving on a sunken ship that had already claimed the life of a diver from another video crew.

In this case there was no need for a proposal and no need to explain why the film should be made. The film was already shot. So the treatment simply had to organize the footage that already existed and describe the script that would be written from it.

The film was organized in acts for commercial television. The following excerpt is from the treatment, act one. In the next chapter we'll look at a piece of the script that resulted from this treatment.

SCRIPT TREATMENT FOR *LOST WARSHIPS—U.S.S.* PERRY

ACT ONE

Fade in on scenes of a World War II Navy task force under way in the Pacific and superimpose the date, September 13, 1944.

We see stock footage of troops aboard ship and maps showing the strategic situation as narration tells us General MacArthur is poised for his return to the Philippines. In two days the First Marine Division will invade Palau to secure MacArthur's right flank.

We see stock footage of two or three minesweepers at work and of a float plane overhead as narration says that ahead of the invasion fleet, U.S.S. *Perry* in company with U.S.S. *Southard* and U.S.S. *Preble* is sweeping for Japanese mines offshore. A scout plane from U.S.S. *Tennessee* reports the area is heavily mined. The *Perry* has already had a mine fouled in its sweeping gear. The mine exploded, destroying the gear, but causing no harm to the *Perry*.

Stock footage of minesweepers turning as narration says that at 1414 the *Perry* turned to the northeast for a final sweep. Stock footage of explosion. Narration says four minutes later, U.S.S. *Perry* struck a Japanese mine and sank in less than two hours.

Stock footage of ships or stills of the actual rescue. Narration tells us that there were several ships in the immediate area and the exact position of the *Perry* was logged to the exact second of latitude and longitude. Even though the logged position placed the *Perry* in a known square about 100 feet on each side, or the size of a small house lot, for more than half a century every effort to find the lost warship had failed.

> Larry Tunks (on camera or V.O.): "As I was doing the plotting on the charts from what I'd learned from the Navy, nothing went together. It just—the numbers weren't right."

> Dissolve to opening titles.

The complete treatment for act one can be found in appendix 8.

By the time I completed the *Perry* treatment, after researching the history of the ship, viewing and logging the footage that had been shot, making a side trip to U.S.S. *Slater,* a destroyer escort that was similar to the *Perry,* organizing all the bits into five acts totaling roughly forty-six minutes, and then doing the actual writing, I had spent a total of 120 hours on the project.

I keep mentioning the amount of time that went into these treatments because some people, including some producers, have the idea that writing a treatment is a sort of pro forma exercise that shouldn't take a lot of time. Actually, the treatment sets the direction for the film. As we've seen, a treatment may be the primary shooting plan for a documentary. It's often used for budgeting. It sets the structure for the film. And it's the template from which the script is written.

All in all, a pretty important document.

20

THE SCRIPT

If you think of the treatment as somewhat similar to an artist's rendering, showing what an architectural project will look like when it's built, then the script would be the architectural drawings that show how to build that project and achieve that look. The script for a documentary visualizes the film that will be shot or—if it is written after principal photography—the film that will be edited from the footage that has been shot.

The previous chapters in this section are all about getting to the point where, if needed, a script can be written. This chapter is about getting it written.

SCRIPT FORMATS

First a small digression into the subject of script formats. Would-be screenwriters have been brainwashed about the importance of formatting. They've been told that every producer receives gazillions of spec scripts, but can produce only one or two films a year. Therefore, in every production office there sits a film school graduate whose job is to reject—for any reason whatsoever—99.9 percent of the spec scripts that come in. One of the reasons for rejection is that the script has not been properly formatted. That may be true in Hollywood for feature film scripts, but . . .

In scripting a documentary, the script format doesn't matter.

If you're going to direct the film, you can write the script in any format you're comfortable with. If you're not the director, find out if the director has a preference and use that.

At one point I favored writing in the straight-down-the-page screenplay format used in Hollywood if there were people involved in the production who were not experienced at reading scripts. If you gave them a side-by-side video script, they often would read just the audio side, thinking that was the important part, and more or less ignore the picture side. With a screenplay format, they had to read down the page and therefore got (I hoped) all the information.

But the truth is, I haven't written a documentary in the screenplay format in years.

The Two-Column Script Format

Figure 20.1 shows an excerpt from the two-column format used for the USS *Perry* script. This was written from the treatment shown in chapter 19. Picture goes on the left, sound on the right. What could be simpler?

How wide are the columns? Doesn't matter. What typeface should you use? Doesn't matter. What does matter is how you approach the writing.

Write the left side first to describe what the audience will see, and then the right side to tell what they will hear. If you do it that way, you'll stay out of trouble. If you start on the right side, you can end up pages later realizing you have no idea what to show to cover all that talk, and may find yourself settling for visual wallpaper.

Where the footage to be used already exists, I indicate the tape number and approximate time code of the shot:

[Tape 20: 00:20:33–20:40]

In the right-hand column at the end of each scene I also indicate approximate running time:

[S=0:07 // RT=00:50]

S equals the estimated length of the scene in minutes and seconds. *RT* equals the estimated total running time for the film from its beginning to the end of this scene. I set my computer formatting to put tape references and running time in hidden type. That way it's easy to cover up so it won't be a distraction to anyone reading the script who doesn't

Figure 20.1. *Two-Column Script Format*

Lost Warships: *U.S.S.* Perry

SCENE	VIDEO	AUDIO

16. Stock footage of a DMS or DD sinking.

    Title:

    ### Lost Warships
    ### U.S.S. Perry
    ### (DMS-17)

    DISSOLVE TO:

MUSIC: In full.

(S=0:10 // RT=02:10)

17. MS of *Ocean Hunter II* under way

    (Tape 05: 00:22:15–22:22)

    SUPERIMPOSE:

    Palau
    March 2005

MUSIC: Continues briefly, then under.

NARRATOR (V.O.): Palau. March 2005.

(S=0:07 // RT=02:17)

18. On board *Ocean Hunter II,* team helping divers prepare to dive.

    (Tape 05: 00:22:15–22:22)

NARRATOR (V.O.): The Lost Warships Team, a group of highly experienced technical divers, came to Palau determined to use the techniques they had developed over three years of training and preparation

(S=0:12 // RT=02:29)

19. Camera handed to diver in the water, second diver in, both swim toward tender.

    (Tape 05: 00:53:07–53:17)

NARRATOR (CONTINUES V.O.): to videotape the valiant ship. The *Perry* had been extremely diffi-cult to find and was equally unforgiving to dive upon.

S=0:10 // RT=02:39)

SCENE	VIDEO	AUDIO
20.	<u>Underwater:</u> Diver with red lift bag. Blows air in and releases it. (Tape 17: 00:05:30–05:37)	NARRATOR (V.O.): The diving conditions were so severe that these experienced divers twice found themselves (S = 0:07 // RT = 02:46)
21.	Red bag pops to surface. (Tape 05: 00:13:10–13:15)	NARRATOR (CONTINUES V.O.): in serious trouble. (S = 0:05 // RT = 01:51)
22.	Tim in boat, pointing at something to port, then turns with urgency and tells crew to go. (Tape 05: 00:16:46–16:50)	TIM O'LEARY (SOT): Let's go! (S = 0:04 // RT = 02:55)

need to be concerned about such things, but it's still available when needed.

The running time for the scene may be determined in several ways:

- For existing footage it's the length of the shot from starting time code to ending time code.
- Where there is narration, I read it out loud, timing it with a stopwatch, and then add a margin of one or two seconds.
- In a scene that has narration plus action without narration, I estimate the running time for the action and add it to the reading time for the narration.
- Timing for all other scenes is an estimate of how long they will—or should—last.

Like everything else in a script, this is liable to change during filming and editing. It is simply a ballpark estimate to keep track of running time and to try to keep the elements of the story in balance.

In the bygone era of typewriters, the speech and narration on the right side was written completely in capital letters. This was done in part to make the words as big as possible so they were easy to read on a TelePrompTer. Today TelePrompTers are computer driven, and you can select the font size, so there's no reason to use all caps. And there's a good reason not to. Letters in upper and lower case are much easier to read than all capital letters.

Some people put narration in italics or a different typeface to make it stand out. I've never done this. You may, if you like.

The complete script for act one of *Lost Warships—USS* Perry can be found in appendix 9.

Storyboards

For some productions—or just for some scenes—a storyboard may be prepared. In its simplest form, a storyboard contains a sketch of what will be seen along with a written description of the sounds that will be heard. Each frame of the storyboard shows a different piece of the action in the film. In a sense, a storyboard is like a slide show about the documentary.

I rarely feel the need for a storyboard, but some directors find them helpful. The reasons to use storyboards are:

- to explain visually a scene that is difficult to understand from words alone
- to help visualize how a scene or sequence should be shot
- to help get approval or financing from a sponsor, funding source, or client

Creating a storyboard is usually the responsibility of the director, not the scriptwriter. If you are an artist, or have access to one, you can make finished storyboards like those ad agencies show their clients for approval. But don't be put off from storyboarding because you're no artist. My occasional stick-figure storyboards have caused actual artists to break out in uncontrollable giggling. Rough as they were, those storyboards did the job for me.

Storyboards are likely to be used for certain scenes either in a historical documentary, to give the feel of the period, or in a documentary about a technical subject, which may be more easily explained in drawings than in words. They are less likely to be used for behavioral documentaries or documentaries of a unique event with the outcome in doubt.

Writing the Script

If there's an approved treatment, start with that. Then script the film scene by scene from the opening FADE IN to the closing FADE OUT. Write the script in master scenes that describe all the action and speech that occur at a specific location at a given point in time. Start a new scene whenever you change the time or place.

A good script may seem a little thin on paper. That's because, as my son Greg has said, the scriptwriter should tell what goes into the documentary, not write "a manual on how to make my movie." It's the director's job to bring the script to life and the editor's job to organize the footage into a film. The director and editor should be allowed some leeway in shooting and editing the film, if for no other reason than because an idea that reads well on paper may not work on the screen.

Writing Description

It is not necessary to detail camera movement, camera angles, close-ups, long shots, and so on, unless the camera work is essential to the understanding of what is being shown. Describe what happens within the scene and leave it up to the director to decide how to photograph it. Obviously, when the sense of the scene demands it, camera directions, such as, "Close-up of an empty boot," should be written into the script. The point is, don't get bogged down in worrying about camera directions, changing angles, reverse shots, and so on. Just tell the story.

And if you're not an experienced filmmaker or videomaker, stay away from terms such as *pan* and *zoom*, because you'll probably use them wrong. In fact, the less you write in terms of what the camera does and the more you write in terms of what the audience will see, the better off you'll be.

On the right side, it's OK to write dialogue for scenes that will be portrayed by actors. But where real people will portray themselves, it's best simply to suggest what they can be expected to say. For instance, if you have a scientist playing herself and telling about an experiment she's done, don't write dialogue. It just makes things harder. Most people will be themselves on camera if you'll let them. But if you try to turn them into actors when they're not trained for it, what you'll get is bad acting and an unacceptable performance. So, just write what they can be expected to say and leave it up to the director to elicit the information from them.

SCRIPTING BEFORE SHOOTING

The amount of detail within the description will vary depending on whether you are scripting prior to principal photography or after it. If the scene has not yet been shot, describe what you hope to shoot. Here's an example from the preproduction script for *Beyond Division: Reunifying the Republic of Cyprus*:

SCENE	VIDEO	AUDIO
54.	Famagusta as seen from an observation point in Deryneia.	NARRATOR (V.O.): This is Famagusta twenty-six years after the invasion. A ghost town. (S = 0:04 // RT = 16:57)
55.	ANNITA, a refugee from Famagusta, who runs the observation point, talks to us.	ANNITA: (Tells us she was seven at the time of the invasion. Her family fled and she has never been able to go back.) (S = 0:13 // RT = 17:10)
56.	From the observation point we see a road overgrown in grass and weeds, running through Famagusta from the seaside up to the Turkish army checkpoint in front of the observation point. To the right of the road we see the hotel buildings standing empty. We can see a crane alongside a hotel building.	ANNITA (V.O.): (Points out the road from seaside running toward us. On the left is the Turkish community, gathered around the mosque. On the right is where the Greek Cypriot community lived. Now empty. Along the beach are the resort hotels. Deserted. The crane was being used to build a new hotel in 1974. It stands where the crew abandoned it to flee the invading Turkish army.) (S = 0:30 // RT = 17:40)

These scenes describe not only what we expect to show, but also what we expect will be said by Annita, the eyewitness to the invasion. Where does this information come from? In this case, script research. Director Peter Vogt and I stood on Annita's observation point overlooking the deserted city of Famagusta—once the most prosperous city in Cyprus—and listened to her talk about the invasion. So I had a very clear idea of what we could show at that location, and what she might be expected to say.

In other cases, you may have to imagine what might be shown and what might be said. For a documentary about the experimental use of electric cars to lower air pollution in India (which I wrote without getting a trip to India) I looked at the research information I'd been given and imagined this:

SCENE	VIDEO	AUDIO
5.	Images of crowded city streets clogged with vehicles producing pollution, visible pollution in the air, people affected by pollution, coughing, turning away.	SOUND: Natural sounds.
6.	Graphic shows that two-thirds of the air pollution in India comes from vehicle emissions.	INDIAN HEALTH OFFICIAL: (Talks about the rise in health problems and deaths related to air pollution caused by vehicle emissions.)

Using this, Mike Buday, who directed the film, brought back some great visual evidence of air pollution.

SCRIPTING AFTER SHOOTING

If you're scripting after principal photography to organize what has been shot, the scene description can be less detailed, but you will include verbatim the sound bites that are used. Here's an example from a script I wrote for an International Association of Fire Fighters film, directed by Marty Sonnenberg:

SCENE	VIDEO	AUDIO
22.	Montage of: fire fighters in the fire house with their families and answering an alarm.	NARRATOR (V.O.): Several IAFF locals and their departments are expanding the scope of traditional CISM and EAP* programs to produce a compre hensive approach to behavioral health—with positive results. (S=0:12 // RT=3:05)
23.	Fire fighters working as a team at a fire or in training.	NARRATOR (V.O.): But trying to get individual fire fighters into counseling has often proven difficult. (S=0:06 // RT=03:11)
24.	Andy Orredondo on camera. (Tape Phoenix 9: 09:14:22-24)	ANDY ORREDONDO: Fire fighters, I think, are a real proud bunch. (S=0:03 // RT=03:14)
25.	Rudy Evesburg on camera. (Tape Arlington 10: 10:07:28-30)	RUDY EVESBURG: It's not cool to ask for help. (S=0:03 // RT=03:17)
26.	Andy Orredondo on camera. (Tape Phoenix 9: 09:14:24-26)	ANDY ORREDONDO: . . . so a lot of times a fire fighter is not going to ask for help. (S=0:03 // RT=03:20)
27.	Frank Jones on camera. (Tape Boston 1: 02:19:10-18)	FRANK JONES: It's not us that are broken. It's somebody else who's broken and we gotta help them. (S=0:08 // RT=03:28)

*The target audience for this knew and used these acronyms. Otherwise I would have written out the words.

SCENE	VIDEO	AUDIO
28.	IAFF behavioral health workshop in Phoenix (where the union manages behavioral health for the city).	NARRATOR (V.O.): The IAFF is committed to delivering behavioral health services that are easily accessible, compre hensive, and free of any stigma.

(S=0:10 // RT=03:38)

Timing

I discussed planning the structure of the film for the proper running time in chapter 18. The documentary normally will have a predetermined length, and the script must be written to match that length. There's no point in writing a brilliant ten-minute scene if the most that can be allowed for the topic covered by that scene is two to three minutes. (I'm making a point of this because overwriting is a sin that most of us must constantly guard against.)

In general, pictures provide more information in less running time than words do. But if you must use words, narration usually can get to the point and cover the topic quicker than a sound bite from an interview. On the other hand, the sound bite could be emotionally stronger or more dramatic than narration. Sometimes a little narration can be used to set up a short, powerful sound bite.

KEEP IT SHORT

Almost always in scripting, you actually need to include less of anything than you think you will. Less narration. Shorter scenes. Less explanation. Less setup. And shorter sound bites. You can usually start a scene later than you think and end it earlier. Try it. You'll be amazed.

Writing the Words That Are Said: Narration

It's helpful to remember that cameras and word processors don't always coexist peacefully. That's because filmmakers create with images, and writers create with words. Words are sometimes easier to understand— and to get approved when that's important—than a string of images written down in sequence. But it's the images that will make the documentary.

The same skill with words that can turn out a sizzling proposal may result in a script that is overwritten, dull, and talky, if the writer fails to make the shift from words to pictures in creating the script.

In a documentary script, words are used to describe what will be shown and to explain the thrust of the film. Be very careful about the use of words in narration and dialogue.

Always let the pictures carry all the meaning they can. I can't say this often enough: *When language is used in narration to evoke images, it can get in the way of the images you are showing on the screen.*

Use simple words and short sentences. Be profound, not elegant.

What to Write

The purpose of narration is to tell the audience the things that they need to know and may not be able to pick up from the footage alone. Its purpose is *not* to fill the sound track with meaningless words like the three guys in the booth on *Monday Night Football.*

My preferred way to handle narration in a documentary has been, wherever possible, not to have any. Life doesn't come with narration or music—or a laugh track, for that matter. Therefore, I reasoned, a film that observes life shouldn't, either. Through several documentaries I stood on principle and avoided narration completely.

The problem is that life also doesn't come with an arbitrary running time, but documentaries do. And a few words of well-chosen narration can often cover what would otherwise take several minutes of footage to explain. So when running time gets short, and the documentary material is rich, even the most committed spontaneous cinema documentarian may type out a narration script.

If the footage is good, the narration can be straightforward, in simple, easy-to-understand English. What belongs in narration? The things the audience needs to know to understand your film that are not covered by the footage itself. And nothing more.

Honest.

Nothing more.

When to Write It

Always write narration as late in the process as possible. Sponsors, clients, even producers love to read the narration ahead of time. It's the one part of the script they feel they truly understand. But the documentary filmmaker who writes the narration before editing picture is borrowing trouble.

In the first place, the lazy person inside all of us is likely to look at a well but prematurely written narration and just select pictures to illustrate it. B-roll. In the second place, your images are the visual evidence of your documentary. They have to be able to stand on their own.

Suggestions for Documentary Scriptwriters

If you're new to documentary, look at documentaries. And look with a critical eye. Documentaries, like any other creative form, range from excellent to lousy. Try to find the ones that appeal to you and analyze what it is you like about them. Do the same with the documentaries you dislike. You can learn a great deal from a film you don't like by analyzing what it is about the way it is made that turns you off.

THINK PICTURES, NOT WRITING

Writing the script for a documentary film or video means thinking in pictures. And that can mean placing yourself mentally in a theater seat looking at a screen, instead of at your desk facing a word processor. If you can't see it, you can't film it. If you are a writer trying to get a handle on how to do a script, remember that the hardest thing to do for a writer beginning to work in film is to stop relying on words.

SHOW THE RESEARCH AS WELL AS THE RESULTS

Take some time to absorb what you've learned and to think about the way in which you learned it. Your problem is to abstract from all that material a sequence of visual events that will show the audience, in a very short time, what you have learned over a period of days or weeks. Take the audience through a process of discovery that is similar to your own. Show the good and the bad. If you have the screen time, you can even take the audience down a few false trails. You may know everything that is going to happen in the film, but you didn't when you started your research. Don't deprive your audience of that delicious uncertainty.

Don't Write a Novel When You
Only Have Room for a Short Story

It's better to develop one theme completely in a short documentary than to try to cram in too much and lose your audience. Resist the pressure to try to make a single film that will be all things to all people. Such a documentary ends up meaning nothing to anyone.

Don't Worry About Transitions

There are two kinds of transitions that may occur in a script. The first is a visual transition such as a dissolve or a wipe. This is used to indicate a change in time or space, for example, dissolving to an event that occurs an hour or a month later than the previous scene or at a new location across the country. Even this is more of a convention than a necessity. You can cut from one location to another without a transition, as long as the difference is clearly evident. A woman can walk out her office door and in the next scene be anywhere—on the moon, in the fourteenth century, or across the country. And the audience will be right there.

The other kind of transition is an event or statement to "ease in" a change of topic. For example, the narrator says, "Now let's turn to a consideration of XYZ." This sort of transition is rarely needed, and when it is, it can often be handled with a superimposed title, such as "XYZ." Or it can be worked into narration while keeping the story moving. For instance, narration might say, "The test results were all positive except for a problem with XYZ." That's usually all the transition you'll need. Audiences raised on television have no problem accommodating abrupt change.

When I started writing for films, I asked a documentary writer-director the best way to get from one scene to another. "That's easy," he said. "Double-space twice."

You Can Hardly Go Wrong if You Write Narration
as if You Were Being Fined $10 a Word

Keep it to the bare essentials. Don't talk it to death. As a writer, I've always looked askance at the statement "A picture is worth a thousand words." As a documentarian, however, I take it literally.

Scripting a Re-creation or Acted Documentary

Most documentaries involving re-creation and scenes played by actors will deal with historical events, including recent events for which no other footage is available. Occasionally, a compelling documentary in search of the truth will deal with events that could occur at some future time. *The War Game* remains the archetype of documentaries of the future.

Even documentaries that rely primarily on visual evidence, sound bites, and narration may include vignettes which provide reenactment of a critical scene for which no footage is available. This is a staple of crime documentaries where the victim is dead and the murderer imprisoned or still at large. For example, *Enron: The Smartest Guys in the Room* reenacts the suicide of Cliff Baxter shortly after the opening of the film.

I think there is room in documentary for more dramatization without falling into the sinkhole of docudrama.

More Than Acted B-roll

The reason to write an acted scene is to bring the subject to life, to let the audience see what did happen—or might have happened. Before you write a scene, be sure you know its purpose in the film. Why is it there and what must it accomplish? Why does the audience need to see this? If you don't know, you probably don't need the scene.

Once you know the purpose of the scene, dramatize it. Don't just seat—or stand—people in a room talking about the problem. At least let someone rush in like Churchy LaFemme in Walt Kelly's *Pogo* comic strip, shouting, "THE JUTE MILL'S EXPLODED!" Then get everybody out of the room and working on the problem.

A documentary with actors is not the same as a feature film about a historical event or person. The script will use documentary structure rather than the three-act structure of a screenplay. Quite often we see reenactors, dressed in the clothes of the time, going through the motions of life back then, while a narrator and various experts tell us the way it was. This is mostly pageantry; there's rarely any dialogue or real drama. Pick the right period and you can find reenactors who love to dress up as Vikings or Romans or Civil War soldiers, have all the gear, and can give a convincing performance.

If you are going to write scenes with actors, you'll benefit from read-
ing some of the excellent books on screenplay writing, such as Linda
Seger's *Creating Unforgettable Characters* and *Making a Good Script
Great,* Syd Field's *Screenplay,* J. Michael Straczynski's *The Complete
Book of Scriptwriting,* and Richard Walter's *Screenwriting.*

Writing the Words That Are Said: Dialogue for Actors

The problem of dialogue in a documentary can usually be decided on the
basis of whether real actors will be used. If they will, you can write dialogue just as you would in a feature film. If not, don't write dialogue.

Even in an acted dialogue scene start with what the viewers will see.
If you tell the story with images you will need fewer words of dialogue.
Keep the audience interested—don't tell them everything all at once.
Pique their curiosity with short sentences and interruptions in dialogue
to let the information come out naturally.

And keep moving. If a character is told that the king wants to see
him tomorrow, the very next scene can be the meeting with the king.
You don't have to let time pass on screen. Get on with it. Only if the
character has to do something critical to the story—that the audience
must know about in advance—do you need an intervening scene.

Put some bumps in the road and bring your characters to life through
disagreement. What makes Aaron Sorkin's dialogue work in films such
as *The American President* and TV series such as *Sports Night* and *The
West Wing* is that he is a master of conflict. "From where I sit," he said,
"put two people in a room who disagree about something—the time of
day—and dialogue will start. And I'll have fun. On the other hand, put
two people in a room who have no conflict, who are in agreement, and I
think you have one character there that you don't need."

THE DIFFERENCE BETWEEN CONVERSATION AND DIALOGUE

Conversation maintains contact among two or more people and sometimes carries information. It is made up of incomplete ideas and frag-
ments of sentences. The parties feel free to interrupt each other, to talk
at the same time, and to change the subject capriciously. Dialogue, on
the other hand, takes place among two or more characters for the purpose of informing a third party—the audience.

Dialogue is artificial speech that must be accepted by an audience as believable. You have to write dialogue the way people *think* they talk and not the way they actually speak.

Keep dialogue believable. Don't use twenty-first-century expressions—or ideas—in a scene set centuries before.

And remember that it never happens in real life that two people who share the same information recite it to each other. That happens only in bad radio commercials.

SAYING THE WORDS THEY WROTE

A device sometimes used to provide dialogue—or at least a narrative monologue—for a historical character is to craft the words that the character says from actual words that the character wrote. The PBS documentary series *Benjamin Franklin,* for example, opens with the statement, "The words spoken by actors in this film are based upon actual writing of the period." Just remember that written language is generally different and often more formal than spoken language, and it can take a very good actor to say those words as if he or she had just thought of them that moment. In *Benjamin Franklin* Richard Easton does this extremely well with Franklin's words, but then he had a good writer—Franklin. In this film, as in *Liberty! The American Revolution,* both directed by Ellen Hovde and Muffie Meyer, the actors speak to the camera, almost as if being interviewed. There is little or no dialogue between characters.

WRITING OUT LOUD

Write narration and dialogue with your ears. Say it as you go. Out loud. Listen to how it sounds. Are there any traps or pitfalls that will cause the unwary to stumble? Fix 'em.

REWRITE

As with proposals and treatments, rewriting will make a script better. Let it sit for a day or two and then take a second look. You will absolutely find things that can be improved. Go ahead and improve them. Save the draft you have and then rewrite in a new draft. That's the beauty of composing on a computer. Anything can be changed. Nothing needs to get lost. And if you don't like the change after you've made it, you can go right back to the way you had it.

PART V

FILMING A DOCUMENTARY

"Let's make a movie!"

. . .

—*Producer Kevin Grant (Peter Haskell)*
in Bracken's World

21

PREPRODUCTION PLANNING

Preproduction planning, or the lack of it, has been the ruination of more films and videos than the combined problems of equipment failure, processing errors, poor lighting, missed cues, and bad acting all put together.

Overplanning squeezes the life out of a film—deprives it of the possibility of spontaneity, the little unplanned touches that add to the documentary's humanity and believability.

Underplanning, on the other hand, carries spontaneity to the point of winging it, which may contribute to grabbing some exciting moments but more often results in a film that is incoherent, lacks essential elements, suffers from technical inadequacy, and is very likely to run over budget.

Up to this point we've looked at the preproduction steps dealing with turning a documentary idea into a filmable project. Now let's look at the final steps in getting ready to make a movie.

SCOUTING

It can be lovely to shoot in a studio with soundproof walls, a level floor for dollying, and lots of electricity available for lights—but I've rarely had the chance. The modern documentary gets shot where the action is, in someone else's home, office, factory, or backyard. In return for a shot at the good stuff, you give up the home court advantage. And this sets up some problems you should be aware of.

When you shoot in a studio, you have total technical control. Lights can be set exactly where you want them. A path is cleared for camera moves. The people stand where you tell them to. Phones are turned off, and no interruptions are permitted. On location, however, you give up a great deal of control.

Everything and everybody that you will need to do the shoot must be brought to the location. If cost were no object, that might mean that you could bring every piece of equipment you can think of, and everyone you know who might be helpful, just in case. But there are few films where cost is no object. If you are renting equipment, you usually pay for what you take along, whether you use it or not. And you can run up a big bill in a hurry with expensive items that you might like to have but don't actually need. As to people, crew costs are the single biggest item in any documentary budget. Most producers have a strong aversion to paying, feeding, housing, and transporting crew members who are just standing around doing nothing. And most directors would rather trade off the cost of an unneeded crew member for additional days of shooting or editing.

Making a documentary on location means that you'll be shooting real people, doing real things—and you have to work with the people who are available. So it's a good idea to find out ahead of time who they are, what they can do, and what they are willing to do.

All of which means you should do some scouting, if at all possible, before you pack up the equipment, gather your crew, and go on location to shoot.

Locations

If you need a particular kind of location, such as a prison or hospital, you'll have to find it. For *Dialogues with Madwomen,* Allie Light needed to re-create her own experience in a mental hospital. She found a hospital, built and equipped but not open, which she could rent by the day. Other scenes were re-created in her veterinarian's examining room, after hours.

More commonly, the documentary concept requires you to work in a specific location, because it is where the people or events that will make up your film are to be found. Some spontaneous cinema documentarians insist on going in cold. They work with a minimum of equipment, use natural light, and feel that any scouting visit will contaminate the situation for filming.

But for most documentary situations, it's better to find out what the location you'll be working in is like. Here are some of the things to look for on a scouting trip.

Lighting

A film or video is made with light. You have to have a certain minimum amount of light, or you won't get any picture. But the type, location, and quality of the light can be equally important. Today's digital video cameras can record an image in very dim light, but they'll record a better image if the lighting is adequate.

INTERIOR LIGHTING

What kind of light does the location have? Most interiors in offices, factories, and public buildings are lit with fluorescent lights—no problem for video, but sometimes a problem for film. My own solution for shooting film with fluorescent lights has been to turn them off, if I can, and bring in my own lights.

Does the room have a lot of windows letting in sunlight? Sunlight doesn't mix well with artificial light. And it is a lot brighter than any normal artificial light source, giving you the possibility of hot spots and dingy areas.

How large an area must be included in the scenes you'll be shooting? It's not a big problem to bring in enough lights to shoot comfortably in anything up to the size of a standard school classroom. Beyond that, video will get you an image in whatever light is available, but film may get iffy.

If you are shooting video, you should be able to white-balance your camera to match the light sources. If there is any question about the quality of mixed-light sources, or the amount of light available, try to bring in a video camera and shoot tests.

Remember that even though your video camera or high-speed film stock may be capable of recording an image in very low light, lens depth of field is inversely related to the amount of light available. In very low light, you may have a problem keeping what you want to shoot in focus.

If you decide to bring in lights, check the availability of electric power. How many circuits are available? What's their capacity? Where is the fuse box or circuit breaker panel located? Will there be an electrician available to help you, or should you plan to hire one as part of your crew?

Exterior Lighting

If you'll be shooting outdoors, what will the light be like at the time of day when you'll be shooting? Direct sunlight? Shadow? Or a combination? Should you plan on bringing in reflectors or some floodlights to fill in the shadow areas? Remember that on a bright sunny day with a clear sky, you can have a difference in exposure of five f-stops between direct sunlight and shadow.

Where will the sun be at the time you'll be shooting?

Shoot Tests Wherever You Can

Scouting for a film shoot, I carry a 35mm still camera with me, loaded with film similar to the motion picture film I'll be using. This gives me a quick way of testing the look of the available light. And it is also a way of keeping a record of what the location looks like. For video, use a small camcorder for tests, or bring in the production camera so you know exactly what you've got.

Write It Down

Keep notes on everything you shoot: where, time of day, exposure information, what the picture is about, and who is in it.

And make diagrams as you go. What are the approximate dimensions of the area, including the height of the ceiling? What color are the walls, ceiling, and floor? Show the location of furniture, doors, windows, electrical outlets, and anything else that may be important.

Sound

What are the acoustics like? Are the rooms lively or dead? What about background noise—not only right where you'll be filming, but other noises, the kind you normally tune out, but a recorder won't. Are there airplanes flying overhead? Is there a lot of traffic noise from the street? Is there piped-in music, and if so, can it be turned off? How about the copy machine in the next room, the refrigerator, nearby bathrooms, people noise in hallways?

What kind of microphones will you need? Will you be recording one person at a time, or several people? Should you plan on a boom mike or shotgun, or will you be better off with wireless lavalieres? Will you need a microphone mixer?

People and Things

You are planning to film at the location for a reason. What is it? What must be shown in the film? Are there important people who must be interviewed—or at least seen? Who are they? When are they available? What will make a visually interesting setting to film them in? Should you do a preinterview while you are scouting? Can you?

Who are the other people you would like to include? People who will look good and talk well on camera? Are there people with an interesting story to tell, or who are doing an interesting piece of work?

What things have to be included at this location? It may be that the location itself is the thing of interest. Or there may be equipment, facilities, or a process that you must document. Investigate it. Plan out the shots you'll need. Find out if you'll be able to film whenever you wish or if you will be limited to certain times of the day or night.

Fees, Permits, and Minders

The use of certain locations may require getting a license or paying a fee. When you take over someone's home to shoot in, you'll normally have to pay them a location fee for the inconvenience, and you'll want to be sure that your liability insurance covers any inadvertent damage that might occur.

If you are working on the street in most cities you'll need to get a shooting permit (with a fee attached), and you may be required—or feel it's a good idea—to hire an off-duty police officer to accompany the crew. State and national parks may hit you with a usage fee or license requirement and may also require you to pay for a park guard or other employee to babysit the production.

Part of scouting is to check out these costs and to be sure that you have covered all jurisdictions. In some locations you may need separate city, county, and state permits to shoot.

Convenience

How easy or how difficult will it be to film at this location? How much cooperation can you expect? How close can you park to unload equipment? Is there good security for equipment left overnight? Will you have a guide or liaison person with you when you are working?

Can you work at your own pace or must you schedule around other activities, which might mean setting up and breaking down equipment several times? Will you have to shoot at unconventional times such as at night, in the early morning, or during lunch hour?

Crew Comfort

What about motels and meals? I once did a shoot in a remote location and didn't bother getting an advance motel reservation for the crew. We got there to discover it was something of a resort area, and all the motels within twenty miles were booked solid.

Is there a place at the shooting location where you can get a meal, snacks, coffee, and cold drinks for the crew, or should you plan on bringing these essential items with you? A hungry or thirsty crew is an unhappy crew.

Out-of-Town Locations

If you'll be shooting at an out-of-town location, what is the availability of rental equipment and freelance crew people? Unless the location is in a major metropolitan area where you are already familiar with the quality of the equipment and people available, you will probably want to bring your own gear and key crew members. But it's nice to know whether there are good rental facilities available in case you need extra lights, lenses, or mikes, or for backup if a piece of equipment goes down. And if you normally rent equipment anyway, the ability to rent on the spot can save you shipping costs and rental fees for the time the equipment would be in transit.

Similarly, you may be able to save on travel and per diem costs by hiring production assistants at the location. When I'm filming in an unfamiliar town, I like to have at least one local person on the crew I can use as a driver, guide, and informant on local customs.

What about buying film or video stock at the location rather than taking a chance on having it pass through airport x-rays? And what about shipping exposed film to your lab? Is there an air freight or express office near the location? What does shipping cost? Can you pay for it by purchase order or check, or will you need cash?

Local Film Commissions

Some cities and most states have a film commission in the state or local government whose purpose is to encourage filming within the area and provide assistance to filmmakers. Film commission staff can usually help you with permits and fees. They may not get you a discount, but they can cut the red tape.

The film commission can often help you find the locations, the people, and things you may need for your film. Filmmakers who travel regularly are considered good customers by the travel industry, and the commission may be able to get you discounts on motels, rental cars, and other location expenses. Sometimes they can point you toward tax incentives that can save you money.

Check it out.

Location Costs

Going on location usually means some out-of-pocket expense. That's obvious when you're headed for an out-of-town location—you know there will be travel expenses, hotels and meals, shipping costs, rental cars, tips, and so on.

Even if the location is close to home base, you want to be prepared for normal costs and have a reserve for unanticipated expenses. Normal costs would include crew meals, gasoline for vehicles, snacks, soft drinks or juice, coffee, and so on. I carry a cooler with me on location and make sure that my driver or one of the production assistants has petty cash to keep it filled with ice and canned drinks.

Unanticipated expenses could range from buying replacement batteries to repair, rental, or even replacement of an essential piece of equipment that has gone down. How you run your budget is your own business. But if I have a crew and equipment in the field, costing hundreds, maybe thousands of dollars a day, I'd rather spend some money to be able to keep shooting and get finished than have to schedule an additional day at the location.

General Considerations

In general, scout the location at the same time of day, and under the same conditions, as when you plan to shoot. You can't tell how much of a hassle shooting will be unless you see the place in operation. This will also let you see how the sunlight comes through the windows and hear how much noise there is.

Planning for Spontaneity

There is nothing like a brilliant spontaneous moment captured by the camera to make a documentary come to life. Just remember that it takes a lot of planning and preparation to have the camera in the right position with the right lighting, and a microphone where it needs to be, in order to capture that spontaneous moment on film or video.

Location scouting is an integral part of that preparation.

SCHEDULING

To schedule a production, include all the necessary steps as outlined in chapter 5. If you have a tight delivery schedule, you must work backward from the delivery date. Never cut corners on processes that are not under your control. You may be able to save a day in shooting or editing, but don't count on the film-processing lab to deliver in less than its usual time or the video post house to have offline and online facilities available exactly when you need them.

Allow time for things to go wrong. They will. Expect it, and don't be thrown by it. If they don't, consider it a gift.

Above all, when the numbers just don't work, be prepared to say to a client or sponsor or your partner, firmly, in a clear voice, "It can't be done."

Preproduction

Occasionally a documentary must go into production on a moment's notice because a unique event is about to take place and you must either cover it as it happens or forget about it. But most documentaries will go into production only after a long period of gestation and fund-raising— the preproduction process.

It takes time to do the research that will result in a well-documented, interesting, and informative film. How much time will it take? *Longer than you think.* Make your best guess as to research time and then double the number. Or at the very least add another 50 percent. You'll need it. Honest. You will.

Out of the research you'll refine the documentary idea, which will lead to a treatment for filming or at least a shot list of visual evidence. You must be prepared for the concept to evolve as you learn more about the topic. And as the concept changes, the scenes you plan to shoot and the way you may plan to shoot them will change also.

It has always amazed me that a director who requires two days to shoot a three-minute scene somehow believes a writer can do thirty minutes of finished script in the same time. Allow enough time for the writer to do a decent first draft, for the producer and director to read and digest it, for some discussion, and for revisions as needed.

Then it takes a lot of phone calls and a lot of scheduling—and revision—before you'll be ready to go into production. You can't assume you'll be able to shoot at a given location whenever you're ready; you need to pin down a time. And if your crew members are freelancers with other commitments, you have to make sure they will be available at the time you want to shoot.

Don't forget equipment checkout, casting as necessary, and rehearsal time.

Production

The shooting schedule presents another set of decisions. Everyone knows that a film is shot out of sequence, *but in what sequence?*

ACTUALITY SITUATIONS

In a behavioral documentary, you have to follow the behavior as it unfolds. If you are doing a documentary of a unique event, you have to cover the event. In each of these cases, people and events beyond your control will affect how you schedule production time. And for the visual evidence to be complete and to make sense, these events or this behavior probably must be shot in the order of occurrence. Not only is it considered cheating to do a reenactment in a behavioral documentary, it just doesn't work. The behavior won't ring true.

But you can distinguish between discretionary scenes and actuality events. You have to shoot behavior and unique events when they are happening rather than when it's convenient. But not everything that goes into an actuality documentary is a hot situation. There are establishing shots, for instance, and background interviews, which you can shoot on a quiet day, or use for backup if the hot stuff doesn't happen when it's supposed to, and you already have the crew scheduled.

PRIORITY SCHEDULING

For more conventional documentary projects, more conventional scheduling strategies can be used.

Schedule critical elements first—the hard-to-get people and hard-to-get locations. You have to take them when they are available.

Schedule exterior filming before interiors, but try to have a backup interior location available if bad weather makes it impossible to work outside.

If a studio will be used at any point in the production, you may have to schedule around studio availability. In scheduling studio time, don't forget to allow time to construct sets—and time to tear them down. Also, you might as well decide in advance what you are going to do with the set once you are finished with it, unless it has been rented and can be returned.

Schedule for economy. Take advantage of discounts for continuous use of rental equipment. Plan for minimum days for freelance crews and for actors.

If the film will take you to several out-of-town locations, try to travel a circular route rather than going back and forth to home base.

Allow for slippage. Everything takes longer than you think it will. Have time to solve problems that arise. If you can, allow time for retakes and cleanup shooting.

LOCATION SHOOTING

Basic to this approach to making a documentary is to plan and organize yourself and your crew so that you will disturb the environment where you are shooting as little as possible. Make no mistake about it: Your very presence is a major disturbance in any location. It may be a welcome distraction or it may be at best an annoyance to those who live or work there.

Your goal, like that of the wildlife photographer, is to become accepted as part of the environment as quickly as possible so that your presence can be more or less ignored by the people in it.

Good location scouting will help you to plan the shoot so that there is a minimum of disturbance and confusion when you arrive with the crew. Allow plenty of time for each setup. You may get what you want in a half hour or less. But you may run into problems and have to take considerably longer. The worst situation you can get into is to start falling behind schedule so that you are still shooting at setup number 1 when you should be at setup number 2, and you are beginning to wonder if you will be able to arrive at setup number 3 before the total time scheduled there has passed, and if you will be able to squeeze in setup number 4 at all. When you get into that situation, you have created a major disturbance in the environment that no amount of excuses and explanation can undo.

Be Honest

Be honest with yourself about how long each scene or setup will take. Then add a little extra time to give yourself a fudge factor.

Be honest with the people at the locations about how long you will take. There is a tendency among producers to minimize the time shooting will take and the disturbance the production crew will cause. Their belief seems to be that if they tell the truth, they won't get permission to shoot. All they really are doing is creating problems for themselves when they get to the location.

I still recall a film—never finished—that I spent one day on as a volunteer lighting director. The members of the congregation of a church came out at nine o'clock on a Saturday morning for what the producer-director had led them to believe would be "about an hour's shooting." And they were still standing in place, grumbling and hungry, long after lunchtime. The producer-director had made two mistakes. First, he had asked the members of the congregation to come at the same time as the crew call, perhaps anticipating that many of them would be late. But they weren't. So they had to stand around with nothing to do while we set lights, laid dolly tracks, and got set to shoot. Second, he hadn't been truthful with himself or with the congregation about how long shooting the sequence would take. It was a very unhappy shoot.

ONE DAY IN A HOSPITAL

Here's the story of a montage we shot in one day in a hospital, using volunteers, for a sequence about patient education. The script called for nine scenes, in the following order:

1. A child being treated in the emergency room.
2. An exterior long shot identifying the hospital and showing several people coming to it to attend health education classes.
3. A reverse shot of the people entering the hospital.
4. A medium shot of a person on hospital scales as part of the hospital's weight management program.
5. A medium close-up of a man filling in a heart disease risk-factor questionnaire.
6. A close-up of a cigarette being stubbed out, to introduce a program to stop smoking.
7. A medium shot of a person eating healthy food as visual evidence for the hospital's better nutrition program.
8. A wide shot of several people and an instructor in a classroom during a health education class.
9. A shot of a patient in a hospital bed, being attended by a nurse.

Planning the Shooting Sequence

We were shooting on a school day, so the child needed for scene 1 wouldn't be available until late afternoon. The emergency room changed shifts at 3:00 P.M., and we wanted to give the new shift time to take over, so we decided that about the earliest we could shoot scene 1 would be 3:30.

Shooting scene 9 was going to depend on the hospital census for the day of the shoot. If all the rooms were full, either we'd have to create a hospital bedroom somewhere or go to an alternative. This could be shot in a corridor, showing a patient on a rolling stretcher being wheeled into a room—without actually showing the room—so that any corridor and any doorway could be used.

The hospital had a large, multipurpose room in which classes were held. It was the proper place to shoot scene 8, but we felt we could also create small sets for scenes 4 through 7 in that same room. And since it had convenient access to a loading ramp at the rear of the hospital, it would make a good base of operations. We asked that it be reserved for us for the entire day.

We needed morning light for the two exterior shots, scenes 2 and 3, as that was when the sun would be behind the camera in the long shot, giving the best illumination on the entrance to the hospital building. So we decided those would be our first shots of the day. We also felt we could use the same volunteers who were extras in scenes 2 and 3 as the students in the classroom for scene 8.

Therefore, we decided that these three scenes—2, 3, and 8—plus one other scene would make up our morning schedule. They required the most setup time, they were the least controllable, and they would let us shoot our large party of volunteers in their three scenes, back-to-back, and then release them for the rest of the day. Also, since morning rain showers were not uncommon, it let us follow the rule of shooting exteriors first with an interior as backup in case of bad weather. If it should be raining, we could start with scene 8 and then, if the rain stopped later in the morning, go outside for scenes 2 and 3.

The production schedule looked like this:

7:45 A.M.	Crew call at the hospital. Set up for scenes 2 and 3.
8:30 A.M.	Volunteers for scenes 2, 3, and 8 meet in the classroom.
9:00 A.M.	Shoot scene 2 in the parking lot.
9:45 A.M.	Shoot scene 3 at the hospital entrance.
10:30 A.M.	Move to the classroom, set up for scene 8.
11:00 A.M.	Shoot scene 8 in the classroom.
11:30 A.M.	Release people for scenes 2, 3, and 8. Set up for scene 6 in the classroom. Call for "person" for scene 6.
12:00 noon	Shoot scene 6 in the classroom.
12:30 P.M.	Lunch.
1:00 P.M.	Set up for scenes 4, 5, and 7 in the classroom.
1:30 P.M.	Call for "persons" for scenes 4, 5, and 7.
2:00 P.M.	Shoot scene 4 in the classroom.
2:20 P.M.	Shoot scene 5 in the classroom.
2:40 P.M.	Shoot scene 7 in the classroom.
3:00 P.M.	Set up for scene 1 in the emergency room.
3:15 P.M.	Location call for child for scene 1.
4:00 P.M.	Shoot scene 1.
4:30 P.M.	Set up for scene 9 (hospital room) wherever the hospital directs.
5:15 P.M.	Shoot scene 9.
6:00 P.M.	Shooting complete.

We set the crew call for 7:45 A.M. on location to give us adequate time to unload and check out the equipment, and get set to roll tape on scene 2 at 9:00 A.M. We asked that the volunteers be available at 8:30 A.M. and plan to stay until noon. This gave us some leeway first thing in the morning, since volunteers are notorious for showing up late or not at all. And it gave the volunteers a realistic picture of how long we'd need them, so they could plan the rest of their day.

How the Day Went

Sure enough, the production crew was delayed and didn't show up until a few minutes after 8:00. And by 8:45 it was clear that we were going to be short on volunteers due to no-shows. But the hospital development office had provided a marvelous liaison person named Hanna, who rustled up some extra extras in a hurry and became one herself. And since we had actually scheduled more checkout and setup time than was absolutely necessary, the crew was still ready to go on time. We rolled tape on scene 2, take 1, at two minutes before 9:00.

The point is: If we had made the schedule based on minimum setup time and had given ourselves a tight shooting schedule to get the scenes done, we would have been running a half hour late before we rolled tape on our first shot.

Even with the delays, we were able to spend about an hour and forty-five minutes shooting the exteriors, including considerable time spent experimenting with a dolly shot that never quite looked right, and eventually was not used. Then we went inside and set up and shot the classroom scene in less than an hour. By 11:45 we were finished with the morning's shooting, in spite of delays, and were ahead of schedule. The volunteers remained cheerful and helpful throughout the morning, and we were able to release them ahead of time. We had a comfortable amount of time for lunch, too, which always helps crew morale.

In the afternoon everything went well and we continued to pick up time on the schedule. This meant we could approach each setup in an unhurried fashion, with plenty of time to think and to make changes or try different approaches if we didn't like what we were getting. We were better than a half hour ahead of schedule when we came to the next-to-last setup, the child in the emergency room.

And then we ran into problems. There were several emergency cases in the emergency room, and there was no way the hospital could spare the space or the staff for us to shoot there for the next hour or so.

Our agreement was that shooting would not interfere with hospital needs. Under different circumstances I would have tried to schedule the emergency room scene for earlier in the day, so that if problems like this developed, we could come back to it later. But that hadn't been possible in this case.

Nevertheless, because we were ahead of schedule and the child who was to be in the scene had not yet arrived, we moved on to the last setup, scene 9, in the hope that by the time we had finished it, the emergency room would be available. Scene 9 went smoothly, and we were ready to do the emergency room scene just fifteen minutes later than the time we had originally scheduled. Unfortunately, business in the emergency room was even brisker than before, and it would still be an hour or more before we could possibly get in there—and even that estimate was contingent on no more emergency cases coming in.

I had budgeted for a ten-hour shoot, so we could have waited another hour without going over budget. But by this time the child who was to be in the scene had arrived and had been waiting for close to half an hour. I was afraid that if we had another hour or more of delay, the little boy would be bored, tired, and cranky when we went to shoot.

Fortunately, our liaison person had an alternative for us—an outpatient surgical room that looked quite similar to the emergency room, and which was not in use. We set up and shot the scene in forty-five minutes, sent the child and his parents home on time, and wrapped the day's shooting an hour and a half ahead of time in a triumph of planning and contingency scheduling.

THEN THERE ARE THOSE OTHER DAYS

Then there are days when everything seems to go wrong, and no matter how much time you've allowed, you seem to be constantly slipping behind schedule. If time and budget will allow it, try to reschedule some of the scenes planned for that day to a later time, to take some pressure off you and your crew. If you can't do that, then at least alert everyone who needs to know that you are running behind and will probably get to their scenes later than originally planned. Then try to get back on schedule.

Make Haste Slowly

The only advice I can give, when you're playing catch-up, is to make haste slowly. If anything, slow down what you are doing. It's when you begin to feel the pressure of time running out that you tend to make mistakes that can cost you even more time, sometimes money, and sometimes even footage that is already shot. Before I learned to hurry up by slowing down, I got into one of these situations and, in the rush to change a magazine of film, I opened the wrong side before putting the magazine into the changing bag, thereby ruining 400 feet of film that had just been shot.

So slow down. Do everything carefully and deliberately. Even call a break for everyone if you think it will help. It just may be that you'll soon find yourself back on schedule.

Staying on schedule is important, not only because you have a job to do and a budget to hold to, but also because you're the stranger in the other fellow's place. You want to keep the inconvenience you cause to a minimum, and you don't want any hard feelings to develop because of your presence.

Scheduling Postproduction

The biggest variable in postproduction is creative editing. If you've shot to a script and will follow the script in editing, then you should be able to get a reasonable time estimate from the editor and director.

But if you've been shooting an actuality documentary whose structure and content will be found in the editing room, it can be hard to estimate how long it will take to put together a decent offline or rough cut.

Here are things that have to be done to complete the documentary after it has been shot:

- Develop film and make a work print or video transfer, or, if you've used video, make a windowprint dub for review.
- Review and log all footage. Eliminate bad shots and identify probable keepers.
- Make a tentative editing plan.
- Offline or rough-cut editing.
- Create titles, graphics, and special effects.
- Record narration, music, and sound effects as needed.
- Online or fine-cut editing.
- Sound mix or sound sweetening.
- Negative cutting and making an answer print for film.
- Audio layback for video.

- Video sweetening.
- Complete video edit master or film release print.

The important thing in scheduling postproduction is to plan for the sequence in which things must be done and to allow enough time to get them done. Again, allow for slippage. Sometimes what seems like a good idea just won't work in editing. Sometimes equipment goes down. Sometimes the editor gets the flu.

And that's the point: Production scheduling is really the art of getting done on time, even when things go wrong.

22

FILMING

There was this great moment that would happen every day or so when we were shooting documentaries on film. It was when the work print—sometimes called "rushes" or "dailies"—came back from the film lab. Those of us involved in the production, and anyone else who was interested, would gather in the room with the projector, dim the lights, and look at what we'd done. This first look at the footage was silent even if we had shot it with sync sound, because transferring and synchronizing the sound was a separate process. So the footage had to stand on its own.

I think the exercise of looking at the silent work print made us better filmmakers. We learned to see what we had before we started listening for what had been said. The best documentary images help the audience to understand the film they are watching, not only factually, but also emotionally.

I started out as a one-man film unit attached to an education center, and had to shoot my own stuff. It was OK, but as I got better as a director, I decided I just wasn't a good enough camera operator to work for me. Since then I've worked with good camera operators, great camera operators, and a couple of pretty bad ones, and what I've learned is that it takes real skill to get consistently good pictures. You have to train yourself to see.

The best shot I ever made in my brief career as a camera operator was a reaction shot I got for the documentary *The Trouble with Adults Is . . .* during a confrontation between student activists and the members of a suburban church. I was filming an earnest young man as he tried to talk about white racism with a well-dressed, middle-aged woman leaving church. She answered him politely, which he mistook for interest, and he went into a monologue about his perception of suburban attitudes. With the film magazine chittering next to my good ear, I couldn't hear the conversation very well, so I had to go by what I saw. This was back when a lady wore a hat and gloves to church, and what I saw was that after about thirty seconds of his monologue, the woman started to put on her white gloves. I moved in for a close-up of her smoothing her gloves carefully down each finger. No one has ever misunderstood that piece of visual evidence. It showed far more eloquently than words that even though he was still talking, she had stopped listening.

Zero-Level Knowledge

This is a great time to be making documentaries. Most of the limitations in the film business that I grew up with have been vanquished by technology. No need for dim, grainy images; video cameras can get a picture in almost any light; and video sweetening can make grab footage look like a studio shot. No need for shaky cam; digital video can make handheld look like a Steadicam shot.

Still, you can't make a documentary without a certain minimum knowledge of the technology that is required. Unless someone on the production team has that knowledge, even the best of ideas won't get recorded. If someone doesn't know how to set the proper exposure, what lens to use and how to get it in focus, and how to record legible sound, it really doesn't matter what you do with the camera. There won't be anything recorded worth showing to an audience.

I call this zero-level knowledge. You have to have it before you can produce anything. In doing documentary, you sometimes have to trade off between technology and ideas. While video cameras can shoot in dim light, someone has to know how a low-light situation will affect your picture. And you can't record audio where the noise level is so high that what you are interested in is drowned out by other sounds. To that extent, technology must inform your documentary idea to make it workable.

Not a Hardware Primer

This chapter is not going to be a primer on production hardware, for several good reasons. The first is that production technology is evolving so rapidly that the half-life of change is roughly equivalent to the time it takes a book to go from manuscript to print. So if I included a lot of information about specific video or film cameras, recorders, and postproduction equipment, at least half of it would be out of date by the time you read this.

The second reason is that while I have performed just about every job on a production crew except makeup artist, for the past several years I've concentrated on writing and directing. I hire a camera crew when I direct, and when I direct postproduction I use a technical editor. Today, I'm neither a shooter nor a film or video editor. And if you want to become expert with a technology, you should learn it from the people who work with it every day.

Fortunately, that's not difficult. You'll find several works on production technology in the bibliography of this book. Or you can take courses. Many college continuing education programs now offer an introduction to video or film production the way they once offered creative writing courses.

Do You Want the Responsibility of Technical Knowledge?

You must decide if you want to be one of the technical people on your documentary crew. If you are the person with the camera, for instance, you have the responsibility of getting good pictures in every shooting situation. If you're the video editor, you not only have to know how to run the editing computer to edit scenes together, you must constantly be aware of color balance, video levels, and a hundred and one other things that have little or nothing to do with the content of your documentary, and everything to do with the technical excellence of the finished piece.

I know people who only want to operate a camera, and others whose joy in life is to record pristine sound. I know creative editors who don't want to shoot or direct, but who love to make the production come to life on the screen. And I know of documentary teams where one person operates the camera and another the sound and they function so closely together that they are codirectors during production and coeditors later in post.

I also know writers who just want to write and do not care to direct. And I know directors who want to put together the best possible technical team on each production so that the documentary they've been imagining becomes the film on the screen.

There are a lot of ways to realize a documentary vision. One is to be able to raise the money. Another is to direct a team of technical people to use their skill and professional knowledge to bring the film you've been dreaming of to the screen. And certainly another is to be a technical participant.

Video and film are corporate media. It is not essential that each person working on a documentary be a master of all the contributing technologies. But, since eventually it all has to fit together, you do need to know how everything works. If you don't, you could end up with a lot of false assumptions that could waste time, cost money, and lose you the respect and cooperation of the skilled people you're working with.

Technology and Art

Back when there was grant money around for any kind of wacky idea that could be expressed in standard English in a proposal with social value overtones, I was invited to a meeting at the Franklin Institute in Philadelphia of an organization composed of artists and engineers. I would be the filmmaker, presumably an artist. The idea for the organization, from whoever wrote the grant proposal and whatever funding agency put up the bucks, was that it would be good for the stuffy, nuts-and-bolts, calculator-toting engineers to be exposed to some artistic ideas. And it would benefit the wooly-headed, esoteric, pie-in-the sky artists to come up against some harsh, realistic, technological concepts. But that's not how it worked.

The engineers—who were all working pros in things like creating animated computer simulations for NASA—didn't waste a second talking about how wire A goes on pin C. They understood all that and assumed everyone else did, too. What they wanted to talk about were the aesthetics of what they were doing.

The artists, on the other hand, had spent years mastering the aesthetics of their work, and therefore only talked technology. They knew what they wanted to do artistically and were spending most of their time mastering the technical demands of their media. And that's all they talked about. They knew that to be good at a craft, it's not enough to have a clear idea of what you want to accomplish. You have to master the tools for doing it.

Filming for Editing

When I started out, I thought a documentary was made with expensive equipment, fast film stock, and something called *content*—which was the result of brilliant directing. I was doing a lot of documentary filming on location—low-light or available-light stuff. The image would look OK in the rushes—not great, but OK; after all, I was doing documentary— but by the time the film went through an internegative to a release print, a number of the scenes in the movie would look strange.

The first thing I had to get over was the idea that a documentary is something you shoot. It isn't. It's what you show.

The main distinction between professional productions and home movies or home videos—quite apart from the cost of the equipment and the skill of the users—is that a professional production is *always* done to be edited and reproduced. A documentary is what the audience sees on the screen. Everything you do in the production process is aimed at getting you and your documentary concept to the point where you have an edited production to show to an audience. So it is important to start with the best possible pictures and sound you can get, using the finest equipment you can get your hands on, recorded on the highest-quality recording media.

A DOCUMENTARY IS MADE WITH LIGHT

It's one thing to understand that it takes a certain minimum amount of illumination to record a video or film, and quite another to accept the fact that a documentary is made with light. I would guess that between the two concepts lie about five years of experience at working with the tools and trying to get the image on the screen to look like the image in your head. If you have a good coach, you may move up in class faster. If you have to do it all on your own, it may take longer.

The *amount* of light available establishes the existence of an image on video or film. If there's not enough light for an exposure—no image.

The *quality* of the light—balance, highlight and shadow areas, position of light sources, lighting contrast ratio, color temperature, and so on—determines the look of the image. The better the lighting, the better the final copies of your documentary.

Location Lighting

On location, it's the quality of the light, far more than the amount of light, that counts.

As a documentarian, you don't normally face the problems of your feature film cousins in trying to match shots made on location exactly to shots made in the studio. In this case, the actuality of documentary works for you. But the fact that your production is a documentary is not an excuse for shoddy lighting.

GOALS IN LIGHTING A DOCUMENTARY

To Achieve Sufficient Light for an Adequate Exposure

This will depend mainly on the recording medium and the camera. The goal is to have a decent depth of field in most situations without requiring an immense amount of light.

To Balance the Light for Proper-Looking Color

You may have more than one kind of light source at the location. For example, in a classroom or office building you might find overhead fluorescents plus sunlight coming in from a bank of windows along one side of the room. And there might still be dark corners that will need additional lighting from your production lights.

Yes, you may be able to white-balance a video camera to accept three different light sources. But as you turn more toward the sunlight coming through the windows—or away from it—you'll go out of balance. To the extent that you are able, you want to reconcile the different light sources so that the camera is essentially working with the same kind of light, no matter where in the room it is pointed.

When Shooting Film, to Minimize High-Contrast Effects

Contrast builds up at every stage of printing as film goes from camera original to printing negative to print, resulting in some loss of detail in highlight and shadow areas. Therefore you usually want to eliminate hot spots and deep shadows, except where you have created them on purpose for dramatic effect.

To Keep Artificial Lighting to a Minimum

Lights are a distraction to your subjects. Lights are hot. Lights draw a lot of electricity and adding lights can easily overload available electrical circuits. Keeping the overall level of illumination as close to the level of the ambient light as possible helps in maintaining a natural look while providing sufficient lighting for good camera and subject freedom.

To Give the Location a Natural, "Unlit" Look

Feature film cinematographers spend a lot of time on each set deciding how to *motivate* the lighting. Even though their lighting instruments may be mounted on an overhead grid or on lighting stands sticking up above the scenery, they have to decide:

- what the theoretical source of the lighting is—sunlight through a window, overhead fluorescents, a chandelier, room lamps on tables, or whatever
- how strong the light from that source should be
- what other sources there might be for fill lights
- how shadows will fall in the scene

As a documentarian lighting a location, you face more or less the same problem, except you are not starting with an empty set. And you may have to use just the natural light that's available.

The location itself can serve as a model for your lighting. Look it over carefully before you begin adding lights. Note the main sources of illumination, and use them to motivate your lighting. Your goal is to increase the illumination in the room to a comfortable level for shooting, without appreciably changing the way the room will look on camera.

To Give the Camera as Much Freedom
as Possible to Follow Action

In certain kinds of documentary shooting, you really don't know what is going to happen next, or where it will happen. So you would like to have enough light everywhere in the area in which you are shooting, so that you can take decent pictures anywhere within that area.

*To Give the People on Camera as Much Freedom
of Movement as Possible*

In many documentaries, you don't want to intrude on your subjects to the point of asking them to "hit a mark" or to remember not to walk out of a certain area. You want to maintain a useful minimum level of shooting illumination throughout the area.

To Provide a Dramatic Effect

It is the play of light and shadow that gives images on video or film their specific look. Not every scene needs to be lit to a flat level of constant illumination. Sometimes, such as in night scenes, you *want* dark areas. Sometimes you may want a subject partially in shadow. Sometimes you might like to have a subject walking from a pool of light into shadow and back into another pool of light. Sometimes you want side lighting, or back lighting, or even lighting from below.

CAMERA WORK

The camera—whether video or film—accumulates the visual evidence that will eventually make up the film you will show to an audience. Like a computer, a camera is a marvelous instrument for the storage and retrieval of information. And like a computer, it can only do what it is told to do—when and how it is told to do it.

Shooting for Showing

The point to all camera work is *to let the audience see the scene* in the way you would like to present it to them. When the image is too dark, or out of focus, or blurred from rapid camera or lens movement, the audience can't see the scene. When it is shot from too close or too far away, the audience may not be able to see what you want them to.

And if the camera work hasn't been done with a sensitivity to the fact that the footage will eventually be edited for presentation to an audience, the editor, the director, and quite possibly the audience, will be painfully aware of the fact.

If you are doing the camera work yourself, you have to keep all these things in mind as you shoot.

Using a Camera Operator

If you are using someone else behind the camera, you have to take time to be sure you both are in basic agreement as to how the footage is to be shot. It is not enough that the camera operator is a professional. In my documentary shot in Wilkes-Barre, I employed two cameramen at one point. Both were professionals, not only in the sense that they were paid for camera work but also in the sense that operating a movie camera was what they did full time to earn a living. But on a scale of one to ten, the footage one of them delivered at the end of the day was a ten, what the other handed in was a two, or at best a three.

One was a truly superb camera operator named Andy Dintenfass, who later became a cinematographer in Hollywood. Andy could start a scene with a wide shot of people talking close to the camera and make an unrehearsed slow pan across the room, tilting up to the audience in the balcony and zooming in for a tight shot of a single person sitting there. And every frame was sharp and legible.

If that doesn't sound so hard, try it sometime.

The other, whose professional experience was gained mainly in shooting TV news, delivered 600 feet of rushes so full of bumpy pans, fast zooms, and focusing adjustments that the footage was almost completely unusable.

In selecting a camera operator, ask to see some unedited footage shot in situations similar to those that may make up your documentary.

And talk. Don't assume that what seems so clear to you is equally clear to your camera operator. If you're using a new camera operator, try to start with some fairly simple things, so that you can see in the footage if there are problems or misunderstandings. You want to get them corrected before you get into the critical stuff. Because, unless you're going to micromanage by headset from a monitor—which I don't recommend—in any hot shooting situation, your camera operator becomes a de facto codirector.

Lenses

Documentaries are normally shot with a camera with a good, fast, sharp zoom lens, because that offers the most convenience and flexibility. I've learned that on location there's not likely to be much light or space. So I prefer a fast zoom lens with the widest possible focal length at the wide angle end.

There's always a trade-off between focal length and depth of field. At the wide angle end you can be in focus almost from the front of the lens to the end of the world. But at too wide a focal length you begin to get wide angle distortion, which makes people's foreheads and noses bulge out while the rest of them drifts away into tinyness. At the other end, long focal lengths can get you close-ups of things far away, but the depth of field shrinks until it may be hard to get everything you want in focus.

Don't assume you're stuck with the zoom lens that comes with the camera until you've discussed what you want to be able to shoot and how you want to shoot it with your camera operator or director of photography.

Camera Support

Andy Dintenfass could shoot rock steady with a twenty-pound camera handheld on his shoulder or under his arm—and did when the situation demanded it. But he would use a tripod for shooting whenever he had the opportunity. His goal, at all times, was to get the best possible images to be edited into the film.

Handheld shooting is fine and often necessary for covering action, for moving quickly from event to event, and even for providing complete coverage of people talking or doing things. An audience will accept a little camera wiggle and bump when the scene reeks of spontaneity. And digital image stabilization has made this less of a problem than it used to be. But your audience doesn't expect to see stationary objects such as buildings, signs, bookcases, furniture, and so on bouncing around on the screen when they don't bounce around in real life—and neither do I. So I have the camera operator use a tripod wherever practical.

In addition to a standard tripod, it can be nice to have a set of baby legs or a high hat along for low-angle shooting with tripod stability.

Today, shaky-cam in documentary is always the result of poor camera work or poor judgment. There's no need for it.

Filming Evidence

The first concern in composing a camera shot for a documentary is to show the evidence.

The second is to show the evidence as artfully as possible.

Always in that order.

Frame the scene so the audience understands what you're showing them, neither so far away that they can't tell what to look at, nor so close that they don't know what they're seeing.

Camera Moves

In general, make all camera moves fairly slow and deliberate—and rare. A sudden zoom, pan, or tilt, followed by refocusing, is distracting to the audience and may make the shot unusable. Let the action take place within the frame. Adjust the composition only when the action changes.

Don't chase the speaker. When you are recording several people and you've been holding close on one person talking, don't think you have to quickly turn the camera to the next person just because he's started talking. Many times you'll pan to him just as he's finished speaking and the person you previously had framed up starts to reply, but you don't have the camera on her anymore. It's much better to slowly come wide until you have both speakers and then think about going for a close-up of one or the other.

If you feel you really must pan or zoom from one composition to another, shoot five to ten seconds of the first composition with the camera still, then do the camera move, and finish with five to ten seconds of the end composition with the camera still. Quite often, when you get in the editing room, you'll find it's better to cut from the still at the start to the still at the end—the pan or zoom takes too long and doesn't show what you want.

Shoot What Matters

If you're filming a dancer, you need to show close-ups of her feet, not her face. Ice skater? Gymnast? They're not performing with their teeth. Yes, we want to see the smile of victory or the frown of defeat when the scores are announced. But the rest of the time we need to see the body working.

Filming a chef? Tilting down from the top of the white hat to the cutting board is a wallpaper shot. How about showing that flashing blade cutting celery, and then giving it to us again in slow motion so we can see exactly how the fingers curl out of the way.

Try to look at the world you are filming with the curious eyes of child seeing it for the first time. And film it that way.

Keep It Visual

Always try to record powerful visual evidence. When you're scouting, look for the pictures that tell the story and then record them when you shoot.

Try to record the unusual and unexpected. If I'm in production and it starts to rain, I shoot. Since most production happens only in good weather under clear skies, a scene in the rain gives a unique look to the film.

Be sure that whatever you shoot yields good imagery. Even if you are shooting an interview, don't just settle for the easy-to-do desk shot. Try to bring more dimension to your pictures. Can you record a hotel executive standing in the hotel's ornate lobby? An industrialist on a catwalk overlooking a manufacturing floor? A teacher on the playground during recess with kids playing in the background?

Learn from What You've Shot

When you are filming a behavioral documentary, you may not know exactly how to approach filming the behavior you want to observe. That's OK. One of the things that should happen is that you'll learn from doing. In a sense the people in the film will teach you how to film them. Study the footage after each day of shooting. When you see something that looks like what you are after, analyze it. Figure out why it works (and why other scenes aren't as good as this) and how you can get more footage like it. Same with the footage that doesn't go where you hoped it would. Analyze why. Ask what you might have done differently. Get better as you go along.

A FEW HINTS

Shoot Enough

Be sure you get enough footage. When I see the same shot repeated two or three times in a documentary, especially as a cutaway, I know the documentarian didn't shoot enough during principal photography. Often it's not sufficient just to shoot whatever the script calls for. Try different angles. Use a low camera or a high one. Get reaction shots—and not just the canned one of the spokesperson listening and nodding. Shoot the kids playing in the sandbox, the dog lying on the rug, the goldfish swimming furiously. You may never use any of it. Or you may be oh-so-glad you shot the extra stuff.

When you are shooting a scripted scene, shoot enough takes. Don't settle for an "acceptable" take; keep shooting until you get what you need. I tell cast and crew, "OK, we've got one we can use. So the pressure's off. Now let's go for great." And I may shoot several more takes. What I've learned is that the take that looks good on the monitor in the field may not be the one I'll elect to use when I get in the editing room. I'm not one to shoot takes excessively—although I've done thirty to forty takes on two or three occasions when something just wouldn't go right, and, on one memorable occasion, more than 150 takes over two days—but I expect to do at least three as we explore the possibilities of the scene and perhaps as many as six or seven until we get something really good.

Record Establishing Shots and Cutaways

Establishing shots set the stage for what is to come. They are, or should be, a part of every documentarian's mental checklist—and written shot list—of what needs to be filmed at any given location. Establishing shots include road signs, exteriors of buildings in which some activity in the film takes place, interiors of rooms such as classrooms or laboratories, and shots used to introduce people in the film (usually before they speak).

Cutaways have the sole function of covering a difficult edit point. Quite often this will be where an interview has been edited to join a statement made at one point in the interview with one made at a different time or to remove an unwanted or irrelevant section from a sound bite. The most common cutaway of this sort is to cut to the interviewer listening intently or nodding. (I didn't say it was the *best,* just the most common.) Ideally, a cutaway will seem appropriate to what is being shown and will go unnoticed by the viewer. Try to find good cutaways in the interview situation that you can shoot when the interview is over.

Shoot for Editing

When I was teaching documentary film, I wouldn't let my students touch a camera until they had learned how to edit. Having editing always in mind changes the way you look at the scene through the viewfinder or on the monitor. It means being sure you have "handles" at the head and tail of each shot so there's room to get in and get out. It means covering the scene with reaction shots, cutaways, and atmosphere shots that suggest the ambience of the location. It means going outside and shooting an establishing shot of the building, even though what you came for was an interview with a doctor in a laboratory.

Camera "Rules"

THE CAMERA IS ALWAYS ON

As far as the people in front of the camera are concerned, my answer to the question "Is the camera on?" is that the camera is always loaded and always on (whether it is or not).

THE CAMERA DOESN'T TALK

Whether you are the camera operator or have hired one, always remember that the camera never talks. Once you start, you'll find it hard to stop. And when you look at the footage, you'll find that the voice from the camera has ruined the scene.

SLATING FILM TAKES

Slate the takes where you can, but don't let the slating process interfere with the spontaneity of the scene. Slating is more important for double-system film than for video, because the slate serves as a reference point for syncing picture and sound. But having someone step out in front of the people whose behavior you want to record, yell, "Scene seven, take one!" and slap a clapstick together is a good way to induce galloping performance anxiety. Remember, you can get a good sync point by shooting a close-up of the sound recordist tapping the microphone. If you have to go in hot, with no chance to slate, you can always slate at the tail.

Look and Practice

There are two things you can do that will help you get what you need when filming. The first is to look at documentaries for evidence of good camera work. Films that don't rely on talk, such as *March of the Penguins, Winged Migration,* and *Baraka* are a good place to start.

Go back and look at *The Endless Summer,* shot with a silent 16mm camera. Bruce Brown made his living showing films of surfing. He had to get good pictures.

Dark Days by Marc Singer takes the viewer into the underground world of squatters who live in the railroad tunnels near Penn Station in New York. Take a look. See what you think.

The Sinking City of Venice (NOVA) has a story to show and does.

Both *The Hobart Shakespeareans* and *A Touch of Greatness* deal with a heroic elementary school teacher, who encourages his students toward excellence. You might compare how each film tells its story using visual evidence.

You might compare the camera work in *The War Room* (1992) with that of *Staffers* (2004) and even go back and take a look at *Primary* (1960) to see how three different filmmakers handled the same subject at three different times.

When you find something more than . . .

- establishing shot
- interview
- B-roll
- more B-roll
- back to interview

. . . make a note of it. What happened that caught your attention? How did they shoot it? Do you think it was a lucky grab, or were they looking for it?

When a great shot jumps off the screen and smacks you in the face, write it down. Analyze it. Learn from it.

Learn from the work of others. That's the first thing.

The second is to take a camera and go practice.

Find something you'd like to show somebody and film it. Think your way into it. What must you do with the camera to make this scene come to life? How does it look in close-up? In long shot? From above? From below?

Then go back and study what you've done. Look with the sound turned off. See if you can tell a story just with the pictures.

Take your time. Just as you can't learn to play the piano in one lesson, it takes time to master camera work.

Hiring a Camera Operator

If you decide to hire someone to shoot for you, don't just look at their finished work. I've sat at an editing console and made several poor-to-mediocre camera operators look good just by plucking their few usable shots out of the sea of blah. Ask to see unedited footage. If the person is any good with a camera most of what you see will be usable, and some should be excellent.

Ask to see what he or she considers the good stuff. If it's blah, the camera operator is blah. But if it's interesting—even if you don't especially like it—look a little deeper. Could be something special in there.

23

RECORDING SOUND

Sound work, like camera work, has as its purpose the recording and accumulation of useful hunks of documentary evidence that can be used in the final edited version of the film.

Be sure that you have provided for good, professional sound recording as part of your production package. At a minimum you need to record legible audio in which the voices and other important sounds are sufficiently separated from the background and from each other that you can recognize and understand them. Which is simply the audio equivalent of saying that you want your pictures properly exposed and in focus so you can tell what you are looking at.

Your ultimate goal, of course, is the cleanest, most natural audio you can possibly get, so that you have the maximum control in editing and the least possible loss of quality in duplication.

Begin by getting rid of unwanted ambient sound, wherever possible, before you shoot. Turn off motors, radios, humming refrigerators, whistling light fixtures, air conditioners, fans, and the like. If the crew has to be able to move around on a bare floor, have them wear soft-soled shoes or go in their stocking feet.

Keep the Sound Clean and Well Separated

Don't record sound on automatic gain control (AGC), which is available on most audio and video recorders. AGC works by boosting the recording level until it reaches some predetermined point. When the sound you want is occurring right in front of the microphone, AGC works fairly well. But when the people stop talking, the AGC immediately raises the level of the background noise as high as it can. This can give you a sound track on which there's a loud whooshing sound in the spaces between people speaking. It sounds terrible, and it's difficult to edit.

You need a sound recordist, someone who will listen to the sounds being recorded to know what is happening on the sound track and keep an eye on the recording level to raise or lower the record volume as necessary to maintain clean sound.

The sound recordist should wear earphones to monitor the quality of what is actually being recorded. Sometimes, while shooting an interview or other sound take, a plane will go over or a truck will drive past making noise that I can hear. When we stop shooting, I'll ask the sound recordist if the noise affected the track. Quite often the answer is that it didn't. The placement of the microphone and the level of sound close to the microphone will often block unwanted noise from recording on the track. But you'll only know this if the sound operator is wearing earphones. Similarly, your sound person may hear offending noises that are not apparent to you.

Do a Reality Check

When I lived in Hawaii, I was asked to produce some documentary-style testimonials for a political candidate on one of the outer islands. The video crew, supplied by the candidate's campaign, was one person from the local cable company, with some obsolete equipment. We shot a potluck dinner and rally for the candidate where there was a lot of background noise. I kept asking the operator how the sound was, as he was shooting, and he said "fine." But we had no playback, so it wasn't until I got back to Honolulu to start editing that I learned what he meant by "fine" sound. He had reproduced the noise in the room faithfully. Unfortunately, that meant we couldn't understand the candidate when he was speaking. The rally footage was good for background and nothing else.

So, if you haven't worked with the sound person before, do some reality checks. Ask for playback at the end of a scene. Listen in on a headset yourself. In planning the shoot, ask if the sound person can give you your own headset.

Microphones

It's almost impossible to record good production sound solely by using the shotgun microphone mounted on the camera. Even TV news, which has never put a premium on quality, uses the camera mike only for ambience or as a last resort in an emergency to capture sound that otherwise would be lost. The closer you can get the microphone to the person speaking, the cleaner and clearer the sound will be. A camera mike just doesn't let you move in close enough.

The choice of microphones for location sound depends on the shooting situation and what you have available. I once thought that the only proper microphone for a documentary crew was a powerful shotgun mike that could reach into the scene and pull out legible audio. Today I mainly use individual wireless lavalieres.

When using a handheld microphone, the sound recordist has to keep out of the way of the camera in two ways. The first is to keep the mike out of the picture, if possible. The second is to stay out of the way of the camera operator. In one of the first documentaries I shot, I had a volunteer sound recordist who would invariably be standing right where I wanted to be to shoot. At the end of the first day's filming, I took him aside and told him, "In each scene, figure out the best place for the camera to be, and don't stand there."

Sound Tracks

If I could have my way, I'd feed each microphone to a different sound track. Sometimes this is possible; sometimes it's not. If there are going to be a lot of audio sources in a situation you're filming, give serious thought to recording audio to a separate multitrack recorder that can be put in sync with the camera.

At a minimum try to separate sound sources to as many different tracks as you have available.

Sound Coverage

Just as you get cover shots for picture, you want to be sure that you have covered the sound situation at each location, and even each setup. At a minimum you need to record a minute or so of the "silence" in the room—that is, what passes for silence when no one is speaking. This is usually called room tone, or ambient sound, and can be a lifesaver in editing.

Also, if there are any erratic sounds, such as a motor that runs intermittently in the background, you may want to record it while it's running, to help even out the editing of an interview where that distinctive sound might be present at the start of the interview, but not in the speech you'd like to cut to.

Sound Sweetening

Just as digital video has made it possible to see in the dark and light like a pro after the scene has been shot, digital audio sweetening can get rid of a lot of the sound problems that may occur during filming. But not all of them. And the best way to handle audio problems is to avoid them in the first place.

Sound Matters

Sound is an important part of the modern documentary. Plan your audio recording as carefully as you plan your camera work. Use the best sound equipment you can manage. And, above all, get the best sound recordist you can find. A poor one can make a day's shooting worthless through unusable sound. A good one can make your film come alive!

24

DIRECTING

Early in my career, a resident in psychiatry, who had become interested in making videos asked me what it took to be a documentary director. I said, "I sometimes think it may be the ability to solve cryptograms in your head." I was half kidding. But I was also half serious. A documentary director has to keep a lot of different elements in mind, mentally putting them together in different ways until they form a clear message.

In making any documentary, but especially an unscripted one, I have a mental checklist of essential elements. So I am always on the lookout for an opening, an ending, and any visual evidence related to the themes of the film. Without these elements there is no documentary. During the course of shooting, I'm constantly revising my mental elements list. We may shoot something that will make a better opening or a better ending than the scene I previously had in mind. That's good. And, of course, in the editing room I may decide to use a different scene entirely.

Which is how you solve a cryptogram, whether you do it with paper and pen or without.

What Does the Director *Do*?

There are few rote memorization rules for directing. It's part management and part creative act. As a director you are in charge. What happens before, during, and after the shoot rests on your decisions. Therefore you need a clear idea of what you are trying to accomplish, even if you are not exactly certain how it will be accomplished.

Equally important, and often overlooked, it helps to be clear about what you are *not* trying to accomplish. During a shoot people may offer suggestions about what to film or how to film it, and you will have to respond to these. Sometimes people will try to "help" you by telling others what to do, and you have to firmly but quietly set them straight.

In preproduction the director may conduct part—or all—of the research, and may either write the script or treatment or work with the writer and approve (or occasionally reject) the treatment and/or script that will be the shooting document for the film. The director will be involved in scouting and selecting locations, auditioning and casting actors, selecting the production crew, and setting the production schedule.

During principal photography, the director has overall responsibility for making sure the footage and sound that will be needed to finish the film (1) get recorded and (2) are recorded in a way that is consistent with the director's vision. This requires giving direction to the camera and sound people on how to record the raw material for the documentary. If actors are used, it will involve rehearsing and directing their performances. The director says when to start filming ("roll and record") and when to stop ("cut").

During postproduction, the director may edit the footage or work with an editor, selecting the bits and pieces that will make up the documentary mosaic and organizing them for presentation to an audience.

The director is responsible for the truthfulness of what is shown.

Directing Filming

Boiled down to basics, someone has to look at what is being shot and say, "Yes, that's what I want," or "No, that's not it." That person is the director.

Behind the Invisible Wall

When filming behavior or a unique event the director may give explicit directions to the people behind the camera and say next to nothing to the people in front of it. It really doesn't matter whether the documentary is a protracted study of whatever happens in the lives of two people (*A Married Couple*), preparation for a spelling bee (*Spellbound*), a year in the life of a fifth-grade class (*The Hobart Shakespeareans*), or an examination of the lives of the various members of an entire community, as in Hubert Smith's Mayan documentary. The goal is to set up an invisible wall between the documentary crew and the subjects so that you intrude as little as possible on what you are there to film, while being prepared to capture whatever events and behavior may occur.

Most of us, most of the time, will be working on less ambitious, if no less worthy projects, so let's examine some different documentary situations, and how they will affect when, where, and how you place the invisible wall.

JUST AN INTERVIEW

In some cases, all you actually want from the shooting situation is an interview with someone. That means someone representing you and the audience is going to conduct the interview. Nevertheless, you want the answers to the interview questions, the way the questions are answered, and the reaction of the person being interviewed to be as spontaneous as possible. I try to do interviews in a location where the subject will be comfortable—which usually means on his or her home ground—and that will be visually interesting for the documentary.

Which means we may intervene in the subject's life to the extent of setting a place for the interview, deciding who is to sit or stand, and where, checking lighting, and even wiring the subject with a lavaliere microphone. But once these preparations are completed, the invisible wall goes up. From then on, no one gives the subject stage directions and no one talks to the subject except the designated interviewer.

FILMING SPECIFIC BEHAVIOR

Sometimes you are looking for certain kinds of behavior. In making *A Young Child Is . . .*, we wanted to show specific examples of development and learning in very young children of different ages. Ideally, we might have spent four or five years tracking the progress of several kids from birth to school age. But in this case, time and budget forced us to select several children of different ages and try to record them in situations in which we thought their behavior would be significant.

Most of the time this meant discussing the kinds of things we would be looking for with the children's parents, and planning the shooting schedule around events that would naturally occur in the lives of the children. We decided what we were going to film, and where. Sometimes we discussed with the parents what might be happening in a given situation, so we'd know where to set lights and the best probable camera location to start with. But this was always done on the basis of, "You tell us where you want to be, and we'll figure out how to shoot it."

We rejected all suggestions from the parents that they could have the child do whatever it was in some other location that would be more convenient for us, or that they could alter the process in some way they thought might make things easier or better for us. This was always the first step in putting up the invisible wall. The parent would make the suggestion. I would ask, "Where (or how) would this normally be done?" They'd tell me. And I'd say, "Then we won't change it. We'll shoot it normally." Once that was made clear, it was relatively easy to put the invisible wall firmly in place for shooting.

Documenting an Event or a Process

Sometimes you are documenting an event or a process, and the *specific* behavior of the people involved in the process is less important than just being certain that *whatever* behavior occurs is valid and spontaneous. This can often be the easiest kind of situation for the behavioral documentarian, because you can claim, with absolute honesty, that you are just interested in shooting whatever happens. And the invisible wall goes up with no problem.

There are exceptions, of course, and you have to deal with them as they come up. There are always the people who will stop in front of the camera and ask when this will be on TV, or what channel you are from. They are usually no real problem, and someone from the crew can take them aside, answer their questions, briefly, and move them out of the way.

There are muggers and show-offs, and you handle them as best you can. Often it's enough just to point the camera in their direction for a few seconds, even if you're not shooting at the time.

You have to be sensitive to what's going on. Sometimes you may get a sense that the whole thing is being staged for the benefit of the camera.

When that happens, if it seems relevant and might fit into your documentary, you may want to capture some show-off behavior.

Or you may just decide to go home.

My Favorite Muggers. The most delightful muggers I ever filmed were some very young kids who found me with a camera on my shoulder and wouldn't let me go.

I was filming at a day-care center for the children of migrant farmworkers. All the kids were outside, and I was shooting them at play. A five-year-old boy appeared in the frame and immediately sat down. Within seconds he was joined by a half-dozen other kids, all sitting, all smiling. No sooner would I point the camera in another direction than the little boy appeared again, soon to be joined by the others, all sitting still on the ground and smiling at the camera. I can only assume that these kids had no experience with motion media, but had learned that if they wanted their pictures taken, they were to sit still and smile.

This went on for about ten minutes, until it seemed to me that the little boy had somehow figured out where I would decide to point the camera next, and was getting there ahead of me. I finally had to quit shooting for a while, until the kids got interested in playing in the sandbox, and then I walked all the way across the playground to an older group of children before I began filming again.

There was no way I could work that 200 feet of film into the final version of *Season for Learning,* but I still have it, and I treasure it as an example of some delightful, spontaneous behavior for which I have never found a use.

You Have to Do It

It sounds easy, but it takes a lot of self-control to keep putting up the invisible wall and to maintain it. But you have to keep doing it, because its existence is really the only answer you have to the critics who question whether anything done in front of a documentary crew can be *real* and to the people who believe that only footage shot with a hidden camera is valid evidence of behavior.

Temptations

Nevertheless, there are many ways in which a documentary crew trying to make an honest record of the behavior that occurs before their camera may be tempted to break through the invisible wall between them and the people whose behavior they are recording.

INTERESTING PEOPLE ARE INTERESTING

The people you are shooting are probably interesting in some way, or they wouldn't have been chosen to be in your documentary. The temptation is always present to try to get to know them better, off camera, than you do on camera. And there's nothing wrong with that, once the film is finished.

When I started making documentaries, I thought it was a nice idea to take the people we were recording out to dinner after the day's shooting was finished. I don't do that anymore—at least not until the end of the last day of shooting. Take the school principal I mentioned in chapter 7 whom I tried to interview for *Schools for Children*. It was at dinner the night before we were to film him that he spoke so eloquently about open education. Possibly, if we had not discussed it in detail in advance, I'd have gotten a better interview the next day.

OUT OR IN?

I got an interesting e-mail from Gentry Underwood, who had read the original edition of this book. At the time, he was a Ph.D. student in ethnography and had been filming the members of a church. He wanted to know if I was familiar with Clifford Geertz's 1958 essay, "Deep Play: Notes on a Balinese Cockfight," because, as he wrote:

> There's a point in the essay when Geertz and his wife are watching a cockfight and the police storm the arena. Like the Balinese, they get up and run away as chaos ensues around them. Prior to this point they had been outsiders in the community, but after they turn tail with the rest of the crowd, they're invited "in" to the community and their work of understanding really begins.
>
> In the past few days of filming, I've been constantly reminded of that story. I'm filming a church community in the DC area, and I'm finding that the more I and my assistant participate in the church activities as one of them, the more they come alive on camera— the more, that is, that they let me "in" to the world I'm hoping to capture.
>
> I write this because I'm torn as I do this between Geertz's recommendations and the suggestions in your book, namely that a real

distance be kept between the filmmakers and the subjects of the film. Your suggestions run pretty counter to what I'm finding is working. Of course, this does mean that sometimes the interviewee or film subject makes references towards myself or the cameraman that are "familiar," and we'll have to edit those out, but what we get in exchange is a closeness and an intimacy that, I believe, would otherwise be impossible.

I posted this letter on my website for this book, makingdocumentaryfilms.com, because I thought it raised an interesting question. This was my reply:

I am of two thoughts. One is that you may not have given the invisible wall a chance to work. People must believe that you are just there to film whatever happens, so that they get accustomed to you and the cameras being around until they ignore you.

The second thought is that in the 21st century the media sophistication of the general public may have reached the point that they believe that the people with the camera are either for you or they are against you. No middle ground.

While I may not have stated it clearly, the invisible wall is a device for objectivity when filming behavior over some period of time. It is not something that is required in all documentary situations. In most cases it is quite appropriate to say this is why we're here and this is what we're doing, and yes, thanks, I'll be glad to have a cup of coffee. But if I want people to reveal themselves in front of my camera over some length of time, I'd prefer if they thought of me as the film guy who is just always there.

FILMING FRIENDS

The people you are recording may already be friends. And it's hard to remain aloof just because you're filming them. Settling in advance how you will relate to each other during filming can help. Each shooting situation is different, and your behavior and that of your crew must be guided by the goals of the film and your purpose in shooting the scene.

You have to construct the invisible wall as high and tight—or as low and neighborly—as the situation requires. Then it's up to you to maintain it. Your subjects will take the cue for their own behavior from the way *you* behave. If you stay on your side of the invisible wall, they'll stay on theirs.

SHOWING OFF AND APOLOGIZING

For relatively inexperienced documentarians there are the twin temptations of showing off while you're working and of apologizing when things don't go according to plan.

The people you are filming assume that you know what you're doing and how to do it. In fact, when you walk through the door with a crew and some expensive equipment, they assume that you know everything there is to know about every aspect of video and film production. This can be a problem if you let them draw you in to a discussion of the last movie they saw, how special effects are done, or the private lives of the people in Hollywood. That's not what you're there for, and it's a kind of showing off.

But the presumption that you know what you are doing can work for you when you have technical problems or something or other starts to go wrong. Generally, there is no need to explain what has happened, let alone apologize for it, to the people you're shooting. Actually, it's when you allow yourself to show off by playing an expert that you then feel some compulsion to explain or apologize when things don't go perfectly. Instead, just stay on your side of the wall.

The best way to show off is just to do the job you came to do in a thoroughly professional manner. If you've prepared carefully for the shoot, briefed your crew thoroughly, and allowed plenty of time to get the job done—including time to solve the problems that inevitably crop up—then you won't have to apologize for anything.

ACCEPTING HOSPITALITY

What about accepting the hospitality of your subjects? It's hard to refuse a cup of coffee when it's already made, or a piece of pie when it's sitting out and being sliced, but if you accept that, where do you then draw the line?

There's a scene in one of the episodes of *An American Family* in which it is clear that Pat Loud and her mother are the only people in the house. But one of the women makes cocktails and pours them into *three* glasses. Who is the third drink for? Pat has one. Her mother has one. So it must be for some member of the production crew. That's a mighty big crack in the invisible wall. Unless it is explained on film—which it wasn't—it alters for all time the way in which we understand the behavior of the people in the scene in relation to the documentarians showing us that behavior.

Adapting to Fit the Filming Process

The temptation to try to bend behavior to fit the filming process—and the catastrophic results that it can produce—has been amply described in the story of the Wilkes-Barre police captain in chapter 7. It can be a perfectly natural error, especially for a crew accustomed to working with professional actors. Still, there can be only one solution for the documentarian: *Never do it*. The moment you ask the people you are recording to be concerned about your production problems, you have torn down the barrier completely, and made your subjects part of your crew.

Getting Things Moving

There is often a powerful temptation to try to get things moving when nothing seems to be happening. *Don't do it*. The moment you start suggesting something to do, you remove the only element that makes the behavioral documentary worth all the time and effort—the spontaneity of the people you're recording.

Even worse than that, however, is the temptation to move into a power vacuum, when one occurs in a project or event you are documenting and try to take charge of the whole thing. Avoiding this may take the most self-control of all. A documentary director is experienced at organizing people and equipment for a specific purpose and is a person who has learned how to make decisions. And sometimes the process or event that you are documenting is being run by people with neither of those skills. If you are documenting the behavior of the people involved in the everyday operation of a project, you may actually spend more time with them and get to know more about what they are doing and how they feel about it than the people who are supposed to be in charge.

Nevertheless, the value of documenting a project in process with the end in doubt is just that—the outcome is uncertain, and the process itself will determine how it all comes out. If you can't make a commitment to documenting the process honestly and accepting the outcome, no matter what it is, then you shouldn't try to shoot it as a behavioral documentary.

Don't Let the Crew Take Over

Finally, don't let your crew take over. This can be a temptation if you are fairly inexperienced as a director and are working with a professional crew. It can be caused by neglect, if you have failed to brief the crew properly. Or it can be the result of a series of bad decisions, perhaps out of a desire not to rock the boat, as happened to me in Wilkes-Barre.

If you're the director, the final decision is always up to you. Some crews will give you everything they've got, all day long and into the evening, and some will spend an enormous amount of effort trying to convince you that the easy way is the best way.

Hints for Documentary Directors

I personally believe documentaries are best directed quietly. Most of the time you are a guest in someone else's personal space. In most documentaries, the people in front of the camera are not actors and are inexperienced at being filmed. Make it easy for them. Quietly get camera and sound rolling and up to speed and then tell the people you are filming to go ahead whenever they are ready. If you must say, "Cut," say it quietly to the crew.

If you are making a historical documentary or reenactment, you probably need a director who is experienced at working with actors. If that's not you, consider hiring one.

As the director, you have the responsibility to get the film made the best way possible. But making a documentary is not all about you. It's all about the film. Keep your ego in check and keep a low profile. That goes for the crew as well.

Review the day's work as soon as you can. This is much easier with video than with film. Bring a playback system with you on location to see what you have recorded. Then plan the next day's shooting accordingly.

Get the shot. You make the final documentary from the footage you've shot. There is no substitute for good footage. And no excuse is adequate for the shot you didn't get. Be sure to shoot cutaways, cover shots, and background. Vary your composition so that you have available master shots, medium shots, and close-ups. Shoot atmosphere as well as action and talk.

Take charge. And remember the advice of an old director to a young person about to direct their first shoot. "If it takes digging a trench to get the shot," he said, "then dig a trench."

25

DIRECTING PEOPLE
WHO ARE NOT ACTORS

Most documentaries feature real people—people who are not actors—functioning in practical situations. If it is a spontaneous cinema documentary, your function as the director is mainly to convince the people in front of the camera that you will *not* direct them—that whatever they do is absolutely OK with you. That they should just get on with it and you'll try to stay out of their way.

But not all documentaries are concerned with human behavior. There are productions in which the primary concern is to document and explain events, processes, and ideas. There are training films and videos using a documentary approach. There are reports on everything from scientific investigations to the release of new industrial or consumer products. And any of these can call for people who are not actors to appear on camera.

Usually you find yourself working with people who are not actors for the very basic reason that they can do whatever it is they do better than an actor could. In a documentary about trucks, for instance, an actor who can speak lines but can't drive an eighteen-wheeler just won't cut it.

And, sometimes, it is this person—who is not an actor—that the documentary is about.

The Right Start

Directing people who are not actors requires a production plan that recognizes the value of these people as well as their limitations. A good shooting plan will emphasize their strengths—the things they know how to do, the things they are able to talk about—but won't call for them to act. You are the professional, and the situation requires you, as the director, to do a lot more than just check lighting and set camera angles. You can't be a control freak; you must be a guide and a nonjudgmental mentor.

HOLD AUDITIONS

Unless you're stuck with the company president, or *must* include the director of research in your film, try people out.

I once had to borrow a school and shoot a film about a seventh-grade class in the middle of July. I had hired a professional actress to play the teacher—she had a lot of lines to say—but I also needed a class for her to teach. We got kids for the film by putting an ad in the local paper, asking anyone interested in being in the film to show up at the school Friday morning. Mostly we needed extras—kids to sit in the seats and look like a class. But there were a few speaking parts where the kids had to appear to be involved in classroom activities.

So I had each youngster practice the single toughest line in the script, and then deliver it in front of the rest of the "class." I figured that anyone who got nervous in front of a bunch of other kids would never make it in front of a camera. In a short time I had gone through twenty-five boys and girls and found out who was going to giggle, who was going to freeze up, and who wouldn't talk above a whisper. I also had a handful of kids who could say the line as if they meant it. And they were just fine, in short scenes, over two days of work.

I hadn't left everything to chance, however. In case I needed someone to say a specific line, I had brought along my own kids who had been drafted into appearing in my films, and those of my students, even before they could walk. Sure enough, there was one bit that caused trouble. It involved a boy taking a survey, who was asking questions of a girl.

BOY: How old do you think you should be to get married?
GIRL: Forty-two.
BOY: Are you kidding?
GIRL: Are you proposing?

None of the local boys seemed to be able to play that scene without breaking up—perhaps because they knew the girls and it was just too close to home. So I used one of my sons, and the scene went off smoothly. Interestingly, none of the girls had any trouble at all in auditioning for this scene—even when they auditioned with the local boys.

AUDITION FOR INTERVIEWS

When all you want is an interview, the principle remains the same: Find the people who will do well and eliminate the ones who won't. Record the auditions on video, if you can. This will let you see if the camera will reveal hidden beards or bulges. And it may give you some fallback footage or sound if the formal interview doesn't go as well as you hoped.

You Have to Be the Professional

Your contract with people who are not actors is that you will not abuse their amateur standing. Right from the start, it is up to you to keep them confident and secure.

KEEP TECHNICAL MANIPULATIONS TO A MINIMUM

Sure, you've got to set the lights and check the sound. Just don't make a big deal about it. If you have come to someone's home or workplace to film, tell them that it's going to take a few minutes to get set up. Let them go for coffee, or go into another office to get some work done while you get ready. Or let them stay on the set and watch. But don't keep them waiting in place while you fiddle around.

PREPARE FOR SOUND CHECKS

Have something ready for the person to say when you go to set the audio level on the recorder. The alphabet is good—almost everybody knows it. Or give the person something written out that he can read. If it's an interview, let the interviewer get in place and ask a few innocuous questions about football, family, or fashions—just something to keep the person talking—but *never* the real interview questions.

And recognize that rigging a lavaliere microphone can be a potential moment of embarrassment for people who are not used to having it done to them. Most sound recordists have developed a deft touch that lets them tape a tiny lavaliere to a woman's skin under her blouse in a to-tally asexual way. But while they're doing it is a good time for the rest of the crew to be busy doing something else.

GROOMING

Even if you don't have a makeup artist on the crew, give your subjects a chance to check their grooming before you shoot. Provide a mirror of decent size if you are on location away from restrooms or dressing rooms.

KEEP THE LIGHTING SOFT, SIMPLE, AND EASY ON THE EYES

Try to avoid hot lights. Actors have to learn how to live with the lights. People who are not actors don't. I use soft lights or umbrellas whenever possible to keep the set cooler and avoid harsh light in the subjects' eyes.

Don't keep people under the lights too long. Call a break when you have to change lighting or tinker with the technology. Light the entire area the subjects will be working in, so that if they have to move—or want to move—they can.

Keep plenty of bottled water on hand for the people in front of the camera as well as the crew.

USE OF A TELEPROMPTER

For those who don't know any better, using a TelePrompTer seems like the perfect solution for getting people who are not actors to say exactly what you would like them to. If it were only so. Unfortunately, some people do not read out loud very well. Even if they say the words exactly as written, they may *sound* like they are reading. Which they are.

But there's another problem. Reading from a TelePrompTer on camera is a professional skill. It takes experience to look natural while doing it. Amateurs often gesture with their heads while their eyes remain fixed on the line they are reading. It looks strange. Professionals know to hold their heads steady so their steady gaze into the camera looks natural.

I try never to use a TelePrompTer with someone who has no prior experience at reading from one. And I use it only reluctantly with an experienced person who is not a professional. It's tough to get a good result.

BE REASSURING ABOUT RETAKES

If the person you are filming gets flustered or stumbles over something he wants to say, tell him it's not a problem, video is cheap, and the whole reason you and the crew are there is to hear what he has to say in the way he wants to say it.

You may also do retakes for reasons that have nothing to do with the person you are recording. Any sort of technical problem can cause a retake. A sound, such as a plane going over, can ruin a perfectly good read. I tell the subject before we start that we will probably do this several times and not to be concerned when I ask for retakes.

Above all, use a good crew that can work around the people you are filming without threatening them or distracting them.

"Acting" Natural

Remember that acting natural on command is the hardest thing in the world to do. It is almost impossible to get a person who is not an actor to walk, sit, or gesture naturally when asked to. So don't ask. If you must have someone enter a room and sit in a chair, don't tell them that's what they're doing. Just say, "Go over to your desk and get to work." They know what that means.

When working with people who are not actors, remember that whatever the person does in the scene is always *right*. If it isn't what you want, *you* have to work out the problem. It is *never* the subject's responsibility.

Here's the difference between professionals and people who are not actors. I was recording a narration track, using an experienced professional narrator. The way he was reading one line bothered me. I knew it wasn't right, but I couldn't quite explain what was wrong—or what I wanted. Finally, I asked him to give me some variations on the line. He read it a half-dozen different ways, putting the emphasis in different places, making his voice go up one time, down the next, and so on. Eventually I heard exactly what I wanted and told him, "That's it." As a pro, he was able to replicate that reading exactly through several more takes.

But you can't expect that from someone who is not an actor. You have to come up with specific, nonacting directions. For example, if you need more time in the shot of the person crossing the room and sitting in the chair, you might have to say, "Go over and get the daily schedule from Mike's desk, then go to your desk and get to work."

Don't Forget the Background

You can get to concentrating so hard on the one or two people you're working with right in front of the camera that you forget there are other people and other things that are—or should be—visible elsewhere in the scene. If there are people back there who are busy doing something, fine. But be sure they know to stay busy. It can be pretty disheartening for a director finally to get a perfect take of the action in the foreground, only to realize that all the people in the background stopped what they were doing to watch.

The purpose of the film you are shooting will determine how far you go in manipulating the situation. For a behavioral documentary, you set up the invisible wall early and keep it in place. Whatever happens in the background happens and is part of the scene. For a more structured investigation or report, you may need a combination of documenting behavior and shooting preplanned shots.

For some kinds of shots you may want to dress the set with some extras. For example, for a health education video I needed a shot of a person having blood drawn for a blood test. I wanted to shoot it right in the laboratory for verisimilitude. But the chair where the person was sitting was against an uninteresting black wall.

By moving the chair to camera left a foot or so, however, we could now look beyond the person having blood drawn into another part of the lab where there was a receiving counter. One end of the counter was partially blocked by a wall. As I was setting up the shot, a woman who was standing and talking on the phone but who had been hidden by the wall took a step backward so that she came into view. It was a nice piece of business, and I incorporated it into the scene. I told her to stand so that she was hidden by the wall and when she heard me say "Action," she was to count two seconds and take a step backwards. That was all. But it added immensely to the verisimilitude of the scene. Even in this case, I wasn't really asking the woman to *act*. Beyond counting, "One-one thousand, two-one thousand," she was simply doing something she did all the time.

Record Your Rehearsals

People who are not actors tend to peak early and then lose their enthusiasm. It can often happen that you'll get the best take the first time they try the scene. I record everything. For the first take, I tell the subjects that this is a rehearsal for the camera. That way, they go through the business of the scene without feeling camera-shy. Then, when they find out I've recorded the rehearsal, they're often relieved. The pressure of doing it right for the camera the first time has been eliminated, and we can go on and do several more takes if necessary with no problem. Even so, it often turns out that the first take is the one that is used in the final production.

Seven Deadly Sins

I originally listed these as seven deadly sins in working with people who are not actors. But, with the exception of the first one, they're really ways you can get in trouble whether you're working with volunteer amateurs or professional actors.

1. TREATING AMATEURS AS ACTORS
The essence of amateur volunteers is that they are not actors. So don't ask them to memorize long speeches, to emote, or, in short, to act. Set up a situation in which they can behave naturally. If they must speak lines, keep the lines short and shoot them in short takes.

2. FAILURE TO EXPLAIN WHAT YOU'RE DOING AND HOW LONG IT WILL TAKE
All directors have a tendency to underestimate the amount of time it will take to shoot a scene, and then to shave it a little more when asking for volunteers to be in the production. Even when you are working with paid actors, common courtesy demands a realistic explanation of the task and the time it will take.

3. FAILURE TO DISCUSS WARDROBE AND MAKEUP
We're past the day of the TV-blue shirt, but checks and patterned fabrics can still cause moiré patterns on video, and some colors may bleed

in reproduction. Makeup is a matter of individual taste, but it should be discussed. Dark beards and transparent skin can still cause problems on film that could be helped with a shave and some makeup.

4. Putting Pressure on the Person

A friend of mine, a physician, was asked to make a statement in a film about patient treatment. Just before the scene was shot, the director said, "We're almost out of film, so we have to do this right." Of course, the doctor fluffed a line, and the director blew up. But being low on film was the director's problem, and he had no right to put the pressure, or the blame, on my friend.

Similarly, failure to explain that retakes have to be made for technical reasons may make people wonder if they've done something wrong.

5. Stopping the Process to Get Them to Do It "Right"

Anything that calls attention to people who are not actors is another way of putting pressure on them for a performance. If they fluff a line, assure them that it's all right, you'll pick it up in the close-up. If they stumble when they enter the room, tell them not to worry, you want to shoot it again from a different angle.

Most professionals will stop when they go up on a line and immediately get ready to shoot another take. In fact, sometimes when they don't like a reading, they'll deliberately fluff a line so you won't use that take. But even with professionals, it's best to keep the pressure off and maintain an attitude of "we're getting closer, and you can do it."

Calling attention to errors just tends to magnify them, until it is the error that the person remembers, not the way to do it right.

6. Letting the Crew Take Over

Make sure the crew understands that when something goes wrong, they are to talk to you, and you'll decide what to say to the talent—regardless of whether you are using a professional or an amateur. It may be that you've been working with your on-camera person, very carefully, building toward something you know you've almost got. That's not the time to burden him or her with a technical something-or-other from your camera operator or sound recordist.

7. Concentrating on Your Needs Instead of Concentrating on How to Get What You Want from the Person You're Directing

Even a professional actor won't give you what you want just because you want it. That's what directing is all about. With a person who is not an actor it's even more important to make no demands and to find a way to get the person to do what you want—naturally and unself-consciously.

Learn from Working with Children

Kids can be totally natural, completely spontaneous, and absolutely gorgeous on film or video. I really enjoy working with children. Some directors don't, probably because they see working with kids as a management or control problem rather than as a creative opportunity.

Here are some of the things I've learned in filming children.

Be Sure They Have Something to Do

A child working on something he or she is interested in will forget the camera. One with nothing to do will mug.

Keep Them Absorbed in What They're Doing

Even if what they're doing is acting in a film. Tell them stories about the part they're playing, explain your technical problems, but keep them interested. Do all you can to treat them as collaborators, not furniture.

Show Them Your Equipment and Explain What You're Going to Do When You Start Shooting

Kids are naturally curious. They're interested in the production process. And if you haven't explained what is going to happen, they'll sneak looks at the camera while you're recording.

Audition for Speaking Parts

Find out who can talk—and is willing to.

Never Talk Down to Kids

Assume that they are intelligent people with a sizable amount of experience with the world. Talk with them exactly as you would with adults and explain anything they don't understand.

Never Lose Your Temper, or You'll Lose Your Actors

Most kids will want to be in the production and will want to cooperate with you. If they don't, do without them.

Be Alert for Signs of Restlessness

When otherwise cooperative kids start to fool around, talk among themselves, or become annoying, they're probably either bored or tired.

Never Keep Kids Working Too Long

Keep lots of snacks on hand. Call frequent breaks. Let the kids relax while you change setups.

Let Them Do It Their Way as Well as Your Way

In my first experience filming children, I used my then-five-year-old son to play the part of a child playing in an abandoned amusement park. I had an idea of what a kid might do with the abandoned equipment. But so did he. So I had to film him doing it his way before he would do it my way. When we cut the film, we used all the takes that were his way. They were better.

Keep Their Speeches Short

Unless you're doing an interview or having the child explain something in his or her own words, keep it brief. A few words are easy to remember and don't call for much acting.

Cover the Scene with Several Takes

To get a master scene plus close-ups of each speaker, shoot the entire scene each time. You can then edit around fluffs and other mistakes. And by shooting close-ups of each speaker, you'll have natural reaction shots without *acting*.

Now Do This with Everyone

Finally, if this makes sense when you're working with kids, then it's a pretty good set of instructions for working with adults, especially adults who are not actors. We're all a bit like children when we get into a new situation. And for most of the people you'll be working with, being in a documentary is definitely a new situation. If you treat them with the courtesy, kindness, consideration, and patience you should extend to children, you'll find that working with people who are not actors can result in excellent footage that could be gotten in no other way.

26

SELECTING AND
DIRECTING ACTORS

The small-crew behavioral documentarian never sees an actor, except for the occasional brief appearance of an on-camera host or spokesperson. But if you are making a historical documentary or reenactment, you'll need to use actors.

CASTING

Where do the actors come from?

In general, when you begin trying to cast actors, you have your choice of three different approaches:

- Doing it all yourself
- Using a casting director
- Using the services of one or more talent agencies

Casting on your own is too difficult and too time-consuming. It's better to turn to an expert.

Using a Casting Director

My preference is to use a casting director. This is a person who keeps up-to-date files on the actors and models available in your locale. You pay the casting director to work for you—either on a daily or hourly rate, or on a flat fee for the production.

The casting director has no special loyalty to any specific actors or talent agencies and can call on anyone, from anywhere, to audition for a part.

The casting director will probably know something about the work experience of any talent you are interested in and can tell you the bad along with the good.

The casting director knows what is a fair rate to pay for the talent you want and should help in negotiating with the talent or his or her agent. In this way the casting director works for you just as a talent agent works for an actor. The casting director may be able to leverage a better rate for your production than you could yourself, simply because you may represent only an occasional opportunity for the talent to work, while the casting director represents a continuous flow of jobs.

Using a Talent Agency

In most metropolitan areas, you can find a list of talent agencies in the Yellow Pages or online, and your city or state film commission also may publish a production directory that lists talent agents and casting directors.

Like a casting director, the agency will make all those phone calls to line up talent for an audition. But unlike a casting director, an agency usually will not make any direct charge to you for its services. It gets paid a commission by the talent you hire. However, if the agency supplies special services, such as recording auditions on video, there may be a charge for these. Ask about that.

In my opinion, using a talent agency is far better than trying to set up your own casting department. But there are drawbacks.

One is that every agency likes to give its newcomers experience. Not just experience in front of the camera, but experience in an audition. So you may find that in order to see the few really qualified candidates for a part, you have to sit through some poor auditions by inexperienced neophytes.

The agency may not have good candidates for all the parts you want to cast. So you face a choice between accepting someone who is not quite what you had in mind or starting all over with another agency.

An agency casting session may not tell you much about an actor's overall experience or how he or she will do on the set as you go through take after take. Unlike a casting director, the agency will want to play up each actor's assets and minimize any liabilities.

Auditions

You may rely on the talent agent or casting director to select a pool of actors for you to consider for the parts you need to cast. But the decision as to whom to cast in what part remains yours. Unless you are thoroughly familiar with each actor's capabilities, you'll want to hold a casting session or audition. The casting director or talent agency may provide facilities for the audition and may offer to record it for you on video. In any event, for a casting session you'll need:

- a room big enough for the candidates to move about in with chairs or other furniture to simulate the set
- a waiting room outside the audition room for the other candidates
- sufficient copies of the script for all those being auditioned to have their own copy for study ahead of time—you don't need to give them a full script, just a page or two with the scene to be auditioned
- props as required by the scene, including costume props

You'll need some kind of an evaluation system. This could be just a tablet on which you write each actor's name and your notes about the performance. Or it could be a more formal set of evaluation criteria.

RECORDING AUDITIONS ON VIDEO

I'm a firm believer in having the auditions recorded. You get a chance to see how the talent behaves in front of a camera—who is mike-shy, who is bothered by the lights, who tenses up under the pressure of being recorded, and on the other hand, who shines through with a better performance when the camera is on.

And you get to see what each actor actually looks like on camera. You may like the way the person reads the lines, but they may not look right. The camera may add weight, making a normal person seem pudgy. The person may not move well in the confined space of a video picture. Or they may tend to overact, which might not be apparent in person but comes across strongly in a camera close-up.

The close-up can also reveal blemishes or other cosmetic problems that may not always be apparent in person. This is critical if you have any thought of shooting in HDTV, which shows everything. For example, I was seriously considering a young woman for a part, until I played back the audition tape. When she smiled in close-up, her teeth, which I didn't remember as having any problem, appeared as sharp, pointy fangs. The camera revealed a flaw that might have been overlooked if we had not videotaped the audition. And if we had selected her, all her scenes might have had to be reshot.

What to Look For

Obviously, you are looking for specific people to play specific parts. But when you start the session, you don't really have any idea which of the people auditioning will be right for which part. You may have a strong preconception of what you want, but you will almost always have to modify this in terms of the talent available.

These are the things you are looking for:

How Does Each Person Move and Speak?

Can this person move and speak at the same time? Block out a scene involving both. Have each person do this same scene, so that you have a standard for comparison.

Can the Actor Remember Lines?

For some people, the script is a real problem. They just can't remember it. Some have an even worse habit—they get the wrong reading seated in their minds, and it is almost impossible to dislodge it. So be sure to have each candidate do at least one bit without the script.

Can the Actor Follow Directions?

I'm willing to give actors a reasonable amount of latitude in interpreting a role. That's their profession. But when a difference exists between the actor's interpretation and the reading I want, the one we're going to go with is mine. So it is critical to find out if the actor can shift gears. And it is important to find out if the actor can understand your directions and follow them. During the audition, change your directions and see if the talent can give you what you ask for. There are actors who can give you only one interpretation of a scene. You ask for something different—they give you the same reading as before. A real pro recognizes that there are a lot of different ways a line can be said.

Does the Person Seem Real or Seem to Be Acting?
Does he or she seem natural? Believable?

Can the Actor Replicate?
Once you have gotten the actor to give you the reading you want, can he or she deliver it consistently, take after take?

How Does the Actor Handle Props?
If business with props is important to the part, get the actor to handle props at the audition. Use the real props if possible. But don't be shy about handing the actor something and saying, "Pretend this is an accordion"—or whatever.

TRY DIFFERENT COMBINATIONS
When you have made preliminary casting decisions, have the people read together. See how they work together. See how one reacts to another's lines. Switch them around to see which is the best combination. Above all, don't be afraid to change your mind. The program you are casting may be around for a long time.

NOTIFYING THE ACTORS
Everyone who auditioned should be notified of the outcome of the casting session immediately after the final casting decisions have been made. Tell the casting director or talent agent the actors you want to use, and let them notify the talent.

Auditioning Voice Talent
Even if you're just casting a voice-over narrator, it's a good idea to do an audition, however short. You just can't rely completely on sample tapes. I had a bad experience this way. I was doing a video for IBM and had selected a narrator I didn't know, based on a sample tape he had sent in. It was a great, strong voice, with a lot of credibility and a good range. The problem was that when I got the talent into the studio, he couldn't deliver.

He had trouble reading basic words about computers. He had a very limited range of expression. And he lacked the professional's ability to bring enthusiasm and emotion to the task. We had to bring in another narrator and do the job over.

DIRECTING ACTORS

The whole purpose in directing actors is to get the actors to create a scene the way you want it.

Therefore, you have to know what you want.

You have to communicate it to the actors.

And you have to keep at it—in rehearsals, retakes, or whatever—until you get what you want.

What Does a Documentarian Know About Actors?

Anyone who has shot and edited a documentary of human behavior probably knows a heckuva lot about how people actually behave. Certainly you know as much or more than most actors do, and probably more than most directors do who work only with actors.

I'm thinking of a high school play in which one of my sons appeared. There was a boy in the play who portrayed a middle-aged New York cab driver. He had the makeup and the props to go with the part. In spite of his youth, he was an experienced actor who had done a number of plays and had made several television appearances. He had most of the traits of his character down cold, but there was something wrong with his performance. It didn't quite permit the willing suspension of disbelief that would have allowed the teenage actor to become the middle-aged cab driver.

As I watched him, I realized what it was. He didn't *walk* like a much older man. He bounced. He moved too quickly. The character he was playing might have an impatient mind that raced ahead at the speed of sound, but his aging body would always hold him back.

A good documentary director would know this.

A good stage or film director who works with actors would know it as well. My point is that a documentary director doesn't have to come in the back door. As you begin working with the actors, you'll discover that you do have something to contribute. Your knowledge of the way the world works, and the way the people in it behave, is something the director of actors spends a lot of time trying to learn.

Try to Budget Extra Time for Rehearsal

I suspect that in most film and video work, not enough time is given to rehearsing the actors. One reason is that you usually record a few lines at a time, and professional actors can get up to performance level in those lines fairly quickly. Another is that there is so much technical stuff to be handled that working with the actors is only one of the director's responsibilities. Another is the idea that film is a director's medium, which would seem to de-emphasize the importance of the actors.

Work out the fine points of performance before you get on the set, if you possibly can, so that the time spent setting lights and planning camera moves is not taken at the actors' expense.

On the set you'll need some full rehearsals of camera, cast, and crew. Record them. You never know when you'll get exactly what you want the first time.

Costume and Makeup

There are no fixed rules about who provides makeup and wardrobe for the actors. In today's documentaries the general rule is that the actors provide their own wardrobe if it's just street clothes for normal wear.

However, if the production calls for special clothing—uniforms, special work clothes, hard hats, boots, heavy gloves, and so forth—then the wardrobe should be provided by the producer. Similarly, if damage to the clothing is a likelihood, the costume should be provided by the producer—or you should arrange in advance to reimburse the actor for cleaning or replacement.

Finding costumes for a period piece is always a problem. If you are putting together a Civil War film, you may have to rent all the costumes, or you may be able to borrow in some cases, rent in others, and even, occasionally, have the actors provide their own. Be sure you are insured against damage to borrowed costumes.

Makeup is another problem. Most experienced actors have learned to do their own. But that doesn't mean they are good at it. Stage actors will tend to go for strong makeup that will hold up under stage lighting.

This may look fine to the audience of a play, viewing from a distance, but it will look coarse and false on camera.

I generally budget for a makeup artist for any production involving actors, unless it is obvious that makeup won't be necessary.

Communicating with Actors

When the actor you are directing gives you exactly what you want and can replicate it all day long through retake after retake, you are in director's heaven. But most of the time it's not so simple.

A common mistake is to look at the script and assume that everyone sees a scene the way you do. They don't. It can come as a great surprise that an actor you have selected, who gave such a great reading at the casting session, could interpret a scene so differently from the way you see it. But it happens all the time.

So, the more specifically you have blocked out exactly what you want—in your mind and on paper—the easier it will be to communicate it to the others involved and to get it in performance. But be flexible. An actor may come up with an interpretation that is exactly what you want. Or he or she may be way off base and in need of direction, or may come up with an interpretation that is not at all what you had in mind, but is just as good—or even better than—your idea.

In short, know what you want, but be open to improvements.

The things an actor may have to do during a scene are:

- move
- look
- do something
- speak
- react

GROSS MOVEMENT—BLOCKING THE SCENE

I generally attend to movement first. Where does each actor start? Where does each actor end up? How does the camera move—if at all— to cover the action? How will you edit within the scene? And how will you edit this scene with the scene that goes before, and the scene that follows?

Generally, you want the motion within the scene to be fluid, well-motivated, and continuous from prior action to following event.

I try to get everyone who has to move in motion before the scene begins. Usually, I'll do a countdown to the start of the scene: "Five . . . four . . . three . . . two . . ." with the count of *one* understood, and the action of the scene itself beginning at *zero*.

As you block the scene, each person, and possibly the camera, will have a number in the countdown on which to start moving. This way all the necessary motion has already been started at the point at which you'll cut into the scene. During rehearsal, I make adjustments to starting positions and starting count until I get the movement within the scene exactly the way I want it.

Where to Look—The Eyes Have It

Where does your actor make eye contact? Is it with the camera, as if he or she were speaking directly to the audience? Is it with another actor, either in the scene or off camera? Or is the actor looking at something else?

Decide in advance, because it has to be correct in the master scene, or you'll find yourself in a lot of trouble when you go for close-ups.

Doing Something

In real life, people can walk, speak, and do things with their hands all at the same time. What does your actor have to do? When is the appropriate time in the scene to do it?

Doing something specific requires planned, fluid movement just like gross movement. It should neither start too soon nor occur too late. When a person walks to a car and opens the door, his hand comes up just before he reaches the car in anticipation of grasping the door handle. When a person spots something on a desk and reaches for it, the sequence must be to see and react to the object before reaching out to get it.

Speaking—Placing Words in Context

I may surprise you by putting speaking lines way down in fourth place on a list of five items. What is said and how it is said are certainly important. But ever since our first kindergarten play, so much emphasis has been placed on remembering and saying the words that we have almost been trained to ignore the other elements that breathe life into a scene.

If, however, we can get the actors moving properly, doing things naturally, and looking in the right places, we'll already be building up a natural rhythm to the scene that will make it easier for them to get the words out properly.

The mark of an amateur is a letter-perfect recitation of the speech—in a vacuum.

Most dialogue is written not the way people actually speak, but the way they wish they did. Just as doing something often involves making awkward movements in a way that looks natural, so it is with speaking. Your actors must take words written by someone else and use them as if they were their own. They must enunciate clearly—without seeming to. They must pause as if to think, even though what they will say next is so well memorized they can say it in their sleep. And they must say the same speech through a hundred retakes if necessary—and make it seem fresh and original each time.

James Garner, a pro at acting natural, calls this saying your lines "as if it were the first time you have ever said those words."

LISTENING AND REACTING

Much of the impact of words comes from the effect they have on someone else, and you'll want to film actors reacting to what another actor says. The obvious way to do this is to shoot a close-up or medium shot as they react to the words that are said. But after you have finished with the scene, you may also want to have them give you a variety of specific reactions from which you can choose in editing the film. To show an amused reaction, you might ask for a long, slow smile, as well as laughter. The important thing to remember is to direct your actors in both the actions and speeches they must perform and in their reactions to the behavior and words of others.

The actor should not anticipate the reaction. Cause first, reaction after.

One-on-One

How do you direct actors? What do you do? What do you say?

Probably at one time or another you'll do just about everything. For some actors you can say as little as, "Let's try it again." For others you may need to give a full-on explanation each time.

In communicating with actors I try not to act out the scene for them. I want the actors to use their skill to interpret my directions. I certainly don't want a good actor trying to imitate my bad acting.

Ego Massage

You usually can't hurt actors by massaging their egos. I've never gotten mad at an actor, yelled at, or belittled one. I've read about directors doing this to get the performance they wanted, but I've never felt I could predict accurately enough what would happen. I go on the theory that if I treat the actors like adult human beings, they'll probably return the favor.

Don't Settle for Less Than You Need

On the other hand, I don't carry ego massage to the point of accepting takes that aren't good enough. I've done that in the past. And each time I do, I relearn, to my sorrow, that when you get into the editing room, you have to live with what you've shot.

There can be a lot of pressure on you to accept a less-than-perfect take. Expense is one. You may have an executive producer or sponsor or boss who doesn't understand what is going on, who wants you to "get on with it." You just have to grit your teeth, broaden your smile, and keep shooting until you've got what you need. The same people who are hurrying you to finish shooting won't for a minute accept any responsibility if you have to go back for retakes.

I don't consider it an insult to the actors to ask for another take—or for several more. I do try to let them know why we're doing retakes. If the reason is technical—sound or picture problems—I tell them that. If it's a fluff in the lines, I tell them that.

I try to get an acceptable take as early as possible. That's one more reason for recording rehearsals. When I have that, I can tell the cast and crew, "OK, we've got an acceptable take, now let's go for perfection."

One important thing to remember is that if you don't like what you're getting, let everyone know. Take a break if you need to. Figure out what's wrong, and what's needed, and then work on getting that.

And realize that your behavior will affect the actors. If you act bored, for instance, they may assume what they're doing is not important. I recall being on the set of a shoot in which the director was not getting the performance he wanted from the actors. It was a comic bit, and what he said he wanted was more excitement, more energy, and a faster pace. He was watching each take as it was shot on a monitor in a room off the set. After the take, he would come out and talk with the actors and crew and then go back for another take. And each time, as he would disappear back toward his video monitor, he would chant in a singsong voice, "Everybody up, now. Lots of energy, lots of excitement."

What he got each time was a singsong performance.

Positive Feedback Can Get You There

Put yourself in an actor's place. Imagine you're standing on your mark while the professionals work the technology to record whatever you do and say. And imagine that two-thirds of the way through your scene, you make a mistake. What would you like to have happen? Actually, the last thing you need is to have a lot of attention drawn to:

- the fact that you made a mistake
- the line or action you did wrong

Whenever I can, I'll let the actor complete the scene, and then ask for a retake. In an interview accompanying the DVD of *The Quiet Man*, Maureen O'Hara talked about flubbing a line and immediately saying "Cut," and stopping to apologize to director John Ford. Ford told her, "There is only one person who is allowed to say 'cut,' and I am that person. If you make a mistake keep going, see if you can work your way out of it."

Good advice. Interesting things can happen when actors have to clean up the mess they've made. Sometimes.

Of course, if there has been a problem with one line or one piece of business, you may want to try picking up a repeat as soon as it goes bad, and keep trying until you get it right. What I'll try to do in this situation is to say, in a calm voice, "Keep rolling. We'll pick it up from the start of your speech. And . . . action." Then if it goes bad again, I'll say, "Again . . . Position One, quickly . . . and . . . action." And we'll keep it going until it either comes out right or becomes clear some other change has to be made.

What I don't do is yell "Cut!" so I can be heard in the next county. I expect that electronic equipment will fail and actors will make mistakes. So there's no reason to act disgusted when predictable events occur.

And every reason to be delighted when they don't.

Ask for What You Want

It can happen that the actor is reading the lines correctly and going through the movement properly, and you're still not happy with what you're getting. Then you have to make a change. And you have to tell the actor what you want changed. Say, "The way we rehearsed it just isn't working. Let's try this."

I've had it happen that I get so focused on what I'm looking for that I forget to tell the actor what I need. Or sometimes a subtle change will creep into the performance. I may notice it and think, "Well, he won't do that next time." But if I don't say anything about it, that little change may become a part of the scene. And I may keep asking for retakes without realizing that I haven't told the actor that I want him or her to quit doing that.

Break Up the Action

One of the things you can do with film and video, of course, is to work in small units of script. This is especially helpful when your actors are not very experienced. You can have the actor say just one line, and say it exactly the way you want it, whether he or she understands it or not. Then you go on to the next line.

Generally, this is the way I plan the shoot, unless I'm thoroughly familiar with the capabilities of the actors. As we gain experience with each other, I'll add length to what we try to accomplish in one take. It sometimes turns out, delightfully, that what I had blocked out as three or four different shots can be done in one long take. I don't count on it; I just accept it with gratitude when it happens.

Film and Video Acting vs. Stage Acting

There are definite differences between acting in films and acting on the stage. And this can cause problems if the actors available to you primarily have stage experience.

THE STAGE IS ONE BIG WIDE SHOT

There's no such thing as a close-up in the theater. You see the whole stage and everyone on it all the time. In general, you are seated somewhat above and looking down. There is very little visual relief. The plot advances mainly through the words said by the actors. That's one reason why the stage is a writer's medium, while film is considered a director's medium.

THE STAGE REQUIRES OVERSTATEMENT

In the theater, everything is aimed at the people in the back seats. Voices project. Gestures are broad. Makeup is strong. What is appropriate for the stage can come across as overdone on film.

ACTING ON THE STAGE IS DONE IN SEQUENCE

A theatrical performance runs from the beginning of the play to the end and is a collaboration between the actors on the stage and the people in the audience. It's live. It's now. The actors build their performance in real time. And once the curtain goes up, the director is out of it. Stage actors may have trouble shooting scenes out of sequence and with the director always there and in control.

A FILM OR VIDEO IS SHOT OUT OF SEQUENCE

The actors in the film may never all be in the same place at the same time. In fact, it's possible—although rarely desirable—to have a dialogue on screen between two actors who actually never were on the same set, in front of the same camera, at the same time.

FILM AND VIDEO BRIDGE TIME AND SPACE

What appears on a movie screen or a TV set can come from anywhere and be made up of anything. You see an actor in close-up, followed by a shot of the Grand Canyon or the mountains of the moon. Film and video are *not* locked into one time, one place, or one dimension.

ACTING ON FILM OR VIDEO TAKES UNDERSTATEMENT

Acting on camera requires a subtle approach, underplaying and reacting rather than projecting. Normal stage projection will come across as overacting, while the powerful language of the stage is often too much for the screen. It seems forced and artificial—which, of course, it is. Different media require different conventions.

You Are the Unifying Force

The audience for a film, while kept in mind from script to screen, comes to view the finished work long after production is over. Because of this, the director is the unifying force in film and video. To provide the integrity and direction that will sustain a work through all the phases of production and postproduction, you must be clear about what you want, and then work with your crew and cast—and later your creative editor—until you achieve it.

27

CONDUCTING AN INTERVIEW

I gave you all the reasons I could think of not to build your film around interviews in chapter 12. I stand by all of them. Still, there are a number of reasons why you may want or need to film an interview:

- Sometimes an interview is used as a substitute for action footage you don't have and can't get. When a ship sinks at sea, you interview the survivors. It's the best evidence you have.
- Sometimes the speaker is an expert on some topic or holds a strong opinion about it, and you want to hear what she has to say, in her own words.
- You may want an on-camera interview to be able to prove that the speaker said whatever he said, especially if the statement is controversial or can be shown to be untrue. You may want to cross-question the speaker to probe his statement for flaws or inaccuracies or for the strength of his convictions.
- You hope that the person being interviewed will reveal her thoughts, hopes, dreams, and feelings as part of the texture of your documentary.
- You may want to use pieces from an interview to supplement or replace narration, in order to give your film a feel of spontaneity and a look of reality.
- Finally, you may just want to show the person on camera. Company presidents, politicians, and celebrities often fall into this category. Their physical presence in the film may be more important than anything they say.

Whatever your reason for shooting an interview, remember that its *use* in the final version of the film has to be justified on the same basis as any other scene. That is, it must present evidence, provide information, or enhance the feel, mood, or flavor of the production, *and* it must help move the documentary along toward its resolution and ending.

Otherwise it belongs on the outs reel with the other shots that didn't work.

Doing a Good Interview

Interviewing is a special skill. Some people do it well, some don't. I think the best interviewers listen intently and speak cautiously—and as little as possible.

Preparation

To do a successful interview, you have to prepare.

Every expert on interviewing says the same thing: Do your home-work. So *do* it. Find out what you can about your subject ahead of time. Most important, find out what you don't know. That's the basis for your questions. Gather documents. No matter what the topic of the in-terview is, something has probably been written about it. Talk to your interviewee's associates. They may give you personal glimpses or a dif-ferent slant that the speaker won't provide.

Quite often you can have the interviewee prepare a list of suggested questions for your use, especially if the interviewee is appearing as an expert. Just make it clear that you won't be limiting the interview to the questions that are provided.

You may want to do a preinterview to find out what the person has to say and how she or he says it. But be careful this doesn't lead to the sit-uation, on camera, in which the speaker begins each statement with, "As I told you before . . ." The preinterview is a good time to get the cor-rect spelling of the speaker's name and exact title. You'll need this for subtitles on the screen.

Take time to explain to the interviewee your purpose, the purpose of the documentary, your slant, if any, who the film is being produced for if there is a sponsor, and the intended audience. If it's a hostile situation, tell your subject what others have said, or are expected to say, and give him or her a chance to refute them.

Explain that it's customary to overshoot an interview. Be sure the person understands that you may shoot a half-hour interview, but you will probably use less than a minute of it in the film.

Get everything—lights, camera, sound equipment, sound checks, lens cleaning, and so on—taken care of ahead of time. Let the interviewee know in advance that you'll need a half hour or so to set up.

Pick Your Spot

You want to do the interview: (1) in an interesting location that helps to build the visual evidence of your film; and (2) in a place where the speaker is comfortable. Try for both. Then:

- Find a comfortable place to sit or stand to ask your questions. You will be there for a while.
- Settle ahead of time whether the interviewee will be talking to you or to the camera.
- Be sure to have each person say and spell his or her name on camera, including rank or title where appropriate.
- And it's always a good idea to have the interviewee give you permission on camera to use the interview.

Avoid Dumb Situations, Dumb Questions, and Dumb Interviewees

The man-in-the-street interview is the classic dumb situation. You grab somebody off the street and ask him what he thinks about something. What you get is noninformation.

Dumb questions are those that elicit no useful information. To avoid them, define your purpose. You can't really ask dumb questions if you know what you're there for.

Every now and then you'll interview a person who is just no good on camera. There's nothing you can do except wind it up quickly and move on. Preinterviews should eliminate the people who will freeze up. But some people go through a personality change when the camera begins to roll.

Shooting Options

Shoot the interview before you shoot other kinds of action with this person. This keeps the behavior of the interviewee fairly spontaneous and free of any bias toward acting you might introduce—through even minimal directions—later on.

While at the interview location, try to get documentary footage that provides visual evidence to go with the interview. You know what the speaker talked about, so you should have no problem planning what to shoot. For example, if you were discussing a sophisticated computer modeling device that is being used to help design and construct a bridge, get some shots of it while you're there at the location.

Shooting to Edit

If you plan to edit out the questions that are asked, have the camera operator change camera angle or focal length only while you are asking questions. This will give you more flexibility in editing the interview down to a short, on-camera sequence without any apparent jump cuts. It may also do away with the use of unmotivated cutaways. An unmotivated cutaway is purely an editing device. It is not used to show the audience something important, but merely to cover a sync-sound edit point and eliminate a jump cut.

If, however, you think you may want to keep the questions as part of the scene, then the reaction of the subject to the questions as they are asked may be as important as his or her answers. You'll want to keep the camera changes to a minimum so that the audience can see the reactions as they happen. Therefore, you may have to cover edit points with cutaways.

If you, or someone, keeps track of the questions that have been asked, you have the option to move the camera around to the subject's point of view after the interview is over and reshoot the interviewer asking the questions on camera.

Shoot cutaways after you have completed the interview. This is the point at which you may be asking the interviewee to *act,* so it should come after you've gotten his or her spontaneous answers and reactions.

Editing Options

Enough has already been said about talking heads. You'll know when the face of the speaker is the most interesting thing you can use, and you'll know when it's dull. Most of the time it is enough to establish the speaker on camera for ten to twenty seconds and then cut away to· something that shows what he or she is talking about. The less you show the person talking, the easier it is to edit the sound track. That's why it's important to shoot that other stuff and not just the moving mouth.

But you don't know while you're recording which sound bites you will want to use on camera. So the camera operator has to stay on the person being interviewed, no matter how long the interview runs. Compose the shot so there is room in the lower third of the picture to superimpose the interviewee's name and title. If the interviewee wants to show you something, fine. Let the camera widen out to include it. But don't push in to a close-up and lose the interviewee. You can shoot close-ups of the items as cutaways after the interview.

One of the problems with the hours and hours of interviews that were shot for *Defenders of Midway* is that they took hours and hours. The camera operator got bored and started being creative—pointing the camera out the window or up at the ceiling and doing a slow pan or tilt to "discover" the interviewee in the middle of a statement. There was a fairly dramatic statement from one of the interviewees that I wrote into the script as voice-over covered by archival footage. The director said he thought it would be better to show that statement on camera. I said, "I do, too. But when he made that statement the camera was filming a blank wall."

Interview Audio

Sound is the heart of an interview. Get the microphone close to the speaker and keep it there. If you're in a grab situation and working with a handheld mike, get it in close to provide good separation between the speaker's voice and the background noise.

But don't hand the mike to the speaker. The person who has it controls the interview, and you may not be able to get it back without yelling, "Cut!" and stopping the entire process.

Ask the Right Questions

Your questions should be specific enough to point a direction for the speaker and vague enough that he or she has to fill in the details. Try to stay away from leading questions, to which the interviewee can answer "yes" or "no." Instead, ask questions such as:

"Tell me what happened."
"How would you explain this situation to people?"
"What would you like people to know about this?"
"What do you see in the future?"
"How did this come about?"

As with a research interview, this is no time to show off your knowledge of the topic. You're asking questions in the name of your audience, and you want answers from the speaker that will inform them. Don't be embarrassed to say, "I don't know about that," or "I don't understand," even if you do. It's a good way to get more information.

Sometimes you have to play devil's advocate and take a position that seems to oppose the speaker's views—or your own—in order to get good explanations and clarification.

THE QUESTION THAT MADE THE VIDEO WORK

My partner Sylvie Hampe and I were asked to produce a series of short, documentary-style vignettes for use on the annual Children's Miracle Network telethon. We were working on the story of a young woman, six months pregnant with her first child, who was hit by a drunken driver, knocked out of her car, dragged more than a hundred feet along the highway, and left for dead.

Through what will pass for a miracle until the real thing comes along, the accident was witnessed by an off-duty policeman, who immediately called for an ambulance. The young mother was rushed to the trauma room at the hospital in cardiac arrest while paramedics kept her body functioning in hopes of saving the baby. The baby, weighing just three pounds one ounce, was delivered by cesarean section and placed in the hospital's neonatal intensive care unit. Then, amazingly, his mother was resuscitated—and lived.

We wanted to shoot the finish of the vignette on a day the mother and her baby, now a healthy nine-pound little boy named William, returned for a visit to the pediatric unit. This was on a day I had managed to come down with the twenty-four-hour flu and wasn't allowed anywhere near patients, especially small babies. Sylvie took the crew in and set up while I sat outside in a family waiting room. She asked Rebecca, the mother, one question, "Tell me what happened the morning William was born," and in one take got the whole story of how the hospital staff saved her and her child. Then, before shutting down, Sylvie asked if there was anything else Rebecca would like to say, and got no indication that there was. At that point, Sylvie looked around to check if the crew had any ideas, and the camera operator volunteered, "Would you like to thank them?"—meaning the hospital staff. That question gave us the ending of the video.

Rebecca looked directly into the camera and said, "Without them, I wouldn't be here. I mean, you know, yeah, God was smiling on me that day, but if it wasn't for them he wouldn't have smiled very long. So I'd like to say thank you. If it wasn't for you all, William wouldn't be the little boy that he is today. [At this point her voice became husky and started to break.] He probably wouldn't be here if it wasn't for you all. So I'd like to say thanks, and [her voice almost a whisper] you guys are so wonderful."

No one has ever watched this with dry eyes.

Listen, Listen, Listen

After you've asked a question, *listen to the answer.* Let the speaker know you're interested. Follow up any interesting points your subject brings up. Don't be ruled by your question list. The reason you have written questions is to have something to go back to if the interview slows down, and to serve as a checklist to be sure you've covered everything before ending the interview.

Don't rush to ask another question as soon as the speaker pauses. Wait a bit. A silence may prompt the interviewee to elaborate on what he or she is saying in important ways that would otherwise be missed. And that can often be better than the first answer given.

The Two Most Important Questions

When you come to the end of everything you've planned for the interview, you still have two questions to ask. I mentioned these in chapter 17, but it won't hurt to repeat them here.

The first is: "Is there anything I should have asked you that I just didn't know enough to ask?" This gives your subject one last chance to show that he or she knows more than you do about the subject.

The second is: "Is there anything that you'd like to say that you haven't had a chance to?" Sometimes your subject has been thinking about the interview and rehearsing little speeches, but feels he or she should only answer the questions you ask.

Occasionally one of these questions may open the floodgates, and you'll get more than you ever dreamed of. But be sure to brief your crew that you're going to do this. One crew shut down the camera and recorder as soon as they heard me ask the first of the questions because they thought I was gathering information off the record. Keep the camera running. You only get one shot at the answer to these questions.

PRACTICE

Finally, if you want to be a good interviewer, practice. The hardest thing to learn to do is to listen. Try to think about what the speaker is saying and where it's leading, not about what you're going to ask next. Learn what kinds of questions prompt good answers and what kinds tend to shut off the response. See if you can't find ways to nudge the speaker into revealing more without asking a direct question. Interview your friends, your relatives, and people you meet at parties. Don't just talk to them, interview them.

And when the time comes to do it on camera, you'll be ready.

28

VERISIMILITUDE IN DOCUMENTARY

Making a documentary requires meticulous attention to what will ultimately be shown to an audience. The verifiable truth of a documentary depends on the honesty of the documentarian in presenting an accurate analog of the situation as he or she understands it. But that alone is no guarantee that the audience will accept what is shown as true—because a documentary, every bit as much as a Hollywood movie or a Broadway play, must work within the framework of audience beliefs, conventions, and expectations. The images on the screen may be both real and true, but if they lack the appearance of truth, the documentarian sets up a credibility gap with the audience that may never be overcome.

An audience comes to any film or video—including a documentary—bringing with it what in the theater is called the willing suspension of disbelief. Violate that and you may lose your audience—sometimes for good. In addition to good visual evidence, structured into a compelling argument, a documentary requires the appearance of truth. The term for this is *verisimilitude*.

In fiction, verisimilitude is generally taken to mean an attention to detail—and to the logic of human behavior—so that the audience will accept what is written or shown as true. That's because fiction is unreal. Even though it never happened, it is expected to have an internal consistency—called the logic of the piece—that will make sense to the audience.

Truth, on the other hand, may well be stranger than fiction. Fiction is bound by rules, whereas truth rests on the chaos of reality. But truth presented without the appearance of truth can raise questions in the minds of your audience.

REENACTMENT AND RE-CREATION

Documentaries using reenactment and re-creation require the conscious use of the techniques of verisimilitude every bit as much as a fiction film does. Because you are reproducing people and events rather than recording them in actuality, you must do nothing to upset your audience's willing suspension of disbelief.

For example, if you're filming a cold winter scene in a studio and you take care that the actor's breath is visible, that's verisimilitude—in a fiction film *or* a reenactment documentary.

Verisimilitude in The War Game

One of the most unrelenting documentaries I know of, Peter Watkins's *The War Game*, explores the implications of an event that never happened—an all-out nuclear war. The setup—that both sides engage in a saber-rattling game of bluffing and escalation from which they are unable to back down—is stated so simply, and is so consistent with what we have come to know about our governments and the people who run them, that it is accepted without a murmur. While *The War Game* documents an event that didn't happen, everything that is shown is either based on actual events—the firestorms caused by bombing in Germany, the effects of radiation in Japan during World War II—or is based on results of the copious government studies done by the nuclear powers in the '50s and '60s.

The theme of the documentary—the outcome of a nuclear attack on England worked out in human terms—is done with a gritty realism that is utterly believable. For instance, there is a firestorm scene in which people are suddenly caught in the grip of a hundred-mile-an-hour wind and flung off their feet. This is what Watkins said about shooting the scene in an interview in Alan Rosenthal's book *The New Documentary in Action* (1971):

> We put a mattress down, and got the people to sort of run and pick themselves up off the mattress. . . . As you are running, you have to

suddenly feel yourself caught and turned by an air current. To achieve this we started pulling them with wires, but finally decided not to do that, as we thought it would hurt them. We also thought it would look false. We also helped the effect by having flares roaring in the background and putting two fans quite close to them to whip bits of shredded paper and flour across, so that you got the visual impression of a sudden whipping across of something. As they ran to a particular spot where their mattress was, the white bits of paper would whip across and catch them. That would be their cue for letting themselves be caught in it and turned. (p. 162)

That's verisimilitude: the appearance of truth—even in an unreal situation—to give the look of realism.

VERISIMILITUDE IN AN ACTUALITY DOCUMENTARY

OK, verisimilitude is useful in a fictional setting or a re-creation to provide a look of realism for a scene that might be the truth but is not real; it's a reenactment. But what is the need for verisimilitude in an actuality documentary where, it is hoped, truth and reality lie nestled in the same set of images?

Mood Music

Paying attention to verisimilitude in a documentary could mean asking whether the use of background music enhances the mood of a scene or detracts from its believability. Since this is a convention from the fiction film, will the audience accept the music as belonging, or are they likely to infer that you are playing on their emotions, perhaps because your facts are thin?

Showing the Crew and Equipment

In a documentary of behavior, I have sometimes included in an early scene a shot of the film crew at work. It serves as a reminder to the audience that what they are seeing occurred in front of a camera, and that they should keep that in mind in evaluating the behavior they see.

But it also helps with what can become a sticky problem of verisimilitude later on. I've done a number of documentaries with little kids, and when a little kid decides to move, he *goes*—sometimes right past the sound tech or the microphone or a light stand that everyone thought would be out of the way. Usually we're able to cut around that and maintain the convention that the crew remains behind the camera while the subjects of the documentary are in front of it. But occasionally the behavior is unique, important, and never repeated. Having already shown the audience the film crew at work, there should be no problem with using the shot, even though the edge of a microphone shows in the picture or part of a light stand is clearly visible in the background.

Showing the crew and equipment is something I'm perfectly willing to do in spontaneous cinema, and something I would never do—not even a glimpse of microphone—in a reenactment or historical documentary. In both cases for the same reason—verisimilitude.

Little Errors, Big Problems

Whenever you're dealing with a specialty or a technical area, it's important to get the details right. Because I'm a former Navy pilot, I often get annoyed when I see a sequence aboard an aircraft carrier that purports to follow a single airplane taxiing forward and launching from the ship. Usually these scenes are edited from stock footage. And all too often the director and editor seem to assume that all blue airplanes with propellers are the same. So we see a World War II Corsair spread its wings, a Hellcat taxi forward, and a Korean War Skyraider take off.

WHAT WERE THEY THINKING?

In the footage I received for *Defenders of Midway,* there was an interview with a man in his seventies who was a Marine dive-bomber pilot at Midway during the battle. The director had gotten permission to use it in our film although it had originally been shot for a different documentary.

For some reason, the director who shot the scene had put this former Marine pilot in an Air Force flight suit and had him wearing a Navy officer's cap, but with no insignia on it. That made no sense at all. And it made the man uncomfortable.

Compounding this silliness, the director asked him not to call his former enemies "Japs," but to refer to them as "Japanese." That's grafting late-twentieth-century sensitivity onto a war that took place in the 1940s. It is correct to say "Japanese" in narration, but senseless to ask a veteran of the war not to call his enemies by the name he always used for them. And when the pilot replied to this request, "That's what I think of them as. I hated them. I wanted to kill them," the director replied, "But you don't now."

"Yes I do," mumbled the pilot, and they went on with the interview.

Why put a seventy-year-old man in a flight suit to talk about something he did when he was twenty? It's terrible verisimilitude. All of the other defenders of Midway were in civilian clothes, even those who were retired military and entitled to wear a uniform. But certainly, if you're going to do it, then the uniform should be correct.

Paying attention to verisimilitude in documentary means you can never assume that close enough is good enough.

Wrong Behavior

When I was shooting a documentary called *Light in Art* for Hawaii Public Television, I had a long sequence showing photographer Brett Weston taking photographs of the work of his friend Henry Bianchini, a sculptor. A verisimilitude problem developed, because each time we began a new setup, they would call each other by name at the start of the shot. It's a small thing, but, in our culture, friends working alone together over a period of time do not normally use each other's name frequently as they talk. They know who they are and whom they are talking with.

I think Brett and Henry fell into the use of this for two reasons. First, there were others in the room, and while we were behind the camera, we *were* there. Social rule says you may need to address someone by name to distinguish him from the others who are also there. Second, what we were videotaping was a scene that had been set up for our film. So it felt to them like a somewhat formal presentation. And social rule says that you may call the other by name at the start of a formal presentation. The problem there was that they treated each take as the start of a new presentation.

I knew that if this continued, when we edited the takes into a sequence, we would have them calling each other Brett and Henry far too often to seem natural. Bad verisimilitude. I asked them to stop using each other's names.

We shot this sequence like a reenactment, not like a behavioral documentary. If I had been shooting a documentary about their behavior,

where we would go in and observe whatever they did and said, I would
have given no such direction. But I also would not have been shooting in
short, slated takes.

More Wrong Talk

In the many hours of the PBS presentation *An American Family,* there's
a scene of Pat Loud visiting her hometown and driving around the community with her mother as they talk about the way things were and the
way things are now. As I watched it, I felt that something didn't ring
true. And as I listened a little longer, I realized it was what they were
saying.

Pat and her mother were overexplaining. Two people simply don't go
into such detail about events that both of them are thoroughly familiar
with *unless* there is a third person in the scene—a stranger who otherwise wouldn't know what they were talking about. And of course there
was. The sequence was shot from the backseat of the car. At a minimum
there were sound and camera people back there, and possibly the director or producer as well. And that's who Pat and her mother were talking
to—not to each other. For a scene that pretended to be a private conversation between mother and daughter, the verisimilitude—in words
and behavior—was wrong.

In this case, as in many instances in this series, the invisible wall between subjects and crew was down—or had never been put up in the
first place.

"Repeat the Question"

What about asking an interview subject to repeat the question before answering it? Obviously, after my experience with the police captain in
Wilkes-Barre, I'm against it. In documentary it puts a burden on the subject, which is not his or her responsibility. But beyond that, it makes the
behavior seem wrong. People rarely repeat questions before they answer
them, unless they are stalling for time while they think of an answer.

So it's bad verisimilitude.

Solving Problems

Suppose you're shooting on location. Off camera there's a machine
making a continuous noise, loud enough to be heard on the sound track,

but not so loud that it interferes with the voices of your subjects. And it can't be shut off while you're shooting.

For the sake of verisimilitude, you might want to include the machine in a shot, so that the noise is explained and your audience can immediately disregard it. Otherwise, that noise may become a question mark that grows in the minds of the audience until they not only stop concentrating on the scene but also may start to question your skill as a documentarian. And when that happens, you're in deep trouble.

Ambient Sound

Verisimilitude is the reason I record ambient sound on everything I shoot, even obviously silent footage. (Silent footage is a film notion, since video is invariably shot with sound.) Suppose I have a scene of people sitting in a room, talking and drinking coffee. Perhaps the importance of the scene is just to show that they are all together and to provide a visual space in the documentary for some essential narration. I still put a microphone into the scene and record sound.

I may have the narration track to cover the entire scene, but the almost subliminal click of a coffee mug against the table and the low murmur of voices in the background increase the believability of the scene. It becomes much more than a visual. It comes to life. Verisimilitude.

Verisimilitude and Editing

Using verisimilitude in editing can mean trying to get into the heads of your audience to see how a sequence will appear to them. Here's where a knowledge of film conventions, and of human belief systems, can help you. It's not only important to communicate the message that you intend, it is equally important *not* to communicate a message that you *don't* intend. What is selected in editing to be shown to the audience is usually a small segment of a much larger hunk of footage. It is abstracted from the event that was recorded and is edited to suggest as much as possible about all that happened in the event itself.

You were there. Your audience wasn't. As you look at the footage, you might recall everything that happened. But your audience knows nothing about the event except what you select to show them from all the footage and sound available. It, alone, has to communicate to the audience what you consider to be important. And it is not enough that it was shot in a real situation. It has to be presented to your audience with the ring of truth.

That means paying attention to verisimilitude.

29

WORKING ON LOCATION

I've always thought that one of the most intriguing titles for a book or movie was *Two Weeks in Another Town,* written by Irwin Shaw. It holds out the promise of something new and different, and the possibility of adventure.

That's working on location.

Preparation

When you go on location, you have to bring just about everything you'll need with you. Don't expect the people at the location to provide anything more than electricity for your lights. And if there's any doubt about that, you'll need to bring along a generator or arrange for an independent hookup from the electric company.

Carry spares of hard-to-get and easy-to-use-up items, such as fuses, batteries, clips, and clamps. You should have a comprehensive supply of audio and video connectors, cords, and adapters.

Unless you have a makeup artist on the crew, you should always bring along a basic makeup kit—a sewing kit and scissors, too, just in case.

Know where the crew is going to live, where you'll eat your first few meals, and where and how you'll handle lunch.

Have your local transportation arrangements made. I prefer a couple of vehicles, such as a car and an SUV, to one large van. That way the equipment vehicle can stay at the shooting location while your gofer or driver uses the other to run errands, pick up lunch, and so on. At an out-of-town location, give serious thought to hiring a driver/gofer/production assistant who knows the local area.

Time Off While on Location

Theoretically, you and the crew are off work between the end of one day's shooting and the start of the next. In practice, the crew gets this time off while the producer-director has a hundred and one things to do, from looking at the day's footage to setting up additional shooting, to putting together the shooting schedule.

Have a clear understanding with the crew ahead of time about how long the working day will be and what is and isn't included. You should expect them to get breakfast before you start the day's work and dinner after you wrap. But if you've got a split day, running into a night shoot, then work out an agreement as to when you'll be working and when the crew will get meals and rest. And stick to it.

CLIENTS, FRIENDS, AND FAMILY

Shooting on location is hard enough without adding a lot of other problems. If you're going out of town and the location is in or near a city where you have other clients or other business, there may be a temptation to try to schedule business meetings while you are there. If you can do so after the obligation to your documentary is complete, fine. But don't get yourself into the position of trying to rush shooting so you won't keep an important client waiting.

By the same token, if the location is attractive as a place to visit, you may be tempted to bring along family or friends to enjoy it with you. If you do, make it clear that they will be on their own, and that they may not see you from the time you arrive until it's time to go.

You never want to find yourself in the editing room wishing you'd gone ahead and shot one more take or filmed the piece of business you'd had in mind, but gave up because it was getting late and you had someone waiting for you. Remember that the real excitement of going on location is in the work—and the work is very demanding.

Some Other Production Considerations

Here are a few other things to think about as you plan and execute a documentary production on location.

It's Hard Physical Work

Making a documentary can be real work, and you need to be in good physical condition to do it. With a small crew, *everyone* ends up carrying equipment from the car or van to the location setup and back. The technical crew may be used to that, while you may not be. And even if you are not carrying equipment, just spending an eight- or ten- or twelve-hour day on your feet can be draining if your normal activity includes lots of sit-down time. You may be a very active person, but if you spend most of your working day in an office, in meetings, or in an editing room, the physical demands of production can be a radical change for your body.

It's hard to be creative—or even effective—when you're fatigued. You make bad decisions. And you tend to skip things that you'll wish later on that you had done. So work out. Do some aerobics. Run. And get in shape for the work ahead.

Dress for the Job

Wear comfortable clothes. All other things being equal, crew people tend to wear jeans, sneakers, and T-shirts and carry along sweatshirts and jackets to layer on if it gets cold. If you are the producer or director, you may not want to be that casual—and under some circumstances you may not want your crew to be that casual, either—but you shouldn't need to spend a long, busy day in a three-piece suit or heels and hose.

Wear comfortable shoes that you can stand in for a long time.

And don't be stupid. If you'll be outside in the sun, wear sunscreen and a hat. If it's cold, wear a hat, coat, and gloves. During my fourteen years in Hawaii I saw a lot of people come from the mainland to do a shoot, and someone on the crew *always* thought it was a great opportunity to get a tan. Of course Hawaii's tropical sun will burn most people crimson in an hour or two. Your job is to do your job, and that's hard when you're badly sunburned.

Or frostbitten.

Get Enough Rest

Shooting a documentary is physically demanding and stressful. You'll burn up a lot more energy through the intense concentration and long hours required during shooting than you may be used to. You need relaxed meals and a good night's sleep to keep in shape. And you need to take short breaks during the day.

When the adrenaline is pumping from excitement and the location clock seems to be dinging away the hours like a runaway gas pump, the tendency is to try to squeeze in just one more location, one more setup, or one more shot. And sometimes you have to.

But my experience is that you lose time when you're fatigued. And you work more quickly and more effectively when you're rested.

Meals, Snacks, and Drinks

Eat well when you're shooting. Coffee and an English muffin may take you easily to lunchtime at your desk, but when you're doing physical work you need fuel.

Eat breakfast. Keep snacks on hand—fresh fruit and health bars as well as donuts and chips. And keep a cooler filled with drinks. Stock it with bottled water and fruit juice as well as sodas. Make sure there's plenty, and make sure that everyone in the cast and crew knows it's available.

Once you've gotten set up on location, you may not want to stop down and lose momentum by going off to a restaurant for lunch. Consider having a caterer bring meals to the set. Or send your driver or gofer for takeout food. But definitely take a break to eat and have some personal time at mealtimes.

Your Hotel or Motel

The ideal place to spend the night is a ground-floor motel room facing a parking lot where you can back the equipment vehicle right up to the door. There's always a lot of stuff to carry from the vehicle to the room at night and from the room to the vehicle at the start of the next day. You don't want to have to haul it up a flight of outside stairs to a second-floor room or even through the lobby to an elevator and from the elevator to your room.

Be a Good Visitor

Your relationship to the people at the location should always be professional, thoughtful, and cordial. Be careful about such things as where to park, observing no smoking rules, not trampling the flowers, and cleaning up the area after you have finished shooting.

Leave the location the way you found it. If you've borrowed furniture or props from other rooms, put them back where they were when you're finished with them.

Be sure you have adequate liability insurance to cover any possible damage you may do in the location. You never know—lights fall down, furniture gets scarred, shrubbery gets mangled—and you have to be prepared. You also *must* be covered by insurance in case someone gets injured.

Almost certainly you will blow a circuit breaker or a fuse at some point. Plan for it. Locate the fuse box or circuit breaker panel ahead of time. And know how to contact an electrician if things go wrong.

Stay on schedule. And if for some reason you can't, immediately let everyone know that you are running behind and will probably be making changes to the schedule.

BE TRUTHFUL AND BE PUNCTUAL

Be honest with people about when you will arrive at their location, how long you'll stay, and how much disturbance you and your crew will create.

And then be punctual.

If you find that your crew tends to arrive at 7:15 for a seven o'clock call, adjust the schedule to get them there on time.

If you find that the production always seems to be running late and that everyone seems to be waiting for you, make some adjustments. Stop trying to squeeze in one extra phone call—or whatever—and start trying to be the first person ready to go.

WRITE THANK-YOU LETTERS

When you've finished with a location, send a thank-you letter to everyone who helped. Don't just blow in, shoot, and vanish.

Do the same with your crew members when shooting is over. Send them a written acknowledgment saying how much you appreciate their contribution to the success of the production.

I promise you that it will pay off big time—you just never know when.

PART VI

POSTPRODUCTION

Postproduction. The time after production, when editing, looping, scoring . . . mixing, etc., are done. In other words, everything you need to finish the film.

. . .

—*Ralph S. Singleton,* Filmmaker's Dictionary

30

PREPARATION FOR POST

At last your documentary is shot. You have the footage. You like what you've done. And you can't wait to begin shaping your documentary.

But you still have a few things to do to get ready for post.

Protect Your Original Footage

Those of us who started in film lived with the constant fear that something bad would happen to the camera original before we finished. We worried that the plane transporting it from the location to the film lab would crash, that the lab would burn down, or more realistically that the camera original would be damaged in processing. We had the lab make a copy, called a work print, and then store the camera original in its vault until it was needed for printing the finished film.

When I switched from film to video I did much the same thing. I had windowprint dubs made from the original camera tapes, and the original tapes were then stored in my safe deposit box.

How you deal with creating work copies and protecting your original depends on the camera system and the offline editing system you're using. You can go from camera medium—and that could be tape, DVD, hard drive, or possibly, by the time you read this, something new and better—directly to the hard drive of your editing system or to DVD or to some other medium.

With film and analog video, the reason to protect the camera original was quite practical. Both image and sound deteriorated with each copy generation away from the original. The original was the best existing recording, and we wanted to save it to use in creating the finished program.

With digital video, copies are clones of the original, rather than second-, third-, or fourth-generation dubs. So, in theory, a full digital copy should be just as good as the digital original. And that's good. But you still have to make a work copy, so that you have a set of camera originals carefully stored out of harm's way and a copy to work with in whatever medium you prefer.

Get Organized

Your footage is only as good as your ability to find what you need. So get it organized. Have a specific place to keep all of the materials related to this documentary. Label all your film or video, both the original and the copies. Put the background information you've collected in file folders and label them.

Logging Footage

Next you need to find out what you've *really* shot. And that means someone has to look at, and log, all of your footage. That someone is probably you, especially if you are the director or editor or both. You need to know everything you have. At the very least you should be able to say to your editor (or director), "Don't we have a shot of _____ that might go in here?"

Logging is simply making a record of what is on the recording medium as it came from the camera. This will include:

- time code at the start of each shot
- scene and take number, if any
- a brief description of what happens in the shot
- any comments you have about the shot

Figure 30.1 shows a page from the log for one videotape from the U.S.S. *Perry* documentary. Figure 30.2 shows a page from the footage log of a scripted documentary shot in a Las Vegas casino. Note that comments haven't been made on every scene. In the casino documentary, each scene has already been fully described in the script and is identified by scene number, so the description is just a brief reminder. Of course if something had changed from what was called

Figure 30.1. Editing Log (Unscripted)

U.S.S. *Perry*	(Tape 12—Underwater John #2) (16 minutes)	Log Page 25 Tape 12

TIME CODE	DESCRIPTION	COMMENT
00:00:00	BARS	
00:00:30	Moving amidships toward stern abovedeck and stub mast1	Good color
00:00:53	Lifeboat support	
00:01:08	Stern lifeboat davit	
00:01:35	Stern 3-inch gun, moving around the gun	
00:03:01	Stern shot with gun, then hull on its side	
00:03:42	Moving starboard from stern toward bow	
00:03:52	Lt. Cdr. Lonnie Sharp swims over wreck	Clear—good color
00:04:20	Moving starboard—low-angle shot of lifeboat davit near stern	
00:05:06	Lonnie swims into frame amidships	Good color on davits
00:05:37	Moving amidships showing collapsed deck areas and large piping	Most likely is engine room C-102 on charts
00:06:18	Diver swims from amidships to stern with paravane cable visible	
00:07:27	Collapsed bridge superstructure debris on sand visible	
00:07:58	Moving from stern toward amidships, bridge debris on left side	
00:08:12	Schooling fish and wreck	Good color and lighting
00:09:10	Ladder on left. Wardroom view from behind	
00:10:18	Penetration of passage 315, Wardroom 312, and possibly the crew's quarters 307 (or boiler room B-103 since the amidships gun is just outside as we exit???)	
00:11:00	With Lonnie swimming up. I think this is the boiler room area just behind where the *Perry* hit the mine	
00:12:03	Shot looking from deck down through ship with fish in background	Nice composition & color
00:12:15	Amidships port gun, swim toward stern	
00:14:10	Good look at the wreck	

TIME CODE	DESCRIPTION	COMMENT
00:14:46	Approaches cameraman (Ray) hanging on anchor line waiting for us to ascend with him	This is standard procedure when dive time is up
00:15:30	Ray on the line (going up?)	
00:16:13	Long shot of bow area from above	Could be establishing shot.
00:16:16	END OF TAPE	

for in the script, that would be indicated in the description or comments. In this log, comments have been made after the description of the scene.

It doesn't matter how you do the log, just as long as you are consistent and thorough, and the way you do it works for you.

COMPUTER LOGGING

I generally type the log into my computer as I view the footage. However, since I'm not a good typist, I sometimes dictate the log into a tape recorder as I view the footage. Then the log can be typed into the computer later. I may have the footage log typed into a database program, which gives me the ability to sort the shots by scene and take number, by location, or by topic. Then, in addition to a sequential log of shots as they occur on the film or video, I can create custom logs that:

- show the scenes in the order in which they will be edited and identify the best takes by location and time code
- show all the footage shot at a specific location, regardless of what tape or other medium it may be on
- show all the shots dealing with a specific topic or person

The better and more versatile your logs are, the easier it is to find a specific shot when you need it or to find a replacement shot when what you thought was a good idea doesn't work.

There are also computer programs for logging. I haven't used them, but changing technology often gives us greater convenience and ease of use, so you may want to investigate what software is available for logging when you are ready for post.

Figure 30.2. Editing Log (Scripted)

Casino Tape #9

TIME CODE	SCENE	TAKE	DESCRIPTION	COMMENT
09:00:50	10	5	Super Suite; model down stairs	no good
09:01:16	10	6	Super Suite; model down stairs	good
09:01:51	10	7	Super Suite; model down stairs	good
09:02:22	10	8	Super Suite; model down stairs	really good
09:02:52	10	9	Super Suite; model down stairs	the best
09:03:18	38	1	Convention Information booth	
09:04:00	38	2	Conven. Info. booth; tilt down	
09:04:53	38	3	Conven. Info. booth; tilt down	
09:05:12	38	4	Conven. Info. booth; static	
09:05:30	38	5	Conven. Info. booth; tilt down	
09:06:11	38	6	Conven. Info booth; talent walking into picture	
09:06:44	38	7	Conven. Info. booth; talent walking into picture from right	good
09:07:12	38	8	Conven. Info. booth; talent walking into picture from right	good
09:08:15	37	1	Allstate car rental;	
09:08:50	43	1	Smiling desk clerk; girl	
09:09:27	01	1	Glimpse of Genie	
09:09:46	01	2	Glimpse of Genie	
09:10:01	01	3	Glimpse of Genie	
09:10:44	42	1	Genie talks animatedly with several people	
09:11:17	02	1	Handsome male genie	

What Is on the Footage?

When you log your footage, you have to forget what you intended to shoot and look critically at what you've actually recorded. People tend to see what they are looking for, not what they are looking at. But if you consider your footage to be visual evidence and build your documentary as a visual argument, then you will rarely make the mistake of putting in a shot that doesn't belong simply because it's a *visual* that seems to *illustrate* something being said on the sound track.

Narration, Graphics, Animation

If your film is fully scripted, you may decide to record narration before you begin editing so that you'll have it for timing as you edit picture. This is common practice in editing commercials and information videos.

In making a documentary, however, I almost always prefer to record the final narration after the program has been edited. There are two reasons:

- When the pictures are strong, you may be able to get away with less narration than was originally written.
- As you edit, you may find you need a few additional words of narration to cover a change from the script or to explain something not covered by the script.

So my choice is to do a scratch track narration for timing during off-line editing and then record the final narration just before the online.

The same is true of creating graphics or animation. If you are certain of exactly what you will need, there's no reason not to have it made before you start editing, so that you'll have it to use as you put the offline together. Except . . .

. . . you rarely know *exactly* what you will need. So, again, my preference is to see how the footage goes together and then have graphics and animation made to fit.

Doing a Paper Edit

Once you have logged and studied your footage, you may want to organize it in a kind of off-offline or paper edit. Sometimes I'll have the computer print out each good take in the log as a small paragraph as if it were on a Post-it or a 3×5 card. Then I'll move these around on a planning board until they form an organization of the material that seems to make sense.

This gives me something to start with when I go into the editing room.

How Long to Allow for Edit Prep

You need a couple of days just to get organized and get things labeled and put away.

Logging will take three to four times the running time of the footage, longer if someone then has to type it into a computer, and even longer for transcribing interviews.

A paper edit can take as long as you want it to. But the longer you take, the better. John Holt, who wrote several excellent books on learning in young children, said that one thing he found from watching kids was that the good problem solvers spent a lot of time just playing aimlessly with whatever it was they were doing. *A lot of time*. Longer than most teachers thought they should. And even longer than Holt thought they would. But at the end of this long process, they had gotten to know whatever they were working with very well. They knew its shape, how it felt in their hands, what it looked like, which things seemed to be like other things, and which seemed to be different.

And when they had gotten to that point, they were usually able to solve the problem quickly and creatively.

The kids who didn't go through this play phase of becoming familiar with the materials, but went right to trying to solve the problem, usually took longer and sometimes never found a solution.

Editing a documentary is often a lot like putting together a jigsaw puzzle. If you take your time and carefully get all of those odd-shaped pieces to fit together the best way, you'll end up with a beautiful picture.

31

EDITING A DOCUMENTARY

There is no escaping the responsibility for the edited film or video. It is the absolute result of the documentarian's judgment as to what to show and how to show it. Since, in editing, you start with an empty "reel"—which may be a file on a computer hard drive—and fill it with images and sound in sequence, there is nothing in the final version of your documentary that is not put there deliberately.

As a director and photographer you work with potential, a lot of ifs— if the light is right, if it doesn't rain, if you can get the shot, if the child actor can remember her lines, if, if, if.

As an editor you work with concrete reality—the footage and recorded sound that exist after shooting is complete. No matter what you intended when you were filming, you have to edit what you actually recorded.

And that can be a lot of stuff. Shooting ratios for documentaries have increased radically as spontaneous cinema ended reliance on shooting from a script and the use of video allowed overshooting to become an inexpensive addiction. You know going into the editing room that you have far more footage than you can actually use. So a major task in creative editing is to cut away the parts you can't use or simply won't have the running time to use.

The story goes that Michelangelo was asked how he could begin with a huge block of solid stone and end with a masterpiece of sculpture such as his *David*.

"It's simple," he answered. "I just chip away everything that isn't David."

In that sense, creative editing is a lot like sculpture. Robert Flaherty, I've been told, edited *Nanook of the North* by projecting his rushes over and over again, gradually taking out the scenes he decided not to use.

A Look Back at Film Editing

Today, editing a documentary—no matter if it was shot on film or video—is much more likely to be done in a video editing room than on a film editing console. And in some ways that's too bad.

Editing film was handwork. You cut the image away from its home on the camera reel and spliced it to another image on an editing reel. You had to physically match the audio track to the roll of picture it went with and then play it to check on the sync. You actually cut the scenes you were not going to use off the camera reel and stored them on an OUTS reel. And you usually took all the scenes that went together, regardless of what camera reel they had come from, and spliced them together creating a new roll of film, which you would label DRUGSTORE or JENNIFER or whatever.

I think old-fashioned film editing had several benefits.

One was that you had to handle the material a lot to get it synced, logged, and sorted. And you got familiar with it as you went along. Because you moved the outs to a separate reel and never looked at them again, you spent most of your time working with and learning about a smaller set of good footage from which the finished film would be made.

Another was simply that it was called *film* editing, and you tended to think in terms of the *pictures* you would use. Few if any film editors would dream of lining up a long sound track from an interview in the synchronizer and then adding in *visuals* to fill out the picture side.

And because it was a hand skill, and was actually referred to as *cutting* the film, you really understood the idea that in editing, you cut what you needed out of everything that had been recorded to create something new that didn't exist before.

Film editing was risky. You actually cut the stuff you were working with. Each time you made a splice, you sacrificed a frame of picture. So just possibly you looked at the footage an extra time or two before committing to a cut.

Video Editing

If editing film made one cautious and thoughtful, video editing offers unlimited possibilities for play. Because you rerecord rather than physically cut the original images, you have the freedom to try *anything*. You can put two scenes together just to see what happens. You can add in a few frames of this or that and possibly create some magic. And since it is all done on a computer, you can save and store all of the permutations for later reference or use.

Certainly digital editing has speeded up the offline editing process without substantially increasing the cost. And if you do your first cut on your own computer there are no editing room charges. So you can allow more time for playing with the footage without actually increasing the cost of the production.

Why the Emphasis on Play?

Good cuts don't just happen. They are the result of knowing what you've got to work with and then experimenting with the ways it might go together. Video editing gives you a free hand to try anything as you revise and refine the way the footage goes together to tell your story. So play with the footage and hold off on making final decisions until you are really familiar with what you've got. It will make you a better editor. And you will make a better documentary.

Transcript Editing

I have no problem with shooting a lot of interviews as part of the process of recording your documentary. I have no problem with having the interviews transcribed so that the log of the interview footage shows what has actually been said. In fact, I like it.

Interviews are research conducted on camera. You shoot them because you hope that in all the talk, you'll find something really good that you can use in the documentary. If you can pull twenty great seconds out of a thirty-minute interview, it was worth shooting the interview. And if you think in that kind of ratio, maybe you won't be tempted to paste pieces of transcript together to create the structure of your documentary.

A good documentary is carefully constructed from visual evidence.

A transcript is almost never visual evidence.

Working with an Editor

As with every other phase of the production process, you have to face the question of who is going to edit your program. Will you do it yourself? Will you hire an experienced creative editor to organize the film? Or will you direct the edit, working with a technical editor who will push the buttons and make the editing system work?

My friend Paul Galan made his early reputation in documentary as a highly skilled film editor. Then he went on to direct a large number of outstanding network documentaries. He told me, "I have learned never to try to edit a documentary that I directed. It's just not as good."

A creative editor brings a fresh set of eyes to the problems you've been wrestling with for months—or even years. Your editor lives in a world of concrete images. All he or she has to work with is what has been recorded. Good intentions no longer count. Footage is everything. And a good creative editor can help you understand exactly what you have and what you don't have—and how to use it.

Editing the Documentary Yourself

Not all of us can afford the luxury of bringing in an editor to cut our documentaries. The trick is to remain objective and still be creative. When you cut your own, you have to step away from the documentary you've been planning all this time, forget everything that happened while it was being shot, and look at it with a different set of eyes—the eyes of the audience.

Also, I think the best way to learn editing is by editing. I relish the hours I have spent at an editing console (with no one looking over my shoulder) trying different combinations of shots to see what would happen. And I definitely learned as much from the edits that didn't work as I learned from those that did.

Editing from a Script

There are two situations in which you would come to postproduction with a finished script. The first is the historical documentary or reenactment that has been fully scripted in advance. The second is the behavioral documentary or documentary of a unique event—such as *Defenders of Midway* or the *Perry* documentary—in which a scriptwriter has been called in after principal photography to write a script from the footage.

Most other documentary projects arrive in the editing room as a mass of footage loosely connected by an idea. This may be a vision residing solely in the director's head, or it may be expressed in a proposal or treatment.

Editing a Reenactment

The problems and challenges of editing a fully scripted documentary are exactly the same as those in editing any other fully scripted production, from a 30-second commercial to a feature film. The script lays down the organization and structure for the program. The footage has been shot to numbered scenes, and each scene has been covered as well or as poorly as the director and crew could manage.

In this situation I might be tempted to hire a creative editor experienced at cutting from a script. The structure is already set and the creativity is in the margins. But even in this situation, the script is a guide to editing the documentary, not an Eleventh Commandment, carved in stone, to be followed at all costs. Obviously, the more detailed the script, the more likely it is that every word and image has been painstakingly approved, and the less freedom you may have to depart from it. But sometimes the scene doesn't work as written and adjustments must be made in editing. That can happen even if *you* wrote the script.

So be flexible.

EDITING A SPONTANEOUS CINEMA DOCUMENTARY

If you are editing a behavioral documentary or a freewheeling documentary of a unique event, you'll rarely see a complete script before postproduction is finished. Instead you'll have a statement of purpose, an indication of style, a suggestion of the flavor of the documentary, and not much else. It will be up to you—or you and your editor—to organize the material and make it work as a visual argument.

What is most important is to have a clear sense of the documentary's purpose—how it is meant to affect an audience. And then to construct a visual argument which supports that purpose.

Editing the Rough Cut

The editing process can be thought of as a series of approximations, each of which should get you closer to the documentary you are trying to make, the documentary that will communicate to your audience what you want it to.

At first, the approximation is very rough—the scenes are too long, they're in the wrong order, the rhythm is off. But in selecting the shots to edit, you have, at the same time, eliminated a whole lot of footage and are now, presumably, working with the best of what you shot. Moreover, the very fact of having edited the documentary into a rough order lets you see better what may not be working and how to fix it.

In the first edited version everything is tentative. You're experimenting with the way images and sounds can be built up into master scenes, and how the master scenes can go together to make the whole documentary.

WORK ON THE WHOLE DOCUMENTARY

Some people like to do a rough assemblage of the footage in the way they think it probably should go. I think this is most useful for scripted documentaries and may be less helpful in editing a spontaneous cinema documentary.

You don't have to start at the opening and slog on through in sequence to the closing titles. You don't even have to edit everything onto the same reel. Start with a sequence that will be easy and fun to put together and go on from there. Build up a sequence in the way you think it should go. Then set it aside and start another. The important thing is to be thinking about the whole film, from beginning to end, even while you're working on a small part of it.

Structure

Everything I wrote about structure in chapter 18 applies not just to writing but also to editing a documentary.

Selecting Footage

As I view and log the footage, I'm constantly looking for pieces that will fit into various parts of the structure. What will make a good opening?

What will make a good ending? What will make an interesting back-ground for opening and closing titles? What should be the first evidence to be presented? What would happen if I ran a piece of this interview right after the mayor's speech? And so on.

At the same time, I try to eliminate the scenes that are no good for one reason or another—scenes that are out of focus, have bad sound, accidentally include people who do not want to be in the documentary, and so forth—and scenes in which nothing of interest happens, or which are otherwise inappropriate.

The Importance of a Good Opening

I'm convinced that what happens in the first few minutes after the initial fade in has an immense bearing on the audience's reaction to the docu-mentary. You've got everything going for you before the program starts. The audience expects the experience they're about to have to be worth-while, or they wouldn't be there. Even captive audiences assume there must be some value, or they wouldn't have been *captured* to look at the production. They assume that the documentary they are about to see is professionally and competently made, and that the documentarian is in control of the material.

Respect the Audience

I have never subscribed to the belief that it is a documentarian's re-sponsibility to do all the work for your audience. You have no business confusing them, of course, but you shouldn't have to do all their think-ing for them. You do, however, have the responsibility to set them on the right track at the start. That's when you teach the audience how to look at your film.

Audiences have come to expect a unity of style and form, an internal logic, which is foreshadowed by the way the documentary opens. And they'll pay close attention to those first couple of minutes as a guide to whether or not there is anything there that is of interest to them. If they see any evidence of lack of control, poor planning, technical problems, inaccurate information, or a dull approach, they're likely to decide their time will be better spent trying to calculate all the prime numbers be-tween one and five hundred.

Where to Start

Don't get locked into thinking that because you filmed in a certain order, or because the events to be shown occurred with a certain chronology, you must present the information in that same order. Starting in the midst of things was a good technique when Spenser wrote *The Faerie Queene,* and it's still a good technique today.

You must first catch the audience's attention and then capture their interest. So ask a question, present opposing points of view, show a problem, or make a statement that goes against common sense—but one that you can back up with documentation later on. Which of these you choose will depend on the rest of the documentary, because the opening, in addition to provoking interest, must be consistent with the style and content of what is to follow.

Edit the Opening Last

I think it's a good rule to edit the opening only after the rest of the documentary has been cut. There are at least two good reasons for this. The first is that the genesis of many films is an imagined opening scene that the filmmaker loves and has planned in meticulous detail. Without the concept of that opening scene, the rest of the film might never have been made. But that opening may no longer have anything to do with the documentary as it has evolved, and should be scrapped. Unfortunately, it has squatter's rights. And there it squats—right at the opening.

The second reason is more formal and has to do with the style, pace, and feel of the documentary. These change as the program goes through the editing process. And an opening scene edited before the style is set may reflect a film that never was, rather than the documentary that is to follow.

Problem Openings

If you want to lose your audience right at the start, here are some ways to do it:

Technically Atrocious

The image is out of focus, the camera shakes, the color is weird, or the sound is impossible to understand. And if this is the best the director could find for the all-important opening scene, the rest of the documentary is likely to be a disaster area.

The Man at the Desk

This used to be a standard opening for nonfiction films. They'd start with some sort of certifiable expert telling you about the documentary that was to follow. You're there to watch a movie, but, instead, he's going to tell you about it, first. I have actually seen programs where the man at the desk doesn't just introduce the film, but draws conclusions for you about a film you have not yet seen.

Panning the Gargoyles

There's music. And there are these images that seem to go on forever—scenery, architecture, close-ups of statue parts—and it is all really rather attractively done. But there's no information. The documentary is supposed to deal with some kind of interesting problem or event. But if it can't get started, how is it ever going to come to grips with anything of substance? Maybe some documentarians feel that if they start with the actual topic, they're being too obvious.

My friend Andy Edwards shot his first documentary in Saudi Arabia—a beautiful video called *Falcons of Arabia*. But for some reason he chose not to show us an actual falcon until four and a half minutes into the program. And the beautiful shot of a falcon flying, which I think should have been the opening, doesn't occur until forty-one minutes into the show. When I asked him about it, he said, "I know. I wouldn't do that now."

Another reason for waiting to edit the opening until the rest of the film is set.

Dumping Exposition

This opening is like the public speaker who stated, "Before I begin my speech, I'd like to say something." There's a whole lot of stuff the documentarian, or someone, thinks you have to know before you can watch the documentary. So they dump it all at the front and pretend the documentary hasn't really started yet. Almost always this sort of thing is not needed. Raise an issue and explore it with good visual evidence, and the audience will stay with you right to the end.

False Starts

It's a human failing. Very likely we all do it. We start the documentary, and then after awhile we start again, and sometimes we start a third time. There's nothing wrong with doing that while the film is taking shape in editing. The fatal flaw is failing to make a decision about which start you like best, so you can drop the others.

Titles with Irrelevant Music

When music is used—with head and tail titles, montage sequences, and so on—it should be appropriate. Better to use musical wallpaper from the stock library, which nobody will notice, than a highly distinctive but totally wrong theme. It's a matter of taste, I'll admit. But when the documentarian and I differ on taste at the opening titles, we're going to have a hard time getting together later on.

Columbus Discovered America!—or, Breathlessly Stating the Obvious

Every manual on effective communication suggests you start with what the audience already knows and build on it. But if you try to play it safe, to be sure you've included something familiar for every member of the audience, you're likely to lose more souls to boredom than you'll save with misplaced relevance.

A film about hurricanes, for instance, began with a scene of Native Americans looking out to sea at fifteenth-century sailing ships, while narration told the audience that when Columbus discovered America, the natives in the Caribbean worshiped the wind god Hudda-kahn. Using the short definition of an opening as the point before which nothing needs to be shown, you can ask, "Do I really have to show this to the audience? Will it be missed if I leave it out?" While it was nice to know the origin of the word *hurricane*, this was not the sort of information that would propel an audience eagerly into the topic.

Middles

The middle is where you present the visual evidence you have recorded, in an organized way that builds the visual argument of your documentary. It is also where you consider opposing evidence and arguments.

Opposing Points of View

If there is an opposing view, it can't be ignored. For instance, *Flock of Dodos,* directed by Randy Olson, an evolutionary ecologist turned documentary filmmaker, is an amusing and highly informative film that explores the campaign by proponents of intelligent design to undermine the theory of evolution as it has evolved over the hundred and fifty years since Charles Darwin wrote *Origin of Species.* In the hands of a docugandist, this would be an attack film, in which all the good people and all the truth are on one side of the argument, while the people on the other side are not only wrong, but *bad.*

Olson is clearly an evolutionist and believes intelligent design is simply creationism dressed up in new clothes to try to appear more scientific to people who don't understand science. Still, in *Flock of Dodos* he treats the other side with the greatest respect, allowing them to present their arguments for intelligent design. One of these arguments is that evolutionists have offered a set of drawings known as "Haekel's Embryos," made in 1874 (fifteen years after Darwin published *Origin of Species*) as evidence for evolutionary development. In Haekel's drawings all embryos start out more or less the same and then grow into quite different animals from frogs to humans.

It turns out these drawings are inaccurate, and embryologists have known they were inaccurate for many years. But John Calvert, director of the Intelligent Design Network, suggests to Olson that Haekel's Embryos are still being taught in biology classes. In a revealing sequence we see Olson and Calvert going through contemporary college biology texts searching for, and failing to find, any reference to Haekel.

The point is made with visual evidence, not rhetoric: The Haekel argument does not hold up. There is never an attack. In fact, Olson says he likes John Calvert very much and finds many points of similarity in their life stories.

Incidentally, the "dodos" in the title seem to be the scientists who have all the knowledge and evidence on their side, but are unable or unwilling to mount a coherent argument against the intelligent design thesis.

Middle Structure

You can go back to chapter 18 on structure and review the section on "The Middle: Presentation of Evidence." The elements for constructing the middle of your documentary are the same whether they are being written into a script or built up shot by shot in editing.

You won't necessarily know the proper order of presentation of this material until you've put the scenes together and looked at them. Quite often, moving a scene to a different place—or sometimes eliminating it—will solve problems of awkwardness and understanding.

BALANCE IN EDITING

Sometimes you have to strike a balance between what actually happened when you were shooting and the way it appears in the edited version of your documentary. I ran into this problem in my first documentary, *The Trouble with Adults Is . . .* , about a group of white high school and college students involved in a summer project on white racism. They were loosely affiliated with a Protestant church group, and in their zeal and immaturity they had alienated the members of a suburban church. This was the church where I filmed the lady with the white gloves (chapter 22).

The climax of the documentary was a confrontation between the kids and the church members at a meeting of the congregation. This erupted into a free-for-all when one of the young people, a seminary student, began reading aloud to the congregation a passage from Claude Brown's *Manchild in the Promised Land* that included the word *fuck*. The church had not permitted us to film the meeting. We did have an audiotape of what happened at the church, and an eleven-minute sequence we had filmed back at the project headquarters immediately after the meeting broke up.

We turned on the camera as the kids stormed into the house very much like combat pilots entering a debriefing room after a mission. They were laughing and talking, and their speech was sprinkled with meaningless profanity and an occasional obscenity. After a couple of minutes, they calmed down and described how they had been threatened, yelled at, and in some cases physically thrown out of the meeting room at the church.

In the rough cut, I left most of this sequence just as it had been filmed. But when I began to show it for comments, I noticed a strange thing. The people who saw it not only missed the point of the scene— my intended point, anyway—but they described it in terms that had very little to do with what happened on the screen. They talked about "a bunch of wiseass kids with no manners, just trying to get a rise out of people." And about "somebody jumping up and yelling an obscenity in church."

It took me almost a month to discover that the edited version was way out of balance with the event it was intended to show. The occasional rough language of the kids as they entered the house was so upsetting to some viewers that they missed the explanation in words—and in pictures taken in the parking lot of the church before the meeting—of how and why this all came about. Quite literally, the viewers went deaf and blind for about two minutes. And just about the time they got their senses back, they heard the young seminarian reading *that word*, and they went off again. Essentially, they weren't *seeing* my documentary.

I wanted the sense of turmoil that the opening of that sequence provided, so I couldn't just eliminate it and start with the calm, rational explanation that followed. The solution I found was to balance the scene according to the expectations and conventions of the intended audience, so that the use of the word *fuck*, when it appeared, would become data, and not just a shocking experience.

I shortened the introductory scene, which trimmed the rough language to two *hell*s and a *damn*. Suddenly, the people I showed it to started talking about what was there, not about some other documentary that existed only in their heads.

Not all of them liked it. But they now understood that sequence as the crucial event of the documentary, against which everything else that happened should be evaluated. If they disliked the kids it was because they found them unlikable throughout the documentary, not because of shock at their language in one scene. And many viewers now found a sympathy for the students' idealism, even though they may have questioned their judgment.

And that's the most I could hope for—a fair presentation of a controversial subject.

The Ending

Build to a climax, resolve the conflict, and get off the stage. Some documentarians have a hard time saying good-bye. They end the film, then they end it again, and sometimes again, and again, and again. Pick your best closing scene, build up to it, show it, and fade out.

Crossing the Line and Other "Rules" of Editing

Like every other aspect of film and video production, editing has become saddled with a list of rules that has grown longer and longer over the hundred-plus years since the invention of motion pictures. One is the rule against crossing the line, which comes from the idea that in order for the audience to understand what they are looking at, the camera should never cross an imaginary line running through the people or event being shown. There are lots of others.

I've never learned them, and I suggest you don't, either. There are a number of principles of good communication that should be followed in editing a documentary. But as for technical rules of editing, there are just two questions you need to answer:

- Can you see what's happening?
- Does it make sense?

Writing Narration as You Edit

Documentary narration, if used at all, should be written as late in the production process as possible. Give the visual evidence a chance to state the case before you feel you need to have a narrator explain anything. And then use narration only to explain whatever the audience needs to know that they can't get from viewing the images.

I try not to write any narration until the fine cut. That's the point at which you can see what information is actually missing or what needs to be explained. Until then make notes as to what narration might be required, but without actually writing the words to be said. Hold off on narration as long as you can. And then write as little as possible.

Seven Sins of Editing

These are some things that can turn your documentary from a fascinating exploration of an important topic into something else entirely.

1. The Documentary Is Too Long

Most documentaries are too long. When you're convinced that your documentary is absolutely and finally completed, go back over it and try to cut it by 10 percent. You'll be amazed at what happens.

2. Relying on Sound to Carry Meaning

Good sound is always a blessing, but a documentary should be a visual experience. Edit the documentary to *show* an audience what you mean, and you'll find there's a lot less you have to tell.

3. Using Inappropriate Images

The use of inappropriate images is often the result of relying on telling instead of showing. Under inappropriate images I'd include B-roll that illustrates the wrong thing, most visual wallpaper, shaky-cam shots, and going from color to black and white without a clear reason for doing so.

4. Repeating the Same Shot for No Reason

Maybe you like the look of it, or maybe you just have to have something to cover a sound edit, but repetition of a shot tells the audience that what they are seeing is important. When it isn't, they wonder what you're up to.

5. False Structure

False structure is putting shots together because they are similar visually but have no good communication reason to be next to each other.

6. Mickey Mousing the Music

You've got a piece of music with a good beat to it, and you think, "I've got a great idea. I'll cut each shot on the downbeat."

Don't.

Why? Because it's cinematically trite, and because it lets the music control the presentation of images, rather than letting the images speak for themselves.

7. Talking Heads

It's so easy to get lots of pictures of the faces of people talking. The problem is when to use them. Occasionally, the most interesting thing you could show your audience is the face of the speaker. Usually it isn't.

Editing the Fine Cut

After the rough cut comes the fine cut, where the documentary is edited to the desired length, awkward cuts are polished, and sequences are trimmed to move faster—or, occasionally, extended to show more.

If time permits, it's a good idea to put the documentary away for a few days. This gives you time to get back your objectivity. It may be that a bothersome scene is bothersome because it actually doesn't belong in the documentary, even though it has been there since the first rough cut. Eliminating the scene entirely or substituting something different may solve the problem for you.

Or it may be that when you show the current edited version, your viewers are missing the point to an important scene, because something in a previous scene is leading them off in the wrong direction.

I cut an opening sequence for *These People,* a documentary about mental health problems, which used a long, slow pan across the empty beds of a crowded ward in a mental institution, ending with one lone mental patient slumped in the shadow. The narrator explained that research showed most patients preferred to be treated in their community rather than in an institution.

This was the point to the documentary, and it was the best opening I've ever done. The scene was so dramatic that everyone who saw it was moved by it. But everything that followed—I mean all the rest of the documentary—seemed an anticlimax.

The problem was that, structurally, that scene was an ending. It completed the visual argument for the audience. So I pulled it out of the opening and used it as the last shot in the film, where it worked beautifully.

Getting Feedback

Show the edited documentary to people with as little comment as possible and try to gauge their reaction to it in terms of the way your intended audience will respond. Seeing the edited version with an audience—even an audience of just one other person—will also help you to see it with fresh eyes.

People asked to look at a cut of a documentary unconsciously cast themselves in the role of experts and feel they have not discharged their obligation to you unless they *help* you. You can't take their comments literally, as instructions on how to change and improve your documentary, but you can learn from them.

I use a four-step method of analyzing audience reaction from the comments people make:

1. Viewer says, "I don't like it" or "I don't understand it." Message: She doesn't like it or doesn't understand it. There's a lot of work left to do.
2. Viewer talks about technical problems, fuzzy sound, abrupt cuts, color, composition, and so on. Message: The documentary doesn't hold interest. He had time to look for technical flaws.
3. Viewer talks about how well made the documentary is and says, "You've done a really good job." Message: The documentary is OK, but not finished. It doesn't move the audience.
4. Viewer doesn't talk about the documentary, but talks about matters related to the problem it explored. She says, "I know a person like that man in the film. He's really hard to get along with." Message: The documentary is getting the desired reaction. It is essentially finished.

It may be a little hard on your ego, but the highest praise is no praise at all. When the viewer ignores all your hard work and starts a discussion where the documentary leaves off, you're communicating.

Don't Expect to Be Loved

One final word of warning. If the documentary deals honestly with a controversial subject, don't expect everyone to like it. In fact, you can expect negative comments from people on all sides of the question—some complaining that the documentary goes too far, others complaining that it doesn't go far enough.

When that happens, you can take it as evidence that you've done an honest job of organizing the material to communicate with an audience.

32

FINISHING THE PRODUCTION

When the reaction to the edited version of your documentary indicates that you've accomplished your goals, it's time to finish up and send your program out into the world.

At this point, your documentary exists either in a film fine cut or a video offline, edited to final length and content. In either case, there still may be some elements to be added.

- titles, both head and tail
- graphics or animation sequences
- photographic or video special effects
- final versions of stock footage or stock photos
- final narration
- sound effects where needed
- final music
- mixed or sweetened sound
- sweetened video if required

Approval Showing

If you have a sponsor, underwriter, or distributor with the right to approve the documentary, this is the point at which you need to hold a formal approval showing to get the money people to sign off on the documentary for content and editing. Even if there are no money people, it's a good idea to hold a formal approval showing for yourself and your colleagues. You are about to go into the last, expensive stage of postproduction, and any changes that have to be made beyond this point could be costly.

Check for Accuracy

You need to be certain that what you have said and what you have shown is accurate:

- Do you have the correct spelling of people's names?
- Do you have their correct titles?
- In editing, have you cut out any explanations or qualifying statements, thereby changing meaning?
- Have you added anything that might change meaning or give the wrong impression?
- Is the narration correctly written and properly recorded?

It's good to have someone who has not been involved in the day-to-day production look at the cut. By this time, you know what you meant to do and assume you have done it. A new viewer may raise questions you thought were already answered.

Final Elements

Now you need to complete all the elements that go into your documentary, so that you will have them to finish the production.

FINAL SOUND

Up to now you may have been getting by on a scratch track narration read by someone on the crew. Now is the time to bring in the good narrator and record a final narration track.

The same with music. Once you have frozen the fine cut or final offline, your music director or composer will have the exact picture and timing to work from.

SOUND SWEETENING

Once you have frozen the offline, you can remix the sound in a sweetening session. This lets you bring in final narration and music, of course, but it also lets you clean up location sound to get rid of unwanted noises. And it lets you add wild sound or sound effects as they are needed and can honestly be included. The final mixed track can go directly to the online as a layback track so that you don't have to spend time rerecording and mixing the sound again in online.

STOCK FOOTAGE AND STILLS

For editing, you may have been getting by with a low-quality dub of whatever stock footage you are using. Now you'll order it in production quality.

The stock library may have given you photocopies of the stills you thought you might use for editing. Now that you know exactly which stills you are going to use, you can order production copies of these.

GRAPHICS AND ANIMATION

Do you have any special graphics planned or computer animation, such as a map with a moving line showing the route that was taken? If so, you have probably already completed these in the last stages of offline editing. In any event, you need the final version for the online.

The Video Online

Whether you do a formal online edit will depend on how you have edited the offline and how you will be distributing your documentary. If you've cut the offline at your desktop computer, or with a bare bones editing system, you'll need to have an online session. If you are preparing the documentary for broadcast, you will probably need to create a finished video master in an online editing suite. On the other hand, if you are working with fairly sophisticated editing equipment already, creating a final video master may only require loading the mastering medium you'll be using into the editing system and pushing a button.

Let's assume you'll be finishing the film in a formal online session.

BE PREPARED

Go into the online with everything you need, properly identified and in a form in which it can be used:

- all your camera footage
- any work footage that may have been created
- whatever stock footage you've ordered

- any stills that you are using, transferred to video using a good camera
- the final script
- all the finished sound

Working from an Edit Decision List

From your final offline, you should have an edit decision list (EDL) that describes the way the documentary goes together. It tells the source for each image and each bit of sound used in the offline. It will not, of course, include images or sounds to be added during the online or during an audio or video sweetening session. The EDL is computer-generated and can be moved electronically or by disk from the offline computer to the online computer.

A digital editing system will assemble the online picture and sound from your source material using the edit decision list. You'll have to add in anything that was not included in the offline, such as superimposed titles from a character generator. And you may have to remake transitions such as dissolves and wipes.

Video Sweetening

Following the online session, you still may want to do some video sweetening. At the most basic level, video sweetening is simply one last pass of the edited master, tweaking the lighting, color, and balance of each of the scenes and the way the scenes flow together. One of the uses of video sweetening is to give footage from several different sources a uniform look, so that there won't be a huge change in the look of the footage from shot to shot. It can also sometimes improve the resolution and sharpness of images that were shot a little soft.

Video sweetening will usually be done after the online, because it's better to work with the edited version, and then color correct all the scenes to blend together. If there is going to be a lot of layering in editing, however, or if the video has come from many sources, it's probably best to make a digital reel of selected takes and color correct those prior to online editing. You should discuss video sweetening with the people at your online editing facility well ahead of doing the online.

And Then Your Documentary Is Done

You'll walk out of the online session—or video sweetening session if you do one—with a finished video master, which is your documentary in all its glory. Done. Finished. Ready for distribution.

Finishing on Film

Most documentaries these days will be finished on video, regardless of how they were shot.

If you have shot on film and intend to finish on film, you are probably thoroughly familiar with the process, which I've reviewed briefly in chapter 5.

Going to Distribution

If you have a sponsor, underwriter, or distributor involved with your documentary, hold a second formal approval showing and get them to sign off on the finished work before it goes into distribution.

Protect Your Master

Once you have a perfect master—either edited film original or digital video—make a protection master from which to make copies. From this point on, you want to handle the camera original as little as possible. So print an internegative of your film or clone dubbing masters of your video. Let the protection master take the wear and tear of making copies. And if something happens to it, take the original out of the vault, make a new protection master, and return the original to safekeeping.

Enjoy It—and Move On

You have been living with this project for months or years, and now, incredibly, it's finished. Enjoy everything that goes with it. The screenings for friends, colleagues, and backers. Entry in film festivals. All the hoopla of theatrical release if that's the direction you are going.

Stand for the applause.

Give the interviews.

And then get back to work.

PART VII

FINAL THOUGHTS

There are no secrets to success. It is the result of
preparation, hard work, and learning from failure.

• • •

—*Colin Powell*

33

GETTING THERE

This final chapter is a response to many e-mails from readers, which in one way or another have asked how to get started in documentary and, by implication, how to do well in the field.

This is a great time to make documentaries. All of the barriers that kept people out of the field have been removed, except for talent and hard work.

Talent: You have to have an interesting idea for a documentary, and you have to execute it skillfully.

Hard work: As I wrote in chapter 1, it looks so easy, but it's not. On the other hand, it can be a lot of fun. Just don't make the mistake of thinking that because making documentaries has now become more accessible, it has also suddenly become easy.

The Low-Budget Documentary

It used to cost a lot of money to make a documentary. Today, technology has made it possible to shoot and edit a low-budget documentary for little more than pocket change. Certainly, if you want to go big time and shoot on location in high-definition video, you still need expensive equipment and a thoroughly professional crew. But if you are willing to start small, shoot with a good but relatively inexpensive camera, and edit on your computer, you can afford to make a first documentary. The technology is not terribly difficult to learn. The cost is manageable.

If you have a specialized knowledge about some topic or an intense interest in exploring and documenting a subject, there is nothing standing in your way other than your own willingness to start. And, I should add, your willingness to continue after you have made a few mistakes. Be comforted by the fact that we have all gone through such a learning process. Throughout this book I've shared some of my learning experiences with you.

There is, of course, no guarantee that your documentary will make any money for you, but there never is. So go. Do. Enjoy.

Work at What You Want to Do

Start with either the documentary process or the documentary topic that you want to become good at, and then keep at it until you are.

Start Where You Are, Do What You Can

If you want to make spontaneous cinema documentaries, just start. Take an idea that you can do close to home and document it. It's a lot easier to do a first documentary about your kid brother's Pop Warner football team, obsessive lawn care in your community, people at the pool, dogs vs. cats, or the people who shop at 7-Eleven, than about brothels in Calcutta, penguins in Antarctica, or life aboard a submarine at sea. The critical factor in almost all documentaries is how the idea is presented on the screen—not the idea itself. A well-executed short film about lawn wars might spark far more interest than a heavy-handed presentation about some vital issue of our time. Show that you know what to do with whatever you have to work with, and you'll find opportunities to move up in class.

Expect that it will take making a couple of documentaries to get to the point where most of the time you will feel confident that you know what you are doing. You have to work past that process of trial and error. Just remember, for the learning process to work, you have to care about those first documentaries and want them to be good. And they can be. The point to a learning process is that you correct the mistakes you've made, and learn from them, so you'll be less likely to make them next time.

The finished production will stand as proof that you not only know how to make this type of documentary, but have stuck it out and completed it. That's a big plus when you're trying to raise money for your next project or trying to get a job with a producer who does the sorts of documentaries you'd like to make.

Get Close to Success

If you want to make documentaries for PBS, then get as close to people making them as you can. There's a lot more to getting a film on the air than just a neat idea and good videography. The competition is fierce, the process may often take a considerable amount of time, and there may well be lots of wrong ways to present a project and few right ways. The people who work for people who make documentaries for PBS learn these things.

The same is true for the History Channel, Discovery Networks, National Geographic, or any of the other cable outlets. It is far, far easier to present a documentary idea to someone at a network who already knows you than to get even a look-in from someone who has never heard of you.

How do you find such employment? Hardly ever by offering to sweep the floors or do any job at all, just so you can learn. People who run production companies, TV stations, and networks are often selfishly fixated on the needs of their organizations. They want to hire people who will contribute to the organization rather than people who want the organization to make a charity contribution to their own career plans.

So you need to figure out what you have to offer. If you lack production skills, you might have talents to offer on the business side, such as bookkeeping or selling, that could get you in the door. Or you may need to take some production courses or make a first documentary on your own before you'll be ready to look for a position close to power.

The same goes for theatrical documentaries. Try to find someone who is doing them and serve an apprenticeship. If, however, what you actually want to do is make feature films, why spend time doing documentaries? Take the low-budget equipment, get a script, find some actors, shoot a feature (or a short), and leave documentaries to those who are obsessed with truth.

You'll find a compilation of useful organizations and associations in appendix 2 that may help you identify potential employers doing the kind of work you are interested in.

What Should You Study?

What interests you? If you are headed to college, are in college now, or are thinking about taking some college courses, you may be wondering where to go and what to study. I regularly get e-mails from readers asking me to recommend a school or a film course for them. All I can tell you is to look for courses offering real, hands-on experience with up-to-date equipment. And talk with former students who have completed the course and are working in the industry. Get their take on how well they feel the course prepared them to (1) get a job; and (2) do the job.

The truth is, the technology of filmmaking at the documentary level is not that difficult to learn, unless your goal is mastery of the technology so you can work as a technical person. I strongly believe that the best preparation for a would-be documentarian is to master one or more academic subjects—history, economics, science—rather than to concentrate on mastering the tools of the trade. In the world of today's documentaries, you constantly will be presented with various forms of evidence, including statements from experts, supporting a specific position. How are you to know if the evidence is any good if all of your training has been about camera angles and digital editing?

Take a few courses to learn the production process from concept to completion, but become an expert on something you want to make films about.

Hard Science

There are not nearly enough filmmakers who actually understand a scientific discipline such as physics, biology, or chemistry. We live in a world of technology that depends on these sciences, and yet we lack communicators who understand them sufficiently to explain to the general public in plain language what current developments in these fields actually mean. Or even what the language of science is actually about. The absolute master at defogging science for a lay audience is Sharon Begley, who as I write this is science editor for *The Wall Street Journal*. Look up some of her articles or her books to see what can be done just with words, remembering that, as a documentarian, you will have visual evidence in addition to words.

Statistics

Learn some statistics. Most people have no idea how to read a statistical report or what statistics—even those that seem very clear—actually mean. If you make documentaries, advocates for various positions are going to wave statistics at you as proof of the validity of their point of view. But as Bjorn Lomborg points out in *The Skeptical Environmentalist: Measuring the Real State of the World,* advocates often use short-term results that tend to confirm their view of things, rather than statistics covering a longer term that might tend to refute their position.

The world has unquestionably grown warmer over the past century than it was at the end of the 300-year-long "little ice age" in 1850. But is it significantly warmer than it has been at various times in the past? Or are both "little ice ages" and periods of "global warming" part of the natural order of things? Can you tell from the data that are presented? Do you know how to test for statistical significance? Are you clear about the difference between models and observations?

Economics

If I were entering college today—but with the knowledge I've gained from a lifetime of reading, writing, and making films—I'd seriously consider minoring in economics. We are way short of people who really understand economic principles. And you're kidding yourself if you think you can do social documentaries in the twenty-first century without correctly accounting for the underlying economic issues.

A good place to start is Thomas Sowell's *Basic Economics.* He actually explains how things work. For enjoyment, take a look at *Freakonomics: A Rogue Economist Explores the Hidden Side of Everything* by Steven D. Levitt and Stephen J. Dubner. It's not only an eye-opener, it offers a technique for finding the unexpected truth underlying common phenomena. For a good read that offers a glimpse of how economists sometimes tackle problems, read Pietra Rivoli's *The Travels of a T-Shirt in the Global Economy.*

History

Most Americans know far less of their own history than they think they do, and very little of the history of the rest of the world. For at least the last two decades, the United States has been doing more business with Asia than with Europe, and yet few Americans have any idea of the complex and fascinating history of the many nations that make up that vast continent.

Africa, the Middle East? The level of ignorance about them is even higher.

Even America's European heritage remains unexplored territory for many college students and college graduates.

There is a world of opportunity waiting for the filmmaker with the knowledge to turn the truth about historical events into great documentary storytelling.

Other Areas

Anthropology and sociology have long been the source of powerful documentary films. Study in these areas provides an entry into the discipline and methodology that separate serious documentary filmmaking from partisan fluff.

The arts are a fertile field for the documentarian who can bring more understanding to painting, sculpture, music, or dance than just lighting and focal lengths. If your knowledge of any form of art goes beyond the surface presentation, so that you can help an audience understand how a specific body of work came about, you can make a serious contribution.

There are countless other areas in which gaining a certain amount of expertise can help you to make a better documentary. Here are a few to stimulate your thinking:

- *The professions.* Medicine, law, architecture, and theology are all fertile areas for a well-informed documentarian.
- *The military.* When I was in college, every family had someone who had served or was serving in the armed forces and who brought home stories about military life. Today, the military is an unknown world to most Americans. If all you know about the armed forces comes from movies, even highly acclaimed movies such as *Saving Private Ryan,* you don't know anything about the military.
- *Education and learning.* More than sixty years ago, writing about the state of education research, the French psychologist and learning theorist Jean Piaget said that we do not even know if the ability to spell is genetic or the result of learning. And today, we still don't know.

  During a period in which we have made astonishing advances in medicine and science; developed the personal computer, the

Internet, and the cell phone to change the way in which we think, work, and communicate; and, oh yes, put some people on the moon; about the best one can say about public education in America is that it has stood still. That's as if U.S. airlines were still flying the Douglas DC-7. Back in the '50s it was the best propeller-driven airliner ever built. But it carried just 110 passengers and had a cruising speed of about 350 miles per hour. Pretty good back then. But today?

- *Government*. Almost all reporting about government, regardless of whether by journalists or documentarians, is about politics, not governance. We hear how this bill or that policy will affect the chance for reelection of some person or party, but rarely do we get any cogent analysis of how it will affect the lives of ordinary people.
- *Aging*. Americans as a people are growing older and living longer. And there is very little research to tell us what that actually means. This is a frontier area.

FOLLOW YOUR INSTINCTS

My point is not to tell you what to study, but to suggest that a concentration on film technique is probably not the best career preparation for a documentarian.

I suspect that most people don't start out to be documentary filmmakers. They start out wanting to explore or expose or recount something they care passionately about. And they want to do it as a film.

What do *you* care about?

Go there.

Good luck with your project.

FEEDBACK

Throughout the book I've mentioned receiving e-mails from readers of the first edition. I value reader feedback. And I am always glad to answer specific questions about the material covered in the book. So far I've been able to reply to all the e-mails I've received. But you should be aware that I don't make recommendations about equipment or funding your documentary.

You can reach me by e-mail at:

writehampe@makingdocumentaryfilms.com

I also have a website devoted to this book. You'll find it at:

www.makingdocumentaryfilms.com

You may also be interested in my writer's website, located at:

www.barryhampe.com

USEFUL ORGANIZATIONS AND WEBSITES

International Documentary Association
This is where a lot of documentary people hang out, with benefits of membership too numerous to list here. If you're serious about making documentaries, you should become a member. Student memberships available. Check it out at:

http://www.documentary.org

Media Communications Association International
What used to be ITVA (the International Television Association) morphed into MCA-I several years ago. Local chapters include the professional production people in your area. Student and local memberships available. On the Web at:

http://www.mca-i.org

Volunteer Lawyers for the Arts
When you have a legal question related to production of your documentary, you may want to turn to the local chapter of Volunteer Lawyers for the Arts nearest you. A listing of chapters by state is posted on the website of the National Association of Independent Artists at:

http://www.naia-artists.org/resources/lawyers.htm

The Association for Women in Communications
A professional organization that champions the advancement of women across all communications disciplines by recognizing excellence, promoting

leadership, and positioning its members at the forefront of the evolving communications era. Find more information at:

http://www.womcom.org

Women in Film and Television

A global network dedicated to advancing professional development and achievement for women working in all areas of film, video, and other screen-based media. WIFTI does not offer individual memberships, but individuals may join local chapters, which are listed at the website:

http://www.wifti.org

National Archives: Motion Picture Films and Sound and Video Recordings

The place to start your search for stock footage, still pictures, and sound:

http://www.archives.gov/research/formats/film-sound-video.html

DEFENDERS AND DEBUNKERS

TruthOrFiction.com

This is the first place to go to check on e-rumors and gotcha stories:

http://TruthOrFiction.com

JunkScience.com

When you hear the phrase, "Scientists agree that . . ." take a look here to find out if scientists really do agree, or if some partisan organization is exaggerating to catch your interest:

http://junkscience.com

Foundation for Individual Rights in Education (FIRE)

The mission of FIRE is to defend and sustain individual rights at America's colleges and universities. These rights include freedom of speech, legal equality, due process, religious liberty, and sanctity of conscience—the essential qualities of individual liberty and dignity. FIRE's core mission is to protect the unprotected and to educate the public and communities of concerned Americans about the threats to these rights on our campuses and about the means to preserve them. Learn more at:

http://www.thefire.org

The World's Smallest Political Quiz
Take the test at:

> http://www.theadvocates.org/

Websites You Probably Know

Amazon.com
One-stop shopping for books, DVDs, and films, both new and used. Go to:

> http://www.amazon.com

Internet Movie Database
If it happened on film or TV, it's probably listed here. Offers a professional membership (IMDbPro) with access to representation listings for over 65,000 people, including actors, directors, and producers, as well as contact details for over 10,000 companies in the entertainment industry. Take a look at:

> http://www.imdb.com

Google
The Internet search engine almost everyone uses:

> http://www.google.com

Ask.com
The other Internet search engine people are using:

> http://www.ask.com

YouTube
As I write this YouTube has become important enough that Google has bought it for $1.65 billion. A source of streaming video and a place to post independent films, including documentaries. As you read this, you probably know more about YouTube than I do. Go to:

> http://youtube.com

LexisNexis AlaCarte!
Designed especially for independent professionals and small- to medium-sized businesses that need answers on the fly, LexisNexis AlaCarte! provides users the information they need through free

searches of premium newspaper and magazine articles, company and industry reports, and legal data. Pay only for what you use. Details at:

http://lexisnexis.com/alacarteinfo/

Netflix

The best place online to rent DVDs. Distributes independent documentaries:

http://www.netflix.com

Wikipedia

The place to start to find out everything about everything. But be aware that folks can more or less post whatever they want. So when you get an interesting lead from Wikipedia, check it out elsewhere before using it. Start at:

http://wikipedia.org

THE DOCUMENTARY CREW

The crew for a behavioral documentary is usually three or four people, depending on the equipment and the requirements of the production. If the location you'll be working in is good sized and you have a lot of different setups to shoot, a larger crew may be justified by the time it will save. But if you are shooting in someone's home or in a small office or store, you don't want to bring a crowd. More than three or four in the crew and you may intimidate the people you're filming and get in each other's way in small spaces. It's a lot easier to maintain the invisible wall between production people and subjects when the crew is small.

Fewer than three or four, however, and you may not have the bodies you need to get the job done. To get something recorded on film or video, you need at least two people—one to run the camera and one to record the sound. Getting decent, legible images and audio is simply too much for one person to handle alone.

Other kinds of productions, such as a historical reenactment, may require a much larger crew.

Who Does What on a Production?

Listed below are some of the people who are likely to be involved with your production. The nucleus of a production crew will be the people who get the stuff recorded: the camera operator, the sound recordist, and the director. Surrounding them may be a lot of other people who contribute to the production.

PRODUCTION PERSONNEL

Producer

The producer is the person who assembles the financing for a project, pays the bills, and handles administrative details from preproduction through to distribution. The producer may hire all or part of the crew. The role of the producer in the creative process varies. Some producers will be intimately involved with the director, crew, and editor at every stage of production; others will leave the creative realization of the production to the people they have hired.

In documentary, the producer will often be a hyphenate—producer-director or producer-writer—directly involved in both the business details of the production and the creative process of bringing it to the screen.

Director

The director is the person in creative control of the documentary. He or she decides when, where, and what to shoot and, in consultation with the camera operator or director of photography, how to shoot it. The director of a documentary will normally stay with the production from preproduction planning through the completion of postproduction. He or she will select the narrator or spokesperson, will supervise recording of narration and music, and will work with the editor in organizing the elements of the documentary for presentation to an audience.

In many cases the director will "own" the idea for the documentary. In that situation, he or she may elect to be a producer-director, or may direct the documentary but hire a producer to handle the business details of the production. The larger the production—and the production budget—the more likely it is that the functions of director and producer will be handled by different people.

Scriptwriter

The scriptwriter researches the content of the documentary and organizes it into a visual argument. For a behavioral documentary or a documentary of a unique event, the scriptwriter may write a treatment or a shot list prior to production and then any necessary narration during postproduction. For a historical documentary or reenactment, the writer will do a finished screenplay. In many documentaries, the writer is also the producer or director.

Director of Photography or Cinematographer

The director of photography has responsibility for the overall look of the production. In consultation with the director, he or she sets the lighting, frames the shot, selects the lenses and film stock to be used, and instructs the camera operator. On a large production, the director of photography does not actually operate the camera. On a small-crew documentary, the functions of director of photography and camera operator will probably be handled by the same person.

Camera Operator

The camera operator must have a professional understanding of the equipment that will record the documentary images. And he or she must know how the lighting in use—whether available light or a lighting setup—will affect the images you are recording. In any hot shooting situation, the camera operator functions as co-director, making crucial decisions about what to shoot and how to shoot it.

Camera Assistant

The camera assistant looks after the camera between setups, keeps the camera log, and generally handles the heavy lifting and detail work so the camera operator is free to be creative. A small-crew documentary may not have a camera assistant, although I think this is an extremely important person on the crew.

Sound Recordist

Recording excellent sound for a documentary is a technical skill that requires both professional knowledge and experience. Your sound person has to be able to record voices in a noisy situation so that they are well separated from the background noise. He or she must know where the camera is pointed at all times and must be sure to record sound that goes with the picture.

Sound Assistant

With a simple one-camera, one-microphone shoot, there is usually no need for a sound assistant. But as the number of audio inputs increases, the sound recordist may need some help. A sound assistant may operate a microphone boom or fish pole to get the microphone close to the people who are speaking.

Video Engineer

In an earlier time, when cameras were less sensitive and tape machines were large and hard to use, location video was shot just like studio video, by taking the studio to the location in a van or trailer. In those days, the person ultimately responsible for the video product was the video engineer. Today's video documentary crew will almost always use a camcorder with an onboard recorder, and responsibility for the quality of the video image passes to the director of photography or camera operator, just as it is in film. If you have a multiple-camera shoot, however, with video feeds coming back to monitors at a single location, or for some reason are shooting switched video, you may require a video engineer.

Electrician or Gaffer

The gaffer is the chief electrician on a film production, working under the direction of the director of photography. The gaffer is responsible for the mechanics of lighting—from providing a power source when necessary to setting and relamping the lighting instruments—and for meeting any other electrical requirements on the production. Most documentary crews will not need an electrician. But if the power requirements are tricky or involve tapping in to a breaker box or other electrical source, an electrician should be used.

Grips

The grips on a production are the heavy lifters. They move and set lights, set up equipment and scenery, lay dolly rails when needed, and push the dolly. Most documentary shoots need at least one grip, who may function as a camera assistant and gofer as well.

Production Manager

A large production will have a person responsible for the business arrangements related to shooting. The production manager, sometimes called the unit manager, will often do the detailed budgeting for the production. He or she breaks down the day's shooting schedule to make the most economical use of crew, cast, locations, and equipment. On a small-crew documentary all of this will be handled by the producer or a production assistant.

Production Assistant(s)

On a documentary, a production assistant is a person who handles detail work, from arranging for the use of a location and getting the appropriate licenses to making sure that releases are signed. In a sense, a production assistant is a white-collar grip, relieving the producer and director of administrative detail. A production may have none, one, or several.

Location Coordinator

This is a special kind of production assistant who is highly knowledgeable about the location in which you will be shooting. The location coordinator knows where you can find a log cabin or a waterfall, how much it will cost to rent, and what permits you will need. Think of a location coordinator as a casting director for places to shoot.

Casting Director

For historical documentaries, reenactments, and other productions in which you will use actors, a casting director can help you find and hire the people you need.

Makeup Artist

Applying makeup for the camera is an art, and the person who does it is a makeup artist. For a spontaneous cinema documentary, you would not use a makeup artist, as that would be breaching the invisible wall. In a documentary with extensive interviews, you might in some cases want to have a makeup artist available to help your subjects look their best. In a reenactment or other documentary with actors, you'll need one or more makeup artists.

Someone to Look After Wardrobe and Props

In a historical documentary involving reenactment, you will have extensive wardrobe and property needs. Unless you have someone to keep track of the wardrobe and props, you're likely to get on location and discover that Abraham Lincoln forgot his top hat and John Wilkes Booth assumed someone else was bringing the pistol. An experienced wardrobe person can help you find the costume items you need and will know how many duplicates of each item of clothing you should keep on hand.

TelePrompTer Operator

If you use an on-camera narrator, host, or spokesperson, you may need to provide a TelePrompTer for them as well as an operator to run it. Today's TelePrompTers are computer-based rather than mechanical. The operator loads the script into the computer and sets up the TelePrompTer. During production, he or she runs the TelePrompTer so that the right words are visible as the talent needs to read them.

Driver(s)

If you are working on location in an area that is new to you, it may be worth it to hire at least one driver from the local area who knows how to get you to the next setup the quickest way without getting lost, and what place serves the best barbecue.

POSTPRODUCTION PERSONNEL

In postproduction you'll become involved with another group of specialists who will help you complete your documentary. In some cases these may be employees of a postproduction house, sound studio, or film lab.

Archival Researcher

An expert who knows where to find the stock footage and still photographs you need to make your documentary.

Creative Editor

A creative editor not only knows the ins and outs of whatever editing system is being used, but also knows how to put the recorded images and sounds of your documentary together to tell your story clearly and artistically.

Technical Editor or Assistant Editor

A technical editor can run the equipment, but generally looks to the director to decide how things go together. As assistant editor, this person helps the creative editor.

Sound Mixer

This is the person who takes all of the various sound sources that make up the sound track of your documentary and skillfully blends them together to go with the images.

Music Director

The music director selects music from various sources, including libraries of stock music, in order to score the film.

Composer

A composer creates original music for the documentary, scored to the picture. It is a joy to work with a good composer.

Narrator

The narrator speaks the narration written into the script.

Video Sweetener or Colorist

A video artist, like the creative editor, who can work wonders with footage shot under rough documentary conditions.

Who Will Do What on Your Production?

I made my first documentary with a borrowed 16mm camera on my shoulder and a friend with absolutely no film experience recording sound. The film was strong on content and well edited, but it was a technical nightmare. I knew *nothing* about shooting 16mm color. And by the time the footage, shot on high-speed reversal color film, went through the several generations to a release print, the scenes shot in available light had become muddy and hard to see, and the scenes shot in sunlight, which seemed so sharp and clear in the rushes, had become contrasty and bizarre, like the colors in a comic book. Most of the location audio was terrible. We simply didn't know enough to do the job right.

CAMERA AND SOUND

In my opinion, it is best if the two critical people in the production phase of a documentary—the camera operator and the sound recordist—are people who practice their craft every day and know exactly what they are doing. This doesn't mean that any professional camera operator can shoot a documentary. In addition to technical skill, it takes a kind of sixth sense for when and where things will happen, an eye for visual evidence, and an optimistic tolerance for the times when the camera is on and nothing seems to be happening.

As for audio—documentaries are often shot in hectic, noisy situations where it is difficult to understand anything. A true documentary sound recordist finds a way to get legible sound, even under atrocious conditions, while keeping the microphone out of the shot. The collaboration between sound and camera often requires ballet-like coordination.

YOUR JOB ON THE CREW

If this is your project, then you are—like it or not—some kind of a producer. You may be executive producer with a host of professionals hired to do the work. You may be line producer, overseeing the task of getting the documentary made. Or you may be producer with a hyphen, as you take on one or more of the technical professional tasks involved in making a documentary.

When I was a documentary film student, *everyone* wanted to run camera. That was the sexy job. And you may be tempted to say, OK, I'm not very experienced at shooting, but I'll know what I want when I see it.

Maybe. What I know is that it is easier to see what is going on all over the shooting situation when you are not trying to view it through the narrow angle of a camera viewfinder. In order to keep the crew small and the shooting situation intimate, sometimes the person functioning as producer or producer-director will run sound. But if you lack the technical experience to run camera or sound well and the expertise to direct, then hire people who know what they are doing until you've had a chance to gain the knowledge and experience yourself.

DIRECTING

Today everyone wants to be a director. Will you direct the documentary yourself, hire a director, or do without? Again, it depends on what your documentary requires and what *you* bring to the project.

If you are making a historical documentary or reenactment, you may need a director who is experienced at working with actors.

FRIENDS AND RELATIVES

Low-budget productions often get made with friends and relatives, and that's the way it is. But the more amateurs you have on the crew, the more problems you may encounter. Just getting a documentary made is a difficult enough task.

Finding and Choosing a Production Crew

How do you find the production people you'll need? One way is to contract with a film or video production company. You'll find them listed by the dozen in the phone book, in the directories of organizations such as the International Documentary Association or the Media Communications Association International, and in directories published by state and city film commissions.

Another way is to look at lots of documentaries. Get the habit of writing down the production credits when you see a documentary you like. Then contact the person or the production company.

It's quite possible that early in your search you may find a producer, production company, or individual crew members who can do exactly what you want. If so, sign them up. You would probably end up hiring them anyway. Otherwise, narrow your list as quickly as possible to a small number of candidates.

DON'T HOLD A COMPETITION

In dealing with production companies, I *do not* recommend holding a competition or sending out a request for proposals (RFP) as a first step. You are likely to eliminate the very people you would most like to talk with, because many excellent filmmakers and videomakers will avoid this kind of competition, for several reasons:

- They feel that an important part of their job is to understand and interpret the needs of your project. This requires the kind of personal contact that is generally eliminated by an RFP.
- They regard a competition involving a large number of production companies as little more than a lottery. It requires a lot of work for which they will not be paid unless they win.
- The best people, once they have established a reputation and a body of films and videos that show what they can do, are unwilling to do any creative work on speculation. And that is what an RFP usually asks for.

Good people are certainly willing to present themselves and their work for your inspection. And they *will* make a proposal and discuss costs when they feel they will be judged on the quality of their existing work, not on how well they guess what you want from an RFP.

Do Look at Their Work

If you are talking with a production company, be sure to find out if the person you are dealing with is in sales or production. Withhold judgment until you've met the production people and seen their work. The best way to find the people you need is to look at the films and videos they've made, because their skill and the nature and quality of their work are the *only things that count.*

Look at complete productions; a composite reel of highlights or best shots tells you nothing about the ability of the crew to sustain a quality effort over a complete production. If you are planning a long documentary of an hour, two hours, or more, you won't learn much by looking at samples of short works. The planning, pacing, and editing of a long documentary is quite different from that of a short production.

Look at the Technical Quality of the Work

If the color is off or the sound is bad, don't accept an explanation such as this is an answer print or an offline edit and all the flaws were corrected in the final version. After all, they are choosing to show you this print and not the final version. And be very leery of anyone who tries to tell you that you have to expect some technical problems in shooting a documentary. That may have been true some time ago, but it is far less true today. Bad picture, bad sound, or bad editing are most likely evidence of a bad production company. Look elsewhere.

When you see a documentary you like, find out:

- How much it cost in current dollars.
- Who directed, shot, and edited it. Are these people still working at the production company listed in the credits? Will they be available for your production? Can you see other work they've done?

Contracting with a production company is one way to find the crew for your documentary. Another is to build the crew yourself, by locating the key individuals you need. You might find a director or camera operator whose work you like and ask him or her to recommend other people to fill out the crew. In general, good people choose to work with other good people. So finding one key player may lead you to everyone else you need. Nevertheless, look at their work, ask for their credits, and check their references.

EQUIPMENT

If you've decided to work with a production company, then the question of where your equipment will come from is solved—the production company will provide it. But you may have some critical decisions to make about what sorts of equipment they should bring.

Again, I want to emphasize that specifying the equipment to use is not what this book is about. The earlier edition, written in 1996, was in print through the transition from Betacam to Beta SP to digital Beta to the actual use and broadcast of HDTV and the advent of mini-DV. There is simply no imagining what the next ten years may bring.

High End or Not?

Film or video was once the critical decision for a documentary film-maker. I started in film and I love film. I like the smell of it when it has just come back from the laboratory. I like to handle it. I like the look of it up on the screen. But I have not directed a documentary shot on film in years.

The question, today, really is: high end or not?

HIGH END

High end is film and HDTV. Film continues to give high-quality images, but expect to do your editing and postproduction on video, even if you plan to release on film. HDTV transfers to film for theatrical release with as good quality as film, and through video sweetening you can even give the video a film look.

Look for theaters to move to digital video. It's perfect for small-room multiplexes where the screen does not have to be huge. It can be auto-mated so there's no need for a projectionist to start and stop the projec-tor and change reels. The cost of duplication will be much less than film. And when digital feature films can be sent to theaters electroni-cally, the immense cost of making hundreds of film prints and of ship-ping the heavy reels of film will be eliminated.

The Other End

The rest, which is not high end, is all other video. This is perfectly fine for all television applications except high quality broadcast HDTV.

You should shoot digital video in the 16×9 format, because that's the standard that broadcast television is moving to.

Camera and Lenses

Use the best camera you can afford to buy or rent. The camera should have a relatively fast, high-quality zoom lens with focal lengths from moderate wide angle to a medium long lens. The video recorder will probably be a part of the camera, making it a camcorder. It may record to tape, to a DVD, to a hard drive or flash drive, or to some other medium not yet in use as I write this.

In some cases you might have need for a small camera, such as a "lip-stick" video camera, that is small enough and light enough to be set on a bookcase or hung from a lamp or a picture frame and can literally be placed in the middle of a scene without being noticed.

Whatever kind of camera you're using, you'll need spare batteries—plenty of them—and a battery charger.

Be sure you have spare parts, including spare batteries and connect-ing cables for *everything*. It can be extremely frustrating to watch a high-priced crew sitting around doing nothing because a twenty-five-dollar cable has malfunctioned.

Most professional camera operators have their own camera and asso-ciated equipment, the cost of which can be included in their daily rate.

Support

You need a good, solid tripod with a smoothly turning head. Yes, a lot of documentary footage is shot handheld. And on-board digital image sta-bilizers have given handheld video a stability equivalent to footage shot with a Steadicam. But certain critical shots must be rock steady. An audience will accept a little shakiness in the handheld footage of people doing things, but they expect inanimate objects to hold absolutely still.

While you will probably never use it in a behavioral documentary, if you are doing a reenactment you may need a dolly or a small crane or jib arm. These let you make smooth camera moves.

Sound Equipment

Basically, you need a recorder and a microphone. But with today's technology, that covers a lot of ground. When you think of a documentary crew, the sound recordist is the person wearing earphones, with a Nagra recorder slung over one shoulder, holding a shotgun microphone wrapped in a windscreen on the end of a fish pole mike holder. And that's still the way a lot of documentaries get made.

But the sound recordist could also be the person sitting at a console watching the dials on a sixteen-track recorder as sound comes in from wireless microphones all over the shooting area.

These are the things you need to know:

- An audio recorder can be synchronized to either a film or video camera by recording a control track or time code on one channel. This can later be matched to the running speed of the film camera or the time code of the video camera to sync the audio to picture. This means you can use any kind of recorder capable of recording a time code track. It also means you can put several of them together.
- A video recorder, whether separate or on board the camera, has a limited number of audio tracks. Each track accepts a separate input. You can use a microphone mixer to meld several inputs onto one track. But it is always better to isolate inputs if possible by giving each its own track. So if you anticipate complex sound, you may need an additional audio recorder capable of giving you as many tracks of audio as you calculate you will need.
- A shotgun or parabolic mike can reach out and isolate sounds from whatever area it is pointed at. It can also sometimes pick up sounds from behind the person you want, even from the other side of the wall.

- The cleanest situation *usually* is to hang a wireless lavaliere micro-phone on each person you want to record. But this is not always possible or desirable. And wireless microphones sometimes will find themselves in conflict with taxi signals, CB radios, and other radio sources.
- You need lots of spare batteries. Lots! More than you think.
- You need a good, basic, backup dynamic microphone that always works when everything else fails. And you need a nice long mike cable to go with it.
- You get the best sound by getting a good microphone close to the person speaking.
- Avoid recording audio using automatic gain control.
- Pick a sound recordist with very good ears, and make sure that he or she wears a good set of headphones.
- Set audio levels manually and visually, using the VU meter on the recorder.

Lighting and Grip Equipment

A film is made with light. It's not that you necessarily need a lot of light, but you need the right kind of light in the right place. Lighting a docu-mentary depends entirely on the style of the film you're making.

Reenactment Lighting

A historical reenactment will be shot like a feature with all the lighting the budget will tolerate. If this is what you are doing, hire a good cine-matographer or lighting director and let him or her go over the script and tell you what you need. Probably you'll do a certain amount of shooting in a studio, where a full lighting array is available. And when you go on location you'll take along a well-equipped grip truck and generator.

Behavioral Documentary Lighting

If you're doing a behavioral documentary, you'll try to work with avail-able light and use as little additional light as possible.

Hard, specular lights—spotlights or floodlights—require careful light-ing and total control of the situation. Otherwise, they give an unnatural "lit" look to the scene, with shadows spilling everywhere. And the people you are filming will seem to move from hot spots to deep shadows in a room in which the audience would expect the lighting to be fairly even. Therefore specular lights are not much use in behavioral documentary situations, other than as bounce lights off the ceiling or to provide a certain look in a static interview situation.

I like to have a couple of soft lights or lights with umbrella reflectors that can be used to increase the overall illumination when necessary without creating a lot of shadow problems.

You may want to have some correcting gels or dichroic filters to help balance your artificial lights with the lighting in the situation, especially if you are shooting film. You'll need some grip stands to hold the lights and gels and flags when required.

A documentarian should always have along a couple of battery lights to use where no electricity is available. And that means bringing spare batteries and a battery charger.

If you'll be filming outdoors, you should have some shiny boards or reflectors that can bounce sunlight into the scene to provide fill light.

Miscellaneous

There are some other things that you may or may not want as part of your equipment.

Monitor and Video Assist

It's your call whether you are going to want to have a video monitor for the director to look at. It's easy enough to install video assist on a film camera to send a video feed from the camera viewing system to a TV monitor. A video camera, of course, provides a video signal, which can be run to a monitor.

This requires wiring the camera to a fixed location. No problem when you have control, as in a reenactment. But it could be a big problem if you're filming the behavior of a two-year-old who suddenly decides to leave the room or go from the front yard to the back of the house, and you have to follow.

What you certainly want is the ability to view what you've shot as soon as possible after you've finished shooting. So you should have decent video playback and an adequate monitor available on location.

TelePrompTer

In some situations you may need a TelePrompTer. This lets your host or spokesperson handle a lengthy explanation or introduction without having to memorize it. As far as I'm concerned, a TelePrompTer can cause as many problems as it alleviates. For me, it is a last resort and should be used only with experienced professional talent who know how to read from one.

Two-way Radios and/or Cellular Phones

When the camera is at the bottom of the hill and the people you are shooting are at the top of the hill, you need some way to communicate with them.

Cars and Trucks

You need to get around from location to location. It's best if you can do it comfortably. At a minimum you need a lockable van for the equipment. It's good to have a separate car with seats for everyone in the crew, which can be used to run errands, pick up talent, whatever, while the van is at the shoot.

Should You Rent or Buy Equipment?

As I have suggested throughout the book, you can make a low-budget documentary with a relatively inexpensive mini-DV camera and a desktop editing system, so it probably makes sense to buy these to learn on. In most other documentary situations, I'm a firm believer in renting equipment, unless you are in production several days a week—every week. Here's why:

- Production technology changes rapidly. This year's new hot camera may be obsolescent in twelve to eighteen months and totally obsolete in two or three years. But you're still stuck with the payments.
- In the past, my friends who signed six-figure notes to get new equipment to work with soon found themselves working to support the equipment rather than the other way around.
- By renting, you can usually work with the latest equipment.
- Even if you eventually want to buy your own equipment, renting is a good way to try before you buy.

- The rental payment and insurance is part of the production budget, and when you're done, you return the equipment to the rental house, pay the bill, and walk away clean.

On the other hand, if you have a long project with a lot of production time, it may be cost-effective to buy the equipment you need, use it for the production, and sell it when the project is over. In essence, you are renting from yourself. And if you really like the equipment, maybe you'll keep it.

Be Sure You Have an Equipment Meister

If possible, you should have someone on the production crew who is really good with equipment. This should be a person who knows a lot about the technology of camera and sound equipment in general and knows the specific equipment you are using. This is the person who will know six good things to try when the camera won't run or the sound won't record.

BUDGETING

A number of considerations go into creating a budget for a documentary.

Who Is Paying?

The first consideration is who is paying to get the documentary made. If this is strictly your project and you are paying the bills, then what you are concerned with is the out-of-pocket cost. If you have your own camera equipment and editing facilities, you don't need to budget for these—or for your time, either—except to determine what the actual cost or fair value of the documentary might be.

On the other hand, if you have a sponsor, a client, or a funding agency, then *everything* becomes a cost, including your time and the use of your equipment. You budget to be sure you don't spend more than you'll receive.

Small Crew or Large Production?

Almost all of my experience is in making behavioral documentaries with a crew of three or four people. And the production budget is basically so much per day for crew, equipment, film or video, steaks, sodas, and mileage.

But if you are undertaking a reenactment, a historical documentary, or a biography with re-creation of events, you'll need to budget like a feature film. The only way to do this is to get an experienced production manager to do your budget for you, once you have a completed script.

Union or Nonunion?

Unless you are doing a large reenactment or are a signatory to a union contract through other work that you've done, your first documentary will probably be nonunion.

A union shoot probably will cost more due to union work rules. You may be required to hire more people than you would use in a nonunion, independent production. And you'll have to pay for travel time, meals, and overtime, as well as union benefits such as health and welfare. On the other hand, using a union crew generally assures a certain level of technical competence. But if you are a union signatory, you undoubtedly already know this.

If you are nonunion and independent, then the cost of everything is the best cost you can negotiate.

Live or Archive?

Where will the footage come from that will be used in your documentary? Will you be shooting it live? Or will it mostly be archival footage? Live productions mean shooting days, followed by review of footage, followed by editing. Productions based on archival footage replace shooting days with the costs of finding, duplicating, and licensing the footage that will be used.

In today's documentary milieu, it can cost far more to make a documentary out of old footage, when you have to buy rights to it, than to go out and shoot everything brand-new.

Above- and Below-the-Line Costs

The budgets for feature films and for some other productions are divided into above-the-line and below-the-line costs. People accustomed to using this system of budgeting tend to think in these terms. It won't be important in planning a documentary unless a funder or sponsor asks you for an above-the-line and below-the-line breakout of your budget.

Above-the-line costs are generally contractual expenses that are negotiated on a run-of-the-production basis. These include the purchase of the script and property rights and the salaries of the producer, director, and cast.

Below-the-line costs are all those costs associated with the production that are calculated on the basis of use. This includes salaries for the crew, cost of equipment and supplies, travel, editing, processing, and postproduction costs, and salaries not agreed upon as above-the-line costs before production starts.

A Budgeting Checklist

Over the years I've developed a number of checklists to try to be sure I account in advance for everything I'm going to have to pay for on a production. I've consolidated these into the checklist that follows. I have tried to make this as comprehensive as possible, so there undoubtedly will be many items on the list that you won't need for a specific production. More important, don't blame me if I've left out something that you do need, because every production is different. Treat this checklist as a starting point and a memory jogger and then add to it the specifics of your production to create your own budgeting system.

At the request of readers, I have posted this checklist on the website for this book:

www.makingdocumentaryfilms.com

so you can download it and modify it for your own needs.

I.   *General (run-of-the-production) expenses*
   A. Production company
      1. Producer
      2. Director
      3. Producer's assistant/secretary
      4. Bookkeeper
      5. Office rent
      6. Telephone
      7. Utilities
      8. Furniture and equipment
      9. Supplies
      10. Licenses
      11. Other
   B. Transportation
      1. Travel costs
      2. Vehicles

C. Legal
   1. Contracts, releases, etc.
   2. Rights
   3. Copyright
D. Insurance
   1. Office and equipment
   2. Errors and omissions
   3. Liability
   4. Production or negative insurance
   5. Completion bond if required
E. Payroll company
   1. Tax, benefits, workers' compensation, etc., throughout the production

II. *Preproduction Expenses*
   A. Research
      1. Text researcher
      2. Cost of books, research materials, microfilm reproduction, photocopying, etc.
      3. Archival researcher
      4. Cost of viewing and duplicating footage and stills for review
   B. Script
      1. Scriptwriter
      2. Interviews
      3. Storyboards if needed
   C. Production planning
      1. Director of photography
      2. Casting
         a) Casting director
         b) Record casting sessions
      3. Locations
         a) Location coordinator
         b) Location research
      4. Others
         a) Sound
         b) Art director

      c) Production manager

      d) Etc.

  D. Travel

  E. Payroll company

    1. Tax, benefits, workers' compensation, etc.

III. *Production Expenses*

  A. Crew and equipment (if contracted as a package)

  B. Crew (individuals as needed)

    1. Assistant director

    2. Director of photography

    3. Camera operator

    4. Camera assistant

    5. Sound recordist

    6. Sound assistant

    7. Electrician/gaffer

    8. Grip(s)

    9. Scriptwriter, if needed during production

    10. Production assistant(s)

    11. Editor, if needed during production

    12. Makeup artist

    13. Property person

    14. Wardrobe person

    15. Driver(s)

    16. TelePrompTer operator

    17. Other

  C. Talent

    1. Host/spokesperson

    2. Featured actors

    3. Extras

    4. Animals

  D. Equipment

    1. Camera and support

      a) Camera(s)

      b) Film magazines

      c) Lenses

      d) Matte box, filters, etc.

      e) Batteries and charger(s)

      f) Tripod(s)

      g) Dolly, Steadicam, crane, jib-arm, etc.

      h) Special mounts (car, helicopter)

      i) Special rigs such as underwater housing

      j) Video recorder(s)

      k) Video playback

      l) Video assist

      m) Monitor(s)

      n) Slate, connectors, etc.

  2. Sound

      a) Recorder(s)

      b) Microphone(s)

      c) Wireless system

      d) Audio mixer

      e) Microphone boom or fish pole

      f) Cables and connectors

  3. Lighting and grip equipment

      a) Grip truck

      b) Lighting instruments

        (1) Spot/flood

        (2) Broad

        (3) Soft lights

        (4) Battery lights

        (5) Other

      c) Grip stands, sandbags

      d) Shiny boards

      e) Cables

      f) Clamps, gels, dichroic filters, etc.

      g) Background paper

      h) Large color-correcting gels for windows

      i) Generator

  4. Miscellaneous

      a) TelePrompTer

      b) Communication (walkie-talkies, headsets, etc.)

      c) Trailers, honey wagons, etc.

E. Transportation

             1. Cars
             2. Vans or trucks
   F. Props and wardrobe
             1. Props as needed
             2. Wardrobe items
             3. Vehicles
   G. Location and studio costs as required
             1. Location fees, including "minders" such as police officers when required
             2. Licenses as needed
             3. Studio rental
             4. Set construction
             5. Set decoration
             6. Storage and transportation
   H. Film processing
             1. Laboratory processing of film
             2. Transfer and sync sound
             3. Work print or transfer to video
             4. Video dubs for review
             5. Shipping
   I. Travel
             1. Travel costs
             2. Rooms
             3. Per diem
             4. Shipping equipment and supplies
   J. Supplies
             1. Film or video medium
             2. Audiotape
             3. Batteries for everything
             4. Gaffer's tape, camera tape, shipping tape, etc.
             5. Replacement lamps
   K. Meals and snacks
             1. Cast and crew meals as required
             2. Snacks and drinks available during production
   L. Contingencies
      A percentage of the production budget set aside to handle unexpected and unbudgeted expense

M. Payroll company
   1. Tax, benefits, workers' compensation, etc.

IV. *Postproduction Expenses*
  A. Stock footage and stills
    1. Work tape
    2. Reproduction quality
    3. Rights
  B. Review of footage
    The director, along with the editor (if the director is not doing the editing) and possibly the producer, will want to review what has been shot to select the best takes, eliminate the unusable footage, and begin to organize the structure of the documentary. Budget time for this.
  C. Editing facilities
    The production company may have editing facilities available, or may rent a film editing room or editing system or a video offline editing room or system by the week or month until postproduction is complete.
  D. Offline editing (video) or rough cut editing (film)
    1. Editor
    2. Assistant editor
    3. Offline (rough cut) editing equipment
    4. Supplies
      a) Splicing tape for film, cores, split reels, marking pencils, etc.
      b) Mastering and work media for video —today this is videotape, tomorrow it may be something else
  E. Graphics and special effects
    1. Animation
    2. Computer graphics, etc.
    3. Special photographic or video effects
    4. Character generator
    5. Other
  F. Music
    1. Composer
    2. Library music

        a) Selection

        b) Rights

    3. Music director

    4. Audiotape as required

G. Audio postproduction

    1. Record narration

    2. Voice talent

    3. Looping if required

    4. Record music

    5. Record sound effects

    6. Audio sweetening and effects (video)

    7. Sound mix (film)

    8. Audio layback

    9. Audiotape and/or video media as required

H. Online editing

    1. Online facility by the hour

    2. Mastering medium

    3. Work medium

    4. Protection master

    5. Video sweetening

    6. Dubs for review

I. Completion on film

    1. Negative cutting

    2. Answer print

    3. Release print

    4. Internegative

    5. Release print from internegative

    6. Shipping and insurance

J. Payroll company

    1. Tax, benefits, workers' compensation, etc.

V. *Distribution Expenses*

A. Prints for release as required

    1. Theatrical standard

    2. Television network standard

    3. DVD authoring

4. Manufacture of initial quantity of release copies, including labels and boxes
5. Shipping

Use this checklist as a starting point. Specific items will change as the technology changes and as your approach to making documentaries evolves. The most important thing is to have a reference point for creating the budget for the documentary. There is so much to do, and there are so many different costs involved, that without some kind of checklist you can easily forget to include something that could cost a lot of money you didn't plan on spending.

And you'll have to live with that.

TREATMENT FOR *TRAVELS OF A T-SHIRT*

THE TRAVELS OF A T-SHIRT IN THE GLOBAL ECONOMY

A Proposal for a Documentary Film
Based on the Book by Pietra Rivoli

The Travels of a T-Shirt in the Global Economy by Pietra Rivoli is a journey in search of the truth, the very essence of documentary filmmaking. It's also a fun read—a rare thing in an economics book—and destined to be a classic. The author's sense of humor shines through as she reveals that many things the popular wisdom assumes to be the case are wrong. That the story of our global economy is often a zany one, full of contradictions and unexpected, sometimes foolish, outcomes. For instance:

- How can the U.S. textile industry be losing jobs to China, when the Chinese textile industry is also losing jobs?
- Trade barriers, erected to protect against foreign competition, have actually increased it.
- Bottlenecks can be good, creating opportunities to improve productivity.
- A worker may prefer working for wages in a sewing factory (read "sweatshop") to the unpaid drudgery of life as a female family member on a subsistence farm.
- Political solutions to economic problems have unintended consequences, which create a host of new problems in what amounts to a jobs program for bureaucrats and lobbyists.
- A lot of "free trade" simply isn't.

The proposed two-hour documentary will follow the form of the book, beginning with a question raised by a student protestor at Georgetown University and traveling from the supermechanized cotton fields of West Texas to the noisy factories of Shanghai, and back to the sunny tourist mecca of Florida where the T-shirt is printed and sold. Total travel: more than 15,000 miles. Then in its second life the shirt joins tons of used clothing moving through a family business in Brooklyn before traveling another 8,000 miles to an open-air market in Dar Es Salaam.

Like the book, the documentary will also move back and forth in time to visit significant, and at times amusing, historical events. For example:

- How government insistence that a generation of Britons wear woolen underwear sparked the Industrial Revolution.
- Peculiar rules that protected U.S. southern cotton growers from the labor market.
- How cheap Asian cotton goods were a "problem" for the West as early as 1701.
- How protectionism enacted in response to change assumes nothing else will change.

Along with the highly visual, often exotic, locations, which will be filmed in high-definition video, the documentary will introduce us to an unforgettable group of unique individuals. As Roger Lowenstein writes in his review of the book in the *New York Times*:

> Ms. Rivoli does her best work at ground level, introducing us to a family farmer outside Lubbock, Tex.; a young woman on the assembly line in Shanghai; a reseller of shirts in Dar Es Salaam, Tanzania; a K Street lobbyist in Washington; not to mention figures from history.

For the viewer, this is, first of all, a good story full of interesting people and exciting locales. At the same time, it functions as a search for truth, replacing myths and assumptions with reality and facts. And, finally, it points to ways in which those who truly want to help the poor and oppressed, both at home and abroad, can actually do so.

TREATMENT

The film opens at Georgetown University where Professor Pietra Rivoli heard a student at a protest against the International Monetary Fund and the World Trade Organization ask the crowd, "Who made your T-shirt? Was it a child in Vietnam, chained to a sewing machine without food or water? Or a young girl in India earning eighteen cents per hour and allowed to visit the bathroom only twice per day?" As the speaker continued to paint a grim picture of the lives of workers in T-shirt factories around the world, Prof. Rivoli reflected, "I did not know all this. And I wondered about the young woman at the microphone. How did she know?" Thus began a search for answers that resulted in the book, *The Travels of a T-Shirt in the Global Economy: An Economist Examines the Markets, Power, and Politics of World Trade.*

Cotton Comes from Teksa

Our protagonist is a cotton T-shirt printed with a colorful parrot and the word *Florida* that Prof. Rivoli selected from a bin at a Walgreen's Drugstore in Fort Lauderdale and set out to trace quite literally to its roots—the cotton plant from which it came and the land in which the cotton was grown. The documentary will use a narrator for essential information. Prof. Rivoli will appear in brief interview sound bites. Wherever possible, narration will use Prof. Rivoli's actual words from her book.

Retracing her steps, we meet <u>Patrick Xu</u> of Shanghai Knitwear, who told her, "Come to China, I will show you everything." Knowing that China is one of the world's largest cotton producers, she asked if she could visit the farm the cotton comes from. "I think the cotton is grown very far from Shanghai," Xu said. "Probably in Teksa." Wondering where that might be, she asked him to show her Teksa on the globe. He spun it to the United States and pointed to—Texas.

Historically, cotton production in the United States, and even today in many parts of the world, is a labor-intensive industry, requiring many human hands to plant, cultivate, hoe, and pick the cotton. But West Texas is the home of factory farming, which began when cotton farmers moving west substituted the tractor for the mule and continued to increase productivity and lower the need for labor. We meet <u>Nelson Reinsch</u>, who farms 1,000 acres of West Texas cotton, mostly by himself.

He is in his early eighties. The story of his life is the story of the evolution of cotton production in the United States, so that it is cost-effective to grow cotton in industrial America and ship it to agrarian China for manufacture.

For historical perspective, we look at the dark side of American cotton production, which runs from slavery to sharecropping to employment of migrant workers. While this is usually seen as exploiting cheap labor for profit, Prof. Rivoli writes that its real purpose was to guarantee that the labor needed to produce cotton would be available at critical times, while avoiding the costs of a free labor market. Mechanization was another way to lower the need for labor. But until recently crowds of workers were still needed to weed and pick the cotton. This decreased the incentive to mechanize the other steps in cotton farming, since the workers had to be kept around so they'd be there at the critical times that hadn't yet been mechanized.

Except in West Texas where, as Prof. Rivoli writes:

> The virtuous circle of scientific discovery and application in American cotton farming has not only done away with many of the risks, it has almost done away with farmers. Today, growing cotton in America is almost a one-man show. Most days, Nelson even takes a nap after lunch.

To keep cotton farming profitable, West Texas farmers are blessed with government subsidies. But they also coax value out of every part of the cotton plant. We see how, from a 22,000-pound module that leaves Nelson's farm, just 5,300 pounds is cotton lint—enough to make about 13,500 T-shirts. But the rest is used in different ways: as cattle feed, cottonseed oil to make peanut butter and Girl Scout cookies, and feed used by catfish farms that are conveniently located near the cotton fields. All of this sorting out and production is done mostly by a series of farmers' cooperatives.

Even if government subsidies to U.S. cotton farmers were removed, which would doubtless lower the world price of cotton, it is not clear that other cotton-producing countries would be able to take advantage of it. They lack the virtuous circle of infrastructure and the mechanization that make Texas cotton farming cost-efficient.

Enter the Dragon

Texas cotton lint travels to China at favorable rates on ships that have come loaded with Chinese goods for sale at America's shopping malls, and because of the trade imbalance might otherwise return with less than a full load. In Shanghai we meet <u>Tao Yong Fang</u>, manager of Number 36 Shanghai Yarn Factory. She is making the difficult transition from years of Communist central planning, which ignored Tao's energy and intelligence, to the world of faster-better-cheaper in which every action is a decision. And we see how Texas cotton becomes Chinese yarn. Then on to Shanghai Brightness Number 3 Garment Factory where the yarn is woven into cloth, which is cut and sewn into T-shirts.

But why is the market for Texas cotton some 7,147 miles away in Shanghai, when there are textile works in the Carolinas no farther away from Lubbock than the ports of California? To understand this we need to look at the long history of textile manufacturing, which Prof. Rivoli characterizes as "the long race to the bottom," after Alan Tonelson's book, *The Race to the Bottom*. Over time, industrial textile production has moved from its preeminent position in Great Britain, first to New England and then to the Carolinas, attracted by low wages and surplus workers who were both docile and desperate. Then Japan became a major player starting in the 1930s, followed by Hong Kong, Korea, and Taiwan in the '70s. And now China.

Back in Number 36 Shanghai Yarn Factory we meet <u>Jiang Lan</u>, who has come to Shanghai from the country. Her story exemplifies the millions of women over the past three centuries and across three continents who left the farm to work in the mills. Why? Often, certainly, for survival. But also because work in the factories, as terrible as it might seem to an outside observer, was perceived by the worker as preferable to life on the farm. As factory workers, these women received a wage, however meager, and a measure of autonomy, unlike anything they experienced on the family farm. For some, the factory became a training ground for better positions. And even when textiles moved on in the never-ending race to the bottom, they would leave behind an experienced workforce and the beginnings of an industrial infrastructure that often appealed to other industries.

Today China. Tomorrow, where?

The Protection Racket

Once the T-shirt is made in China, it must find its way through an ever-changing maze of arcane regulations and quotas before it can be admitted to the United States. So, as the T-shirt boards a ship in Shanghai, we switch our focus to Washington—the Congress and the K Street offices of lobbyists and trade associations. It is a curious fact that every administration from that of Dwight D. Eisenhower to the present has dealt in protectionist regulations for the textile industry as a trade-off for liberalizing free trade in other areas.

In Washington we meet Augie Tantillo, who has grown up in protectionist politics, starting as an aide to Senator Strom Thurmond. Through his recollections and the historical perspective of Prof. Rivoli, we learn how politicians responding to "the groans of the weavers" enacted protectionist policies. And, as Prof. Rivoli tells us:

> In what would become a long epic of unintended consequences, the politics served to accelerate rather than slow the race to the bottom. The VER (Voluntary Export Restraint), which limited imports from Japan, supplied not so much protection for the U.S. textile industry as an opening for Japan's competitors in the race—especially Hong Kong and Taiwan—to supply the U.S. market. In a pattern that continues to this day, the effect of plugging one hole in the dike was to increase the force of imports gushing through others.

We see how quotas, erected to protect against cheap goods from China (shades of England in 1701) have become an international marketing currency, adding to the cost of goods. Far from benefiting U.S. workers, they have actually aided dozens of small developing countries whose textile and apparel industries were created in response to the quotas. In a historical footnote we learn how rules to protect British woolens from cotton launched the modern industrial world. And we revisit the question of loss of jobs. Nelson Reinsch, farming virtually by himself, represents the loss of many jobs historically associated with raising cotton. They didn't go somewhere else. They just went away. So it is in the textile industry. Increased productivity usually means fewer workers. And this is true not only in the U.S., but also in China.

We meet Senator Jim DeMint (R-SC), who broke rank with every senator from the Carolinas over the past 50 years and not only failed to support the protectionist position but went to the other extreme and campaigned openly as a free trader—but was nonetheless elected in 2004.

We then turn to the social consequences of the race to the bottom. Prof. Rivoli writes, "While free trade increases global welfare, some local workers, companies, and communities are the losers; the economic benefits of free trade are diffuse, while the costs are typically concentrated." Where protectionism fails to benefit the local community, other policies are needed to compensate for the loss. Policies that don't just sound good, but actually work.

In Miami we meet <u>Gary Sandler</u>, who has learned to negotiate the protectionist maze to keep his company stocked with blank shirts which it screen prints and sends to market. He buys shirts from China—and a dozen other countries. By the time the T-shirt reaches him, it has navigated more than 15,000 miles through the global economy.

Afterlife—A Free Market

Americans don't wear out their clothes, they tire of them. The T-shirt begins its final journey when it is donated to the Salvation Army. It probably won't go to clothe a poor or homeless person—there aren't enough of those to handle the glut of castoffs. Instead it will be bundled with other donated clothes and sold in bulk for five to seven cents a pound to the recycling industry. And, Prof. Rivoli reveals, "Unlike the U.S. cotton producers, North Carolina textile mills, or the Chinese sewing factories, the clothing recyclers are on their own, without help, or even notice, from governments or lobbyists."

In Brooklyn we meet <u>Ed Stubin</u>, who runs Trans-Americas Trading Company, a family business, as are most in this industry. We see how success depends on mining the 70,000 pounds of used clothing Trans-Americas receives each day for "snowflakes," unique items with a decent resale value, and sorting the rest either for shipment to Africa or to be cut into rags or shredded and processed as "shoddy," which is used in such things as carpet pads, mattresses, and insulation.

Our T-shirt travels in a bale of used clothing from Brooklyn to Dar Es Salaam, Tanzania, where it reemerges in an open-air market as *mitumba*, clothing thrown away by Americans and Europeans. Here we meet <u>Geofrey Milonge</u>, who runs a T-shirt stall and survives in a free market by being faster-better-cheaper. And we learn how American castoffs are clothing a nation. Prof. Rivoli tells us, "Whatever the economic costs and benefits of the trade, it is clearly true as well that mitumba is fun. I found that taxi drivers, shopkeepers, and high school students—far from being embarrassed—delight in talking about mitumba."

Back in Brooklyn, Ed Stubin counts the ships arriving full of goods from China and looking for cargo for the return trip. He wonders how long it might be before the clothing recycling industry might shift to China.

Conclusion

"As I followed my T-shirt around the globe," Prof. Rivoli writes, "each person introduced me to the next and then the next until I had a chain of friends that stretched all the way around the world: Nelson and Ruth Reinsch, Gary Sandler, Patrick and Jennifer Xu, Mohammed and Gulam Dewji, Geofrey Milonge, Augie Tantillo, Ed Stubin, Su Qin, and Tao Yong Fang. . . . The Texans, Chinese, Jews, Sicilians, Tanzanians, Muslims, Christians, whites, blacks, and browns who passed my T-shirt around the global economy get along just fine. Actually, much, much better than fine, thank you very much. All of these people, and millions more like them, are bound together by trade in cotton, yarn, fabric, and T-shirts. I believe that each of them, as they touch the next one, is doing their part to keep the peace."

Potential for a Miniseries

While the proposed film will make a taut, informative, and entertaining two-hour documentary, the material is so rich and the people and locations so interesting that it could easily be expanded to a miniseries of as many as five one-hour programs. Once a crew is on location in Texas or China or Tanzania, it costs very little to add a day or two of additional shooting and explore the topic of that location in greater depth.

The introduction and the first section, "Cotton Comes from Teksa," could be spilt into two one-hour programs:

A Florida T-Shirt Made in China from Texas Cotton. Introduction to *The Travels of a T-Shirt in the Global Economy.* The evolution of cotton farming from the slave days of the antebellum South to the incredibly efficient one-man farm of Nelson Reinsch in Texas. Bottlenecks and productivity: How the invention of the cotton gin began the mechanization of cotton farming. Mules, literacy, and tractors: The end of sharecropping and the rise of the factory farm.

The Virtuous Circle. Profitably combining scientific discovery, government subsidy, cooperative leverage, and efficient marketing of everything produced in order to rule the market. How to farm 1,000 acres all by yourself. Using the waste products of cotton farming to feed cattle, feed fish, and feed people. How cooperatives changed the market. A look at the question of what would happen to world cotton markets if U.S. subsidies to cotton farmers were removed, and the surprising reasons why many developing countries still would not be competitive.

Each of the remaining three sections would expand to an hour, giving more opportunity to explore these topics:

Enter the Dragon. More detail on: (1) How America stole the textile industry from England long before China did it to us. (2) The infrastructure left behind when textiles move on. (3) The pros and cons of sweatshops. (4) How both social activists and corporations can actually help the workers.

The Protection Racket. Expanding to an hour will permit a stronger exploration of the perils of protectionism and especially the many unintended consequences of the quota system. Who benefits and what it costs.

Afterlife—A Free Market. This is such a delightful section of the story that it deserves an hour.

Production Considerations

The proposed documentary will be filmed in high-definition video in locations across the country and around the world. Professor Pietra Rivoli will participate in the production of the film, and the filmmakers will have access to the individuals and locations she profiles in the book.

The documentary is planned to have a running time of approximately 112 minutes.

For a follow-up DVD, it would be possible to include longer versions of interviews with key individuals shown in the film, as well as a spectacular travelogue of the locations visited.

TREATMENT FOR *A YOUNG CHILD IS . . .*

TREATMENT FOR A FILM ABOUT HOW VERY YOUNG CHILDREN LEARN

Purpose of the Film

1. To focus on young children from birth to the age at which they begin school.
2. To show the tremendous amount of learning accomplished by these very young children before they ever come in contact with schools and teachers.
3. To foster an attitude of respect for the learning ability, and the accomplishments, of young children.
4. To show some of the processes young children use in learning on their own, which differ from the processes schools use to "teach" children.
5. To show the ways in which young children grow and develop.
6. To include on the agenda of learning not only that which is abstract, cognitive, and "school-like," but also that which is emotional, social, and decisional.
7. To explore the validity of concepts such as "attention span" and "failure" in the context of preschool learning.
8. To promote respect for the young child as a human being, a person, and an individual. To lay a foundation for the second film (*Schools for Children*), which will take the approach of seeking educational programs that match the way children actually are.

Approach to the Film

The approach to filming will be open and documentary in style. We wish to observe the behavior of very young children, recording it on color film with synchronous sound. We wish to explore and document what children actually do, including, if appropriate, what they do in the presence of cameras. Little or no attempt will be made to direct the children's activities, and, in no case, will children be asked or encouraged to "act out" some preconceived activity to illustrate what children are supposed to do.

What we get is what you see.

Content of the Film

Filming situations will include, but not be limited to:

1. The behavior of babies less than a year old.* We shall be looking for the development of language—patterning sentences, experimentation with words, feedback and reward—the development of motor ability, trial-and-error efforts toward walking and crawling, and the emotional environment of the very young child.

2. The behavior of toddlers. We shall be looking for concrete examples of exploratory learning, of "play," which gains the child a familiarity with the object or task and gets him "ready" to use it. We shall also be looking at attention span and the ways in which these very young children learn from failure, without being defeated by it.

3. The trusting environment. As we film babies and toddlers, we shall be looking for examples of "trust" built into their environment, and the ways in which these children develop a sense of trust.

4. Two-year-olds and the sense of autonomy. In filming children roughly two years old, we shall be looking for the ways in which these children attempt to separate themselves from the background—to define themselves as unique, as individuals—to

---

*I think I had in mind that the paragraph headings I used in describing content might become divisions within the documentary. It didn't work out that way in editing. Nevertheless, in this treatment I have developed a possible organization of the material, through these headings, without being unalterably committed to it.

use as examples of the ways children develop a sense of autonomy. At the same time we shall be looking for examples of sophisticated development of verbal behavior, the self-correcting mechanism that turns "baby talk" into a reasonable facsimile of adult speech.

5. The Age of "Why?" Here we're dealing with two-, three-, and four-year-olds, looking for some replacement of trial-and-error learning with verbal interaction. Let us be clear about what we expect to find: We do not expect that every "Why?" is a reasoned request for information. But, as in patterning sentences before the child has words to fill them with meaning, we do expect to find a new emphasis on verbal behavior—practicing, playing with it—so that he will have the form ready when he wants to fill it with content.

6. Curiosity. This exists at all age levels, and we want to capitalize on it wherever we find it. We want to look for curiosity as it develops, to see how it develops and how it is turned off.

7. Creativity. Again, one can find examples, perhaps, at all age levels. We shall be looking for them. By "creativity" we do not mean merely artwork, or singing, or anything particularly related to the creative arts. We shall be looking for evidence of children taking what they know and reformulating it into something new, the creative solution to a problem, the development of a "new" word of precise meaning out of two old words, etc.

8. The Age of Initiative. Here we are looking for examples to show that the child has learned to trust his environment and has gained a sufficient sense of himself that he can now try on other roles. He can begin to accept others and interact with them. He can play with other children instead of alongside others.

9. Verbal behavior of five-year-olds. We want to observe five-year-olds talking with each other and with adults. Our premise is that their verbal behavior can be quite sophisticated, and is a necessary part of the readiness in communication which will lead them naturally into other communication skills such as reading and writing.

10. Decision making. At all levels we shall be looking for evidence of very young children making decisions on their own, guiding and directing their own behavior.

11. Repetition, familiarity, mastery. We want to show the way in which young children approach novelty. If they don't like it, they have "a short attention span." But if they do like it, they want it repeated, and repeated, until it becomes familiar and they have a feeling of mastery over it. Examples might be a parent reading a story, and when he has finished the child says, "Read it again," perhaps preferring it to a new story he hasn't heard. Or a young child going down a sliding board. As soon as he has convinced himself he won't be hurt, he wants to slide again, and again, and again.*

12. The effects of frustration on young children. In our filming, we expect to find instances where a child finds himself frustrated at what he intends to do. We want to observe this, to see how children deal with frustration.

13. Abstract learning—the learning of colors, numbers, letters, etc. How does a child learn these concepts? What does it mean to say, "He knows the alphabet," or "He knows how to count"? What is evidence that he does, and what is evidence that he doesn't?

14. Learning vs. "Right Answers." Again, we shall be looking for evidence of the difference between learning something, and learning how to give right answers about it. As an example of what we shall be looking for, we have a film clip, five minutes in length, shot in a classroom this past summer. In it, a teacher is working with two seven-year-olds, trying to teach the concept: "2+3=5." She has a filmstrip projector with a picture of two red chickens and three white chickens on it and a box of blocks set before the children. At the beginning of the clip, she points to the two red chickens and asks Johnny (his name, *really!*), "How many chickens do you see?" Johnny answers, "Five." He has solved the problem, but she doesn't know it. She is looking for the answer "Two," which is the right answer as far as she is concerned. She says, "No. How many do you see here?" She then goes through the entire process,

---

*This is the way you indicate the kinds of images you'll be looking for. It doesn't mean you will use these exact images. As it happens, we never even tried to film a parent reading a story. We did shoot in a playground, where we got some film of kids going down slides. But I didn't use it in the finished film.

counting two red chickens, counting three white chickens, counting blocks for red chickens, "1–2," counting blocks for white chickens, "1–2–3," counting all the chickens, "1–2–3–4–5," counting all the blocks, "1–2–3–4–5." She then says, "So, two plus three equals how much, Johnny?" And Johnny answers, "Four!" He has learned to look for "right answers" and has lost the ability to solve the problem.

U.S.S. *PERRY* SCRIPT TREATMENT

SCRIPT TREATMENT FOR *LOST WARSHIPS—U.S.S.* PERRY

ACT ONE

Fade in on scenes of a World War II Navy task force under way in the Pacific and superimpose the date, September 13, 1944.

We see stock footage of troops aboard ship and maps showing the strategic situation as narration tells us General MacArthur is poised for his return to the Philippines. In two days the First Marine Division will invade Palau to secure MacArthur's right flank.

We see stock footage of two or three minesweepers at work and of a float plane overhead as narration says that ahead of the invasion fleet, U.S.S. *Perry* in company with U.S.S. *Southard* and U.S.S. *Preble* is sweeping for Japanese mines offshore. A scout plane from U.S.S. *Tennessee* reports the area is heavily mined. The *Perry* has already had a mine fouled in its sweeping gear. The mine exploded, destroying the gear, but causing no harm to the *Perry*.

Stock footage of minesweepers turning as narration says that at 1414 the *Perry* turned to the northeast for a final sweep. Stock footage of explosion. Narration says four minutes later, U.S.S. *Perry* struck a Japanese mine and sank in less than two hours.

Stock footage of ships or stills of the actual rescue. Narration tells us that there were several ships in the immediate area and the exact position of the *Perry* was logged to the exact second of latitude and longitude. Even though the logged position placed the *Perry* in a known square about 100 feet on each side, or the size of a small house lot, for more than half a century every effort to find the lost warship had failed.

> Larry Tunks (on camera or V.O.): "As I was doing the plotting on the charts from what I'd learned from the Navy, nothing went together. It just—the numbers weren't right."

Dissolve to opening titles.

Dissolve to the Lost Warships Team in Palau. Narration says that in March 2005 a team of highly experienced technical divers—after nearly three years of preparation—came to Palau determined to videotape the valiant ship and to test the techniques they had developed. The *Perry* had been difficult to find and was extremely difficult to dive on.

We see diving footage as narration continues: The conditions were so severe that the divers twice found themselves in serious trouble. In developing an innovative approach to open-ocean diving and videotaping, the team placed an emphasis on operating safely under "must dive" conditions. U.S.S. *Perry* would present the team with its first challenge.

We see stills (and video if it exists) of Larry Tunks's expedition to find the *Perry* along with footage of *Ocean Hunter II*. Narration says that the *Perry* had finally been located when one of its survivors, Larry Tunks, who believed he had a mental image of the ship's location at the time of the explosion . . .

> Tunks: And in just a few seconds I recovered, I was fine. But in the process—in that process, I just willed in my mind where that island was in relationship to me. And 60 years later, I was able to go almost exactly to the spot just where the ship's at.

. . . teamed with an experienced underwater explorer, Navot Bornovski, who knew how to survey the bottom.

> Navot: Main advantage that I had, I was captain on an oceanographer for many years and I know the waters of Palau.

Stills (and video if it exists) of the discovery of the *Perry* intercut with the interview with Larry Tunks.

Tunks: When they come to the surface, they're yelling and screaming, putting their hands up like that. And again I did it, in a flash—I didn't have a stitch of clothes on. I jumped over to swim . . .
Tunks: And that was on the 1st of May. 2nd of May was my birthday.

Narration continues: After the *Perry* was found in the year 2000, attempts to dive to the ship and videotape it ended in tragedy.

Tunks: History Channel, they sent men over, ten of them, just before Christmas, and I went with them. That's when the diver got killed. They couldn't go down. They tried it for three days, and they couldn't make it.

Dissolve to the Lost Warships Team at Roatan, re-creating the training process. This will be about 2–3 minutes and will include:

• Scenes of the team training together, developing the methods that would be used in Palau.
• A quick resumé check introducing the team members and briefly giving their experience.
• A sound bite on CCR and the decompression algorithm.
• A sound bite on the difficulties of doing work in current. (Tim O'Leary says it's like being towed behind a speedboat.)
• A sound bite from John about videotaping lost warships.
• The importance of boats and safety divers in a "must dive" situation.
• Anything else we need to squeeze in here.

Dissolve to minesweeping footage. Narration says that the *Perry* was inside the sweep of U.S.S. *Southard*, an area which should have been free of mines. So where did the mine come from that sank the ship? The likely answer was discovered by the Lost Warships Team in diving on the *Perry*.

Bump out to commercial with a Lost Warships bumper graphic. In a window in the graphic are scenes of the Pearl Harbor attack. Narration says the *Perry* won six battle stars for combat in World War II.

Fade out.

End of Act One

(Approximate time: 8 minutes)

U.S.S. *PERRY* SCRIPT FOR ACT ONE

LOST WARSHIPS: U.S.S. *PERRY* (DMS-17)

Act One

SCENE	VIDEO	AUDIO
1.	FADE IN	FADE IN
	Stock footage of a World War II Navy task force under way in the Pacific.	Music: opening theme.
		(S=0:04 // RT=00:04)
2.	Stock footage of General MacArthur, aboard ship if possible.	Music: Fades under.
		Narrator (V.O.): By September of 1944, General Douglas MacArthur was poised to keep his promise to return to the Philippines.
		(S=0:08 // RT=00:12)
3.	Stock footage of invasion ships and Marines aboard ship.	Narrator (V.O.): Under his command he had an invasion force of seven hundred vessels holding one hundred seventy-five thousand soldiers and sailors.
		(S=0:09 // RT=00:21)

SCENE	VIDEO	AUDIO

4. Graphic:

Map showing the Philippines, and the direction of MacArthur's invasion, with Palau on its right flank. Arrows indicate MacArthur's approach to the Philippines and the First Marine Division's approach to Palau.

NARRATOR (V.O.): To the east, the First Marine Division was scheduled to invade Palau to secure MacArthur's right flank.

(S=0:08 // RT=00:29)

5. Stock footage of two or three minesweepers sweeping for mines offshore.

SUPERIMPOSE:

Palau
September 13, 1944

NARRATOR (V.O.): To prepare the way for the Marine landing, the destroyer-minesweeper U.S.S. *Perry*, in company with the U.S.S. *Southard* and the U.S.S. *Preble,* was sweeping the waters offshore for Japanese mines.

(S=0:14 // RT=0:43)

6. Stock footage showing an observation float plane from a U.S. battleship.

NARRATOR (V.O.): A scout plane from the U.S.S. *Tennessee* reported that the area was heavily mined.

(S=0:07 // RT=00:50)

7. Stock footage of minesweepers, showing a mine exploding in the wake of a ship.

NARRATOR (V.O.): The *Perry* had already had a mine become trapped in its sweeping gear and explode, destroying the gear, but causing no harm to the ship.

(S=0:09 // RT=00:59)

8. Stock footage of minesweepers turning.

NARRATOR (V.O.): At 1414 the ships turned to the northeast for a final sweep.

(S=0:07 // RT=01:06)

SCENE	VIDEO	AUDIO

9.   <u>Stock footage</u> of a DMS or DD exploding starboard side amidships.

Narrator (V.O.): Four minutes later, the U.S.S. *Perry* struck a Japanese mine—and sank in less than two hours.

(S=0:09 // RT=01:15)

10.   <u>Stock footage</u> of ships engaged in a rescue.

Or

<u>Stills</u> of the actual rescue of the men from the *Perry*.

Narrator (V.O.): Several ships that were engaged in rescue efforts logged the position of the *Perry* to the exact second of latitude and longitude.

(S=0:10 // RT=01:25)

11.   <u>Stock footage:</u> Close-up of a hand marking a position on a chart.

IRIS OPEN TO:

Narrator (V.O.): Even though these positions placed the *Perry* in a known square about one hundred feet on each side,

(S=0:09 // RT=01:34)

12.   <u>Graphic:</u>

Baseball diamond, highlight the 90 × 90 infield, with an overlap of an extra 5 feet on each side.

IRIS CLOSED TO:

Narrator (Continues V.O.): or slightly larger than a baseball infield,

(S=0:05 // RT=01:39)

13.   <u>Stock footage</u> of a sonar screen.

Narrator (Continues V.O.): for more than half a century, every effort

(S=0:04 // RT=01:43)

14.   Divers underwater.

Narrator (Continues V.O.): to find the lost warship had failed.

(S=0:04 // RT=01:47)

SCENE	VIDEO	AUDIO

15. Larry Tunks on camera.

(Tape 22: 00:48:15–48:27)

SUPERIMPOSE:

Larry Tunks
U.S.S. *Perry* Crewman

DISSOLVE TO:

LARRY TUNKS (SOT): As I was doing the plotting on the charts— from what I'd learned from the Navy—nothing went together. The numbers weren't right.

(S=0:13 // RT=02:00)

16. Stock footage of a DMS or DD sinking.

Title:

Lost Warships

U.S.S. *Perry*
(DMS-17)

DISSOLVE TO:

MUSIC: In full.

(S=0:10 // RT=02:1U)

17. MS of *Ocean Hunter II* under way

(Tape 05: 00:22:15–22:22)

SUPERIMPOSE:

Palau
March 2005

MUSIC: Continues briefly, then under.

NARRATOR (V.O.): Palau. March 2005.

(S=0:07 // RT=02:17)

18. On board *Ocean Hunter II*, team helping divers prepare to dive.

(Tape 05: 00:22:15–22:22)

NARRATOR (V.O.): The Lost Warships Team, a group of highly experienced technical divers, came to Palau determined to use the techniques they had developed over three years of training and preparation

(S=0:12 // RT=02:29)

SCENE	VIDEO	AUDIO
19.	Camera handed to diver in the water, second diver in, both swim toward tender. (Tape 05: 00:53:07–53:17)	NARRATOR (CONTINUES V.O.): to videotape the valiant ship. The *Perry* had been extremely difficult to find and was equally unforgiving to dive upon. (S=0:10 // RT=02:39)
20.	Underwater: Diver with red lift bag. Blows air in and releases it. (Tape 17: 00:05:30–05:37)	NARRATOR (V.O.): The diving conditions were so severe that these experienced divers twice found themselves (S=0:07 // RT=02:46)
21.	Red bag pops to surface. (Tape 05: 00:13:10–13:15)	NARRATOR (CONTINUES V.O.): in serious trouble. (S=0:05 // RT=01:51)
22.	Tim in boat, pointing at something to port, then turns with urgency and tells crew to go. (Tape 05: 00:16:46–16:50)	TIM O'LEARY (SOT): Let's go! (S=0:04 // RT=02:55)
23.	LS swimmer in the water near red bag. (Tape 05: 00:19:13–19:17)	NARRATOR (V.O.): In developing an innovative approach (S=0:04 // RT=02:59)
24.	Looking from one small boat to the other small boat. (Tape 05: 00:19:31–19:41)	NARRATOR (CONTINUES V.O.): to open-ocean diving and videotaping, the team placed an emphasis on operating safely under "must dive" conditions. TIM O'LEARY (SOT OFF CAMERA): Call the ship. Tell them everybody's OK. (S=0:11 // RT=03:10)

SCENE	VIDEO	AUDIO

25.   <u>Underwater:</u>

NATURAL SOUND:

      Diver enters water from boat.
         (Tape 02: 00:00:32–00:37)

(S=0:04 // RT=03:14)

26.   Divers going down anchor line.
      Lots of bubbles coming up.

NARRATOR (V.O.): The U.S.S. *Perry*
would present the team with its
first challenge.

      (Tape 16 (second part): 00:05:26–05:33)

      DISSOLVE TO:

(S=0:06 // RT=03:20)

27.   Photo of Larry Tunks as a sailor
      in WWII and/or photos of the
      Perry in WWII.

NARRATOR (V.O.): The *Perry* had
finally been located when one of
its survivors, Larry Tunks, who
believed he had a mental image of
the ship's location at the time of
the explosion . . .

      DISSOLVE TO:

(S=0:12 // RT=03:32)

28.   Larry Tunks on camera.

LARRY TUNKS (SOT): I just willed
in my mind where that island was
in relationship to me. And 60
years later, I was able to go almost
exactly to the spot just where the
ship's at.

         (Tape 22: 00:23:36–23:55)

(S=0:20 // RT=03:52)

29.   Navot from below.

NARRATOR (CONTINUES V.O.): . . .
teamed with an experienced
underwater explorer, Navot
Bornovski, who knew how to
survey the bottom.

         (Tape 09: 00:24:42–24:49)

(S=0:08 // RT=04:00)

<u>SCENE</u>	<u>VIDEO</u>	<u>AUDIO</u>
30.	2S Navot and John Bell.	<u>Navot Bornovski (SOT)</u>: I think the benefit I had was I was captain on our dive boat *Ocean Hunter* for many years and I know the waters of Palau.
	(Tape 20: 00:20:33–20:40)	
	<u>Superimpose</u>:	
	Navot Bornovski Captain *Ocean Hunter II*	
		(S=0:08 // RT=04:08)
31.	<u>Stills</u> of the discovery of U.S.S. *Perry*.	<u>Larry Tunks (SOT)</u>: When they come to the surface, they're yelling and screaming, putting their hands up like that. And again I did it, in a flash—I didn't have a stitch of clothes on. I jumped over to swim; we've got pictures of this, of course.
	Intercut with:	
	The interview with Larry Tunks.	
		(Tape 23: 00:06:20–06:37)
		I went out, got around these two guys—and they're big, big, much bigger guys than me. And we're just screaming our heads off like that.
		(Tape 23: 00:06:40–06:48)
		(S=0:20 // RT=04:28)
32.	<u>Stills</u> from Navot of History Channel attempts.	<u>Narrator (V.O.)</u>: The *Perry* was found in the year 2000, but subsequent attempts to dive to the ship—in order to videotape it—ended in tragedy.
	Or generic images of divers.	
		(S=0:10 // RT=o4:38)

SCENE	VIDEO	AUDIO

33.   Larry Tunks on camera.

      (Tape 23: 00:15:30–15:47)

LARRY TUNKS (SOT): History Channel, they sent men over, ten of them, just before Christmas, and I went with them. That's when the diver got killed. They couldn't go down. They tried it for three days, and they couldn't make it.

DISSOLVE TO:

(S=0:18 // RT=04:56)

34.   Roatan Island, Honduras. Establishing shot of members of the Lost Warships Team training together.

SUPERIMPOSE:

Roatan Island Honduras

MUSIC: Bridge.

NARRATOR (V.O.): Long before their rendezvous with the U.S.S. *Perry* in Palau, the Lost Warships Team began training for "must dive" situations at Roatan Island in Honduras. Training that would be invaluable in the waters off Palau.

(S=0:19 // RT=05:15)

35.   Tim O'Leary on camera.

      (Tape 30: 00:05:47–06:02 Take 4)

TIM O'LEARY: Diving the U.S.S. *Perry* can be an extremely dangerous dive because of the high flow current, coming around . . . that can come around the island. The divers must work and dive as a team and train as a team, so that under stressful conditions, they can make the dive successful.

(S=0:16 // RT=05:31)

SCENE	VIDEO	AUDIO

36.   Ray Hunley on camera.

(Tape 30: 00:12:43–12:57 Take 3)

RAY HUNLEY: CCR diving for us is a much safer form of diving. We have a longer gas supply, so that we could stay down longer if we needed to. And we have a much shorter decompression obligation so that we can get out of the water quicker, and we are not exposed to the strong current for as long a period of time.

(S=0:15 // RT=05:46)

37.   Tim O'Leary on camera.

(Tape 30: 00:07:49–08:02
Second Take 2)

TIM O'LEARY: In order to reduce the risk of decompression illness, we'll be using a cutting edge algorithm known as RGBM. This will stop us deeper, but bring us out of that killer current much faster than standard decompression tables.

(S=0:14 // RT=06:00)

38.   Ray Hunley on camera.

(Tape 30: 00:13:14–13:37
Slates as Scene 39, Take 1)

RAY HUNLEY: We need a chase boat to be able to follow the divers in a drift dive situation. If we can't stay on top of them, then we wouldn't be able to assist them. Safety divers are an integral part of the team, because anybody who goes down in those kind of environments may run into problems, and they need somebody to assist them by bringing them extra gas supply or whatever they may need.

(S=0:24 // RT=06:24)

<u>SCENE</u>	<u>VIDEO</u>	<u>AUDIO</u>

39. Tim O'Leary on camera.

(Tape 30: 00:09:22–09:33
Recorded as Scene 38—4th take,
no slate)

TIM O'LEARY: Descending into a high flow current can be deadly. We know that the currents around this island can reach upwards of five knots. That'd be much like dragging a person behind a boat at six miles an hour.

(S=0:12 // RT=06:36)

40. John Bell with underwater video camera.

(Tape 30: 00:16:12–16:26
Take 3)

JOHN BELL: Tim and I came up with the idea of creating a worldwide dive team of closed circuit divers who could go to extreme exposure and dive sunken ships. Our first choice was the U.S.S. *Perry*, which we'll do in about two weeks.

DISSOLVE TO:

(S=0:14 // RT=06:50)

41. <u>Stock footage</u> of a minesweeper following in the safe area of another minesweeper.

MUSIC: Bridge.

NARRATOR (V.O.): When the *Perry* struck the mine that sank her, she was inside the sweep of the U.S.S. *Southard*— an area which should have been free of mines. So where did the mine come from that sank the ship? The likely answer was discovered by the Lost Warships Team in diving on the *Perry*.

(S=0:20 // RT=07:10)

42. Bump out to black with the Lost Warships bumper graphic. In a window in the graphic are identifiable scenes from World War II.

MUSIC: In full.

NARRATOR (V.O.): The *Perry* won six battle stars for combat in World War II.

(S=0:10 // RT=07:20)

End of Act One

BIBLIOGRAPHY

Bernard, Sheila Curran. *Documentary Storytelling*. Burlington, Mass.: Focal Press, 2004, 2007.

Burkett, Elinor. *Another Planet*. New York: HarperCollins, 2001.

Collier, Maxie D. *The ifilm Digital Video Filmmaker's Handbook*. Hollywood, Calif.: Lone Eagle Publishing Company, 2001.

Crichton, Michael. *Rising Sun*. New York. Ballantine Books, 1992.

Field, Syd. *Screenplay: The Foundations of Screenwriting*. New York: Dell Publishing, 2005.

Geertz, Clifford. "Deep Play: Notes on a Balinese Cockfight," in *The Interpretation of Cultures: Selected Essays*. New York: Basic Books, 1973.

Hampe, Barry. *Video Scriptwriting: How to Write for the $4 Billion Commercial Video Market*. New York: Plume/Penguin, 1993.

Kelly, Walt. *Pogo,* vol. 2. Seattle: Fantagraphics Books, 1994.

Konigsberg, Ira. *The Complete Film Dictionary*. New York: Meridian/Penguin Books, 1987, 1989.

Levitt, Steven D., and Stephen J. Dubner. *Freakonomics: A Rogue Economist Explores the Hidden Side of Everything*. New York: William Morrow, 2005.

Lipton, Lenny. *Independent Filmmaking*, rev. ed. New York: Simon & Schuster, 1983.

Loewen, James. *Lies My Teacher Told Me: Everything Your American History Textbook Got Wrong*. New York: Touchstone, 1996.

Lomborg, Bjorn. *The Skeptical Environmentalist: Measuring the Real State of the World*. New York: Cambridge University Press, 2001.

Michaels, Patrick C. *Meltdown: The Predictable Distortion of Global Warming by Scientists, Politicians, and the Media*. Washington, D.C.: Cato Institute, 2004.

Newton, Dale, and John Gaspard. *Digital Filmmaking 101: An Essential Guide to Producing Low-Budget Movies*. Studio City, Calif.: Michael Wiese Productions, 2001.

O'Connell, P. J. *Robert Drew and the Development of Cinema Vérité in America*. Carbondale: Southern Illinois University Press, 1992.

Pryluck, Calvin. "Ultimately We Are All Outsiders: The Ethics of Documentary Filming." *Journal of the University Film Association* 28, no. 1 (Winter 1976), repr. in Alan Rosenthal, ed., *New Challenges to Documentary*.

Rabinger, Michael. *Directing the Documentary*. 4th ed. New York: Focal Press, 2004.

Rivoli, Pietra. *Travels of a T-Shirt in a Global Economy*. New York: John Wiley & Sons, 2005.

Rosenthal, Alan. *New Challenges to Documentary*. Berkeley: University of California Press, 1987.

———. *The New Documentary in Action: A Casebook in Film Making*. Berkeley: University of California Press, 1972.

———. *Writing, Directing, and Producing Documentary Films*. 3rd ed. Carbondale and Edwardsville: Southern Illinois University Press, 2002.

Seger, Linda. *Creating Unforgettable Characters*. New York: Owl/Henry Holt, 1990.

———. *Making a Good Script Great*. 2nd ed. Hollywood, Calif.: Samuel French Trade, 1987, 1994.

Singleton, Ralph S. *Filmmaker's Dictionary*. Hollywood, Calif.: Lone Eagle Publishing, 1986, 2000.

Sowell, Thomas. *Basic Economics*. New York: Basic Books, 2003.

Walter, Richard. *Screenwriting: The Art, Craft and Business of Film and Television Writing*. New York: Plume/New American Library, 1988.

Weart, Spencer R. *The Discovery of Global Warming*. Cambridge, Mass.: Harvard University Press, 2003.

Worth, Sol, and John Adair. *Through Navajo Eyes: An Exploration in Film Communication and Anthropology*. Bloomington: Indiana University Press, 1972.

Zettl, Herbert. *Television Production Handbook*. Belmont, Calif.: Wadsworth Publishing Company, 2006.

———. *Video Basics* 5. Belmont, Calif.: Wadsworth Publishing Company, 2007.

FILMOGRAPHY

This is a list of the films mentioned in the text. Many are available on DVD and can be rented from DVD sources, such as Netflix, or bought or ordered from Amazon, Borders, and other sources. Where I have not been able to find a DVD source, I've tried to indicate where the film might be bought or rented on VHS. Some of these documentaries are either no longer available or can be found (if at all) only on film.

Documentaries

89 mm from Europe (1995) Written and directed by Marcel Lozinski, this beautiful short film received a 1995 IDA Distinguished Documentary Achievement Award. Distributed by Studio Filmowe Kalejdoskop (Poland) and Direct Cinema Limited.

9/11 (2002) The definitive film of the World Trade Center disaster by Jules and Gideon Naudet and James Hanlon. [DVD]

Ages and Stages (1950s) This series of films on behavior in early childhood was produced and distributed by McGraw-Hill. It is responsible for perpetuating a libel against two-year-olds, by titling the film on that age *The Terrible Twos*. An example of visuals illustrating the sound track.

An American Family (1973) Shot and directed by Susan and Alan Raymond, this series for PBS was a landmark event in the evolution of direct cinema. The Museum of Television and Radio has some episodes. IMDb shows a DVD release.

Baraka (1992) Directed by Ron Fricke. Pure visual. [DVD]

Baseball: A Film by Ken Burns (1994) Directed by Ken Burns, this is a very long, very eclectic look at the game which used to be known as the national pastime. [DVD]

Basic Training: The Making of a Warrior (1994) Produced by Kevin Stead and directed by Ari Golan. Not in release.

The Battle of Midway (1942) The most decisive sea battle of World War II, filmed as it happened by John Ford. [DVD]

Battleship Potemkin (1925) Classic reenactment documentary directed by Sergei Eisenstein. [DVD]

Benjamin Franklin (2002) Miniseries for PBS directed by Ellen Hovde and Muffie Meyer. [DVD]

The Berkeley Rebels (c. 1964) Directed by Arthur Barron, this early-sixties documentary appeared on CBS. I have found no distributor.

Berlin, Symphony of a Great City (1927) A classic silent film, directed by Walter Ruttman, which has become a model for all city films. [DVD]

Beyond Division: Reuniting the Republic of Cyprus (2001) Directed by Peter Vogt and written by Barry Hampe. May be available through the Embassy of the Republic of Cyprus.

The Birth of Aphrodite (date unknown) I don't know where you're likely to find this film. I got it out of the Philadelphia Public Library many years ago.

The Borinqueneers (c. 2006) Produced by Noemi Figueroa Soulet and Raquel Ortiz. The story of the 65th Infantry Regiment, the only Hispanic-segregated unit in U.S. military history. El Pozo Productions, http://www.prsoldier.com.

Bowling for Columbine (2002) A film by Michael Moore. [DVD]

The Bridge (1928) A beautifully realized, classic documentary directed by Joris Ivens, who gives a clinic on how to observe an object with a camera. Available from the Museum of Modern Art.

Celsius 41.11: The Temperature at Which the Brain . . . Begins to Die (2004) One of three rebuttal films to *Fahrenheit 9/11,* directed by Kevin Knoblock. [DVD]

Chronique d'un été (Chronicle of a Summer) (1961) This is an early and exciting example of cinéma vérité in France from Jean Rouch and Edgar Morin. I saw the film in French with English subtitles. As of this writing I have been unable to find a distributor.

The City (1939) Willard Van Dyke directed this classic American city film, which follows the format established by Ruttman with *Berlin.* Look for it on VHS or at the Museum of Modern Art.

The Civil War (1990) The PBS series that made director Ken Burns a household name. [DVD]

The Cliburn: Playing on the Edge (2001) Documentary follows the performers in the prestigious piano competition. Produced and directed by Peter Rosen. [DVD]

Connections (1979) An incredible series of programs, starting in 1979, written and hosted by James Burke and directed by Mick Jackson. [DVD]

Crumb (1995) Terry Zwigoff conceived and directed this offbeat theatrical documentary about underground artist Robert Crumb and his family. [DVD]

Dark Days (2000) Marc Singer went underground to document the lives of people living in the railway tunnels under New York City. [DVD]

Defenders of Midway (1994) Directed by Tim Bradley and written by Barry Hampe, this one-hour documentary on the greatest naval battle in American history was funded by the Department of Defense Legacy Resources Management Program. It had its world premiere at the Arizona Memorial and then vanished into the bureaucratic mist.

Devil's Playground (2002) Amish teenagers experience life outside the Amish community in a documentary directed by Lucy Walker. [DVD]

Dialogues with Madwomen (1994) Director Allie Light's documentary of emotion is available through Women Make Movies, 225 Lafayette Street, #207, New York, NY 10012.

The Endless Summer (1966) Bruce Brown's classic film about surfing, shows how to tell a story with good footage and no sync sound. [DVD]

Eyes on the Prize (1987) Award-winning PBS documentary about the civil rights movement; Henry Hampton, executive producer. [DVD]

FDR (1995) This four-and-a-half-hour documentary, made for the PBS series *American Experience,* was produced and directed by David Grubin. [DVD]

Fahrenheit 9/11 (2004) The film Michael Moore made to prevent the election of George Bush. Failed at that but made Moore a millionaire. [DVD]

Fahrenhype 9/11 (2004) One of three rebuttal films to *Fahrenheit 9/11,* directed by Alan Peterson. [DVD]

Falcons of Arabia (1994) This is an interesting first documentary, shot, directed, and edited by Andrew Edwards. No distribution.

Flock of Dodos: The Evolution-Intelligent Design Circus (2006) Documentary at its best; a marvelous investigation of a controversial issue, written and directed by Randy Olson. Prairie Starfish Productions, Los Angeles, http://www.flockofdodos.com. May be available on DVD by the time you read this.

The French Revolution (2005) Directed by Doug Schultz. [DVD]

Harvest of Shame (1960) An early award-winning television documentary for CBS Reports from the team of Edward R. Murrow and Fred Friendly. [DVD]

High School (1968) A spontaneous cinema documentary directed by Frederick Wiseman, filmed at Northeast High School in Philadelphia. Wiseman's films are distributed by Zipporah Films, Cambridge, Mass., http://www.zipporah.com.

The Hobart Shakespeareans (2005) Praise for a hero teacher, directed by Mel Stuart. See it. [DVD]

Hoop Dreams (1994) The most talked-about documentary never to get an Academy Award nomination started out to be a TV half hour, and became instead a longish theatrical documentary and PBS special. [DVD]

Hospital (1970) Fourth in a series of spontaneous cinema documentaries about institutions directed by Frederick Wiseman, filmed at Metropolitan Hospital in New York City. Wiseman's films are distributed by Zipporah Films, Cambridge, Mass., http://www.zipporah.com.

An Inconvenient Truth (2006) Directed by Davis Guggenheim. Al Gore's environmental message set to video. [DVD]

In the Street (1952) An early experiment in concealed photography, by Helen Levitt, Janice Loeb, and James Agee. Available from the Museum of Modern Art.

Is Wal-Mart Good for America? (2004) PBS's *Frontline* takes on Wal-Mart and tries to be fair about it. Directed by Rick Young. [DVD]

It Was a Wonderful Life (1993) They were women with a comfortable middle-class life. And then they were homeless. Directed by Michèle Ohayon. [DVD]

The Kidnapping of Ingrid Betancourt (a.k.a. *Missing Peace*) (2003) A first documentary by Victoria Bruce and Karin Hayes, who triumphed over everything going wrong. Shown on Cinemax.

Lalee's Kin: The Legacy of Cotton (2001) A behavioral documentary about a family living in poverty in the Mississippi Delta. Directed by Deborah Dickson, Susan Frömke, and the legendary Albert Maysles. This should eventually be on DVD.

Liberty! The American Revolution (1997) Documentary miniseries directed by Ellen Hovde and Muffie Meyer. [DVD]

Light in Art (1988) A documentary directed by Holly Richards and written by Barry Hampe. Not distributed.

Lonely Boy (1961) Wolf Koenig at the National Film Board of Canada set the mold for films about entertainers and musicians with this direct cinema study of Paul Anka. Various distributors including the Museum of Modern Art and the National Film Board of Canada.

Mad Hot Ballroom (2005) A delightful film about kids in several New York elementary schools learning ballroom dancing and taking part in a citywide competition. Directed by Marilyn Agrelo. [DVD]

March of the Penguins (2005) A nature documentary directed by Luc Jacquet under incredibly harsh conditions. If you haven't seen it, go get it. [DVD]

A Married Couple (1969) An early direct cinema behavioral documentary directed by Alan King. I have found no distributor.

Michael Moore Hates America (2004) One of three rebuttal films to *Fahrenheit 9/11*, directed by Michael Wilson. [DVD]

Mother Washing a Baby (c. 1896) This short observation of behavior was made at the Edison Studios at the turn of the century and can be found in a compilation called *Early Edison Shorts*.

My Brother's Keeper (1992) A film by Joe Berlinger and Bruce Sinofsky about the murder trial of Delbert Ward, one of four hermit brothers in rural New York State. [DVD]

Nanook of the North (1922) Robert Flaherty's classic film is arguably the first behavioral documentary. [DVD]

Natasha and the Wolf (1995) A strange documentary for the PBS *Frontline* series by Kevin Sim and Olga Budashevska, set in Russia and full of interviews with simultaneous translation. Not in distribution at time of publication; check PBS Video.

Night Mail (1936) John Grierson carried the show-and-tell documentary about as far it could go with this classic film about a train. [DVD]

Nuit et Brouillard (*Night and Fog*) (1955) Alain Resnais's documentary of the Auschwitz death camp. [DVD]

October: Ten Days That Shook the World (1927) Sergei Eisenstein's re-creation of the Bolshevik Revolution. [DVD]

Outfoxed: Rupert Murdoch's War on Journalism (2004) One of several attack documentaries directed by Robert Greenwald. [DVD]

The Plow That Broke the Plains (1934) Pare Lorentz made this film about the drought in the Great Plains and its causes at the height of the Great Depression. [DVD]

Primary (1960) Robert Drew thought there had to be a better way to document unique events than the standard show-and-tell documentary, and this film was the visual evidence. [DVD]

Referred for Underachievement (c. 1966) Dr. Ed Mason, a psychiatrist, made this documentary record of an intake interview with a patient and her family. I have found no distributor.

The River (1937) Another Depression-era documentary directed by Pare Lorentz, showing a flood on the Mississippi and its causes. [DVD]

Roger & Me (1989) Director Michael Moore uses his quest to bring GM chairman Roger Smith to Flint, Michigan, as a metaphor to show hard times in his hometown. [DVD]

Salesman (1968) Albert and David Maysles filmed this behavioral documentary about door-to-door Bible salesmen and shared the directing credit with editor Charlotte Zwerin. [DVD]

San Pietro (1945) John Huston directed this classic documentary about a single battle in the Italian campaign during World War II. IMDb shows it available on VHS.

Schools for Children (1973) Second of two films on learning in children, directed by Barry Hampe. Not in distribution.

Season for Learning (1972) A documentary about a summer educational program for children of migrant workers, directed by Barry Hampe. Not in distribution.

Sex in a Cold Climate (1998) Documentary about Irish girls interred in various Magdalene asylums and/or orphanages because of out-of-wedlock pregnancies, being sexually assaulted, or just being "too pretty" (believe it or not). Directed by Steve Humphries. This documentary led to the feature film *The Magdalene Sisters* and is included on the DVD for that film. [DVD]

Sexual Intercourse (c. 1970) An observation on film of a couple making love, made for a medical school in the early 1970s. No information on distribution.

Sinking City of Venice (2002) An outstanding science film in the *NOVA* series and a primer on visual evidence, produced by Marco Visalberghi and Julia Cort. Available only on VHS at time of publication from http://shop.wgbh.org/. Also check PBS Video.

Six Days to Sunday (1995) Documentary of a unique event with the outcome unknown as the Dallas Cowboys and Minnesota Vikings prepare for Sunday's game. NFL Films.

The Sorrow and the Pity (1970) Marcel Ophuls directed this landmark documentary that explored anti-Semitism in France during World War II. [DVD]

Spellbound (2002) Unquestionably the film that should have won the 2003 Academy Award for documentary. Directed by Jeffrey Blitz, it follows eight youngsters headed for the 1999 National Spelling Bee. [DVD]

Staffers '04 (2004) This was a TV series following staffers for Democratic presidential candidates. [DVD]

Stolen Honor (2004) Carleton Sherwood's attack film aimed at John Kerry's presidential campaign. Vietnam War POWs blame Kerry for their harsh treatment. On DVD from http://www.stolenhonor.com.

These People (1976) A documentary about the controversy over community care vs. institutionalization of mental patients, directed by Barry Hampe for Horizon House, Philadelphia. Not in distribution.

Titicut Follies (1967) The first and perhaps the best known of Frederick Wiseman's spontaneous cinema documentaries. Filmed inside the Massachusetts Correctional Institution at Bridgewater, a prison hospital for the criminally insane. Wiseman's films are distributed by Zipporah Films, Cambridge, Mass., http://www.zipporah.com.

A Touch of Greatness (2005) The story of Albert Cullum, a remarkable teacher in the 1960s and '70s. Directed by Leslie Sullivan, with archival footage by Robert Downey, Sr. [DVD]

Triumph des Willens (*Triumph of the Will*) (1935) Docuganda for the Third Reich, directed by Leni Riefenstahl. [DVD]

The Trouble with Adults Is . . . (1968) A well-edited, technically atrocious documentary about a group of students in the summer of 1968, directed by Barry Hampe for the United Church of Christ. Not in distribution.

Uncovered: The Whole Truth About the Iraq War (2003) Another attack film by Robert Greenwald in which the truth is the first casualty. [DVD]

Unzipped (1995) Douglas Keeve directed this theatrical documentary about fashion designer Isaac Mizrahi. [DVD]

Victory at Sea (series) (1952) The story of the U.S. Navy in World War II, compiled from archival and combat footage. [DVD]

VolcanoScapes (c. 1990) One of a series of documentaries about Kilauea volcano, produced by Artemis and Mick Kalber, Tropical Visions Video, http://www.tropicalvisions.com.

Wal-Mart: The High Cost of Low Price (2005) Robert Greenwald attacks Wal-Mart. [DVD]

The War Game (1966) Peter Watkins directed this speculative documentary about the effects of a future nuclear war. [DVD]

The War Room (1993) A film by Chris Hegedus and D. A. Pennebaker that follows the Clinton campaign from the New Hampshire primary to the election. [DVD]

Watermarks (2004) Yaron Zilberman's loving portrait of the Hakoah Vienna Jewish women's swim team of the 1930s. [DVD]

What the #$*! Do We (K)now!? (2004) New Age speculation on the nature of everything. [DVD]

Winged Migration (2001) Where do the birds go? This beautiful film shot over three years follows migratory patterns of birds. Proof that you don't need interviews to tell a story. Directed by Jacques Perrin with co-directors Jacques Cluzaud and Michel Debats. [DVD]

Woodstock (1970) The first of the great concert films, directed by Michael Wadleigh. [DVD]

A Young Child Is . . . (1973) A behavioral documentary about early learning in young children, the first of two films on learning in children directed by Barry Hampe. Not in distribution.

Feature Films Mentioned

The American President   *A League of Their Own*
The Aviator   *The Longest Day*
The Birth of a Nation   *The Magdalene Sisters*
Cromwell   *Munich*
The Day After Tomorrow   *My Darling Clementine*
Gunfight at the OK Corral   *Patton*
Hotel Rwanda   *Queen Elizabeth*
In the Name of the Father   *The Quiet Man*
Jeanne d'Arc   *Quiz Show*
JFK   *Revolution in Russia*
Kinsey

INDEX

ABOUT THE AUTHOR

BARRY HAMPE has made more than 200 documentary films and information videos as director or scriptwriter or both. He lives in Northern Virginia with his wife and business partner, Sylvie Leith Hampe, where he now concentrates on writing books and documentary scripts. At various times in the past, Hampe has owned production companies in Philadelphia, Honolulu, and Las Vegas and has taught documentary filmmaking at the University of Pennsylvania and writing and documentary film theory at the University of Nevada, Las Vegas.

www.barryhampe.com